FINDING THE TARGET

FREDERICK W. KAGAN

Finding the Target

THE TRANSFORMATION OF AMERICAN MILITARY POLICY

Encounter Books · New York

FOR H. R. MCMASTER

Commander, Historian, Teacher, and Friend

First edition published in 2006 by Encounter Books,
an activity of Encounter for Culture and Education, Inc.,
a nonprofit, tax exempt corporation.
Encounter Books website address: www.encounterbooks.com

Manufactured in the United States and printed on
acid-free paper. The paper used in this publication meets
the minimum requirements of ANSI/NISO Z39.48–1992
(R 1997) (Permanence of Paper).

FIRST EDITION

LIBRARY OF CONGRESS CATALOGING-IN-PUBLICATION DATA
Kagan, Frederick W.
Finding the Target: The Transformation of American
Military Policy/Frederick W. Kagan
p.   cm.
ISBN 1-59403-150-9
1. Military art and science—United States—History—20th century
2. Military art and science—United States—History—21st century.
3. United States—Military policy. 4. United States—
Armed Forces—Reorganization.
UA23.K24 2006
355'.033573 22   2006012792

10 9 8 7 6 5 4 3 2 1

CONTENTS

LIST OF ABBREVIATIONS

AAA   Anti-aircraft Artillery

AAM   Air-to-air Missile

AAN   Army After Next

ABM   Anti-Ballistic Missile

ACR   Armored Cavalry Regiment

ALB   AirLand Battle

ALFA   Air Land Forces Application Agency

AMRAAM   Advanced Medium-Range Air-to-air Missile

ARTEP   Army Training and Evaluation Program

ASW   Anti-Submarine Warfare

ATGM   Anti-tank Guided Missile

AVF   All-Volunteer Force

AWACS   Airborne Warning and Control System

BAI   Battlefield Air Interdiction

BUR   Bottom-Up Review

C^2 Command and Control

C^3 Command, Control, and Communications

C^4I Command, Control, Communications, Computers, and Information

C^4ISR C4I plus Surveillance and Reconnaissance

CAS   Close Air Support

CENTAF   Commander, Air Forces, U.S. Central Command

CENTCOM   U.S. Central Command

CFLCC   Combined Forces Land Component Commander

CJTF   Combined Joint Task Force

COG   Center of Gravity

CORM   Commission on Roles and Missions

DBK   Dominant Battlespace Knowledge

DCSOPS   Deputy Chief of Staff for Operations

DOC   Designed Operational Capability

EUCOM   U.S. European Command

FCS   Future Combat System

FM   Field Manual

GDP   Gross Domestic Product

GNP   Gross National Product

HMMWV   High-Mobility, Multi-Wheeled Vehicle (Humvee)

HPM   High-Power Microwave

IADS   Integrated Air-Defense System

IAEA   International Atomic Energy Agency

ICBM   Intercontinental Ballistic Missile

ID   Infantry Division

INTRODUCTION

ON NOVEMBER 5, 2001, a small Afghan force under the command of General Abdul Rashid Dostum faced a mixed collection of Taliban and al Qaeda troops dug into defensive positions near the village of Bai Beche, outside of Mazar-e Sharif. Dostum's troops rode horses, wore traditional Afghan garb, and were armed with AK-47s and the other light hand weapons that Afghans had been using against the Soviets and each other for decades. One prepared to ride into combat with only one leg. The defenders, similarly armed, occupied an extensive and complex Soviet-built trench system. Since November 3, U.S. Special Forces troops embedded within Dostum's militia had been calling in bombing attacks against these positions, but no one knew what the effect of that bombing had been.

The Americans and Dostum developed a plan of attack: U.S. aircraft would bomb the position once more just before the Afghan leader launched his cavalry into a charge. At the designated time, Dostum's men spurred their mounts and galloped at the trenches, only to be met with withering fire from the defenders—the American bombers had, for some reason, failed to attack on time. A furious Dostum rode back to confront his Special Forces comrades, demanding to know what had happened. They apologized and assured him that the bombs were on the way. Somewhat placated, Dostum took up his position again and waited for the signal, but confusion reigned once more. Apparently mistaking the signal for "get ready" as the signal for "attack," Dostum charged the trenches again just as the bombs began to land. The horrified Special Forces soldiers thought they had just wiped out Dostum's command, but the timing was accidentally perfect. Just after the last bombs hit, Dostum's cavalry charged through the cloud of smoke and dust and drove easily through the stunned and disoriented defenders, routing them utterly. Unable to regroup from this debacle, the Taliban and al Qaeda troops soon yielded Mazar-e Sharif itself, and their entire position in Afghanistan began to unravel.

Secretary of Defense Donald Rumsfeld seized eagerly upon this incident as proof of the validity of the "transformation" program he had been pursuing since taking office at the beginning of the year. He declared the "first cavalry charge of the twenty-first century" was "precisely what transformation is about." With this statement, Rumsfeld took the already vague and confused concept of military transformation and contorted it still further even as he worked feverishly to lock in a particular vision of the U.S. military based upon that shaky conceptual foundation. The confusion within the concept, however, has largely escaped serious consideration, overshadowed as it has been by the counter-insurgency operations in Iraq and Afghanistan from which it seems at first glance to be distinct. In the pages that follow, we will see that transformation is not at all separate from the problems the U.S. has encountered following two apparently successful wars. It is, on the contrary, one of the most basic causes of those problems and of the general national security crisis in which the nation finds itself today.

The idea of military transformation has a fairly long lineage. Gustavus Adolphus, Frederick the Great, and Napoleon were all thought to have changed warfare fundamentally in their own eras. Attempts to comprehend the new nature of warfare during and after the French Revolution became a cottage industry nearly on the scale of the current transformation debate. The Franco–Prussian War and World War I were widely seen as marking dramatic shifts in the way war was fought, and World War II did so in at least three ways—with the advent of mass tank warfare, strategic bombing on a vast scale, and atomic weapons.

The first real effort to define a "military revolution" resulted from attempts to understand the introduction of gunpowder to warfare in the early modern period. The focus of this discussion was primarily on the way the development of gunpowder armies affected developments in civilian society, rather than specifically on the ways in which gunpowder transformed war itself. The discussion about changes in warfare at that time, confined more narrowly to the military history community, focused instead on the so-called "infantry revolution" starting in the fifteenth century, which ended the days of feudal knights, mainly through the skillful use of formations of pikemen, and on the "artillery" revolution begun somewhat later.

Both of these discussions took place within fairly limited and specialized scholarly communities, and whatever general insights they might have developed about how war changes were largely lost beyond those small groups.[1] Before the 1980s, the American military did not concern itself deeply with this developing concept and did not explore the ways in which war had changed or might change with any seriousness. The real theoretical basis of the current debates about transformation therefore developed, oddly enough, in the Soviet Union in the 1960s in the concept of a "*revoliutsiia voennykh del*," generally translated as "revolution in military affairs," or RMA.[2] It is this Soviet concept that entered the Western dialogue about war in the 1970s and 1980s, and revolutionized that dialogue in the 1990s.

The Soviets argued that the first use of atomic weapons over Hiroshima and Nagasaki had not, in fact, brought about any fundamental change in the nature of warfare. The bombs had still to be delivered by bombers, which could be shot down by skillful defenses. Therefore, the problem of penetrating the enemy's air defenses was just the same as it had previously been. The bombs themselves, moreover, although large, did not do more damage than the thousand-bomber raids at the height of the allied strategic bombing campaign had done. Considering that the (conventional) bombing of Dresden had generated ground winds of up to 300 miles per hour in the resulting conflagration, there was some validity to this insight. True, the consequences of allowing one atomic-armed bomber through were much greater than those of allowing a single conventionally armed plane through, but the Soviets believed that the basic strategic considerations of World War II bombing continued to hold even after 1945.

The real revolution, they believed, resulted from the marriage of thermonuclear warheads to intercontinental ballistic missiles. An atomic bomb, of the type used at Hiroshima, relies on the simple explosion of a critical mass of enriched uranium. A thermonuclear bomb harnesses that explosion to create an even larger blast resulting from the fusion of hydrogen nuclei. Atomic bombs could generate explosions equivalent to tens of thousands of tons of TNT. Thermonuclear bombs could generate explosions three orders of magnitude larger—the Soviets once detonated a weapon equivalent to 60 *million* tons of TNT, and throughout the Cold War warheads equivalent to one or two million tons of TNT were quite common.

The Soviets argued that the damage such weapons could do to their targets was beyond all comparison with what conventional bombers could achieve, however prolonged the bombing campaign. With an atomic bomb, for example, the placement of the weapon and the details of the terrain still mattered a great deal—hills could shelter the areas behind them and if the bomb landed significantly off-target, it might well fail to destroy whatever it had been aimed at. This was not true of large thermo-nuclear weapons. Detonated in the air above their targets, these weapons were almost immune to terrain effects and could miss their aim points by large margins and still destroy whatever they aimed at—and much else besides.

But the Soviets believed that even these awful weapons were not enough by themselves to transform war—they just required that the air defenders be perfect in their job of shooting down incoming bombers. When the technology allowed the place-ment of thermonuclear warheads on intercontinental ballistic missiles (ICBMs), however, the game changed completely. There was and is no reliable defense against ICBMs. The potential victim of those weapons must assume that they will all strike their targets and work as intended, because there is virtually nothing he can do to prevent that from happening. Because there is no defending against ICBMs, and because of the destructive capability of thermonuclear warheads, the Sovi-ets believed that war had been transformed completely. The old balance between offense and defense had been shattered and the timeframe of war had been dramatically shortened. A ther-monuclear exchange would last perhaps an hour, perhaps less, and all would be determined by the end of it. War as humanity had known it for tens of thousands of years had suddenly and completely altered in this first RMA.

As a description of military events in the 1960s and after, there was more than a little wrong with this Soviet analysis. First and foremost, there has never been a thermonuclear exchange. Although the Soviets were right that such an exchange would look nothing like anything that had come before, the emphasis on the total transformation of warfare resulting from the *existence* of such weapons proved misplaced. Armored warfare supported by aircraft and strategic bombing campaigns continued to be the norm, and the wars in Korea, Vietnam, and Afghanistan looked very much like campaigns of the pre-nuclear era. Second, the

Soviets almost certainly underestimated the changes in strategic bombing already wrought by the atomic weapon, a mistake that resulted from their tendency to underestimate the damage, short-term and long, that was done to Hiroshima and Nagasaki. Third, by insisting upon a complete transformation in the nature of warfare, the Soviets set the bar too high for their concept to be truly useful. If the test of an RMA is that few or none of the old rules of war apply anymore, then there has never been and probably never will be an RMA. Fourth, by defining the RMA in this fashion, the Soviets relied uncharacteristically on a technologically deterministic view of war. Their RMA resulted purely from a technological development, and the concept did not really depend in any important way on social, economic, political, doctrinal, or other changes. Considering the Soviets' normal manic focus on such issues, the development of the RMA concept was an anomaly even for them.

It should be no surprise, therefore, that the concept lay relatively dormant for the next three decades. Some Westerners picked it up in a bastardized version, translated from the Polish equivalent as a "military-technical revolution," but it gained no real headway among U.S. military leaders or civilian military analysts until the 1980s. A few visionaries of that time picked it up, but made little progress until the wake of Operation Desert Storm, when the concept, dramatically modified, took flight as we shall see.

The inherent flaws in the Soviet concept and the hyper-enthusiasm with which it was embraced by certain military communities in the 1990s have led some eminent students of war to declare on the contrary that the whole idea of "revolutionizing" war is meaningless.[3] They point out that military transformations do not occur overnight but take decades to work out and ask how such a prolonged process could possibly be called a "revolution." They also point out the enormous number of continuities that link all epochs of warfare together. The old rules never really do give way to entirely new principles and, if one takes a sufficiently long and abstracted view, war really has not changed very much at all for many centuries—if it ever did.

These critiques of the concept are very valuable. They offer important correctives to the tendency of RMA-enthusiasts to dismiss all previous history as irrelevant to the "new" way of thinking. They also highlight the tremendous complexity of war and the ways in which it might or might not change over time, fighting both technological determinism and simplistic reductionism. As usual, however, the truth really does lie between the two extremes.

War, as a human activity, is subject to the dictates of human nature. Since that nature has changed very little over the ages, war itself has remained very stable in certain critical ways. Ideas about how to fight wars based upon an understanding of human psychology have generally remained valid for all of human existence. The notion that surprising the enemy is a good thing; the desirability of concentrating efforts on a few important objectives rather than spreading them out over the entire theater, of moving more rapidly than the enemy, of being better protected, better armed, better organized, and better trained; the belief in the importance of supply and well-planned movement —all of these and many more ideals have formed the core of military manuals for as long as people have been writing them. To the extent that ancient theorists such as Sun Tsu and Vegetius still offer valuable lessons for warriors today, their relevance results from their insights into how humans and human organizations work, what tasks they must perform, and the inherent limitations on human (not technological) capabilities. Theorists, like Clausewitz and Sun Tsu, for example, who placed human beings at the center of their study of war will continue to offer insights for as long as human nature remains constant. Those, like the French fortress-designer Vauban, the French artillery revolutionary Gribeauval, the Prussian railroad revolutionary Helmuth von Moltke the Elder, and the British tank-enthusiast J. F. C. Fuller, who focused more narrowly on the revolutionary capabilities of the technology of their day, have much less to offer as the world has moved away from their technological levels.

The fact that certain central elements of war remain relatively constant over the ages does not, however, mean that war does not change. The fact that the First World War looked nothing like the Wars of German Unification; that World War II looked nothing like World War I; and that Desert Storm looked nothing like World War II is surely important. Each of these wars saw orders-of-magnitude improvements in the ability of armies to move large distances, to attack the enemy with volumes of firepower, to place that firepower precisely on designated targets, to communicate among their different components, to sustain themselves in both attack and defense, and in a host of other vital areas. The search for timeless continuities among these struggles is valid and important, but to ignore the enormous differences among them would be misguided.

It is easy enough to develop a more circumscribed definition of a revolution in military affairs that requires not a complete transformation in the *nature* of war, but only a substantial one. Critics will say that the nature of war never changes, only its particular and superficial manifestations. It is more accurate to say that the definition of war does not change—war is the organized, purposeful use of violence to achieve a political objective. But the nature of war involves more than that definition. It involves the way states create and sustain armies, and the way that effort in turn affects the state. It involves the size, scale, and expense of combat both in treasure and in blood. It involves the speed of military actions and the interaction between war and politics. All of these things can change dramatically, even over fairly short periods of time, and it is both valid and useful to define such changes as military transformations or even revolutions in military affairs.

The difficulty of developing a clear definition for this concept and of identifying specific historical eras and events to which it applies is nothing compared to the problem of recognizing and reacting to a transformation in war while it is occurring. Historically, few states have done that successfully without suffering long periods of danger and even defeat. France in the Interwar Years is the classic example of a state that simply misread the direction war was taking, and the 1940 campaign is the standard text for what the resulting defeat might look like. It is possible, however, to be less wrong than the French and still suffer badly, as the British did in 1940 and 1941 despite having invented the tank and having led the world in strategic bombing theory in the previous two decades.

More worrisome still, in many respects, was the German experience in World War II. The Germans developed a sophisticated theoretical understanding of the nature of war in their time, and adapted the tank and the military airplane to new ideas of fighting pioneered at the end of World War I and improved upon consistently thereafter. They were successful enough to destroy Poland and France with almost unheard-of speed, and thereby to drive Britain to the brink of collapse as well. But errors in their doctrine and its execution led to spectacular failure in 1941—and subsequently to the occupation of Berlin by a Red Army that had developed an even more sophisticated and effective understanding of the new ways of war. It emerges from this example and from others that it is not enough to get it about right—the difference between the 90 percent solution and the 100 percent solution can be the difference between victory and defeat in war.

There is, therefore, a great deal at stake in the effort to comprehend how war is changing at the moment. The importance of the task does not, however, make the task itself any easier. Understanding the changing nature of war requires not merely exploring the trendlines of technology, but also comprehending war's interactive nature. Revolutions in military affairs do not occur as the result of the actions of a single state, but as the result of the interactions between multiple states. Attempts to change warfare through an inwardly focused transformation, looking only at one's own capabilities and programs, are unlikely to succeed—and have never done so in the past. Accurately predicting the future course of military development is, thus, impossible.

The only way to proceed is with an open mind. Visionaries, like Fuller, who develop and pursue a single concept and then cling to it despite changes in the international military situation, rarely succeed. Those, like the German blitzkrieg theorists, who adapt their developing ideas to changing realities, are more successful. Ironically enough, it was the Soviets who proved most flexible of all, repeatedly reconceiving their own "deep battle" armored doctrine and developing it to a point of excellence similar in essence, but wildly different in detail, from the original concepts. Vision is important, but so is flexibility and a realistic appraisal of the outside world.

The pages that follow are critical of certain key attributes of current transformation theory, and the last chapter proposes a fundamental change in the way Americans think about the military tasks that lie before them. It is not that the authors of the transformation program are inept or ill-intentioned—on the contrary, they are senior military and civilian leaders with decades of experience, the best educations available in their fields, and years of thinking about these problems behind them. And they are all, without any question, devoted to doing what they think is best for the nation.

The problem from which they suffer is excessive exposure to a particular line of thought that has been predominant for more than a decade. Certain assumptions about war and about human society that formed the basis for early transformation efforts were accepted too uncritically. These assumptions are now so deeply rooted in the way people think about transformation that few even recognize that they were nothing but assumptions to begin with—now they seem to be axiomatic facts. To evaluate the current transformation program in a meaningful way requires stepping back from it and exploring its historical development in detail. We must identify and examine each assumption as it enters the developing conception of war and transformation. We must avoid the polemics and politicization of the study of recent experiences in war that have become so common in the polarized debates of the day. We must hold open equally the possibility that the current transformation visions are wrong, and that they might be right. Above all, we must recognize that the truth is nearly certain to be in between, and that no one should be forced either to accept completely or reject utterly any idea about how to transform the U.S. military, or the nature of war. For our goal should be simply to find the best way forward from here to establish the long-term security and well-being of our nation, and that will be the aim of the work that follows.

FINDING THE TARGET

CHAPTER ONE

Recovering from Vietnam

THE VIETNAM WAR hurt the American armed forces badly. The first experience of defeat in a major war combined with the severe stresses placed on the military crushed morale. The war's unpopularity produced unprecedented opposition to the draft and to the military as an institution. For the first time in many decades, the military felt distrusted and despised by mainstream America. Many officers believed that the defeat resulted from political betrayals by the country's elected leaders; others traced the causes to failures within the military itself. Most of those who served in the military of the early 1970s remember it as among the worst times in their careers.

The Vietnam War also led, however, to the transformation of the U.S. military. The renaissance was amazingly rapid. Within a decade, the U.S. military had completely reformed its manpower policies, training, doctrine, and equipment, and was on the road to becoming the most effective armed force in modern history. This transformation resulted from a complex interplay of forces, some political, some intellectual, and some military-technical. Every part of the change was subject to criticism and doubt. Experts in the late 1970s were indeed largely skeptical of the military's ability to recover even its former standards of effectiveness. Virtually no one saw that the efforts to recover from Vietnam and develop an All-Volunteer Force (AVF) would change the very nature of warfare within two decades.

The story of the origins of this transformation commands our attention today for a number of reasons. First, the 1970s was the last time that the ultimate size, composition, and capabilities of the U.S. military were considered in all of their detail and complexity. Many key assumptions that still shape the American armed forces today are now lost in the history of this period. They must be recovered and re-examined as America reshapes its military for the new challenges of the post–9/11 world. Second, the 1970s was not only a time of strain and recovery, but also a time of fiscal stringency. Like policy-makers today, the leaders of the 1970s were fixated on the problem of reducing the cost of the defense establishment while trying to increase its combat effectiveness to meet a growing threat. In the course of that effort, policy-makers in the 1970s addressed many of the solutions that are currently being considered to address today's problems—returning to conscription to cope with recruiting problems; finding technological answers to strategic challenges; meeting an enemy's quantitative advantage with qualitative superiority and so on. Some were implemented, others rejected, but the overall discourse can powerfully inform today's debate.

Third, the transformation of the 1970s was one of the most complete and successful military transformations in history. Its success resulted from its all-encompassing nature and from the fortunate synergy that developed between divergent paths of reform adopted for diverse reasons. It is an unheralded transformation, moreover—few students of military history even include it in the list of "revolutions in military affairs" of the twentieth century. The long-lasting predominance that this transformation produced for the military forces of the United States, however, shows that it not only deserves recognition alongside of the blitzkrieg revolution or the development of Soviet deep battle doctrine, but that it also demands close study for the lessons it offers about how to transform militaries.

Finally, the developments of the 1980s that led directly to the creation of the armed forces that smashed Saddam Hussein's regime twice grew out of the transformation of the 1970s that made them possible. We simply cannot understand how the armed forces reached their current state of excellence and strain without a careful consideration of their rebirth after failure.

GRAND STRATEGY

The innovations of the 1970s came at a moment when the American armed forces faced one of the worst crises in their history. The Soviet Union seemed to be expanding its military power far beyond the point of parity at which American observers had expected the U.S.S.R. to stop. It seemed to many that the Soviet leadership was seeking the sort of dominance that might make a pre-emptive attack possible. There was general consensus that NATO would be hard-pressed to stop such an attack with conventional forces and that a significant U.S. military expansion was required to meet this growing threat. The presence of vast Soviet and Warsaw Pact ground forces just across the inter-German border from American troop concentrations lent urgency to the problem, as it had done throughout the Cold War years. A similar, if smaller, danger existed on the unstable Korean peninsula, where U.S. forces also faced a much more numerous and hostile enemy separated from them by only a narrow demilitarized zone.

The Vietnam War had severely circumscribed possible responses to these growing dangers, however. In the closing years of that conflict, discontent with military service threatened to tear American society itself apart. Before the war had even ended, Richard Nixon had already decided that he must abandon conscription completely and quickly. By 1973, it was gone. The U.S. would have to find a way to meet the Soviet threat with an all-volunteer force that was both smaller and more expensive than the conscript armies it had used for the previous two and a half decades.

The 1973 Arab oil embargo and the economic downturn that it intensified led to a further restriction of the political possibilities for restoring America's military strength. Unrestrained defense spending was simply not politically acceptable in the 1970s and neither Democratic nor Republican administrations were willing to try to fight for dramatically increased defense expenditures. The social revolution that had accompanied the last years of the Vietnam War added to this problem by creating a political environment in which spending on domestic programs had much more priority than spending on defense. The widespread expectation of a "peace dividend" following the end of hostilities in Southeast Asia added to this shift in priorities.

The need to rein in defense spending interacted badly with the shift to the AVF. Volunteer militaries require significantly higher expenditures on personnel than conscript militaries. Salary and benefits packages must be good enough to lure healthy young men and women away from non-military occupations and keep a substantial number of them in the armed forces beyond their first enlistment tours. The transition to the AVF reoriented spending priorities within the military, therefore, away from a traditional focus on equipment, training, and readiness and toward a high focus on recruitment and retention of enlisted personnel. The initial result was to put even greater strain on the defense budget at a time of seemingly high risk.

There was no ready solution to these tensions. Various expedients were considered and some were tried, but none could rescue the armed forces from the paradox of having to face a growing threat with diminishing resources and capability. The de facto solution adopted throughout the 1970s was the acceptance of an extremely high amount of risk at the conventional level while relying on America's nuclear deterrent to make it good.

THE SOVIET THREAT

It has become commonplace in the post-Cold War world to look back at the Soviet threat with something like nostalgia. "At least we knew where and how we were going to fight" is a common refrain now among military theorists trying to understand and deal with today's threat from terrorism. Even today Army officers will take guests to places in Germany and declare, "This is where I was going to die." An analogous line of argument is that the U.S. armed forces during the late Cold War focused exclusively on defeating large Soviet armored formations in Central Europe because that was the main and obvious threat they faced and no other was worth considering. None of these common beliefs is valid.

The Soviet threat to the U.S. in the 1970s was vast, complex, amorphous, and unpredictable. It ranged from the danger of a full thermonuclear exchange to their support of small bands of revolutionaries around the world. The challenge of balancing the capabilities required to defeat the high-end Soviet nuclear or conventional threat with those required to respond to the lower-end challenges of unconventional warfare without bankrupting the U.S. and its allies was the central problem of American grand strategy during the Cold War. It was never satisfactorily resolved.

The Soviet Union was neither a predictable nor a consistent enemy. At times the Soviets pursued a cautiously aggressive policy focused on Europe. At other times, Soviet leaders focused their efforts on revolutionary movements in the Third World. Sometimes they prioritized conventional forces, sometimes nuclear forces. During the Brezhnev years, especially the 1970s, they seemed to be prioritizing everything at once. The 1970s saw a dramatic expansion of Soviet nuclear and conventional capabilities in Europe and the U.S.S.R., both qualitatively and quantitatively, as well as continuing efforts to support revolution in Asia, Africa, and the Americas.

The Soviet Union was not a straightforward Evil Empire, however. Coincident with the increases in military armament and support for insurgencies, Soviet leaders negotiated and signed a number of dramatic arms limitation treaties, including SALT I, the Anti-Ballistic Missile Treaty, and SALT II. Some saw in these negotiations a cynical ploy to gain even greater advantages by forcing the West to adhere to treaties the Soviets intended to violate; others saw in them a legitimate chance to begin a negotiated settlement to the Cold War. These negotiations were, at all events, a skillful effort to use diplomacy and world public opinion to support Soviet grand strategy, still further complicating American efforts to devise an appropriate counter-strategy.

The multifarious nature of the Communist threat forced U.S. grand strategists to consider their responses to a wide variety of possible dangers. The Central Front in Europe was thought to be the most dangerous, and sometimes the most likely, threat facing America and her allies. The Vietnam War had seriously distracted attention from the European theater, however. Troops and equipment moved from Europe to East Asia, reinforcements destined for European units were sent to fight the ongoing war, the development and fielding of new equipment was delayed. By the early 1970s, the combat capabilities of American forces in or destined to reinforce Europe were thought to have been seriously degraded as a result of the Vietnam War. The U.S. had faced the problem of balancing threats in multiple theaters by accepting risk in what had been thought to be the "main theater" in order to support operations in a secondary theater.

The complexities of U.S. grand strategy were not restricted to the balancing of U.S. military operations in various active or potential theaters of war. The Arab-Israeli War of 1973 also placed a strain on U.S. forces in Europe, as a substantial portion of the equipment pre-positioned there to facilitate the rapid reinforcement of the theater by forces based in the continental United States was rushed to Israel to make good Israeli losses in the early stages of the war. This diversion of resources taught a troubling lesson: U.S. forces had accepted such a fine strategic balance that even actions undertaken against America's allies not at the behest of the Soviet leadership could undermine U.S. forces' ability to accomplish their most central mission.

The Yom Kippur War of 1973 saw America's most reliable ally in the Middle East threatened with extermination. The Arab oil embargo of 1972–73 was another ominous development in this decade of instability, showing the vulnerability of the U.S. (and world) economy to the actions of Arab states not controlled or prompted by the U.S.S.R. And 1979, of course, saw the collapse of the Iranian monarchy, upon which the U.S. had built much of its Middle Eastern policy, in the face of radical Islamist revolution—that was neither controlled nor supported by the U.S.S.R.

The threat the U.S. faced was therefore complex, multi-dimensional, and unpredictable. Above all, the U.S. military posture in the 1970s was thought to be clearly inadequate to deal with the threats facing America in the way that Kennedy and Johnson had approached that problem. Moreover, changes resulting from the Vietnam War seemed to be increasing that inadequacy rather than redressing it. U.S. grand strategy and security policy faced a real crisis.

The administrations of the 1970s, unable or unwilling to respond to this crisis by increasing expenditures on national security significantly, instead tried to reduce the threat through

9

other means. Nixon made the most dramatic changes. His famous approach to China was intended to strip the U.S.S.R. of a potentially powerful ally and to create a new U.S.–Sino–Soviet relationship in which it would be easier to balance threats without having to face each one down individually. This approach also reflected the fact that the Nixon administration had largely given up on defending U.S. interests in Asia. That decision was highlighted by Nixon's determination to abandon the old two-and-a-half-war standard for maintaining U.S. armed forces that dated back to Kennedy's time in favor of a one-and-a-half-war standard.[1] Jimmy Carter's abortive efforts to reduce the presence of U.S. military forces in Korea were another step in the policy of abandoning East Asia through the 1970s.[2]

The pursuit of a serious diplomatic track with the Soviet Union was another part of the U.S. effort to match ends with means by reducing threats. The Nixon/Kissinger policy of "linkage" aimed to barter U.S. diplomatic and economic concessions in return for reductions in the Soviet threat. The SALT negotiations, initially a part of this policy, acquired a momentum of their own, continuing into the late Carter administration. These negotiations sought to mitigate the Soviet thermonuclear threat through diplomacy, thus avoiding the need to increase defense spending to match the Soviet build-up.

At no time did U.S. military capabilities dip below the point at which the Soviets might have decided to risk all-out war—deterrence was maintained throughout the period. Nonetheless, the 1970s ended with a series of catastrophes for American foreign policy. In 1979, a revolutionary movement soon dominated by the communist Sandinistas ousted the U.S.-backed president of Nicaragua, Anastasio Somoza. That same year, the forces of Ayatollah Khomeini took power in Iran, as we have already noted, not only unseating the American-backed Shah, but also taking numerous hostages from the American embassy in Teheran. At the end of the year, finally, Soviet forces invaded

Afghanistan, assassinating the unreliable communist ruler of that state who had been making overtures to the U.S. (which the humanitarian-focused administration of Jimmy Carter had rebuffed), and installing a new puppet backed by Soviet tanks.

The causal relationships between the changed U.S. grand strategy and these events are far from clear. It is hard to imagine U.S. troops invading Iran to preserve the Shah's power, still harder to see them trekking to Afghanistan to fight the Soviets on their own border. Previous decades might have seen American military intervention in Nicaragua, but that defeat was by far the least important of the three. The only real connection lay in the fact that many domestic and foreign observers saw in the more cautious grand strategy of the 1970s a weakness bred of fear, domestic turmoil, economic stagnation, and military incapacity. That fear permeated the senior military leadership, which was well aware of the fact that diplomacy was holding threats in abeyance without eliminating them, and that the U.S. military was badly equipped to respond to those threats or to any others that might unexpectedly emerge which were clearly beyond the reach of diplomacy.

The rapid deterioration of the U.S. security situation at the end of the 1970s ensured that fears that the military would not be able to accomplish tasks vital to American national security would persist. The environment of fiscal stringency forced those pushing for a military transformation to find creative solutions. The political determination to move to the AVF ensured that those solutions would be novel. U.S. military transformation in the 1970s thus emerged from a powerful nexus of forces including domestic political, economic, social, diplomatic, military technical, and so on. The misfortunes of the 1970s that instigated transformation turned out to be good fortune for the nation that would reap the benefits of that transformation.

⋆   ⋆   ⋆

Finding the Target

The Transformation

The U.S. military responded to the crisis of the 1970s with several initiatives, including the creation of the All-Volunteer Force, the fielding of new generations of equipment in all of the armed services, a major revolution in training throughout the armed forces, and a renaissance of intellectual development and sophisticated arguments about military doctrine. The initial impetuses for each of these transformations were different and largely independent of one another. Luckily, they operated synergistically to produce a fundamental change in the nature of warfare, a Revolution in Military Affairs.

The All-Volunteer Force

The idea of conscription came under ferocious attack in the late 1960s for several reasons. The unpleasantness of a jungle counter-insurgency, the growing mistrust of the Johnson administration (which had been less than honest with the American people about the war), and the fact that the war seemed to be both endless and hopeless: all were factors that certainly played powerful roles in the anti-draft agitation that began to rock the nation at the end of the decade. A more subtle and complex problem also came into play, however: the draft seemed extremely unfair.[3]

A country the size of the United States sees far more young men come of draftable age every year than it actually needs in any but the most total of wars. The deployment of 550,000 soldiers to Vietnam did not come close to requiring such a total mobilization—President Johnson did not even find it necessary to call up the Reserves to maintain that level of force in combat.[4] As a result, it became necessary to choose who would serve and who would not at a moment when the stakes were very high. At first the decisions were made based on a system of deferments that had been designed to direct young men into desirable occupations by exempting those working in such occupations from immediate military service. This attempt to control the labor pool with the threat of conscription was one of the major attractions of conscription for many of its advocates.

By the end of the 1960s, however, hostility about the unfairness of the deferment system led to pressure to adopt a lottery system in place of occupational or educational exemptions. This effort ran into trouble not only because it exposed the children of the wealthy (and increasingly anti-war) elite more to the dangers of conscription and war, but also because it would have stripped control of the conscription process from local communities through the elimination or severe reduction of their draft boards. Despite the fact that by the end of the war almost all automatic deferments had been eliminated, the sense that the selective draft produced lucky winners and unfortunate losers prevailed.

Nixon had run for president on a platform of significant draft reform and the elimination of conscription at the end of the war. He followed through rapidly on these promises, spurred by the growing anti-war and anti-draft sentiment in the country. In the early days of his 1972 re-election campaign, Nixon announced that the last inductees would enter the military in December 1972. The draft had died a rapid death.[5]

Supporters of conscription made a number of arguments in defense of the increasingly unpopular system. They argued that it would be impossible to attract enough young people to volunteer for military service to maintain America's defense posture at an adequate level. They particularly feared that the end of the draft would eliminate the country's ability to mobilize rapidly in the event of a major war. Many lamented the collapse of the deferment system that had allowed the government to focus labor resources into either defense-related industries or community-service jobs, although that argument had largely collapsed by the 1970s. Some noted with concern the dramatically increased costs of maintaining a volunteer force.[6]

As the 1970s progressed, the fears of the pro-draft advocates only grew, and experience emphasized still other concerns. The first years of the AVF saw an influx of both blacks and women into the armed forces, because those were demographic groups most easily induced to volunteer—blacks because of their relative poverty and women because of the new opportunities that a manpower-hungry military began to open to them. The changing demographics of the military raised hackles even higher among draft-supporters. The increase in the percentage of women seemed to them to raise the specter of the introduction of women into combat, which many regarded as a social evil. The large number of blacks in uniform, especially in the enlisted ranks, seemed to some to raise the danger that Army units might become unusable against civil disturbances which, at the time, frequently took the form of race riots. Still another fear was that an increasingly professional military would chafe at civilian control. The draft had ensured that the majority of soldiers in uniform had come recently from civilian life and could expect to return to it in a few years. Their lack of military professionalism was seen as a virtue that tied them to their communities and ensured their loyalty to the civilian leadership of the state. As the rank-and-file of the armed forces became long-service professional soldiers, it was argued, their loyalty would shift from the nation to their military leadership. Such soldiers would be much more apt, it was thought, to support unconstitutional actions on the part of military leaders emboldened by that shift of loyalty.

Some observers pointed out that the early years of the AVF, when recruiting goals were met with relative ease, had coincided with a significant economic downturn and also with a bulge in the eighteen- to twenty-one-year-old population. Over the next decade and more, they argued, not only would the economy improve, but the number of military-aged youth would decline in accord with changed demographic trends. It might become impossible, they feared, to find enough willing young men and women to meet even the most modest enlistment targets.

Yet another predicted difficulty with the AVF was that the quality of the recruits would be rather lower than had been the case with the conscript military. There were two main reasons for this belief. First, conscription had drawn from a broad segment of society, especially after the elimination of deferments, thus pulling into the military many well-educated young men who otherwise would never have joined the colors. Second, the difficulty of meeting recruiting goals required the lowering of quality standards for recruits. In the age of conscription, the problem had been sifting out the best conscripts from a large pool. In the age of volunteers, the problem was fighting for every possible recruit. A resulting drop in average quality seemed inevitable.

Finally, the adoption of an all-volunteer military would, it was feared, seriously reduce the nation's reserve mobilization capability. Congress was unwilling to maintain local draft boards, agencies, and personnel at the levels that would have been necessary to renew conscription rapidly in the event of an emergency. During the time of the draft, young men had frequently joined the Reserves or the National Guard in the hope of escaping service with the active forces as a result of exemptions passed into law in 1963.[7] Those who had made this decision fared well, on the whole, during the war years, since Johnson's determination to avoid a reserve call-up allowed most of them to stay at home. But that decision also seriously undercut morale in the Reserves and National Guard. With the end of the war and the draft, it was thought that the attractiveness of the Reserves would diminish markedly, as young men no longer saw the need to protect themselves from conscription by joining the Reserves. Reserve recruitment in the early years of the AVF was, therefore, predicted to be extremely low, with the nation's ability to mobilize manpower rapidly in the event of crisis correspondingly reduced.

Of these various objections to the AVF, several have proven completely invalid over the thirty years since the end of conscription. The racial make-up of the military has not in any way reduced its utility either in domestic crisis or foreign wars, and the armed forces have been astonishingly successful at developing strategies and education programs that integrate not only blacks, but growing numbers of Hispanics and other ethnic minorities into an increasingly color-blind force.[8] Although the percentage of women in uniform has grown dramatically, moreover, that growth has not led to the integration of women into combat units in the Army. Women have been allowed to fly combat missions in the Navy and the Air Force, however, and female soldiers have seen combat in Iraq and elsewhere as part of military police, aviation, and other forward-deployed combat service support units. Their presence has coincided with a dramatic increase in the combat effectiveness of the American military, though, making it impossible to argue that they have harmed combat capability in any important way. It is easier to argue that they have improved it.

Dire predictions about the impossibility of meeting recruiting quotas have also proved largely unfounded. Recruitment has been harder or easier over the past three decades depending on the state of the economy and the nature of the conflicts the armed forces were engaged in or preparing for, but the military has never yet been unable to sustain itself at or near its programmed end-strength with recruits of an acceptable level of quality. Problems with Reserve and National Guard recruitment have also proven largely ephemeral, at least until very recently.

Nor has the elimination of conscripts weakened the military's commitment to civilian control in any noticeable way. Although

Colin Powell's public opposition to President Bill Clinton over the issue of homosexuals in the military caused some to warn darkly of imminent military coups, it must be remembered that the "revolt of the admirals" in 1949 and MacArthur's obvious and dangerous insubordination toward Truman both occurred within the context of conscript forces. After the Powell controversy, moreover, the senior military leadership has proven extremely docile in the face of mounting tensions and controversies. Since the U.S. officer corps has been made up of long-service professionals since the Civil War, finally, it is no surprise that the elimination of conscripts from the rank-and-file has had no important effect in this area.

Not all of the fears of AVF opponents have proven baseless, however. Even AVF advocates admitted at the time that the new military structure did not provide adequate manpower for large-scale rapidly developing crises. As the military abandoned the draft, it transitioned to a new organization based on what was called the "total force" concept. This organization relied on various categories of Reservists to fill out peacetime units to their wartime strengths and to add new units in wartime. The idea was that only when the Reserves were exhausted or totally mobilized for war would the nation turn to conscription.[9] In effect, this concept turned the Vietnam experience on its head by requiring the president to mobilize the Reserves and preventing him from resorting to conscription instead, as Lyndon Johnson had done.

The Army added its own twist to this policy in the early 1970s, as Chief of Staff General Creighton Abrams shifted most of the forces' essential combat service support units (military police, logistics, civil affairs, and other similar units) into the Reserves. His motivation in this decision is unclear. Some have suggested that he intended to make it impossible for a president to go to war in the future without support from the nation by requiring him to mobilize the Reserves for any deployment. His subordinates at the time certainly realized that this would be the effect of the new force structure, although it is not at all clear that Abrams intentionally adopted it for the purpose of tying the president's hands.[10] In truth, the focus on the Army's internal organization obscures the larger context of this debate. The entire "total force" concept was, in effect, designed to prevent any future president from repeating Johnson's method of waging war. Its originators always foresaw that any serious deployment overseas would require substantial reserve mobilization.

Whatever the details of the Army leadership's intentions, however, the net result of the transition to the "total force" concept was that the burden of mobilization shifted from conscription to the Reserves. This shift immediately raised important questions about the nature and availability of the reserve. What percentage of those on the reserve rolls would actually show up at their units when called? How long would it take them to arrive there? How long after their arrival would those units be ready for combat or combat support operations? How would the military make up deficiencies if there were not enough Reservists? These were the key questions of the day.

The initial answers were not encouraging. Because Johnson had not used the Reserves, there was virtually no historical experience in the 1970s for estimating what percentage would actually be available when called up. A 1975 Department of Defense study estimated that availability rates would vary from 95 percent of some categories to 10 percent of others, but a study the following year found these estimates to be highly questionable. Among other things, the study estimated that as a result of problems of recruiting into the Reserves, two categories of Reserves would "cease to be viable resources of mobilization manpower by FY 1980."[11] Nor would these Reserves be able to report to their units very rapidly. It was estimated that Reservists would need at least sixty days to fill out their units, and that some Reserve units might require months of training beyond that before they would be able to perform their wartime tasks. These estimates were regarded as "very optimistic" even by AVF-advocates.[12] In other words, the active forces deploying to meet a large-scale threat had to expect significant shortfalls in reinforcements and replacements in the first several months of deployment. Moreoever, it might even be necessary to resort to some form of conscription again just to complete that initial reinforcement.

This reflection would have been disturbing enough at any time, but it was particularly disturbing in the mid-1970s. The Yom Kippur War of 1973 had rocked the American defense establishment to its foundations. In a matter of weeks, Arab and Israeli forces destroyed thousands of tanks and hundreds of combat aircraft, moving rapidly over many miles of desert. The speed and lethality of this short war, which featured recent-model U.S. and Soviet equipment, led to a re-evaluation of the threat on the Central Front in Europe. If Arabs using Soviet tanks and aircraft could drive so rapidly and inflict so many casualties on Israelis, then what would the Soviets be able to do with their vastly superior stockpiles and much greater manpower? The effects of this war played an important role in spurring technological developments in the U.S. armed forces, as we shall see, but it also affected the early development of the AVF in an important way.[13]

The increasing size of the Soviet military combined with the U.S. forces' new respect for the speed and lethality of war persuaded the leadership that NATO forces in Central Europe were in grave danger. Donald Rumsfeld, in his first tour as Secretary of Defense in 1976, noted that "The force balance [between NATO and the Warsaw Pact] reaches an acceptable level of risk with the arrival of U.S. reinforcements, but only after a very critical period in the first few days when the force ratio could reach dangerously high levels."[14] This was an understatement, especially considering the time it would take to bring reinforcements to bear in many likely crisis scenarios, a time that would be measured in weeks, at least, rather than days.

The dilemma was apparent. U.S. active forces readily available for combat in Europe were not adequate to defend themselves in the face of Soviet attack. Only with the arrival of substantial reinforcements from the continental United States, including hundreds of thousands of Reservists, would NATO stand a chance of holding off a Warsaw Pact onslaught. But the arrival of those reinforcements would take weeks or months at the most optimistic estimates, and would almost certainly fall short of the necessary numbers of men because of the limitations of the reserve system. And it was virtually certain that the war would be over long before the Department of Defense could resurrect the defunct Selective Service System and even begin a new conscription. The solution was obvious: the active forces had to be increased. The problem was that there was no money in the defense budget for such an expansion, no likelihood of increasing the budget, and no certain way to increase recruitment at a difficult time even if the money had appeared. The military found another way.

A perennial tension in any military organization is the ratio of actual combat forces to troops in supporting services—the ratio of "tooth to tail." Military analysts and historians generally regard a high "tooth to tail" ratio as optimal, seeing in excessive support structures wasteful inefficiency that detracts from combat capability at a high cost to the state. The reality is considerably more complicated, particularly in modern armies that rely on vast and sophisticated support structures to function at all. At times of high threat and constrained resources, however, the "tail" frequently seems an attractive area for retrenchment in order to free up resources for the "teeth." So it was in the 1970s.

The Army of 1974 consisted of thirteen and a third active divisions. In Congressional hearings of that year, Abrams testified that this force offered a "marginal chance of succeeding" without using nuclear weapons. He also feared forces within the Congressional budget community to cut the Army down to "an elite professional force with as few as eight army divisions."[15] He determined, accordingly, to increase the size of the active Army's combat troops, both in order to stave off calls for a reduction and in order to enable the force to meet its requirements to defend the nation's interests in war. Based on no very detailed examination of the problem and without having informed his subordinates, he decided to aim for a sixteen-division active Army.[16] But he determined to achieve this objective without increasing the overall size of the active force.

Abrams accomplished his goal. By the early 1980s, there were sixteen divisions in the Active Army, while the end strength of the active force remained almost perfectly constant from 1975 to the end of the 1980s, when it began to decline.[17] Abrams' success resulted from an assault on the "tail" of the active Army. The decision to rely on combat service support troops in the reserve allowed him to reduce dramatically the number of such forces in the Active Army. At the same time, Abrams fought hard to scale back what he regarded as bloated headquarters staffs throughout the Army, restoring the slots occupied by those staffs to the combat units of the active force as well. The Army received significant assistance in this task in 1976, when Congress required the service to convert 18,000 support slots in the European forces to combat billets—or else to lose the slots.[18] The Army thus increased its combat forces within a few years by more than 20 percent without adding a single soldier to its ranks.[19]

By the end of the 1970s, the AVF had settled down. Recruiting had become stabilized, the combat power of the force was increased, and the advent of new technologies (which we will consider below) was helping to reassure nervous commanders about their ability to meet the challenges they faced. Reforms to the reserve system increased the likelihood that the Reserves would be able to play their designated role and began to repair the critical manpower shortages that resulted from the reserve recruiting disasters of the first years of the AVF. The AVF had survived its birthing and growing pains and was beginning to mature into a powerful and reliable military force.

As a program for maximizing immediate combat power in an era of tight fiscal constraints, the "total force" concept was excellent. It offered the Army the best chance to meet the first powerful blows of the Warsaw Pact with the best possible forces in a timely fashion. But the "total force" and the AVF accomplished that goal at a very high price. The reliance on the Reserves to provide combat service support critical for the functioning of the active Army dramatically reduced the Reserves' ability to provide new combat forces as reinforcements or replacements. In the case of a large-scale conflict, the system would not have been able to meet the demand for military manpower for very long at all before it became necessary to resort once again to conscription. The atrophy of the mechanisms of conscription, however, made that last resort seem very unreliable. The nation continued to accept a very high degree of risk in its military manpower policies in order to preserve the desired financial equilibrium.

The shift of combat service support to the Reserves created another problem not visible at the time. It meant that the Active Force could not sustain an overseas deployment of any size for any length of time without relying on significant Reserve support. Since the focus in the 1970s was on short, sharp, massive wars that would either end or go nuclear very quickly, this was not an important consideration at the time. As the U.S. transitioned away from the prospect of such wars following the fall of the Soviet Union, however, it would become very important indeed.

The slashing of "tail" to provide more "tooth" was a mixed omen. On the one hand, it showed that such a transformation of "fat" to "muscle" was possible, thereby providing modern-day advocates of similar measures with some historical backing. On the other hand, the Army of the 1970s went as far as it could possibly go in this direction, and perhaps even farther than it should have. Current discussions of slashing the support services to provide more combat power rarely consider the fact that the current force structure emerged from precisely such an effort, raising the possibility that further dramatic shifting of resources from support to combat elements will not be possible.

The controversies of the 1970s focused on the problems of transitioning to the AVF. The defenders of the concept had to do relatively little to win their battle considering the political climate of the time. As a result, the debate largely missed one of the most important consequences of the elimination of conscription. It turns out that a long-service professional military can be vastly more effective in combat than a conscript force. Long service provides much greater time for assimilation and acculturation of recruits, as well as for their education, training, and professional development. It facilitates the growth of unit cohesion and the sort of large-unit training that is very difficult in a force that has to concentrate on bringing new conscripts up to minimal standards in basic skills. It also changes the leadership dynamic of the force fundamentally.

In a conscript military, junior officers and NCOs spend a great deal of their time attempting to motivate and discipline their soldiers. These activities distract those officers from their own professional development and frequently lead to a stifling of subordinates' initiative. The advantages of a professional military began to make themselves felt in the 1980s. Volunteers are far easier to motivate than conscripts. As they gain experience and confidence, they are more able and willing to take the initiative, and their superiors are readier to trust them to do so. That experience and growing expertise in their specialties also makes it easier for volunteers to master ever more complex military technology. Freedom from having to motivate unwilling soldiers, finally, frees officers to focus more steadily on their own professional and intellectual development. Although few saw it at the time, the advent of the AVF created an opportunity for the military to increase its combat effectiveness dramatically, and enabled it to take the best possible advantage of changes in military technology, doctrine, and training that had come about for independent reasons.

MILITARY TECHNOLOGY

It has become so commonplace in the current defense debate to focus on technology that it is important to remember that the technological developments of the 1960s and 1970s were only one part of the story of military transformation then and subsequently. The improvement of U.S. military technology after Vietnam would certainly have led to increased combat effectiveness if nothing else had happened. The combination of that technological growth with the establishment of an all-volunteer service and with the developments in training and doctrine described below, however, allowed the U.S. to change the face of warfare fundamentally within the space of two decades.

The adoption of the AVF had hit the various armed services differentially, in part based on the Vietnam experience. Whereas the Army and Marines had expanded during the war by 61 percent and 63 percent respectively between 1965 and their wartime highs, the Navy increased by only 15 percent, and the Air Force by less than 10 percent.[20] The question of conscription was clearly much more urgent for the land forces than for the Navy and the Air Force, although the end of conscription affected those services in complex ways as well.[21] This fact was especially true in light of the different service cultures. The Army and Marines have traditionally valued and prioritized people, both in budgetary decisions and in leader education

24

and training. The Navy and the Air Force normally prioritize weapons systems. The technological transformation of the military therefore affected the airpower services much more immediately and dramatically, although the real impact it had also had on the Army and the Marines emerged starkly in the first Gulf War.

The Air Power Services

Vietnam was nearly as much of a catastrophe for the airpower services as it was for the land forces. A lethal combination of Soviet-made surface-to-air missiles (SAMs), traditional anti-aircraft artillery (AAA), and MiG fighters led to staggering losses in aircraft and crews. Two thousand five hundred and sixty-one aircraft and 3,587 helicopters fell to enemy fire, and roughly another 1,200 planes and 1,300 choppers crashed due to non-combat causes. Three hundred and eighty-three Air Force F-105 fighters were lost out of a total of 833 that had been built. Half of the aircrews of these lost planes were never recovered.[22] In addition to these horrifying losses, Vietnam severely compromised airpower theories and many of the justifications for airpower that had become so prominent in the nuclear era. Although the American military dropped 8,000,000 tons of bombs on Vietnam (and some of its neighbors)—twice the tonnage used in World War II by all the combatants—the war was a disastrous failure. Unlike the Army and Marines, moreover, which could at least claim never to have lost a battle in this last war, the Air Force fared far worse against the Vietnamese fighter pilots than it had against any other adversary in its history. Kill ratios in the skies over Vietnam were a mere 2.4 to 1, dropping at times to an even exchange. They had been 8 to 1 in World War II, and 10 to 1, sometimes as high as 14 to 1, in Korea.[23] The Vietnam War induced a real sense of failure and crisis in the airpower services.

As was the case with the Army, the Air Force and Navy responded to that crisis in many dimensions, and we will explore changes in training and doctrine below. Service leaders put the greatest effort, however, into refitting their forces with new technology designed to solve as many of the problems they had encountered in Vietnam as possible, and to secure for the U.S. an airpower advantage that would last for a decade or more.

American air forces had found it difficult to penetrate the Vietnamese anti-aircraft defenses, to shoot down enemy fighters, to identify and locate meaningful targets, and to hit those targets with any reasonable accuracy. Although many factors caused these difficulties, they all shared at least one common root. The U.S. fixation with nuclear weapons during the Eisenhower administration had left a legacy of poorly chosen technology and mistaken attitudes in the airpower services. It took defeat in Vietnam to free the services from that legacy.

Eisenhower had adopted a policy called "massive retaliation" as the basis of his Cold War grand strategy. This policy relied upon the U.S. nuclear advantage to protect America and her allies, and that reliance, in turn, allowed Eisenhower to reduce the conventional armed forces and thereby save money.[24] The Air Force embraced this policy to such an extent that even the tactical air force units focused primarily on the mission of delivering nuclear weapons against an enemy, and both the Air Force and the Navy thought of defense only in terms of flights of large, slow-moving, and poorly maneuvering bombers. U.S. aircraft were not designed to engage in dogfights or even in complicated multi-aircraft missile engagements with enemy fighters. The main criterion for the selection of any airframe was whether or not it could deliver a nuclear weapon.[25]

As a result, American fighters over Vietnam frequently found themselves outmaneuvered by obsolescent Soviet aircraft that had been designed to engage in single combat. The U.S. Air Force might have taken much longer to resolve this problem had it not been for an intellectual breakthrough by a trouble-some maverick fighter jock named John Boyd. Boyd had cut his teeth flying combat missions in Korea, and then had spent considerable time at Air Force training bases. As a major, he had gone back to college to earn a degree in engineering, which allowed him to make a discovery that would revolutionize combat aircraft design and air-to-air combat tactics. He called his breakthrough "Energy Maneuverability." The key was the application of physics, engineering, mathematics, and computers to generate graphic pictures of the maneuverability characteristics of aircraft in various different conditions (altitude, speed, etc.). By generating these images for U.S. and Soviet aircraft, Boyd discovered that American fighters were markedly inferior to their Soviet counterparts when it came to air-to-air combat. This observation in itself was not remarkable (although it earned Boyd a great deal of initial hostility within the Air Force) because pilots flying combat missions over Vietnam at the time were discovering the same thing in real time. But Boyd's application of mechanics and cybernetics to the problem allowed him and a small team of intellectual mavericks to discover a solution.[26]

In the mid-1960s, Boyd and his cohort, who came to be called the "Fighter Mafia," managed in effect to hijack the development of a new fighter then being designed to replace the F-111. The F-111 had resulted from the confluence of two trends. The focus on nuclear war led its designers to emphasize payload, in part because of the belief that even in the fight for air superiority it was more important to be able to destroy the enemy's planes on the ground than to have to fight them in the air. Secretary of Defense Robert S. McNamara's emphasis on efficiency in management and procurement reinforced this trend. The F-111 was supposed to become the mainstay not only of the Air Force, but of the Navy as well. It was designed to accomplish five separate missions: "air superiority, close air support, all weather attack, nuclear attack, and all weather intercept."[27] A plane that could execute five different missions for two different services was unlikely to do anything very well. At two-and-a-half times the size of a B-17 bomber, it certainly was not going to be a nimble dogfighter.

The combination of the poor showing of American fighters in the skies over Vietnam and Boyd's Energy Maneuverability theory allowed the Fighter Mafia to take control of the development of the follow-on to the F-111. The result was the F-15 Eagle, the first Air Force plane in many years designed primarily to win air superiority in the skies. It featured two powerful engines and aerodynamics that gave it significant performance advantages over other U.S. and foreign planes. With an internal 20 mm cannon and the capacity to carry eight air-to-air missiles, it could use its advanced targeting radar system to engage the enemy from a great distance or to outfly almost anything else in the sky in a dogfight.[28] These advantages were made possible in part because it was the first fighter for a long time not designed to carry nuclear weapons.

But the F-15 was still a relatively large aircraft, and the Fighter Mafia immediately pushed for the development of a lightweight airframe designed to be the perfect dogfighter. The result of this effort was the F-16 Falcon. The Navy, meanwhile, pursued parallel efforts to develop its own replacement for the F-111, which it had never adopted. That development produced the F-14 Tomcat, another aircraft designed to win air superiority by defeating enemy fighters in the sky. The F-14 is a highly maneuverable airframe, even though it was not designed in accord with Boyd's theories. The Navy insisted on a swing-wing configuration, which Boyd argued added considerable weight to the airframe in exchange for marginal overall improvements in performance. The Navy's haste to fill the gap left by the decision not to acquire the F-111 also led it to accept engines for the F-14 that were considerably less efficient and powerful than those of the F-15. The focus on air superiority, however, still made the F-14 a superb combat aircraft. The subsequent reluctance of Congress to accept the F-14's high price tag led to the development of the F/A-18 Hornet, designed to accomplish both the air superiority and the ground attack missions at a lower unit cost than the F-14, and the Navy ultimately adopted a mix of F-14s and F/A-18s for its carrier air fleet.[29]

The refocusing of the fighter community on securing air superiority in the sky was accompanied by the development of dedicated bombers to fill the roles of long-range penetrator and close air supporter. Thus the Air Force began the development of the B-1 bomber and the A-10 ground-attack aircraft. Neither aircraft proved as successful in its role as the "superfighters" did in theirs. The B-1 program was bedeviled by problems from the start and the Air Force bought very few of the airplanes in the end. The A-10 was more successful. It was designed to be a tank killer, using both an internal 30 mm cannon (very large for an airplane) and specially designed Maverick television-guided missiles. It is heavily armored and designed to be able to survive intense ground fire while it flies slowly at low altitudes hunting for and destroying enemy tanks. It performed this mission extremely well in the first Gulf War, although it did suffer from higher-than-desirable loss rates.[30] The ability of the F-15 (especially configured as the F-15E Strike Eagle), the F/A-18, and the F-16 to conduct ground-attack missions with accurate missile fire led to a tension about the need for the A-10 within the Air Force community, especially as elements in the service desired to turn away from the close air support role in the 1980s and 1990s.

The net result of these developments in aircraft design produced a suite of airplanes unmatched by any power in the world. In the 1970s, the U.S. definitively reclaimed the technological advantage in air superiority aircraft, and there was every reason to believe that the new generation of "superfighters" would bring U.S. kill ratios up to and beyond the highest levels in

American history. That reflection did not induce complacency in the service, however, for two reasons. First, the Soviets were known to possess several times as many fighters as the U.S. could afford to produce, and although American planes were now superior, the Soviets were working feverishly to catch up. Second, the Soviet historical emphasis on integrated, multi-layer air defense systems posed a significant challenge to American pilots who wanted to do more than fly over their own troops. The airpower services attacked the first problem through the development of missile, radar, and radar-tracking technology in the 1970s. The solution to the second problem, stealth technology, largely emerged in the 1980s.

The performance of American air-to-air missiles had left a lot to be desired in the Vietnam War. In the first several years of U.S. active involvement in the war, the hit rates of American air-to-air missiles (AAMs) ranged between 9 percent and 16 percent. The problem was that U.S. air-to-air missiles had been designed for use against slow-moving and poorly maneuvering Soviet bombers from considerable distances. They were not useful when fired at close range against hard-flying MIGs engaged in intense dogfights. Problems in maintenance and doctrine also reduced the performance of these missiles, exposing U.S. aircrews to excessive losses in air-to-air combat.[31] Over the course of the war and afterwards, therefore, the Air Force put a great deal of effort into upgrading its AAM capability. This effort produced a suite of three missiles: the Sidewinder (dramatically improved over the versions used in Vietnam), the Phoenix, and the Advanced Medium-Range Air-to-Air Missile (AMRAAM). The development of these missiles was greatly facilitated by the establishment of an advanced air combat training center at Nellis Air Force Base in 1970.[32] One of the problems with the previous generations of American AAMs had been the failure of designers to test them in realistic combat scenarios. Their inability to match the maneuvers of the agile

MiGs was not apparent in the sort of long-range static engagements used to validate them before large-scale buys. Once it became possible to test the missiles realistically, developers were able to perfect the technology of engaging and destroying enemy aircraft at all ranges.

These developments resulted in missiles that could begin destroying enemy aircraft at a range of one hundred miles (the Phoenix), at thirty miles or more (the AMRAAM), or in the close fight (the Sidewinder). The reliability of the weapons and their ability to maintain their lock on even hard-maneuvering enemy aircraft increased dramatically to the point where American pilots could reasonably assume that any missile they fired would hit and destroy its target. In the long run, these developments in missile technology probably reduced the significance of the maneuverability characteristics of the superfighters. It was becoming increasingly unlikely that enemy aircraft could even get close enough to U.S. planes to force them to maneuver.

Vietnam also revealed shortcomings in the management of aerial combat. Although designated ships and aircraft maintained a radar watch on North Vietnamese airbases to provide early warning of MiG launches, they were not able to provide continual coverage of the movement of enemy aircraft or to communicate that knowledge to U.S. aircraft in a timely and efficient manner. As a result, American pilots were frequently surprised by MiG attacks and engaged at close range. The Air Force began developing an Airborne Warning and Control System (AWACS) in 1961, but the system did not come on line until 1977. When it did, it provided U.S. aircraft with a revolutionary capability. The more than twenty crewmembers of an AWACS flying command were able to track many enemy and friendly aircraft simultaneously over an extensive area, warning U.S. pilots of approaching enemies planes and vectoring them in to attack enemy formations.[33] The AWACS enabled the superfighters to use their long-range missiles to best effect, reducing the number and intensity of dogfights and preventing enemy pilots from achieving surprise. Developments in the avionics and radar tracking systems of the superfighters themselves, which allowed pilots to track and engage multiple targets simultaneously, also helped expand their ability to offset superior Soviet numbers.

The increased maneuverability of the superfighters did not sufficiently protect them from the threat of SAMs and anti-aircraft artillery that had brought down so many American pilots over Vietnam. The Vietnamese air defense system was extensive, moreover, but primitive compared to the vast air defenses the Soviet Union was building to protect its own territory and its forward-deployed troops in Eastern Europe. If the U.S. Air Force wanted to be able to conduct strikes in the rear of Soviet forces, it would have to improve its ability to get through an integrated, multi-layer air defense system with limited losses. U.S. pilots in the early years of the Vietnam War had suffered from serious handicaps in this effort. Restrictions on their rules of engagement prohibited them from attacking enemy MiG bases, radar sites, and even SAM batteries under many circumstances. Aerial countermeasures, especially electronic countermeasures, were primitive and limited, and the mania for centralized control led to stereotyped attack patterns that the North Vietnamese quickly learned how to punish.[34]

The dramatic easing of the rules of engagement and centralization that characterized attacks in the 1970s reduced these problems significantly, but the Air Force also worked hard to develop effective counter-measures to reduce the SAM threat to its aircraft. By the end of the war, improvements in anti-radiation missiles (those designed to locate and destroy enemy radar sites) and the development of dedicated SAM jammers (like the F-104 Wild Weasel and its descendants), reduced American aircraft losses to SAMs significantly. These technological capabilities and the fear of continuously improving Soviet SAM systems also led to the development of an air superiority doctrine focused on eliminating enemy air defenses as a first priority, along with the fielding of additional systems, like the Stealth fighter and bomber, to do it.[35]

The inefficiency of U.S. bombing in Vietnam was the final problem the Air Force set about solving. Despite the vast tonnage of bombs dropped on North Vietnam, the Ho Chi Minh trail, and enemy positions in South Vietnam, U.S. forces had great difficulty destroying their targets. Part of the problem was simply that Vietnam provided few large, easily visible targets for the "dumb bombs" dropped by American planes in a ferocious SAM and Anti-Aircraft Artillery (AAA) environment. As a result, the Air Force worked feverishly to develop and field laser-guided bombs (LGBs) that could home in on laser beams pointed at their targets. The results were impressive. Years of attacks with "dumb bombs" against the Paul Doumer bridge in Hanoi had done little more than chip its paint. But in May 1972, four F-4s carrying eight laser-guided bombs destroyed it in a single flight.[36] Throughout the 1970s, the Air Force worked feverishly to improve the accuracy and reliability of its LGBs and to develop missiles like the Maverick, a television-guided missile that an attacking pilot could literally steer into the target. These improvements in the accuracy and effectiveness of missiles and bombs against ground targets would lead to a fundamental reconsideration of the nature of bombing campaigns in the 1980s and 1990s.

The development of aerial technology in the 1960s and 1970s offers a number of important lessons about the technological basis of military transformation. First and foremost, the improvements in America's aircraft resulted from a decision to stop trying to produce single airframes to accomplish all conceivable missions for all services but instead to produce the best planes for a discreet number of critical tasks. These improvements also resulted from the rejection of a focus on a single type of warfare—nuclear war—and the determination to prepare instead to fight many kinds of conflicts against various different enemies. The resulting panoply of aircraft provided the airpower services with a great deal of versatility and redundancy. If one airframe proved less capable in certain roles than anticipated, or if the development of enemy capabilities reduced its safety or effectiveness, other aircraft and missiles could cover the deficiencies. Furthermore, this panoply of aircraft and missile types allowed the development of a synergistic approach to air warfare far superior to anything seen before. Having more types of planes and missiles is less fiscally and bureaucratically efficient, but it can be militarily more effective. Focusing on a single primary mission may ease the task of developers and budgeters, but it can gravely compromise the success and safety of warriors.

Second, the renaissance of American airpower resulted partly from lessons learned in a lost war and partly from the sense of urgency that resulted from the vast and growing Soviet threat. Both parts of the equation were necessary for the success of this technological growth. It is highly unlikely that Congress would have funded multiple competing airframe and missile upgrades in the absence of the Soviet threat, and only the airpower failures in Vietnam could have broken the services out of their traditional and conservative mindsets.

The third lesson shows how the intellectual development of a single individual on active duty could play a critical role in making this transformation possible. John Boyd had to fight hard for the opportunity to go to Georgia Tech to learn the abstract skills necessary to turn his instinctive understanding of air combat into a systematic approach that would help change the future of aircraft design and aerial combat. He teamed up with civilian scientists, and subsequently received help from a number of military and civilian personnel working for the Air Force, but the intellectual breakthrough required an officer experienced in combat but able also to grasp the abstract theories of mathematics, engineering, physics, and cybernetics. The probability of similar breakthroughs in various aspects of warfare increases as more officers are sent for additional civil schooling and decreases when civil schooling programs are curtailed or eliminated.

Fourth, the pressure of the Soviet threat and the defeat in Vietnam combined to make possible the development of new aircraft within remarkably short periods of time. The F-14 went from a proposal to first delivery in less than four years; the F-15 and F-16 each took six years; and the F/A-18 nine years.[37] This rapid ability to produce entirely new aircraft using revolutionary technology and design techniques meant that the planes arrived with the Air Force when they were still relevant to the missions and threats for which they had been designed. It also avoided the dangers of exponential growth in research and development costs that can accompany protracted developments and raise the unit cost of new purchases to unacceptable levels.

One of the reasons for the speed of these development cycles was that none of these planes relied upon "leap-ahead" technologies. The F-14 suffered from using inferior engines, but it remains to this day a superb aircraft capable of meeting all the challenges it might face. The F-15 used available technology to improve its engines, avionics, and radar suite. Additional delays might well have produced still better technologies but at the cost of raising the price and delaying the arrival of a desperately needed aircraft. The technology used in the end, again, proved to be more than adequate to secure the F-15's place as the world's premier air superiority fighter.

At all events, shame from defeat and fear of a powerful enemy combined to break through service culture, military conservatism, and fiscal constraint and allowed the airpower services to transform the technology of aerial warfare forever.

★   ★   ★

35

The Army

The end of the Vietnam War found the Army in an equipment crisis as serious as that which faced the air power services. Vietnam had highlighted the utility of helicopters in providing mobility and mobile fire support to dispersed troops, although it had also revealed some of the shortcomings of available helicopter models. The renewed focus on war against the Soviet Union that accompanied the Army's withdrawal from Vietnam, however, quickly drew attention to the clear inferiority of American tanks to the new model Soviet armor. By the 1970s it was becoming clear that American tanks, already far inferior in number to those of the Warsaw Pact, could not reasonably hope to survive on the battlefield against such excellent designs as the T-64 and the T-72. These reflections helped generate a sense of crisis in the Army materiel community similar to that which prevailed in the air power community, even though the Army had not been defeated on the battlefield because of these problems.

Army efforts to modernize its tank fleet since the Second World War had been problematic. The M4 Sherman had been badly outclassed in the waning years of that conflict by a series of German and even Soviet tanks. Subsequent models (all dubbed the "Patton") had been largely incremental improvements on the inadequate Sherman, culminating in the M60, which first appeared in 1959. The Army's efforts to improve upon the M60 coincided with Robert McNamara's tenure as Secretary of Defense. Interested as always in efficiencies and economies, McNamara directed that the Army work jointly with the Germans in developing a tank to serve both forces. The effort, which lasted throughout the 1960s, was a complete disaster. The proposed tank was extremely complex, relied on unproven technology, and was very expensive. A brief effort to salvage something from this program in a purely American tank at the turn of the decade also failed. The Army approached the task of building a successor to the M60 in the early 1970s, therefore, with a great deal of nervousness. Improvements in Soviet tank technology made success in this effort critical, but past attempts had left the Army badly burned.

Part of the problem lay in the belief of many Army officers that the tank had outlived its usefulness. The improvement of missile technology, shaped-charge explosives, and even of extremely effective kinetic energy rounds seemed to have tilted the traditional struggle between armor and firepower decisively in the direction of firepower. It seemed that no amount of armor could reliably protect a tank from the menaces it would now face on the battlefield. As the 1973 Arab-Israeli War demonstrated, even a man-portable anti-tank guided missile was capable of destroying modern tanks. A 1972 article in *Armor*, the Army's professional journal for tankers, was titled, "The Death of the Tank."[38]

This fixation with the killing power of modern anti-tank systems led to two emphases in tank development in the 1960s and early 1970s. First, tanks should be small, lightweight, and fast rather than heavily armored. Since armor could not protect against the anti-tank threat, tanks would have to be able to avoid making themselves targets. This proposition made the more sense in light of the second emphasis of tank designers in this period—missiles. Anti-tank guided missiles (ATGMs) have the advantages of much greater range than conventional tank main guns and dramatically improved accuracy at the full extent of those ranges. They have the disadvantage, however, of being relatively slow—a missile can take as long as fifteen seconds or more to reach its target. That is theoretically enough time for a tank to identify an oncoming missile and maneuver to avoid it or kill its operator. The Army therefore sought to arm its tanks with missiles rather than guns, and to make them light and quick enough to defend themselves against missile attack.[39]

Two factors combined to revise this approach. First, experiments conducted at Fort Knox using sophisticated (for the time) computer analysis focused the attention of the Army's designers on the importance of crew survivability rather than simply getting in the first shot (the traditional priority of tank warfare). This focus made additional sense when the designers reflected on the fact that, even apart from the obvious humanitarian concerns, it takes longer and costs more to make a tank crew than to make a tank. Real cost effectiveness would come from a vehicle that would preserve its crew.[40] This reflection might not have had much result but for the fact that one frustrated Army designer learned accidentally that the British had invented a new type of armor that would provide enormously greater protection at a reasonable weight. This new armor, called alternatively "Chobham" after the laboratory where it was made, or "Burlington," "Starlight," or any of another code-names, revolutionized tank design. General Creighton Abrams, Army Chief of Staff from 1972 to 1974, saw a demonstration of the new armor and declared, "The tank is back in business."[41]

The use of the new armor did add to the planned weight of the tank, however, pushing it well past the upper limit the Army designers had been prepared to accept. Many officers dug in their heels, clinging to the notion that agility was more important than armor protection. Abrams resolved the argument by deciding to accept the higher weight of new armor. The difficulties of fielding a weightier tank were mitigated by advances in engine design. Over the course of M1 development in the 1970s, two engines were produced, both capable of propelling the nearly 60-ton tank at high speed. One was an innovative but still fairly traditional diesel; the other was a gas-turbine that applied aircraft engine technology to the tank.

The turbine offered a number of important advantages over the diesel. It generated high horsepower and very good pick-up, could use a wide variety of fuels, produced little smoke, and was extremely quiet. The diesel, by contrast, was loud and smoky, thus advertising the tank's position to the enemy from a great distance. But the gas turbine engine consumes great quantities of fuel; in fact, it uses almost as much fuel idling as it does at full power. Diesel engines are, by their nature, among the most fuel efficient. The designers of the M1 wrestled over these issues but finally decided to select the gas turbine engine for the new tank.

The last major decision was the selection of the gun. The Army had long since adopted a British-designed 105 mm gun for its tanks, and tests against more advanced German 120 mm and British guns showed that the 105 performed well. The M1 design team strongly favored the 105, both because it was American and because they hoped that new "leap-ahead" technologies would soon promise much greater performance. The German 120 mm was still under development, however, and the designers did not want to get locked into a weapons system only marginally better than their current systems when new technologies beckoned.

In the end, the decision to select the 120 mm gun was largely political. Secretary of Defense Donald Rumsfeld was determined, as McNamara had been before him, to try to standardize NATO combat equipment. The idea of using the German gun also appealed to him as a way of luring the Germans into using the American gas turbine engine. These measures would have allowed German and American armored units to standardize fuel and ammunition, and would also have signaled effective inter-allied cooperation. Rumsfeld was willing to sacrifice the promise of leap-ahead technologies in the future for these current benefits.

The M1 that appeared at the end of the 1970s was an impressive machine. Its armor could stop both kinetic energy and shaped-charge warheads. Its engine was powerful enough that M1 drivers racing their tanks over bumps in the ground could become airborne. It also incorporated a new fire control technology relying for the first time on a digital computer. This system allowed the gunner to identify a target and fire at once, while the computer accounted for a myriad of factors, including wind speed and direction, distance, elevation, and even the droop of the main gun as it heated up from repeated firing. As a result, a trained M1 crew could expect to hit a target the first time, every time, even when moving at top speed over rough terrain.

The adoption of this digital fire control computer represented a reach for an untested technology just barely mature enough to integrate into a current system. This was precisely the sort of technology used throughout the M1. Ironically, the effort to avoid "leap-ahead" technologies that were insufficiently mature to offer confidence in their ultimate success produced a tank that has revolutionized land warfare.

Army officers in the 1950s and 1960s concerned about missile technology had not been entirely wrong in their thinking. Anti-tank guided missiles were one of the waves of the future, and the advantages of missiles in range and in long-range accuracy were very important. Efforts to combine missiles with tank main guns in order to produce all-purpose armored vehicles had failed, however, and Chobham armor combined with advances in fire control and ammunition technology convinced the Army to design the tank around a kinetic energy main gun. But just as the Air Force broke multi-purpose aircraft design programs into smaller programs aimed at producing several different aircraft models maximized for different purposes, so the Army found other ways to incorporate the potential of missile technology into the force without compromising the effectiveness of the tank.

The collapse of the earlier efforts to modernize the M60 tank, combined with a general lack of direction in the post-Vietnam Army, had created great confusion in Army procurement programs by the early 1970s. No fewer than nine major weapons systems were competing with one another for scarce

Congressional support. The Assistant Vice Chief of Staff, Lieutenant General William E. DePuy, took matters into his own hands in early 1972, forcing the senior Army leadership to settle on the five key programs it would pursue. The result was a determination to proceed with what would become the M1 tank, the Bradley Infantry Fighting Vehicle, the Blackhawk transport and Apache attack helicopters, and the Patriot anti-aircraft missile.[42]

The most important aspect of these systems, apart from the M1, was not their individual specifications, but the way they formed an integrated suite of complementary capabilities for the service. The Bradley was fundamentally different from the M113 Armored Personnel Carrier that it had replaced. The M113 was really just a lightly armored taxi for soldiers; the Bradley was meant to participate directly in armored warfare. Although itself not armored heavily enough to withstand tank or missile rounds, the Bradley boasts a TOW (tube-launched, optically-tracked, wire-guided) missile launcher of its own. When operating in conjunction with M1s, the Bradley brought the long range and accuracy of the anti-tank missile to the fight as units approached the enemy, while the M1 could provide protection and certain destruction in closer combat.[43] The Apache attack helicopter provided direct fire support from the air using both Hellfire missiles and its own 30 mm gun.

Military transformation enthusiasts of the 1990s coined the term "systems of systems" to describe the interlinked surveillance, target-acquisition and tracking, and attack systems they favored. The coinage was new, but the concept was not. The Bradley, M1, Apache, and other Army programs also formed a system of systems. Each separately suffered from numerous important vulnerabilities. When combined intelligently, the strengths of one system masked the weaknesses of the others. Armored units in the U.S. Army now routinely travel with their Bradleys in the lead, able to identify enemy armor quickly and engage it at extreme range with the accurate and lethal TOW missile. As the units close to gun range, the thinner skinned Bradley slips to the rear as the M I s advance, confident that their armor will protect them from enemy missiles and main gun rounds while their own stabilized and computer-targeted main gun wreaks havoc on enemy armored formations. When necessary, the infantry traveling in the backs of the Bradleys emerges to engage other enemy infantry, supported by the Bradley's 25 mm stabilized machine-gun, or to investigate and clear suspected strongpoints before remounting for the continued advance. Apaches flying overhead provide immediate support to units engaged in combat, and can also theoretically fly into the rear of enemy formations to locate and disrupt reserves before they arrive to participate in the close fight.

These systems operate on different principles using different advantages to cover their various vulnerabilities. The armor of the M I allows its crews to advance without fear. Its main gun is virtually unstoppable and instantaneous. The Bradley uses missile technology, which is slower and more vulnerable to counter-measures, but offers much greater range, using the M I 's armor and the range of its weapon to offset its own vulnerability to enemy tank guns and missiles. The Apache mounts both missiles and guns on a heavily armored helicopter that offers mobility and the ability to loiter in a given area for a long time —something that fixed-wing aircraft cannot do. The range of threats this array of systems poses gravely complicates the enemy's ability to defend against U.S. forces, and the various modes of protection complicate the enemy's efforts to destroy American troops. It is not enough for the enemy to solve one problem—penetrating the M I 's armor, say, or defeating the Bradley's missiles—since the force can compensate for inadequacies in one area by using advantages in others. The enemy would have to defeat all of the U.S. advantages or find a way to prevent American troops from coordinating their activities effectively—hard to do against well-trained troops—to defeat a

U.S. heavy unit in combat. As with the Air Force technological revolution, the decision to build multiple, diverse weapons systems with complementary capabilities offsetting individual vulnerabilities presents the enemy with a nearly insuperable set of challenges he must resolve in order to survive.

THE TRAINING REVOLUTION

But even the best technology means little in the hands of unskilled soldiers. Fortunately, the 1970s and early 1980s also saw a fundamental revolution in the way the U.S. armed forces trained for war. Parlaying the transition to the all-volunteer military, this training allowed the military to develop soldiers and airmen capable of taking full advantage of the advanced new technology being developed and fielded at the same time. It was a critical part of the transformation of the American armed forces.

The training revolution took different courses in the airpower services and the land forces, stemming from the different experiences in Vietnam. The sense of tactical defeat in the air power services led to crash programs. The Army's relatively greater satisfaction with its tactical performance and its disorganization following the end of the war delayed the development of the land forces training revolution.

Air Power Training

The same casualty rates in Vietnam that had led the Air Force and the Navy to insist upon new fighter and attack aircraft drove them to examine the performance of their pilots even in the older airframes. The Navy acted first, commissioning the Ault Report in 1968 to study the appalling loss rates Navy pilots were suffering in the skies over North Vietnam. This report recommended a series of sweeping changes, particularly

43

in the way the Navy trained its aircrews. As a result, by 1969 the Navy had begun developing much more sophisticated training programs in air-to-air combat. The first "graduates" of this program left in March 1969, and by the end of the war the Navy's kill ratio was up to 12 to 1. In 1972, this program received a permanent home at Naval Air Station Miramar, and the informal name of "Topgun."[44]

The Air Force followed suit more slowly, establishing its first "Aggressor Squadron" at Nellis Air Force Base in 1972 and beginning a program of realistic air-to-air combat training partly based upon Topgun. The Air Force rapidly outstripped the Navy in the scale and complexity of its air combat training, however. While Topgun initially focused on "dissimilar air combat training" in which "aggressor" pilots flew different types of U.S. aircraft at the limits of their performance in an effort to push the pilot trainees to the limits of their skill, the Air Force focused on a more realistic approach, requiring "aggressor" pilots to adopt known Soviet tactics and formations in their missions. In this way, the Air Force worked hard to train pilots as closely as possible to the way they would actually fight.[45]

But even as the aggressor squadron program was getting underway at Nellis, the Air Force remained dissatisfied with its aircrew training programs. A symposium held at Nellis in late 1972 concluded that Tactical Air Command " 'may have concentrated too extensively on improving the machine and have not spent enough effort on the man who must fly it or on the training which he must have to make that machine an exploitable advantage.' "[46] The result of these reflections was the establishment of the Red Flag program in 1975. Red Flag rested on the recognition that most aircrew losses occurred within the first eight-to-ten missions a pilot flew. The Air Force hoped that by developing very realistic training programs, it could in effect give the pilot experience without the risk of combat, thereby both improving pilot performance in combat and dramatically reducing casualties.

The Red Flag exercises involved the planning and execution of full-scale realistic combat missions. Air Force bombers attacked simulated targets including SAM sites and anti-aircraft artillery emplacements in "force packages" (groups of different types of aircraft) similar to what they would use in real combat. They practiced cooperation with spotter aircraft and AWACS, electronic counter-measures, and even pilot survival skills— "downed" pilots were taken into the middle of the desert training area and compelled to survive and escape using only the contents of their own survival kits. The Red Flag program rapidly expanded to include ever larger and more realistic force packages and target sets, and it was copied at a number of different airbases around the U.S. and even in Canada, in cooperation with the Canadian armed forces.[47] From 1975 on, the Air Force ran an average of five Red Flag exercises a year.[48]

The training revolution relied upon a revolution in technology. In the 1970s both the Air Force and the Navy developed systems to capture every aspect of an aircraft's performance, the position of every switch in the cockpit, videotape of the pilot's displays, and, of course, the position of every aircraft in the exercise at any given moment. This technology allowed Air Force and Navy trainers to conduct completely objective evaluations of pilot performance without allowing emotionalism or machismo to interfere with the learning of lessons from both success and failure.

The regular conduct of highly realistic force-on-force exercises in multiple locations throughout the United States greatly facilitated improvements in airpower doctrine at the tactical level.[49] The Air Force abandoned the rigid formations it had used to such poor effect in Vietnam and allowed its pilots, already benefiting from their superior training, much greater initiative in air-to-air combat. The synergy between realistic training and improved doctrine was very powerful.

At the same time, the training program helped to underline the fact that it was unrealistic to expect every aircrew to be excellent at every task. The F-15 might perform equally well as an air superiority fighter or a ground-attack aircraft, but its aircrews could not maintain excellence at both skills all the time. The Air Force therefore adopted an approach called Designed Operational Capability (DOC), in which particular squadrons focused on different air combat skills. An air superiority squadron would also train for ground-attack missions, but on a much reduced scale. Its focus would be on keeping enemy aircraft out of the skies. This approach also allowed the Air Force to refine training programs and standards of training, making it easier for aircrews to understand the tasks they needed to accomplish and for the Air Force leadership to evaluate their level of accomplishment of those tasks. The move away from commonality and homogeneity in the force allowed more units to be excellent at their primary tasks and avoided the danger of creating a service in which all aircrews were mediocre at everything.[50]

The improvements in training in the Air Force were not without controversy. The more realistic flying conducted at Nellis resulted at first in an increase in training casualties and aircraft damage.[51] There were two ways to look at this problem: one was that the training was unnecessarily harsh and dangerous and deprived the force of aircraft and aircrews that would be needed in combat; the other was that it was far better to take those limited losses in training accidents than the far higher losses that inexperienced pilots would suffer in combat. The Air Force leadership courageously took the second view, and accepted the increase in training mishaps. They were quickly rewarded for this decision—by 1995, the incidence of training accidents had declined precipitously—Air Force major incidents were down by nearly 70 percent in that time. This reduction in the accident rate was itself a dramatic testimony to the efficacy of realistic training, and a harbinger for the survivability and skill of U.S. aircrews in real combat situations.[52]

Army Training

The impetus for the revolution in Army training was somewhat different from the one that drove changes in training in the air power services. It arose from several sources. First, the transition to an all-volunteer force entirely invalidated the training model the Army had been using for decades that sought to prepare officers and soldiers for service in a mass-mobilization force. Second, the Army's return from Vietnam led to a refocus both on the likelihood of war in Central Europe and on the prospects for smaller conflicts outside of Southeast Asia. That change of focus also changed the Army leadership's ideas of how war would be fought, which led in turn to the need for further changes in training. Third, the Yom Kippur War of 1973 provided a powerful spur to thinking about training for future war. And, finally, the success of the air power services' new training systems and the promise of new training technologies offered the promise of dramatically improved training for the ground forces as well.[53]

As the Army moved toward the AVF and the prospect of major mobilization for conflicts diminished, Army leaders realized that the old training models—preparing officers and soldiers for jobs far above their present rank—would not do. General William E. DePuy, first commander of the U.S. Army Training and Doctrine Command (TRADOC), established in 1973, believed that future wars would be short, sharp affairs in which the Army would not have time to mobilize, even if civilian leaders wanted to do so. The example of the Yom Kippur War reinforced this line of thinking, although DePuy and others had come to these conclusions even before that war had begun. It became vitally necessary, therefore, for the Army to be able to win the first battles of any future war—something it had not been able to do in any conflict with the possible exception of Vietnam. So powerful was this line of thinking that in 1986 it produced a volume entitled *America's First Battles, 1776–1965* that made a strong historical case for the problems the U.S. Army traditionally encountered at the start of each war—and for the continuing need to solve those problems in advance of future conflicts.[54] The Army leaders of the 1970s suddenly began to place much greater emphasis on peacetime training than they had ever done before.

The creation of TRADOC made it much easier for the Army to address this problem directly. DePuy and his assistant Major General Paul Gorman took advantage of the new-found centralization of the Army's training and educational institutions to revolutionize the Army's training programs. DePuy and Gorman believed that the Army had gone too far in the direction of educating officers rather than training them, a profound but too infrequently noticed difference. An officer or soldier is trained to master a particular set of skills, either physical or intellectual, so that they can be executed and repeated easily and flawlessly; he is educated to be able to make complex decisions in unpredictable circumstances with a solid historical, philosophical, cultural, and general intellectual background.

Gorman and DePuy argued that the Army had gone too far in the direction of education by the 1970s, and was doing very little to train its personnel to meet obvious and foreseeable challenges that they would certainly face. There is a discrete set of tasks that a platoon leader or company commander will certainly have to perform both in peacetime and in war, and many of those tasks are both perfectly predictable and readily trainable. DePuy and Gorman believed that the Army was not doing enough to meet this obvious challenge, leaving the mastering of these skills to a mobilization period that would no longer exist—or to the beginning of a conflict that was not likely to last long enough to allow U.S. forces any meaningful "learning curve." Soldiers and officers, they believed, should leave their schools ready to move at once into positions of responsibility and to function effectively at a high level. If that meant spending less time and effort preparing personnel for unpredictable challenges or for situations they would encounter years down the road in their careers, Gorman and DePuy were willing to make that sacrifice.

They accordingly developed a set of training standards and a program for continuing to improve and refine Army training called the Army Training and Evaluation Program (ARTEP). The most important feature of the ARTEP was that it provided clear standards by which to evaluate individual and unit training performance. Its advent introduced into Army wisdom the platitude "train to standard, not to time," which still echoes in the halls of Army units around the world.

The initial focus of the Army's training revolution was on training conducted at units' home stations. The budgetary restrictions of the early and mid-1970s were simply too great to imagine establishing larger or more centralized training areas, and the perceived urgency of improving Army training was too great to allow a significant delay in responding to the problem. By the middle of the decade, however, a movement was growing within the Army leadership to consider establishing one or more large-scale National Training Centers in the U.S.

This movement sprang largely from the reflection that warfare had changed so much in recent years that few Army posts had the capabilities necessary to train their units properly to prosper in the first battle of the next conflict. The Yom Kippur war had dramatically underlined the lethality of the new warfare—the Arab and Israeli forces together *lost* more tanks in the space of two weeks than the entire U.S. Army contingent in Europe *possessed*.[55] The range of modern tank and artillery tubes, of man-portable anti-tank missiles, and of modern combat aircraft, helicopters, and the tactical missiles they carried, moreover, meant that training facilities adequate for 20,000 World War II-era soldiers could not accommodate the needs of a modern 600-man battalion. Fiscal constraints and the growing opposition of the neighbors of many Army posts to the existing training at those training areas precluded dramatically increasing the size of training areas throughout the Army. The successes of the Air Force and Navy at Nellis and Miramar, respectively, also encouraged the Army leadership to seek to emulate their model of vastly improved centralized training bases. By 1977, therefore, the Army began to pursue the development of "one or more" National Training Centers in the Continental U.S.[56]

As at Nellis AFB, the emphasis at the National Training Center (NTC) eventually created at Fort Irwin, California in the early 1980s was on conducting the most realistic combined-arms training possible. Technological advances again facilitated this effort, allowing the Army to field the MILES laser-tag system for simulating combat. When a soldier or tanker fired a gun, a laser beam was fired from the weapon at the target. If the beam struck any of a number of special sensors worn on the body of infantrymen or attached to vehicles, a computerized system determined what the effect of the shot would have been. "Dead" or "wounded" soldiers or "destroyed" or "damaged" vehicles were immediately put out of action both literally on the field and symbolically in the computer system. This system removed much of the guesswork and subjectivity from the evaluation of simulated combat results, and created a more realistic battle-field littered with "casualties" to be evacuated and "damaged" or "destroyed" vehicles to impede further movement. Innovations added over time were smoke-production teams to simulate the steady obscuring of the battlefield that occurs during combat and techniques for integrating artillery and aircraft attacks, as well as anti-aircraft fires. For many soldiers and officers, the sheer ability to take a full battalion (subsequently brigade) combat team into the field and maneuver it against an enemy trained in Soviet-style tactics and formations was a revelation. Over the course of the 1980s, centers were set up to distill the lessons from these mock combats to enable the Army to improve both its future training and its doctrine for future warfighting, just as the Air Force did based on the Red Flag exercises.

Valuable as the Army's new training programs were, however, they were not without cost. DePuy and Gorman were aggressively present-focused in the development of the Army's training, doctrine, materiel, and education systems. DePuy explicitly rejected the notion that the Army should attempt to foresee and prepare for future combat. His comments in this regard are worth noting: "[P]eople aren't smart enough to see what we'll need in the year 2000. The reason we aren't smart enough to do that is that people we ask in 1979, for instance, to look at the shape of the Army in the year 2000, possess a 1979 mentality. So the Army they see out there is simply a reflection of the 1979 Army with some gimmicks." He also rejected the notion of Army personnel trying to determine the future course of weapons development: "Somebody was supposed to sit down and visualize the perfect weapon of the future. Then, after you have visualized and described it, you turned it over to the engineers and the scientists and asked them to make one. Well, in the first place, there isn't anybody in TRADOC or [Combat Development Command] who can see further than the scientists or the engineers *have already seen.* Secondly, [this process] constituted a hunting license for the scientists and the engineers in the labs to spend a lot of money seeking a vague objective."[57]

So DePuy focused instead on determining what was technically feasible at the moment that would upgrade immediate Army capabilities, and fielding that technology. His and Gorman's focus on training soldiers and officers to perform the tasks they would immediately face, rather than on educating them for the future, helped to create an Army that was amazingly proficient at the tactical level. Its continued intellectual development—of the sort that permitted DePuy, Gorman, and others to make such important and fundamental changes—would receive much less emphasis as time went on, however, with consequences as hard to measure as they are potentially devastating.

Nonetheless, the net result of all of these changes in the air power services and the Army was to create an American military able for the first time in its history to take the field on very short notice with a superb standard of training and a good deal of experience in highly realistic simulated combat. Officers and soldiers who fought in Operation Desert Storm and in subsequent operations repeatedly expressed their amazement that real combat seemed to be *easier* than the simulated combat they had been through many times. This level of technical and tactical proficiency translated into enormous self-confidence on the battlefield as well. For the first time in our history, American troops going to war in 1990 rightly felt that they had very little to fear from their enemies.

THE REBIRTH OF MILITARY DOCTRINE

Success in war depends on more than equipment or even quality personnel. It also depends upon a clear, reasonable, and well-articulated notion of how to fight. The Army's efforts to overhaul its doctrine resulted from the same sense of crisis that was driving the equipment and training revolutions that occurred simultaneously. The three were, in fact, closely interrelated.

Active Defense

General DePuy, the first head of TRADOC from 1973 to 1977, had been instrumental in selecting and pushing for the adoption of the Army's "Big Five" weapons systems, as we have seen. He was also intimately involved in early discussions that laid the groundwork for the establishment of the National Training Center. When he turned to the problem of reformulating the Army's doctrine, he naturally focused his efforts on developing a body of writing that would justify the Army's new programs in the extremely austere fiscal environment of the mid-1970s. From the first, therefore, the institutional priority of defending costly weapons systems and training areas played a critical role in the drafting of the Army's warfighting doctrine.[58]

The other priority driving the revision of the doctrine was fear. As DePuy's manual itself declared:

[W]e must assume the enemy we face will possess weapons generally as effective as our own. And we must calculate that he will have them in greater numbers than we will be able to deploy. . . . Because the lethality of modern weapons continues to increase sharply, we can expect very high losses to occur in short periods of time. Entire forces could be destroyed quickly if they are improperly employed.

Therefore the first battle of our next war could well be its last battle. . . . The United States could find itself in a short, intense war, the outcome of which may be dictated by the results of initial combat. This circumstance is unprecedented: We are an Army historically unprepared for its first battle. We are accustomed to victory wrought with the weight of material and population brought to bear after the onset of hostilities. Today the U.S. Army must above all else, *prepare to win the first battle of the next war.*[59]

This conviction led DePuy to launch a crusade to reorient the Army's thinking, procurement, organization, and training to focus, for the first time, on initial success in unanticipated

combat. He waged that crusade through an extreme centralization of intellectual effort, the suppression or attempted destruction of countervailing arguments, and through the application
of the "systems analysis" approach that Robert McNamara had
brought to the Defense Department as Secretary of Defense.

As we have already seen, DePuy was present-focused and
rejected the idea of attempting to discern and prepare for the
future of land combat. His determination to apply systems
analysis to the development of doctrine required taking that
presentist approach even further. He ordered the development
of a number of specific scenarios which could be wargamed.
He drew a great deal of support for his doctrine from the
analysis of the results of those wargames, building a doctrine,
in the end, that seemed ideally suited to a particular variant of
the possible future war in Central Europe—but utterly unsuited
even to other possible variants of that war, let alone other kinds
of wars.

DePuy was also highly tactically-focused. He recognized
and feared the enormous Soviet superiorities in tanks, artillery,
and manpower, and he sought to counteract that superiority by
improving U.S. Army tactics. When American officers could
locate, maneuver, and command their units well enough to inflict high enough loss rates on their Soviet adversaries, he reasoned, the Soviet numerical superiorities would be overcome.

DePuy's mistrust of the capacities of his subordinates led
him to remove responsibility for writing the doctrine from the
officer whose job it should have been because of intellectual
disagreements with that general. Instead, DePuy took personal
control over the document, conferring with only a handful of
trusted aides, and ensuring that the doctrine reflected his own
experiences in combat and beliefs about the future of war,
modified by the "systems analysis" evaluations of wargames
and tactical experiments. As a result, the doctrine was not
informed by any clear sense of historical development, and was

not placed in any historical context. Neither did it have any broad support within an officer corps on whom DePuy aimed simply to impose it.

Apart from the systems analysts, only the Germans and the Air Force had a substantial impact on the new doctrine. DePuy was a great fan of German tactical skill and imported *Panzergrenadier* tactics almost unchanged from German manuals into FM 100–5.[60] He also worked to coordinate the doctrine with his counterpart in the Air Force, General Dixon. We will consider the results of this collaboration in greater detail below. DePuy used both of his "allies" as leverage to ram the body of his doctrine down the throats of his peers in the Army. When the Supreme Allied Commander in Europe Alexander M. Haig Jr. presumed to criticize the proposed doctrine, for example, DePuy chastised him for failing to understand the international political consequences of rejecting or even criticizing a doctrine so similar to that of our German allies.[61]

The doctrine that DePuy drove home relied upon a very specific notion of the Soviet threat the Army faced. DePuy imagined that the Soviets would mass forces against predetermined sectors of the allied lines, attack with enormous artillery concentrations at designated breakthrough sectors, and attempt to roll over the stunned defenders. The task of those defenders, therefore, became identifying the intended breakthrough points as quickly as possible and massing all available combat power against them. DePuy saw allied forces moving aggressively, but laterally, along the front line of battle in order to stop the Soviets in their efforts to blast holes in the NATO defense.

The assumptions that NATO would stand on the defensive and that allied forces would attempt to hold right at the international borders rather than adopting a defense-in-depth resulted from DePuy's analysis of the political climate of the era —and perhaps also from his closeness to his German counterparts, who certainly did not want to see their country's space traded for time. These assumptions were probably realistic, but the notion that the Soviets would not respond to the allies' denuding of other sectors of the battlefield in order to concentrate against the initial breakthrough areas was not. The specific force-ratio calculations that emerged from the systems analysis evaluations of the wargames were also far from reliable guides to what actual battlefield conditions would produce. DePuy's eagerness to eliminate tactical and even operational reserve forces, finally, would have left the allies with virtually no ability to respond had any of the tenuous assumptions that underlay his doctrine fallen down.

These obvious flaws of the new doctrine did not escape the Army leadership and outside analysts, and a veritable torrent of criticism was unleashed against the new doctrine, which DePuy "marketed" aggressively. Even General Don Starry, one of DePuy's most eager assistants with the project, quickly came to doubt its feasibility. As a corps commander in the mid-1970s, as the doctrine was being unveiled, Starry realized that it was too tactical and too stereotyped to be of much use to corps commanders or their superiors.[62] These flaws and critiques would have become apparent, of course, had DePuy solicited meaningful comment from his peers and subordinates before pressing the document on the Army—but then he would almost certainly have been forced to make "compromises" he found unacceptable, and he preferred to insist upon the literal implementation of a flawed doctrine rather than to risk derailing his proposed reform of the Army.

It is very easy to be too hard on DePuy, and on other leaders who have made similar decisions subsequently. The task of crafting Army doctrine and operating procedures is complex and fraught with bureaucratic pitfalls. Approaches that are too open and solicit too much input run two risks: they may result in "committee" documents that embody so many compromises as to have lost all meaning, or they may become so entangled in intra-bureaucratic conflict that they never see the light of day at all. DePuy rightly sensed that he held command at a time of crisis in the Army, and that it was his duty to see a meaningful doctrine successfully through the process. He did, however, go too far in relying on his own experience and in using the urgency of the time to avoid forcing himself to answer hard questions about his product.

As a result, the product, FM 100–5, *Operations*, 1976 edition, satisfied virtually no one. DePuy spent a considerable amount of time and effort in a rearguard effort to save it from its vociferous critics, but he was unable to do so even before it became clear that the ideas of Soviet doctrine on which FM 100–5 was built were out of date. Ironically, the fiasco of "Active Defense," as DePuy's approach came to be called, spurred an intense discussion and argument about the future of war and the right way to design Army doctrine, and led to the development by 1982 of a wholly new way of imagining how the Army would fight the Soviets—or any other adversary.

AirLand Battle

The most serious flaw in the 1976 doctrine was that it envisioned a more or less stationary allied force standing on the international borders slugging it out with oncoming echelons of Warsaw Pact troops until the Soviets tired of the game. DePuy was so focused on the tactical problems of killing more Soviets in the main battle area that he largely ignored the development of capabilities to strike Soviet reserve or "second echelon" forces before they were within range of allied troops. This tactical fixation not only produced an unworkable Army doctrine, but also hampered coordination with the Air Force.

The Air Force emerged from the Vietnam conflict divided about its future missions. Some senior leaders saw the end of the Vietnam war as the opportunity to return to a focus on strategic

57

bombing and nuclear war. Air Force manuals in the mid-1970s placed strategic attack at the top of their lists of critical missions, declaring "the region above the earth's surface permits largely unhindered access to any point on or above the earth, thus provides a unique opportunity to apply aerospace power against all elements of an enemy's resources, regardless of their location," and a 1979 manual proclaimed that the Air Force aimed at "devastating bases or industrial centers behind enemy lines."[63]

But the major weapons systems the Air Force developed at this time supported operational missions within the European theater far more than deep penetration into Soviet territory, and the Tactical Air Command leadership took away from Vietnam a belief in the critical importance of close air support. Air Force generals declared, "The primary purpose of tactical air forces is to provide the necessary protection and support to ground and sea forces to allow them to control their environment," and "Our first job in the tac air is to help blunt and stop the armored thrust."[64] To this end, the Air Force championed the development of the A-10, an aircraft specifically designed to kill Soviet tanks in the high-threat counter-air environment of Central Europe.

The Army had also emerged from Vietnam with a healthy respect for the importance of close air support and a desire to cement solid links with its sister service. DePuy wanted to ensure that the Army did not waste money fielding systems that duplicated Air Force capabilities.[65] Army Chief of Staff Creighton Abrams also wanted to avoid inter-service fighting over Army helicopter programs and other budgetary issues.[66] The circumstances for a real growing-together of the Army and the Air Force were propitious, and senior leaders in both services took advantage of them. From 1973 to 1975, TRADOC and the Tactical Air Command (TAC) developed a number of working groups to iron out problems in advance of coordination in the use of air power in support of ground forces. In

1975 these initiative blossomed into the Air Land Forces Application Agency (ALFA), which was to facilitate even greater coordination.[67]

Attempts to accomplish these laudable aims generated relatively little practical result, however. When TRADOC officers attempted to brief an air–land coordination doctrine based on their own scenarios and wargames, Air Force officers at all levels were skeptical and even nervous. The TRADOC officer in charge of the liaison effort, moreover, did not have DePuy's confidence, having crossed his chief over the nature and purpose of the doctrine then under development. As a result, the coordination effort largely languished.[68] The main practical result was a series of joint experiments combining Air Force attack planes with Army helicopters and ground controllers. These experiments helped facilitate cooperation in the Close Air Support mission, but little else.[69]

It is likely that the tactical focus of Active Defense was one of the reasons for the relative ineffectiveness of these early efforts at Army–Air Force integration. Since the Active Defense did not look beyond the echelon of Soviet forces in contact with allied troops, the only pressing coordination task was that of true close air support (CAS)—U.S. Air Force missions undertaken in direct support of ground units fighting for their lives against a much larger foe. DePuy had no doctrinal basis for interfering in the deep attack missions into the rear of the Warsaw Pact that some in the Air Force community preferred, and so provided only a limited impetus to his subordinates' efforts to coordinate those attacks with Army operations. The Active Defense battlefield continued to be divided neatly into Army sectors and Air Force sectors with the exception of CAS.

The development of AirLand Battle (ALB) doctrine changed all that. When Don Starry took command of TRADOC in 1977, he had already come to see some of the flaws in the Active Defense. He increasingly turned his attention to the problem of reducing the combat power of Soviet follow-on forces before they could arrive within range of allied ground units, and thus helped to generate a fundamental revolution in Army thinking.

The new thinking drew heavily not so much on German or British operational principles, which had guided American doctrinal development for decades, but on the Soviets' own theories about the operational level of war. The operational level is the level between tactics and strategy. At this level strategic tasks are broken down into missions that tactical units can accomplish, and tactical successes are integrated to achieve strategic goals. As the tactical level is concerned with battles, the operational level is concerned with linking battles together into one or more campaigns in a theater. The view of the operational commander is wide and deep—he sees not just the portion of the theater directly in front of him, but the entire theater as it relates to his undertaking. The transition from the tactical focus of Active Defense to the operational focus of AirLand Battle opened up new ways of thinking about warfare, and new modes of Army–Air Force cooperation—and conflict.[70]

Between 1977 and 1981, Starry and a team of doctrine writers including Lieutenant Colonels Huba Wass de Czege and Don Holder steadily refined a vision of warfare that considered the entire theater. They argued that allied forces standing in more or less static positions and awaiting the arrival of Soviet attackers would inevitably be overrun, even if they succeeded in winning the "first battle." To have a chance, the allies would have to delay the arrival of second echelon Soviet forces, attrit those forces before they arrived, and destroy their command, control, and communications (c3) infrastructures to disrupt them as much as possible, thereby reducing their combat power when they did arrive.

The doctrine was notable at the time for its insistence on the importance of integrating nuclear and even chemical weapons into allied defensive plans, but the real breakthrough was more profound. The Soviets had for decades advocated viewing the enemy as a system, not a monolith or a collection of military units strung together. The system was bound together by its C3 systems and by its own internal cohesiveness. By attacking critical communications nodes, reserve forces, and command centers deep in the rear even as the front line troops advanced, the Soviets argued, it would be possible to induce a state of systemic shock in the enemy. Friendly forces could then take advantage of that shock to defeat enemy units operating far below their normal levels of efficiency and determination. The idea of attacking the enemy simultaneously throughout the entire depth of his defensive deployment was at the cornerstone of Soviet military thinking from the 1930s on. By the end of the 1970s, it also lay at the root of American AirLand Battle doctrine.[71]

AirLand Battle doctrine proposed to use long-range Army assets, such as the Multiple-Launch Rocket System (MLRS) then under development, attack helicopters such as the Apache, and, primarily, Air Force assets of every variety to attack Soviet second echelon forces as they began to move toward the front line. This doctrine was popular in the Army because it seemed to restore an offensive focus to Army doctrine so conspicuously absent in Active Defense. By advocating the movement of ground units in support of these deep attacks, it returned maneuver to a place of honor that Active Defense had reserved for pure firepower. The true significance of the new doctrine, however, was that it drove the Army to take a holistic view of the entire theater of operations, considering all of the Soviet forces and using all of the resources of the allied armies and air forces from the first moment of the struggle to the last. It integrated the deep attack of the Air Force with the "close fight" the Army would be engaged in, and theoretically eliminated the neat division of the theater into Army and Air Force sectors.

One of the virtues of AirLand Battle doctrine was that it was not specific to the European theater. It was designed based on a general understanding of the problem of fighting a numerically superior enemy, and was not tied to specific scenarios, systems analysis evaluations of wargames and force ratios, or the particular terrain of Western Europe. It was as applicable to warfare on the Korean peninsula or in the Middle East as it was to Europe, even though it was preeminently intended to guide the struggle in Germany. Because it was based on a more timeless appreciation of the nature of war and its basic challenges, moreover, AirLand Battle was itself more timeless. Indeed it continues to offer many valuable insights into the nature of certain kinds of warfare even today, long after Active Defense has lost all possible meaning.

The Army's adoption of ALB facilitated closer ties with the Air Force, but also introduced new strains. Because the Army was now thinking of the theater as a whole, rather than focusing only on the line of battle, it was easier for the Army and the Air Force to merge their warfighting approaches. A series of agreements between the Army and Air Force staffs hammered out the details of theater-wide cooperation between the services, and the SHAPE headquarters in Europe began developing concrete plans for what was called follow-on forces attack (FOFA) using all of the Army and Air Force equipment and personnel available. The Army agreed to assist the Air Force in the growing problem of suppressing enemy air defense capabilities and the Air Force committed to the Army's vision of attacking Soviet reserves. The Air Force coined a new term to describe this effort to isolate the front line from the interference of Soviet reserves, which it now called "battlefield air interdiction" (BAI). In the two years following the publication of FM 100-5, the Army and the Air Force agreed on the "thirty-one initiatives," aimed at improving coordination between ground and air forces throughout the theater. These programs laid the basis for the successful integration of air and land power in the Gulf War of 1991.[72]

The growing Army concern with the entire theater of war

was not an unmixed blessing for the Air Force, however. In the first place, General Creighton Abrams had reorganized the Army in the early 1970s to support his effort to increase the number of active divisions without increasing Army active end-strength. He focused particularly on abolishing or dramatically reducing headquarters and headquarter staffs, including the "army" level of command at the theater level. Thenceforth the highest operational Army command was the corps, and the Army continued to maintain two corps headquarters in Europe (V Corps and VII Corps) throughout the rest of the Cold War.

AirLand Battle doctrine naturally focused on the corps level of leadership in its consideration of the theater as a whole, since that was the highest command echelon in the Army. That focus, however, meant that at least two Army commanders would be competing for Air Force support both in the form of CAS and in the form of battlefield air interdiction or follow-on forces attack. Depending upon how the Army and the Air Force developed mechanisms for coordinating Army requests for both forms of air support, this situation might not have been that problematic.

But the Air Force had learned a powerful lesson from the Vietnam War—the fragmentation of the theater into different air power sub-theaters badly hindered the planning of air operations overall. The different procedures and even rules of engagement used in the various parts of the Vietnam theater led to confusion and inefficiency. The Air Force was determined to ensure that henceforth a single manager oversaw the planning and conduct of all air operations in any theater, and therefore viewed the Army's apparent plans to split theater-level thinking along corps boundaries with distaste.

The Army's growing concern with coordinating the activities of all air and ground assets in a theater, rational as it might seem at first, also posed a significant challenge to the Air Force leadership's view of the role of air operations. Army commanders naturally saw the Air Force as an element that supported ground operations. The experience of Vietnam had highlighted to a generation of Air Force leaders that when U.S. forces were engaged on the ground, all other missions became subordinated to supporting them. This approach not only generated its own inefficiencies as aircraft responded to emergency requests for help, but also severely limited the air power services' ability to plan and conduct theater-wide bombing campaigns.

The Air Force therefore wanted to ensure sufficient autonomy in its operations to be able to plan and conduct coherent theater-wide bombing campaigns. The Active Defense doctrine had facilitated this approach, since it left the entire theater beyond the engaged forces to the discretion of the air commanders. AirLand Battle seemed to allow corps commanders to require the coordination of air missions 300 kilometers or more into the enemy's rear areas. As one student of this history noted, "The dominance of ALB over more classic interdiction strategy in air allocation decisions, by fragmenting the theater air campaign, would undermine the ability of the air component commander to mass resources to engage and destroy enemy ground-force concentrations as needed throughout the theater." The Air Force and its historians see in AirLand Battle "an explicit effort by the Army to gain greater control of the air assets to be used in the now-extended battlespace within his purview."[73] Even as AirLand Battle dramatically increased air-ground cooperation throughout the theater, and even as it drove both services to think ever more coherently and complexly about the theater of war as a whole, therefore, it also increased the traditional friction and even rivalry between the two services for predominance in establishing missions and coordinating operations. Subsequent developments in both services have only exacerbated this problem, as we shall see.

The development of AirLand Battle doctrine was an enormously positive development in the Army's thinking about war.

It is not merely that the doctrine is superior to what came before. The method of its development was also superior. Starry did not repeat DePuy's mistakes of over-centralizing the process. Instead he repeatedly circulated drafts of critical concepts throughout relevant parts of the force, and listened carefully to the response that came back. As a result, not only was the doctrine improved, but the Army also came to feel ownership over the changes as a whole. When the document was finally promulgated in 1982 there was no sense that TRADOC was ramming its product down the throats of unwilling officers and soldiers.

The doctrine's superiority also resulted from the complexity of its view of war. The focus on the immediate Soviet threat was important in maintaining the urgency for change and in providing a set of enemy characteristics against which to posture U.S. forces and measure their likely success. But ALB was explicitly developed not simply to meet the obvious Soviet threat, but to solve fundamental problems inherent in the nature of war at that time. How can U.S. forces, possibly equipped with more advanced technology, defeat enemies who would almost inevitably have significant numerical superiority? How can American troops harness their growing advantages in air power and long-range weapons systems to restore maneuver to what looked as though it might become an attrition-based battlefield? How can the U.S. disrupt enemy attacking forces and their reserves before American troops have to meet them in close combat? These were the basic questions AirLand Battle addressed, and it did so independent of the specifics of terrain and force ratios that had so bound the development of Active Defense.

AirLand Battle also rejected the systems analysis approach to doctrinal development. It did not attempt to specify the precise force ratios in attack or defense that would lead to success, or to determine how many Soviet tanks U.S. tankers had to kill for each loss of their own. It restored considerations of morale and cohesion to the battlefield by recognizing that the force that gained and held the initiative also secured a moral advantage over its opponent. Even as AirLand Battle saw the enemy more as a system to be shocked and then shattered, it also recognized that that system consisted of human beings, with all their strengths and weaknesses. AirLand Battle was a model both of doctrinal development, and of doctrine itself. It played a critical role in preparing U.S. ground forces for success in future war.

CONCLUSIONS

The reforms of the 1970s affected every aspect of the U.S. military and marked a true watershed in the history of the military art. Their effects were not seen until the 1991 Gulf War, by which point certain expansions and new ideas had entered into the equation, blurring the importance of the 1970s changes themselves. But just as wise historians of the Wehrmacht recognize that the reforms and ideas developed by Hans von Seeckt, Groener, and others in the 1920s were the true origins of the blitzkrieg techniques that led to such success in 1939 and 1940, so historians of the current epoch will recognize that the 1970s reforms established all of the essential preconditions for the changes in warfare wrought by the U.S. armed forces in the 1990s and early twenty-first century. And those changes were so great that, right or wrong, virtually every major military in the world today believes that the U.S. inaugurated a revolution in military affairs to which potential foes of America will have to adapt or perish.

These reforms offer an interesting set of insights to those concerned with military transformation today. Amazingly, the people who set them in motion did not do so with the intention of transforming warfare or generating a revolution in military affairs—that term, in fact, had not yet come into common parlance outside the Soviet Union nor was the concept it denoted widespread in the U.S. military. The proponents of change in the 1970s acted primarily through fear and out of a feeling of failure, and both elements were essential to the reforms' success. The geopolitical and military-strategic world environment of the 1970s presented U.S. force planners with a clear, if daunting, set of problems they needed to solve. The problems were partially connected—all services faced growing Soviet threats that could overwhelm them with superior numbers, for example. The development and increasing sophistication of missile systems was another example of connectivity among the problems. The air power services had to respond to changes in the SAM threat just as the land power services had to fear man-portable anti-tank missiles. All services had come to recognize that traditional American ways of fighting that included looking very bad at the beginning of each war would not do in the future, so that U.S. peacetime forces had to be combat-ready at all times.

The specific impetuses for each of the reforms were diverse, however. The air power services really felt that they had failed during at least the early stages of the Vietnam War; the Army and Marines did not. The Army felt that the shift to the AVF required fundamental changes in the way it trained and fought; the air power services did not share that view. The air power services' fears for the future were based heavily on their own combat experience; the Army's fears came primarily from watching the Yom Kippur War and extrapolating its effects to the Central Front in Europe. The air power services defended their new technological programs with reference to specific Soviet air frames and capabilities; the Army developed an entire doctrine to justify its stated requirements. Although AirLand Battle came closer than any doctrine has then or since to creating a common view of war between the Army and the Air Force, the services continued to compete with one another for control of operations, for resources, and for visions of war. They were not coordinated or on the "same sheet of music" about how U.S. armed forces should be designed or used. They did not learn the same lessons from their own wars, or from the Arab–Israeli conflict. Yet the result was one of the most successful military transformations of all time. Why?

The Value of Diversity

First, diversity can be a virtue in military affairs. The services, indeed, different factions within each service, identified various different critical problems that needed to be solved, and then various ways of solving them. In some cases, different services identified the same problem in different ways—attacking Soviet follow-on forces, for instance—and developed different notions of how to deal with that problem. The result was the development of balanced military power—military power that addressed multiple threats with multiple responses. Inefficiency resulted from this approach—the Air Force probably did not need four different high-performance fighter aircraft, for example, to secure air superiority. The Army could probably have mounted the TOW missile on the MI tank, reducing the Bradley to a much cheaper armored personnel carrier rather than "infantry fighting vehicle." Using a sort of logic prevalent today, as we shall see, the Army certainly did not need the Apache attack helicopter to perform missions for which Air Force and Navy aircraft were reasonably well suited. The reforms of the 1970s wasted a great deal of money on redundant programs. Or did they?

It turns out that the Air Force's and Navy's various fighters are not exactly redundant, because all perform somewhat differently and bring different capabilities to combat, both in the air and on the ground. An enemy seeking to challenge the U.S. in the air must not only defeat the F-15's missiles and superb guidance radar, but must also be prepared to out-dogfight the F-16, arguably the most maneuverable fighter flying today. The

F-14 is not simply an Air Force plane jury-rigged to land on aircraft carriers, but a superb purpose-built carrier-based fighter that can hold its own in a wide variety of engagements, as it has proven repeatedly since its deployment. The combination of all of these platforms with their overlapping capabilities is so impressive that virtually no one has bothered even to attempt to challenge American control of the air. It is far from certain that a single "perfect" airplane, which would inevitably have to make compromises to perform too many roles at once, would have achieved this level of air dominance and retained it for so long.

The Army's "redundancy" has also proven a source of great strength. Although the Apache in principle provides no capabilities that an F-15 or A-10 does not have, in reality its ability to loiter on the battlefield and immediately to the rear of the enemy's front line, to operate in poor visibility, and to work effectively in concert with a wide variety of ground units, creates a synergy that fixed-wing aircraft cannot sustain over long periods of time. The Bradley proved itself so well in both Iraq wars and elsewhere as a unique capability that greatly augmented the power and capability of U.S. heavy armored units that it hardly requires defense any more. Above all, the Army's varied capabilities ensure that even without air support, an armored unit need not fear anything it might encounter on the battlefield. The Air Force's daunting array of capabilities ensures that there is no single threat that can unhinge the U.S. air campaign, and only a rare enemy will be able to create the cluster of capabilities necessary even to challenge American air supremacy. There is as much to be said for redundancy in military systems as in space launch systems—and no sane NASA engineer would rely on a single system with no backup to perform any mission-critical task.

★   ★   ★

FINDING THE TARGET

*The Importance of Directing Transformation
at Specific Challenges*

The second major reason for the success of the transformation
of the 1970s was that it was focused on threats and challenges
rather than capabilities. In the 1990s, as we shall see, there was
a tendency to create a dichotomy between threat-based transformation and capabilities-based transformation. The former
was thought to address specific problems posed by particular
enemies. The latter was thought alternately to build on advantages the U.S. already held in certain capabilities, or to create a
given set of capabilities thought to be necessary for success in
war. In truth, the successful portions of the 1970s transformation were neither threat- nor capabilities-based. They were
based, instead, on attempts to resolve particular challenges
inherent in the geostrategic and military-technical environment of the time.

The closest approach to a threat-based transformation in this
period was the development of Active Defense doctrine. DePuy
explicitly built that doctrine on assumptions about the specific
Soviet threat the Army was facing in the Fulda Gap, and he justified Army systems by reference to particular scenarios used to
model that threat. The result was a fiasco—not even the Army
accepted the doctrine or its underlying concepts, and outside
the service it was entirely stillborn.

Both AirLand Battle and the Air Force and Navy transformation programs were not so clearly or directly tied to particular
threats. They addressed the much more general problems of how
to fight outnumbered and win and how to succeed in the early
battles of the next war. DePuy had focused on these questions
too, of course, but the answers he found were specific to the
Central European theater (if they would have worked even
there). The answers the developers of AirLand Battle and air
power transformation programs arrived at were more general.

They applied as well to the Korean peninsula and the Middle East as they did to fighting the Soviet Union.

They were not so generic, however, that they did not address any particular threat at all, which is a great danger with capabilities-based transformations, as we shall see. They remained focused not on a particular threat or set of threats, but on a particular set of challenges that had to be resolved. They then worked to find solutions to those problems that were generalizable, rather than being tied to the specifics of particular scenarios. This is the way of most successful military transformations.

The Danger of Seeking Leap-Ahead Technologies

Third, the transformation of the 1970s relied neither on off-the-shelf technology nor on leap-ahead technology, but on that narrow sliver of technological development that is just visible at the horizon. The superfighters' fly-by-wire avionics, the M1's targeting computer and armor, the air-to-air missiles' tracking and maneuvering capabilities were all new and untried technologies, but they had been under development for a while and were sufficiently close to reality that incorporating them in the new systems did not entail a great deal of risk. Consistently throughout this transformation, military and civilian leaders refused to accept the risks of waiting for pie-in-the-sky leap-ahead technologies because of the urgency of rapid transformation. The result, ironically, was almost certainly a more successful and fundamental transformation than would have occurred had they waited for or tried to incorporate leap-ahead systems.

The Importance of Holistic Transformation

Finally, the transformation was, albeit almost unintentionally, all-encompassing. It was not merely technological, organizational, or procedural, but affected every aspect of military life and function. Not all changes were positive; even those that were positive sometimes carried bitter trade-offs. But just about everything changed, and the net result was the creation of a transformational synergy that produced much greater and more positive change than any individual initiative could have done.

The reasons for the success of this transformation, in the end, were the burden of failure and the fear of the future operating together. The military would have reformed after Vietnam even had the Cold War suddenly and unexpectedly ended. The transition to an AVF—a political inevitability at the end of that conflict—would have required such change if nothing else, but the air power services would just as inevitably have changed in response to perceived failure in the skies over Vietnam. The Navy's reforms, indeed, began even during that conflict. The reforms of all of the services would never have been so deep or expansive, however, without the climate of fear and urgency resulting from the geostrategic situation of the late 1970s. Internal and Congressional opposition to change and to spending money was repeatedly beaten down with reference to the enormous danger facing U.S. forces across the Inter-German and Czechoslovak borders. That threat alone would not have generated sufficient reform within the military without the recent experience of military defeat. Both factors were absolutely necessary to bring about the epochal changes of the 1970s.

This reflection should be unsettling to those who worry about U.S. military transformation today. It is always much harder to learn from and build on success than from failure, and as we shall see the U.S. military's legacies of success in Iraq and Afghanistan have greatly complicated the problem of military reform. The absence of a clear and overpowering threat, moreover, makes it ever more difficult to transform institutions as inherently conservative as the military, or to convince political leaders rightly desirous of spending wisely to expend valuable dollars on seemingly unnecessary programs. The liberation of military thinkers from the tyranny of a clear enemy, moreover, can be a dangerous trap. It can also liberate them not only from reality, but from the sense of urgency that is an essential precondition of any successful military transformation. It remains to be seen how the U.S. will fare in this most difficult of undertakings: the effort to transform while at the height of power and conventional success.

CHAPTER TWO

The Reagan Revolution

THE PERCEPTION OF a growing Soviet threat combined with a sense of failure drove the Army and the air power services to reform themselves in the 1970s. The modernization programs begun then laid the essential groundwork for a fundamental transformation of the U.S. military. That transformation was only just beginning when Ronald Reagan took office in January 1981, however, and it could still have faltered if Reagan had not supported it and even worked to expand it. But his enthusiastic backing ensured the completion of the transformation effort already underway. Changing perceptions of the threat and even continued military failure played a critical role in sustaining these efforts over his two terms.

Despite the promising initiatives begun after Vietnam, the U.S. military entered the 1980s in a difficult position. Carter had consistently played down the importance of military power and attempted to keep defense budgets low throughout the first three years of his term. Although the Soviet invasion of Afghanistan at the end of 1979 changed Carter's outlook and led to a reevaluation of the importance of defense and a change in defense priorities, Reagan inherited a military long starved of resources and just starting to see a reversal of years of neglect.

74

The growth in defense budgets during Reagan's tenure was impressive and important. Even more important, however, was the development of American grand strategy in the 1980s. Carter had not had time to create or establish the intellectual underpinnings for the alteration of the American military posture he had belatedly seen as necessary. Reagan's efforts to do so also proved incomplete and, ultimately, inadequate to resolve critical problems in the U.S. grand strategic thinking and planning. They were sufficient, however, to provide a justification and a vision for the future development of the armed forces and a different strategic paradigm for thinking about their possible use.

At the same time, the military in the 1980s saw a dramatic increase in the tension between the threats and tasks for which it was designed and those it actually faced and performed. The armed forces may have decided that they would "never again" fight a confused, drawn-out, and indecisive war like Vietnam, but they found themselves engaged in precisely such a struggle against Muslim terrorism in the 1980s. The military operations were almost all small in scale and short in duration, and so did not place a great strain on armed forces designed to meet greater challenges. The natural focus on the Soviet threat, more ominous because of failure in Vietnam, prevented the timely recognition of the early stages of the problem that would come rapidly to dominate the post-Cold War American national security discussion and acquire a critical role after 9/11.

A New Grand Strategy

At a time when other politicians wavered, Reagan believed that the U.S. would inevitably win the Cold War. He was convinced of the weakness of the Soviet economic and political system and the friability of the Soviet alliance structure. He was confident that the skillful application of superior American economic capability, the greater attractiveness of the ideas of freedom and democracy to those of tyranny and centralized control, and the greater technological capabilities of the West would eventually lead to victory. He also felt that the Soviet Union was approaching a point of crisis in its own affairs, and doubted that Brezhnev or his likely successors could reverse the trend.[1]

The fact that the Soviet Union was nearly certain to collapse of its own flaws did not, however, reduce the immediate threat Soviet arms posed to the United States and its allies. Despite the growing weakness of the Soviet state, the Soviets continued to pour vast resources into modernizing and expanding their military. In the 1970s the Soviet nuclear arsenal had equaled and then surpassed that of the United States, and the Russians seemed determined to continue to widen the gap in their favor. They simultaneously undertook a series of efforts to improve their conventional forces. By 1981 the Reagan administration believed that the United States would soon face a deadly crisis. Soviet nuclear strength precluded any reliance on the American nuclear force to deter Soviet conventional attacks, and it was by no means clear that American forces even in conjunction with their allies could withstand such attacks conventionally. There was a danger that aggressive young Soviet leaders would push for drastic external solutions to the U.S.S.R.'s domestic problems. The U.S. needed to revitalize its armed forces across the board in order to restore the value of the nuclear deterrent and also to emancipate conventional deterrence from its reliance on nuclear weapons.

But the U.S. economy in the early 1980s was very weak and it was by no means certain that it would recover rapidly. At early cabinet meetings, Reagan faced considerable opposition to plans for an aggressive program of defense spending. The 1982 National Security Strategy described of an era of constrained resources that would force the administration to make hard choices about military spending.[2] Although Reagan did increase the U.S. defense budget dramatically, therefore, he attempted to do so intelligently, targeting funds to solve the most urgent problems facing the armed forces rather than simply expanding the military across the board. He also worked hard to revitalize American thinking about defense and national security.

To begin with, Reagan revolutionized American grand strategy for dealing with the Soviet Union, rejecting not only Carter's approach, but key aspects of the containment strategy established in the late 1940s. The grand strategy that Carter had relied on for the first three years of his presidency rested on three main bases. First, the U.S. could best meet the Soviet threat with a combination of political, economic, and military pressures of which the military component would not necessarily be the most important. (The Carter administration even believed that it would be able to work cooperatively with the Soviets to defuse and contain crises in certain areas of the world. This assumption flowed from the belief that although Soviet military capabilities had expanded, U.S. advantages in economic, political, and moral strength more than balanced the brute force the Russians had to rely upon.[3]) Second, the decisive point of any U.S.–Soviet war would be Europe, and that other theaters would be largely irrelevant to the outcome. Third, any major war would be short.[4]

Reagan rejected all three of these premises. He thought that authentic cooperation with the Soviets was not feasible and that the best way to use the U.S. economic advantages was through the expansion of the American military. And he also believed that the U.S. had to prepare for a protracted and global war, however much he might prefer to deter war or to keep it limited and local if deterrence failed.[5]

Reagan went even further rejecting one of the core tenets of U.S. grand strategy since 1945. He did not aim simply to contain the Soviet Union, but actually to "roll back" Soviet control, an idea that American grand strategists had considered and rejected at the start of the Cold War. A military strategy document written in 1981 established as an objective of U.S. foreign policy to "*Reverse* the geographic expansion of Soviet control and military presence throughout the world."[6] A 1983 National Security Decision Directive declared that the U.S. must work "To contain *and reverse* the expansion of Soviet control and military presence throughout the world."[7] To give reality to these pronouncements, Reagan not only spoke openly of liberating Eastern Europe and imposed a variety of sanctions on the Soviet Union during the Solidarity uprising in Poland, but he also undertook a series of military operations designed to challenge Soviet claims to exclusive control of various bodies of water off the Russian coastline.[8] The Soviets got the message, and East–West tensions rose to a point unprecedented at least since the Cuban Missile Crisis of 1962.

Reagan matched his grand strategic pronouncements by increasing defense spending by nearly one-third between 1981 and 1987, relying on the new fear of the Soviet Union generated by the invasion of Afghanistan to overcome the stigmatization of the military following the Vietnam War.[9] This increase is less dramatic placed in a larger perspective, however. Defense spending in 1981 accounted for 23 percent of the federal budget and 5.2 percent of the GNP; in 1987, the high-point of the build-up, the percentages were 27.3 percent and 6.2 percent respectively. By contrast, the U.S. spent 8.2 percent of its GNP and 45 percent of the federal budget on defense in 1960 after eight years of Eisenhower's efforts to rein in military spending.[10]

Reagan targeted this spending increase on the specific areas he felt were most out of kilter with the requirements of the new grand strategy. He therefore focused on the size and composition of the Navy in order to allow it to compete with the Soviets in multiple theaters simultaneously or sequentially (we will consider the Naval build-up in more detail below). He dramatically expanded the military reserve components, especially the Army National Guard and Reserve, in order to make it possible for the

U.S. armed forces to sustain themselves in a protracted struggle. He sought to expand U.S. airpower capabilities as well, since those would be essential in stopping or slowing an enemy attack in the early days before reinforcements could arrive. And he sought to increase the amount of air- and sealift available to transport those reinforcements to threatened sectors rapidly.[11]

Reagan also paid particular attention to critical problem areas that had emerged during the second half of the 1970s by increasing operations and maintenance (O&M) accounts by 75 percent, and research, development, procurement, and military construction accounts by 73 percent between 1980 and 1988.[12] Operations and maintenance accounts fund training and normal maintenance and repairs to equipment. When budgets are tight, militaries frequently raid these accounts first, because doing so has the least dramatic and immediate impact on military power. Over time, however, low O&M accounts lead to atrophied training and increasing stockpiles of useless equipment, so the long-term consequences of such raiding can be devastating. The military had gone through just such a period of O&M raiding in the late 1970s, and Reagan worked hard to repair the damage virtually from the moment he took office.[13]

He also worked to repair another casualty of the late 1970s —the all-volunteer force. By 1980, the AVF had reached a crisis. Recruiting and retention were dramatically down, and the quality of recruits joining the force was also very low. After the promising initial years of the AVF, the last half of the 1970s seemed to portend disaster for the concept, and the very validity of an all-volunteer military came under increasing attack by those who had always been skeptical of the idea.[14]

Reagan had turned this situation around completely by 1984, improving enlisted and officer recruitment and retention, both qualitatively and quantitatively across the board. Many have argued that changes in recruitment patterns depend much more heavily on the state of the economy, the size of the adolescent population, and general attitudes toward military service than on specific Department of Defense programs, and these arguments are frequently used to "document" the impossibility of maintaining an AVF of the necessary size at any given moment. Government programs, however, do seem to matter a very great deal in determining the success or failure of military recruiting and the long-term retention of officers and NCOs.

One of the reasons for the fall-off of military manpower in the late 1970s had been the collapse of recruiting, retention, and quality-of-life programs, largely for lack of funds. Reagan increased the budgets for these programs, as he did generally in the Defense Department, but he did not simply throw money at the problem. Instead of blanket enlistment bonuses or extensions to the universal GI bill, both of which had been traditional and inefficient means of attracting qualified recruits, Reagan supported targeted bonuses and educational opportunities aimed at the best candidates and designed to draw them into the most under-staffed military specialties. Because of the renewed focus on protracted war, Reagan paid particular attention to the Army National Guard and Reserve, and his attentions reaped substantial rewards. Intelligent, focused, and moderate spending increases can have dramatic effects in recruitment and retention, whatever the economic or demographic situation of the U.S. overall.[15]

Reagan also worked to restore the nuclear balance that he feared was tilting too heavily in the Soviets' favor. He fought hard to expand the M-X missile program, although he ultimately had to retreat from the notion of mobile basing for those missiles that he had demanded during his first campaign. He also won a bitter struggle to emplace intermediate-range nuclear missiles in Western Europe. Neither of these efforts was particularly novel, since both had long traditions in U.S. Cold War grand strategy, and the M-X concept had been developed during Carter's presidency.[16]

Reagan also attacked the problem of the nuclear balance from a unique direction, however, by insisting upon a large-scale effort to develop a ballistic missile defense system. This effort, the Strategic Defense Initiative (SDI), ran directly counter to two decades of U.S. thought about nuclear weapons that insisted that any such attempt to defend against Soviet missiles would destabilize the arms race and make war more likely. It also drove U.S. policy dangerously close to (some would even say over) the line established by the Anti-Ballistic Missile (ABM) Treaty of 1972, which forbade certain such efforts. The Strategic Defense Initiative was a dramatic new departure for U.S. Cold War grand strategy, and there is considerable evidence that it had precisely the effect Reagan had intended: the Soviets were aghast at the prospect of seeing even part of their strategic nuclear force neutralized and especially at the economic price repairing that damage would impose on their already weakened economy.[17]

The Reagan defense build-up therefore aimed primarily at making good deficiencies he saw in the armed forces that Carter, Ford, and Nixon had bequeathed to him in light of the changing Soviet threat. It did not fundamentally transform the U.S. military—almost all of the weapons systems, training programs, and doctrinal concepts fielded or used in the Reagan years had been developed in the 1970s. It did, however, create an environment in which the seeds of the 1970s transformation could grow and develop further. Without that build-up, it is not clear that the systems put in place in the earlier decade would have reached their full potential.

For all that, Reagan and his advisors did not feel in any way secure about the situation they faced in the first half of the 1980s. They did not believe that even the expanded military they were fielding could meet the Soviet threat in every theater or even support commitments to U.S. allies. They knew that virtually any large-scale operation, even against a non-Soviet adversary, would require a significant mobilization of the reserves, and might require a return to conscription. They were far from sanguine that the technological developments of the 1970s would be enough to maintain the necessary advantage in that area, considering the efforts the Soviets were visibly putting into matching them.

In sum, Reagan, like Carter, Ford, and Nixon before him, believed that U.S. grand strategy entailed significant risks. The image of the Reagan years as a time of unconstrained resources and limitless defense programs has permanently obscured this fact and allowed the myth to arise that the U.S. defense posture of the 1980s was clearly sufficient to meet the challenges it faced.

NAVAL RENAISSANCE

The Navy was by far the greatest institutional beneficiary of Reagan's defense largesse. The story of the Navy's collapse in the 1970s and its rebirth in the 1980s is important not only because of the critical role that service has played in recent operations, but also because of the transformation in naval strategic thinking that accompanied it. Frustrated by their inability to communicate with the Carter administration, the Navy's leaders worked tirelessly from 1978 on to develop a sophisticated and coherent body of strategic thought that would, among other things, justify the changes they sought in the defense program. Those efforts succeeded beyond the expectations of their initiators and incidentally helped create the basis for some of the most important central trends in current U.S. transformation policy.

However bad the focus on a short war, whether nuclear or conventional, was for the Army, it was much worse for the Navy. Carter's military strategy assumed that the Navy would not have the time or the need to move its forces from theater to theater, or to play an important role in the decisive ground combats expected to occur in Europe. It therefore effectively ceded the Pacific and Indian Oceans to the Soviets in the event of hostilities.[18] Carter's desire to maintain the most economical possible military structure was naturally reflected in the continuous underfunding of the Navy, therefore, and an almost fanatical opposition to building large aircraft carriers of the Nimitz class. He even once vetoed a defense appropriations bill because it included funding for such an aircraft carrier against his wishes.[19] He and others argued that advances in missile technology had turned carriers into nothing more than large targets that could not survive anywhere close enough to shore to be effective, but the conviction that Europe was the only important theater and that the war would be brief actually made this technical argument almost irrelevant. The Navy's combatant ships could play no meaningful role in such a war no matter how invulnerable the aircraft carriers were. The Reagan administration's willingness to contemplate a protracted conflict and to see the problem as global rather than Eurocentric facilitated a complete renaissance of maritime strategy and a massive shipbuilding program aimed at producing a 600-ship Navy.

Collapse and Rebirth

The Navy traditionally faces a broad set of missions that do not complement one another very well. It must defend the sea lines of communication between the U.S. and its principal allies around the world, deter nuclear attack with its own strategic nuclear forces, support Army and Marine operations on and near the coast of enemy states, protect the U.S. homeland from enemy sea- and airborne attack, support U.S. interests by maintaining a visible naval presence in troubled waters, and, at times, conduct its own deep strike missions. In addition, the fleet must be able to defend itself against a wide variety of potential threats ranging from submarines to nuclear attack.

The American political leadership does not necessarily value all of these missions equally or consistently over time. Nor does the civilian leadership's valuation always match that of the Navy leadership. This mismatch, especially sharp during the 1970s, led to a significant decline in the Navy's influence on national policy, budget share, and combat strength.

From the time of the launching of the first Polaris missile from a submarine in 1960, the Navy had entered the business of strategic nuclear deterrence. The decision to pursue this weapons system had at that time generated great discord within a service then dominated by a fixation with carrier air power. It was tightly in line with the priorities of the national political leadership throughout the Cold War, however, and political support and funding for the Navy's ballistic missile submarine programs remained consistently high.[20]

Support for the Navy's carriers, on the other hand, varied much more dramatically with circumstance. During the conflicts of the 1960s, both in the Caribbean and in Southeast Asia, the carrier, and the blue-water Navy in general, played a prominent and successful part. The Navy prided itself on its central role in the Cuban Missile Crisis of 1962, when its perfectly executed blockade of Cuba seemingly forced Khrushchev to back down. Throughout Vietnam, Navy aircraft flew thousands of sorties from carriers close off the Vietnamese coast in support of ground combat operations and in independent strikes against targets throughout the theater. Despite the difficulties they encountered in defeating North Vietnam's MiGs and air defenses, these experiences cheered naval aviators on another level because they seemed to promise a future of political support and a congenial style of warfare.

The tactical and operational problems Navy pilots encountered in the skies over Southeast Asia received enormous study, as we have seen, and great efforts were made to resolve them. The Navy's maritime difficulties in the Vietnam War received far less attention, however. The Navy's attempt to maintain a close blockade off the Vietnamese coast to offset the unwillingness of the political leadership to mine Vietnam's harbors was far less successful than that of Cuba. The Navy was never able to shut down the movement of supplies through its own cordon completely, although it reduced that movement dramatically. More importantly, the coastal blockade simply drove the North Vietnamese to change their patterns of supply. They sent their ships to harbors in Cambodia and increased the movement of supplies along the Ho Chi Minh trail, relying heavily on Vietnam's many rivers to disperse those supplies to units throughout the country. Although the Navy responded by patrolling the rivers and deltas aggressively (in part through the "Swift Boat" squadrons of which John Kerry was a member), these patrols were not successful in shutting down the North Vietnamese logistics system. The Navy was never willing to devote enough resources to make them effective, and failures of cooperation between the riverine patrols and U.S. ground forces further hindered their effectiveness. Although the Navy had made much in the early 1960s of its commitment to small wars, flaunting its Seabees and special operations forces, the service remained dominated by its aviators and would not deviate from its focus on force projection to give adequate resources to the less glamorous "brown water" missions it faced in the war. The Navy paid very little price for its failure in littoral operations in Vietnam, since subsequent administrations rejected the idea of fighting wars like Vietnam again at all. But Vietnam and its legacy posed a much more insidious danger to the Navy.

Throughout the 1960s naval analysts had come increasingly to fear that the Soviet focus on long-range surface-to-surface missiles (SSMs), both nuclear and conventional, would make carriers obsolete. The Soviets had chosen to focus on such weapons because they could not afford to build a blue water carrier fleet to oppose U.S. aircraft carriers with similar capabilities. They instead built numerous guided-missile cruisers and destroyers, and developed a doctrine of missile salvoes that they hoped would destroy U.S. carriers from afar without having to engage their protective aircraft. By 1970, many in Washington as well as Moscow believed that this approach would succeed.

Had the American political leadership continued to focus on power projection against Third World states, this growing threat would not have loomed so ominously. Vietnam did not have such SSM capability, and no state outside of the Soviet Union was working on it seriously enough to pose any threat for years to come. Navy ships had operated off the coasts of Vietnam, Cuba, and Korea with near-impunity. They could expect to do so against similar enemies for the indefinite future.

As Nixon, Ford, and Carter refocused their attention on Central Europe and the Middle East, however, the capabilities of the Soviet Navy came very much to the fore. Would U.S. aircraft carriers be able to get close enough to Europe to operate safely in the face of massive Soviet efforts to deny them access? Would they be able to operate in the confined waters of the Eastern Mediterranean at all? Since the primary advantage of an aircraft carrier is its ability to provide a politically neutral and highly developed mobile base for aircraft, moreover, their utility in such conflicts was minimal. Moreover, American planes operated freely from bases throughout Europe and the Mediterranean already, bases that could not be sunk with SSMs. To many outside the Navy, these facts appeared to undermine most of the traditional arguments for the large and expensive carrier fleet the Navy consistently sought.

Most Naval leaders saw the problem somewhat differently. They noted with alarm that the Soviets had launched a massive shipbuilding program in the 1960s and continued it in the 1970s. The U.S.S.R. also fielded very long range bombers like the Backfire, which could strike U.S. SLOCs from bases in

Eastern Europe. For the first time since World War II, the Navy faced a challenge in its traditional primary role—control of the seas.[22] Unfortunately for the service, the leadership split over how to respond to this challenge.

Admiral Elmo Zumwalt, Chief of Naval Operations from 1970 to 1974, basically accepted the argument that the carrier had lost its significance. He favored the construction of a much larger fleet of smaller, simpler, and cheaper ships that each held a small number of vertical/short take-off and landing (V/STOL) aircraft. These ships could hold the line in the narrow seas of the Mediterranean and the northern European littoral, while a smaller number of true carriers fought their way back to the front line from safer positions in the rear. Zumwalt slowed or cancelled construction of a number of classes of ships in order to preserve the resources for this modernization program in a time of fiscal constraint.

Zumwalt's approach was not popular within the Navy, however, and his authoritarian manner of implementing it contributed to the hostility that might have been expected from a service dominated by its aviators. Opponents argued that such small ships and aircraft of such limited capabilities could not possibly hold out in waters where much more powerful carriers could not. The best way to defeat the Soviet threat, they further argued, was to destroy it at its bases. The Soviet danger to the carrier was turned into a further justification for the naval deep strike mission already favored by naval aviators.

This argument for building an offensively-minded and extremely expensive Navy did not succeed with political leaders such as Jimmy Carter bent on dealing with the Soviet threat through negotiations, détente, and disarmament. As one prominent historian argues, the Navy's focus in the 1970s on weapons systems rather than on national strategy, on threats rather than coordinated responses to them, destroyed the service's credibility with Congress and successive administrations. As a result, the Navy got the worst of both worlds. Zumwalt's program failed partly through the efforts of his own subordinates to undermine it, but the aviators could not sell their competing vision of carrier-based deep strike either. The Navy shrank to its lowest levels since before the Korean War, its ships aged steadily as the Soviets laid down new keels, and its ability to perform its traditional missions rapidly eroded.

At the same time, the transition to an all-volunteer force hit the Navy badly. Navy recruiters had benefited from the draft because large numbers of qualified young men who wished to avoid serving with infantry units volunteered for the Navy instead. With the end of conscription, the quality of Navy recruits dropped significantly. The lingering effects of the Vietnam War were also felt in the flight of experienced NCOs and a general drop in morale accompanied by dramatic increases in drug and alcohol abuse. Inadequate budgets across the board cut into steaming time, and an inability to find qualified sailors even prevented some ships from sailing at all.[22]

These critical problems, combined with tensions between and within the Navy's various sub-communities, prevented the Naval leadership of the 1970s from focusing on the problem of developing a meaningful maritime strategy to incorporate into a larger national military or grand strategy. At the moment when the Navy most needed attention and increased funding, its own problems prevented its leaders from making the arguments necessary to justify any increases. Just as the Army found the impetus for major change in a reevaluation of the Soviet threat, so too did changes in Soviet naval doctrine shake the Navy from its stagnation. Throughout the 1970s, Naval leaders had come increasingly to the conclusion that the U.S. could not confidently protect even the most vital sea lanes across the Atlantic in time of war, and certainly would have to cede the Pacific and Indian Oceans, and even possibly the North Sea, to the Red Fleet. These conclusions were based on the belief that the Soviets would pursue an offensive maritime strategy designed to cut those SLOCs and drive the U.S. fleet from contested waters. By the end of the 1970s, however, some intelligence analysts and admirals were realizing that Soviet strategy was changing.

Admiral Sergei Gorshkov, the legendary head of the Red Fleet, and his advisors apparently decided that sending the Soviet ballistic missile submarines (SSBNs) out into the open ocean would expose them excessively to allied anti-submarine warfare (ASW) efforts designed to keep the sea lanes clear. He opted instead to concentrate the SSBN force in the White Sea and the Sea of Okhotsk, and to use a large portion of the rest of the Soviet fleet to protect them in those bastions. There the SSBNs would be able to serve as a reliable and survivable deterrent to any American escalation of conflict to the strategic nuclear level, or as a safe second-strike force to be held in reserve in the event of a limited nuclear exchange.[23]

The initial implications for the Navy's budget woes were discouraging—a Soviet shift to a defensive orientation would destroy any sense of urgency in the political leadership about building a fleet to match the growing Soviet navy. But Admiral Thomas Hayward, CNO from 1978 to 1982, did not see it that way. He had already come to the conclusion that the Navy's most important lack was not money, but strategic thought. In Hayward's opinion, the service's inability to articulate an overriding vision that might justify its existence, let alone expansion, made the budget battle hopeless from the start. He therefore set in motion a series of efforts to reconsider and, in fact, develop from scratch a maritime strategy. He was even willing to accept a maritime strategy that seemed to contradict the prevailing short-war, Europe-focused strategic concepts then prevalent in the Carter administration.[24]

Hayward argued that the notion of simply abandoning the Pacific and Indian Oceans, to say nothing of the North Sea, to the Soviet fleet was folly, as was the idea of shifting the Pacific

Fleet to the Atlantic in time of war. If nothing else, such a shift would simply ensure that a large portion of the Navy would be out of action for weeks—the weeks in which, according to Secretary of Defense Harold Brown, the war would have been decided in Europe once and for all. Nor could the NATO alliance calmly contemplate a Soviet seizure of the North Sea and the dire threat to the critical SLOCs that would pose.

But the American Navy was too small to face the Soviets everywhere in the late 1970s, and Hayward and others felt that that numerical inferiority militated strongly against a defensive posture. Only by striking decisively in one theater first and then shifting to another could the U.S. fleet hope to defeat its larger nemesis. Hints of the change in Soviet strategy and doctrine, far from discouraging Hayward in this reappraisal, seemed to him and others to provide an opportunity. If the Soviets could be made to fear that their ballistic missile submarines were in danger even in their secured bastions, some reasoned, then they would redouble their efforts to protect them, thereby effectively ceding the world's oceans to the U.S. and her allies. Numerical inferiority and perceptions of the enemy strategy combined to reinforce the trend already well underway toward an offensively oriented U.S. maritime strategy. The development of the Aegis fleet defense cruiser, able to track and shoot down incoming anti-shipping missiles, was also critical in supporting this new approach, answering the argument that carriers were too vulnerable even as the new offensive strategy gave them a central role in any fleet operations.[25]

The new maritime strategy suffered from a number of important flaws. First and foremost, it was an attempt to circumvent the absence of a clear national military strategy in the hope that the higher-level strategy would follow the Navy's lead. In this respect, Hayward and his successor, James D. Watkins, were only partly successful. The Reagan administration accepted the vision of global and protracted war that underlay the Navy's assumptions, but it never clearly ruled on the Navy's concept of attacking the Soviet SSBN force in its bastions. Neither did it integrate the Navy's proposed maritime strategy, which focused heavily on the extra-European problem, with the Army's completely European focus, and the Air Force's emphasis on the delivery of strategic nuclear weapons. The Navy's effort to force Reagan to adopt a clear national strategy that would harmonize service strategies therefore clearly failed.[26]

Hayward and Watkins were very successful, however, in providing a sophisticated intellectual justification for the building and deployment programs they preferred. By 1990 the Navy fielded fifteen attack carriers, one hundred attack submarines, and adequate cruisers, destroyers, and support ships to maintain and defend them at sea. If Reagan had not explicitly endorsed the strategy of striking the Soviets in their bastions, he had not rejected it either. The Navy thus organized itself around an offensive mission of taking the fight to the Soviets using carrier-based aircraft and the Tomahawk sea-launched cruise missile (SLCM—now frequently called the TLAM for Tomahawk Land Attack Missile) that came on line in the decade as well. There is no way of knowing how well this posture would have fared in battle against the Soviets, but it turned out to be perfect for the sorts of missions the Navy would actually perform in the 1980s—and in the years that followed.

The Navy's renaissance in the Reagan years offers a number of important lessons. First, although Naval leaders focused heavily on the problem of purchasing and maintaining hardware, the only major new technology fielded was the Aegis defense system, which had been under development for years. Unlike the Army's rebirth, the naval renaissance resulted from an intellectual revolution within the service.

Second, that strategy did not spring fully formed from the head of a CNO or his advisory team. Hayward took the lead, to be sure, but he focused primarily on establishing organizations within the Navy that could conduct coherent long-term thinking and planning. He revitalized the Naval War College and worked hard to make it an intellectual center and the home of maritime strategic thinking. This effort paid dividends at once, as Newport faculty and staff, together with world-class wargaming facilities, developed and fleshed out the basic concepts of the maritime strategy that Hayward and Watkins used. But it also encouraged the development of a longer-term ability to conduct strategic thinking within the Navy, while preparing junior officers for such endeavors later in their careers. It was a way of institutionalizing creativity and intellectual support for transformation within the service.

Like the transformations in the Army and the airpower communities following Vietnam, therefore, the Navy's transformation in the 1980s was broad-based, threat-driven, and supported by a sophisticated intellectual effort. Fear of the Red Fleet drove first the Naval leadership and then the national leadership to make hard choices. Recognition of the many areas in which the Navy was suffering ruled out attempts at easier partial solutions. Above all, Hayward's realization that the Navy's greatest weakness was its strategic thinking made possible a fundamental transformation of the Navy's capabilities with very few new technologies. As a result, the Navy regained a considerable degree of balance against a waning Soviet threat. For all the promise of Hayward's efforts to revitalize maritime strategic thinking, however, the Navy's ability to continue to meet the changing world that followed the collapse of that threat remained to be seen.

THE GEOSTRATEGIC REALITIES OF THE 1980S

The Reagan administration rightly focused on the Soviet Union, but the 1980s found American forces repeatedly engaged with a series of enemies related only peripherally to the Cold War.

Some of the crises of this time were sui generis, such as the invasion of Grenada in 1983. Others were part of what we can now see as the first stages of a long-term trend of growing American involvement in the Muslim world. In particular, Reagan was the first modern American president to undertake repeated and significant military operations designed to deter or punish terrorists and their state sponsors.

Reagan and his advisors knew that the threats they confronted did not all tie directly back to the Soviet Union—the Soviets had certainly not put Khomeini in power, for instance, nor did their agents blow up the Marine barracks in Lebanon in 1983, and they did not direct Moammar Qaddafi to undertake his attacks on American citizens throughout Europe and the Mediterranean region.[27] But the Reagan administration continued to see even these relatively new threats strictly within a Cold War paradigm. States might fail for a variety of independent reasons, but America's interest lay in the fact that the Soviets might benefit from the resulting chaos. Khomeini's revolution was worrisome, after he had released the hostages, primarily because the Soviets might use it as a pretext to invade Iran. The Iran–Iraq war that began in 1980 offered similar possibilities to the U.S.S.R., and therefore presented similar dangers to the United States.[28] In retrospect it is easy to see that there were more fundamental trends at work that transcended the Cold War framework, but in scrutinizing Reagan's policies for missed opportunities it is equally important to remember that if the Soviet Union had not collapsed in 1991, these trends would still be second- or third-order priorities.

Throughout the 1980s, therefore, all of the military operations the armed forces undertook were seen as lesser included missions within the overall strategy of preparing to deter or defeat the Soviet Union. The desultory efforts begun by Carter and continued in the early 1980s to establish a Rapid Deployment Joint Task Force to respond to crises in the Persian Gulf reflected the fact that overall U.S. strategy saw the Middle East as a very low priority in the general contest with the Soviets.[29] Reagan's emphasis on preparing for a protracted and global war, moreover, did not directly support a series of operations designed to be short, sharp conflicts. Since the U.S. did not, in fact, have to face a serious Soviet military challenge in this period and since each of the military contests of the Reagan years were brief and pitted American forces against much less well-prepared enemies, the tensions between U.S. grand strategy and the realities of the world were not important. Because the size of U.S. forces shrank in the post-Cold War years, however, and the scale and duration of the contingencies increased dramatically, we can now see the Reagan years as the beginning of this growing trend in U.S. military policy.

It has become customary to portray the military operations between 1975 and 1990, and, indeed, to 2003, as a triumphant progression from incompetence to unchallengeable dominance, particularly in the airpower community.[30] From the low point of Operation Eagle Claw, the Iranian hostage-rescue mission in 1980, U.S. military capabilities seem to have improved steadily through conflicts with Libya, the invasion of Grenada, operations in the Persian Gulf, and, finally, Operations Just Cause in Panama and Desert Storm in Iraq.

There is a certain amount of validity to this view. Certain aspects of American military technique improved dramatically over the course of the 1980s, particularly the penetration of hostile airspace. There is a limit, however, to the relevance of these operations for subsequent missions, both in the 1990s and after 9/11. Because the nature of the operations changed so radically over the course of the quarter century between 1980 and today, the simple triumphalist interpretation can be misleading.

U.S. troops went into action in 1975 against Cambodian pirates who had seized a container ship, the USS Mayaguez. In 1980, Special Forces attempted to rescue the hostages Kho-

meini's henchmen were holding in Teheran. In 1981, naval airmen clashed with Libyan pilots over the Gulf of Sidra in defense
of the principles of naval law. In 1983 Marines became victims
of Muslim terrorism in Beirut, which carrier-based aircraft
then attempted to avenge. At about the same time, U.S. forces
invaded Grenada in another massive hostage-rescue mission
that almost incidentally deposed a nascent communist regime.
In 1985, carrier aircraft forced down an airliner carrying the
hijackers of the Achille Lauro. The following year, Reagan
launched a large-scale air strike against Libya in retaliation for
Qaddafi's support of terrorism. In 1987–88, the U.S. conducted a large-scale exercise to protect shipments of oil from
the war-torn Persian Gulf that included the reflagging and protection of Kuwaiti tankers. And in 1989, George Bush deposed
Noriega's regime in Panama in Operation Just Cause.

Apart from Just Cause, these operations all had several things
in common. They were all primarily air-sea operations with little
or no ground participation. Of the ground forces that were involved, the vast majority were Marines. All ground combat was
conducted by and against light infantry with little or no armored
support and, in most cases, no room for significant maneuver
on the ground anyway. With the exception of the Beirut mission, all were very short operations conducted with little notice
and quickly finished. All were also highly limited operations in
which the U.S. refrained from using much of its available military power against enemies that could not have hoped to match
any substantial commitment of that power. These operations,
finally, were not part of any coherent strategy except in the sense
that they were all intended to show American strength and
resolve. The extrapolation of lessons from these operations to
major wars such as the Gulf War, or even to the scattered and
smaller missions that the war on terror might require, is therefore extremely problematic.

Between 1975 and 1985, the major terrorist threat the U.S.

faced took the form of hostage-taking. The Mayaguez affair, the Iranian hostage crisis, Operation Urgent Fury in Grenada, and the Achille Lauro hijacking and its consequences all revolved around the seizure or possible seizure of American citizens as hostages. This terrorist technique was not confined to American targets, of course, but the Israeli actions during the Entebbe raid of 1976 served as a strong deterrent to later hostage-taking attempts against citizens of that state. The success of that raid and its deterrent effects remained green in the minds of American leaders for years thereafter, who hoped by similar decisive action to achieve similar protection for U.S. citizens.

In the wake of the 9/11 attacks, which followed more than a decade of terrorist attacks focused on blowing up buildings, aircraft, or even individuals, hostage-taking has come to seem both less likely and less dangerous than the more recent variation of terrorism. Even the seizure and execution of individual hostages in Iraq has generated far less comment than the earlier undertakings did despite extensive self-promotion by the terrorists themselves.

There is good reason to continue to fear a renewal of such efforts on a broader scale, however. Hostage seizures are inherently dramatic, suspenseful, and longer-lived than simple bombings. They place a much heavier burden on the victimized government to take action, and to do so rapidly. This burden offers the terrorists the hope, on the one hand, that the government will take no effective action, thereby harming its legitimacy in the eyes of its people and the world, or, even better, that it will take unwise action that will promote the terrorists' cause directly or indirectly. It is the pressure of time and the need to respond urgently to the unforeseen attack that makes this method of terrorism potentially more attractive than a simple bombing, in the aftermath of which governments are much more likely to take the time to reflect seriously and choose a better course of action.

Hostage-taking also places advanced militaries that rely on speed and firepower for success at a disadvantage. The task of locating hostages and extracting them without allowing their captors, usually intermingled with them, to kill them is extraordinarily difficult. In evaluating U.S. military operations between 1975 and 1986, therefore, it is essential to bear in mind that the missions they faced were among the most demanding any military could face, at least at comparable scales.

This stricture is nowhere more true than in the evaluation of Operation Eagle Claw of 1980. This mission—the attempt to free the hostages Khomeini's minions were holding in Teheran —has served as the exemplar of all that was wrong with the U.S. military at the end of the 1970s. At first glance, this view seems valid—not only did the rescue attempt fail, and fail in a public way that precluded any further attempts, but a helicopter–airplane crash as the troops were attempting to leave after aborting the mission left eight Americans dead, five wounded, and a considerable amount of hardware on the Iranian desert.[31]

Much has been made of the fact that the wrong helicopters or pilots were used, that the equipment had not been well-enough maintained, that the airmen were not skilled enough at their jobs, and so on, and there is no doubt some truth to each of these accusations. It is equally true that restrictions placed upon the mission by the political leadership left an unacceptably small margin for error. The mission was so challenging in itself, however, and the obstacles so formidable that it is difficult to imagine its success under even the best possible circumstances. The troops had to fly from carriers nearly a thousand miles across hostile countryside and desert, establish two intermediate base camps and defend them without being detected, infiltrate a hostile and suspicious—and very large—city by vehicle, penetrate a heavily defended compound, rescue hostages spread out in at least two different locations, rendezvous with vehicles, and escape from the heart of an alerted enemy country for a 1,200-mile flight to safety in Egypt. It was a mission that would have seemed incredible in a Rambo movie, and there was little reason to believe that it would have worked in reality even with the best soldiers and equipment.[32]

The Carter administration adopted it for lack of any better alternative, because the political pressure of the situation was becoming unbearable. It was precisely the sort of mistaken action that can be expected in a protracted hostage-crisis situation. It nevertheless came to be seen as the proof of the collapse of American military power following the Vietnam War, helped lose the election for Carter, and provided Reagan with a rallying cry for the restoration of the military that Carter had already begun—and which would almost certainly have had little effect on the conduct of a similar mission in the future.

The Marine barracks bombing of 1983 is another exemplar of military unreadiness, but there too the picture is less clear than might at first appear. The Reagan administration found it very difficult to establish clear goals for its intervention in Lebanon, perhaps because it was not clearly connected to the Cold War. Reagan had sent a small force of Marines as part of an international peacekeeping force to restore order in Lebanon in the aftermath of the Israeli invasion of 1982. Initially, the objective was to maintain a completely even-handed approach, which even involved rejecting Israeli demands for cooperation and special privileges. No one imagined at first that the Marines were in any danger; indeed, relations with the local Lebanese were initially very positive.

As the situation grew more complicated, however, the Marines found it impossible to avoid seeming to take sides, even as they strove to remain impartial. As a result, they started to become targets of radicals in the area. Unfortunately, the Marine and Naval commanders on the scene, as well as the political leadership in the region and in the U.S., did not see that the changing situation was putting the Marines increasingly at risk. Mistakes by the local Marine commander, who focused too heavily on maintaining a peaceful posture aimed at securing good will with the locals, badly exacerbated this situation so that a terrorist was able to drive a truck full of explosives right up to a virtually undefended compound housing hundreds of Marines. Two hundred and thirty-nine American servicemen died.[33]

The comparison of this catastrophe with the failed Special Forces raid in Somalia in 1993 or with the Khobar Towers bombing in Saudi Arabia two years later shows that even the most professional American forces, fresh from one of the most dramatic victories in their history, can make mistakes that permit terrorists or hostile local tribesmen to inflict unacceptable casualties on them. To use the Marine barracks bombing as an indictment of U.S. military capabilities in general would be highly unfair.

It reflected a more serious problem, that was seen again in Somalia and elsewhere. The line between peacekeepers and combatants, at least in the eyes of militants in a complicated situation, can be very thin. A mission that the American leadership sees as entirely peaceful and nonthreatening may not seem this way to local leaders. Worst of all, local leaders who initially welcome an American presence can over time change their minds.

It seems logical to argue that the military of the 1990s handled Operation Desert Storm much better than the military of 1980 would have, but there really is no clear benchmark for making an honest comparison. The military of 1980 would almost certainly have performed better in a Desert Storm-type operation than it did in Eagle Claw or Beirut. In the same way, some of the problems the military is experiencing in Iraq today surely reflect the drawdown of the 1990s and other recent problems, but some of them have also been endemic in the force since the 1970s or earlier. One of the greatest dangers in military analysis is to look at any given operation as the vindication or indictment of the military as a whole. Each operation is unique and stresses the military differently. The trick is to understand first what lessons we can expect to learn from a given operation and only then to study the lessons themselves.

One aspect of U.S. military capability that clearly did improve over the course of the 1980s was the conduct of deep-strike missions into defended airspace. The capabilities for such missions had existed since the 1970s—especially precision-guided munitions and anti-radiation missiles that could track and destroy SAM radars. It took the airpower services some time, however, to learn how to integrate all of their capabilities in a successful strike with low casualties and low collateral damage.

The effort to punish Lebanese factions for the Marine barracks bombing in 1983 was not successful. Errors of many varieties led to an ineffective air strike that lost several aircraft.[34] The effort to punish Qaddafi for his support of anti-U.S. terrorism in 1986 was much more successful. To many it now seems to have been the graduating exercise for American airpower before the real-world test of Desert Storm. The hallmark of this operation was careful planning to ensure that Libyan air defenses and the Libyan air force would be neutralized before the vulnerable bombers came into range of their weapons. Greater use of precision bombing capabilities reduced collateral damage and time-over-target for the attackers. The result was a nearly picture-perfect strike in which U.S. forces suffered no losses and hit all their targets. Qaddafi was so stunned by the strike, and by his helplessness before U.S. airpower, that he dramatically scaled back his terrorist operations.[35] There is a world of difference, nevertheless, between this very brief and small-scale strike and the prolonged and massive bombing campaign against Iraq in 1990, and a linear extrapolation from the one to the other is impossible and inappropriate.

★   ★   ★

CONCLUSION

Reagan completed the military transformation begun in the 1970s. One key to this success was a new look at grand strategy and national military strategy, and a willingness to maintain current programs while increasing spending to make up for deficiencies elsewhere. The continued presence of a massive Soviet threat was another critical part of this effort. In the shadow of that threat there was little room for abstract arguments about what an individual weapons system might or might not do in theory. And in fact, the Navy's attempts in the 1970s to make such arguments nearly destroyed the service. By the 1980s, all of the services were sharply focused on the specific geostrategic problems that the nation faced, and worked to fit their own strategies and then their procurement, training, and doctrinal decisions into that geostrategic context. In this respect, the presence of the Soviet enemy made military planning easier than it is in many respects today.

The scale and imminence of the Soviet threat was also important. The fear of falling behind an aggressive enemy, of being unable to accomplish core military missions, including defending the American homeland, put great pressure on military and political leaders alike to identify and solve problems. It created an environment in which "making the hard decisions" was not simply code for killing defense programs, as it is today, but actually meant choosing wisely among both domestic and national security priorities. Pressed to hold the defense budget at stable levels when he took office, Reagan replied, "Look, I am the President of the United States, the commander in chief; my primary responsibility is the security of the United States. . . . If we don't have our security, we'll have no need for social programs."[36] Much of this emphasis was peculiar to Reagan, of course, but the context of the time, including the recent Soviet invasion of Afghanistan, the Soviet nuclear and naval buildups, and so forth, had made the issue of defense pressing even for Carter. In the absence of such a clear and ominous threat it is difficult to imagine even Reagan driving through such an aggressive military program, whatever the objective needs of the armed forces.

Because of that threat, however, Reagan was able to increase the defense budget to the minimum levels necessary to maintain and improve the existing force as well as to make up for certain obvious shortfalls in major programs, especially nuclear forces and the Navy. He did not, therefore, force the military to choose between sustaining current readiness and working on "transformational" programs. The large increases in O&M and procurement accounts made good critical deficiencies in the day-to-day preparedness of the armed forces to fight.

At the same time, Reagan completed development and deployment of the M-X missile and began an entirely new program, the Strategic Defense Initiative, as well as aggressively furthering the development of precision-guided munitions and stealth aircraft (which we will consider in more detail below). Had Reagan forced the military to make choices among these various programs and efforts, the completion of the transformation begun in the 1970s would surely have been set back substantially and the armed forces' ability to undertake the demanding missions of the 1990s would have been seriously undermined. Sometimes it is important not to make choices, even in times of apparent fiscal constraint.

Even so, the U.S. military at the end of Reagan's presidency was not yet ready to change the nature of warfare. A series of further intellectual breakthroughs was required to take the technologies and capabilities just coming to fruition in the force to the next level.

A Revolution in Airpower Theory

THE PRECISE U.S. air attacks in 1991 and 2003 on Iraqi military and leadership targets and the extreme efforts made to avoid collateral damage and civilian casualties, seem in one sense to be merely extensions of U.S. strategic bombing theory going back to World War II adapted to the age of precision-guided munitions and the "CNN effect." The innovations in airpower theory of the past twenty five years have in fact transformed it almost beyond recognition, however. The relatively simplistic attempts of World War II planners to identify "bottlenecks" in the German economic system whose destruction would paralyze that economy have given way to sophisticated efforts to understand the entire enemy government, economy, society, and military as a system. We shall explore the consequences of this view, both positive and negative, throughout much of the rest of this work, for U.S. military transformation in all services has come to rely on it as an intellectual foundation. First we must consider its origins.

JOHN BOYD

The most articulate early spokesman for this radical new way of thinking about war in the U.S. was John Boyd, whom we last met as the architect of the superfighters, but who then retired from the Air Force as a colonel in 1975.[1] Boyd was more than just a maverick fighter jock. He was a synthesizing thinker who read broadly in many disciplines and connected disparate ideas that would have seemed totally unrelated to one another to other people. He compiled his thoughts into a series of presentations that, together, take fifteen or sixteen hours to hear. They have survived in a compilation of hundreds of slides under the title "A Discourse on Winning and Losing."[2]

The Discourse is difficult to read, partly because of its format and partly because of the eccentricity of Boyd's manner of thinking, but its core concepts are very powerful. Although Boyd was a superb engineer and an excellent student of physics, he found biological analogies much more helpful for understanding human systems such as states and armed forces.

All human organizations, like human beings themselves, can exist only within an environment with which they must interact, Boyd argued. To do so, they must understand that environment accurately and be able to act upon it in ways that enhance their survival. This biological fact offers a number of important vulnerabilities for an adversary to exploit. One can try to distort the enemy's perception of the environment, try to cut the enemy off from necessary connections with that environment, or simply work to have a more accurate perception and better connections oneself.

Boyd formalized his notion of how individuals and groups interacted with one another and their environment in the concept of the "OODA loop." OODA stands for observation, orientation, decision, and action. The idea is that one observes an event or situation, evaluates the observation in light of genetic, cultural, psychological, and other mental predispositions, decides upon an appropriate action to take in response, and then acts. The process then repeats indefinitely. Boyd believed that all living organisms and human groups interact with each other and their environment in accord with this paradigm. Complex organizations like armies, he argued, can have multiple OODA loops operating simultaneously—those at lower levels moving generally faster than those at higher levels, but all interconnected in complex ways.

It is obvious that some organisms can observe-orient-decide-and-act faster than others. The ideal, Boyd believed, was to move through the loop so much faster than the enemy that the enemy's attempts to observe, orient, and decide become hopelessly obsolete even as they are taking place. As the enemy attempts to take an action in response to one event, our own OODA loop would have completed another iteration, thus presenting the enemy with a changed situation in which his original response is outdated and therefore inappropriate. As the enemy falls behind, his ability to take purposeful action vanishes and his will even to try erodes.

To accomplish this result, Boyd believed that it was essential to maintain the highest possible levels of flexibility and initiative in order to make one's actions unpredictable and rapid. He believed that internal friction was the enemy of flexibility and rapidity of decision and action, and that centralization of command contributed to that friction. People in a rigid hierarchical organization, he felt, focus too much on problems internal to that organization and insufficiently on interacting with the enemy or the environment. The more complex and hierarchical the organization, furthermore, the longer it takes to execute an OODA loop. Drawing heavily on the example of German doctrine between 1917 and 1945, Boyd believed that adherence to a common doctrine and training paradigm would allow superiors to give their subordinates maximum flexibility to make decisions on their own, thus increasing the speed of the OODA cycle. He even argued, in fact, that "command and control" as a concept should be replaced by "leadership and appreciation," two qualities more in keeping with an initiative-based, decentralized organization.

The idea of the OODA loop and the idea of cycling through it faster than the enemy caught fire within military circles and continues to have a profound effect on the way officers and analysts think about war. But Boyd did not stop there. He also argued that the very complexity of human organizations such as armies and states offers an additional vulnerability. Such complex organisms can only function if their parts work together harmoniously. An enemy who understood how those parts interacted with one another—and particularly their vital interconnections—could break them apart into isolated components that could neither communicate nor coordinate actions with one another. Having accomplished this, the attacker would have the enemy entirely at his mercy.

This idea offered a profound set of insights into the nature of war, even if they were not entirely new. It was not necessary, Boyd was arguing, to defeat the enemy's armed forces or destroy his state or society. The careful targeting of these vital but vulnerable interconnections among what he called "centers of gravity" would leave the enemy helpless, whatever the many military forces that remained to him. An enemy army whose commanders cannot speak with their subordinates, whose intermediate leaders do not understand the situation and tasks they face, whose soldiers do not receive direction from above, is not an army, but a mob waiting to collapse.

It is not a new vision. As early as 1918, J. F. C. Fuller developed a concept for tank warfare that he called "Plan 1919" aiming to accomplish a similar goal using rapid tank strikes to decapitate the enemy. Soviet "deep battle" theory of the 1920s and 1930s intended to use deep air and artillery strikes to paralyze enemy reserves and command and control centers to facilitate the destruction of enemy forces by rapid armored thrusts;

German armored doctrine pursued a similar, if more limited, approach.[3] None of these theories, however, considered the problem on the breadth and scale of Boyd's ideas—the level of the entire state and even society backing the armed forces. In the context of traditional American thinking about war, moreover, Boyd's theories were a real revelation.

They were not, however, without flaws. Boyd's use of the term "center of gravity" has proven to be especially problematic, as have almost all recent attempts to use or define this concept. The term is Clausewitzian in origin, and represents that great thinker's efforts to find physical analogies to describe warfare. Over the past decade, in fact, a substantial debate has emerged about what Clausewitz really meant and how the term can best be applied to modern warfare.[4] There is still no clear consensus, and it must be admitted that even Clausewitz's definitions are not entirely clear and unambiguous, the claims of certain recent entries into this debate notwithstanding.[5]

Clausewitz uses "*Schwerpunkt*" (German for "center of gravity") consistently with its physical meaning for the most part—the balancing point of an object, or the point at which, if all of the object's mass were concentrated there, the Newtonian properties of the object would be unchanged.[6] In this regard, there can obviously be only one center of gravity in any given object, although Clausewitz recognized that states and coalitions —or even large military forces dispersed over wide areas—may be regarded as collections of objects and, therefore, have multiple centers of gravity.[7]

Boyd introduced a significant level of confusion into the discussion by using "center of gravity" and "*schwerpunkt*" to mean two different things and by failing to define center of gravity at all. His only direct statement about the meaning of the term simply rejects Clausewitz's definition: "Clausewitz incorrectly stated: 'a center of gravity is always found where the mass is concentrated most densely'—then argued that this is the place where the blows must be aimed and where the decision should be reached. He failed to develop [the] idea of generating many non-cooperative centers of gravity by striking at those vulnerable, yet critical, tendons, connections, and activities that permit a larger system center of gravity to exist."[8] Thereafter, he repeatedly spoke of the need to generate "non-cooperative centers of gravity," but made no further effort to describe what he meant by that term.[9]

Boyd put more effort into defining the concept of *schwerpunkt*: "*Schwerpunkt* acts as a center or axis or harmonizing agent that is used to help shape commitment and convey or carry-out intent, at all levels from theater to platoon. . . . In this sense *Schwerpunkt* can be thought of as a focusing agent that naturally produces an unequal distribution of effort as a basis to generate superiority in some sectors by thinning-out others as well as a medium to realize superior intent without impeding initiative of many subordinates."[10] Boyd used the concept both positively and negatively, advocating the development of a clear *schwerpunkt* to facilitate one's own harmonious interactions and to break the enemy apart into multiple *schwerpunkten*. He seems to have meant for *schwerpunkt* to stand for main effort or primary mission. Its quality of organizing a decentralized force resulted from the fact that if subordinates understand the overall main goal or mission of the operation, then they can operate with much greater freedom of action and initiative—and their superiors can trust them to do so.

Boyd did not, however, consider the relationship between *schwerpunkt* and center of gravity very carefully. Did each center of gravity, by which he seems frequently to mean force or part of a force, have its own *schwerpunkt* or did all share a common *schwerpunkt*? What did Boyd mean by "striking at those vulnerable, yet critical, tendons, connections, and activities that permit a larger system center of gravity to exist"? He offers no clear explanation.

The mismatch between Clausewitz's definition and Boyd's usage is important. To Clausewitz, an enemy's center of gravity was the object that, once destroyed, would entail the destruction, or at least material reduction, of his ability to continue fighting. He made it clear that he thought that the enemy's largest concentration of combat forces would almost inevitably be his center of gravity, at least in a conventional conflict. When that had been destroyed, the enemy would no longer be capable of continuing to fight and hostilities would almost certainly end.

Boyd clearly did not see centers of gravity in this light. He advocated destroying the *connections between* centers of gravity, which would then become "non-cooperative" and hinder rather than help the enemy's cause. It is not surprising that he thought in this way and Clausewitz did not. The Prussian theorist was advanced for his day, but no one at that time had begun to think of armies as systems that could be shattered by cutting the sinews that bound part to part. Such thinking could only really emerge with the advent of air power and could come to reality only with the increasing availability of precision-guided munitions.

The fact that Boyd used the term "center of gravity" to mean something other than the object or objects to be destroyed that will likely lead to victory, however, began a process of confusing the use of this concept that only grew worse as time went on, however. The problem was not that Boyd did not use Clausewitz's definition for the term—for all his brilliance, Clausewitz is not the final word on war, and deviation from his word is not the inevitable road to failure. The problem was that Boyd used a term, referring explicitly to Clausewitz, that Clausewitz had imbued with certain connotations, but used it to apply to a different concept without explicitly accepting or rejecting the connotations. Those who read a discussion about striking centers of gravity with Clausewitz in mind imagine that doing so will lead directly to victory. Boyd's vision of striking the *connections* between centers of gravity, however, was both more sophisticated and less clear in its implications for the outcome of the conflict. That conceptual elision has helped to generate a great deal of the confusion in the critical discussion about centers of gravity in war.

Clausewitz also emphasized two other important factors in the discussion of center of gravity, moreover, that Boyd largely ignored or distorted. First, center of gravity is a concept that only has meaning in a total war according to Clausewitz. Only such a conflict, he wrote, forces nations to mobilize their strength and will sufficiently to create true centers of gravity.[11] Second, only cohesive organizations can have centers of gravity. An opponent whose component parts do not interact with each other in important ways—a weak coalition, for example— will not offer a center of gravity whose destruction will lead to victory. It is very important, using the Clausewitzian definition, to examine whether the concept is even appropriate to the war under consideration.[12] Boyd's theories apply the concept to every enemy and every situation, explicitly including revolutionary war, upon which Clausewitz only touched briefly.[13]

Clausewitz did see the center of gravity as something that bound a state or coalition together, but his way of envisioning this process was different from Boyd's notion of attacking the sinews that bound the pieces of the enemy together.[14] As an example, Clausewitz describes part of the 1814 campaign against Napoleon. Two major allied armies advanced against Napoleon, one commanded by the eccentric, dashing, and aggressive Prussian Fieldmarshal Blücher, the other by the cautious and conservative Austrian Fieldmarshal Schwarzenberg. Although Schwarzenberg's army was the larger, Clausewitz writes, Blücher's was the true center of gravity: "Even though Blücher was weaker than Schwarzenberg, his enterprising spirit made him more important. The center of gravity lay with him, and he pulled the other forces in his direction."[15] Napoleon, Clausewitz argues, should have continued attacking Blücher

after initially defeating him, rather than turning on Schwarzenberg as he subsequently did. Clausewitz saw Blücher's army as
a force that served to unify the coalition army. Its destruction,
he believed, would shatter that cohesiveness and, since the cohesiveness of the coalition was a critical center of gravity,
would have served his purpose much better than the attack on
Schwarzenberg's army, even though it was larger. The center of
gravity that pulls a force, nation, or coalition together, therefore, is not the same as the literal methods of communication
that tie people to people and armies to armies.

It is worth noting that nineteenth-century military theory
offered an alternative to this viewpoint. Baron Henri Antoine
de Jomini, following a relatively long tradition with which
Clausewitz was well familiar, argued that an army could be
defeated by attacks on its communications. He, and other similar theorists, might well have argued that, rather than continuing to hammer at Blücher's army, Napoleon would have been
better advised to cut it off from Schwarzenberg, thereby sever-
ing the communication between the two and shattering the
cohesiveness of the coalition without having to fight a battle.
There was, thus, a notion of striking at the enemy's communications directly that Clausewitz explicitly rejected both in this
passage and throughout *On War*.[16] Boyd's development of the
concept, therefore, used a Clausewitzian concept and argument to support a fundamentally Jominian vision of war that
Clausewitz rejected.

Boyd transformed the idea of center of gravity from the center of the enemy's capabilities to fight to the organizing principles that held the enemy together. He and others nevertheless
continued to assume that, those centers once destroyed, the
enemy would no longer be capable of continuing the fight and
hostilities would necessarily end. This assumption is unwar-
ranted, because it ignores the fact that biological systems naturally seek to repair themselves once damaged. The reconstruction

of the main body of an army is too slow and laborious a process to be undertaken in all but the longest and slowest-paced of conflicts. The reconstruction of command, control, and communications links and the re-integration of "non-cooperative centers of gravity" can take place much more rapidly, however. Boyd's own theories, in fact, suggest that such a reconstruction would be the primary goal of an organization shattered as he described, and that human organizations should, in fact, excel in such tasks. Boyd never considered the problem that the disaggregation of the enemy system he proposed was likely to be fleeting rather than permanent, and he did not therefore consider how to follow up on that success in order to achieve victory. These problems would come to be central in the development of American airpower thought in the years to come, and they remain central to much thinking about military transformation today, as we shall see.

Despite these problems, Boyd's ideas breathed new intellectual life into the way American officers, civilian leaders, and military analysts thought about war. Boyd aggressively marketed his ideas throughout the 1980s, giving his increasingly long briefings to anyone who would listen to him—and many people did. He helped influence the development of AirLand Battle doctrine directly, and he helped begin a new way of thinking about air warfare. The theoretical nature of his own writings limited their direct impact on U.S. strategy and planning, but Boyd had a worthy successor in Colonel John Warden, whose theories and active participation led to the air campaign against Iraq of 1991.

JOHN WARDEN

John Warden was an Air Force fighter pilot whose career as a senior officer was spent mainly in the Pentagon. In the winter of 1988 he became the Deputy Director for Warfighting under the Deputy Chief of Staff for Plans and Operations, General Michael Dugan. From that position, Warden and his subordinates prepared a plan for the air war in Iraq based upon ideas he had developed in the mid-1980s, some of which formed the basis of his 1988 book, *The Air Campaign*.[17] Warden wrote *The Air Campaign* in less than a year while a student at the National War College.[18] It is not surprising, therefore, that the concepts he developed in that work are less sophisticated and holistic than Boyd's theories.[19] Warden, for his part, explicitly set himself the task of writing about the use of airpower at the operational level. His work was practical rather than philosophical, and airpower-focused rather than ecumenical. It was, nevertheless, an insightful and important approach that began the process of changing the way American military leaders of all services thought about war.

The main thrust of Warden's work was that air superiority was the single most essential requirement for victory in modern war. He believed that all of the resources of the airpower services certainly, possibly even of the other services as well, should be devoted to securing air superiority from the first moments of the struggle. Only when air superiority was obtained, he argued, should the military contemplate using air resources for other missions. There might be times that seemed to call for an exception to this rule, he noted, but "when it seems most obvious that the rule should be disobeyed, it is most likely that it should not be."[20]

Warden based this argument on an extensive review of recent military history. No state, he claimed, has ever won a war without obtaining air superiority and, conversely, no state that had air superiority has ever lost a war.[21] He did recognize, however, that airpower can play only a very limited role in a counterinsurgency struggle. In the context of the late 1980s, when the military was determined not to fight another Vietnam and the problem of the day was the Soviet army, Warden can be excused for not focusing his thoughts on this issue.

The Air Campaign is thus a cogent argument with substantial historical basis for the need to subordinate both close air support missions (CAS) and air interdiction missions to the task of gaining and keeping air superiority. It is also, therefore, an argument for an autonomous commander for the air campaign and even for the subordination of ground operations to air objectives, at least at the beginning of a conflict. It is as bold a statement for airpower dominance within the U.S. military as the Navy's maritime strategy was for complete naval autonomy and somewhat bolder than the Army's claim in AirLand Battle doctrine for the subordination of all efforts to the land fight.

Like Boyd, Warden was taken with the Clausewitzian concept of "center of gravity," and he emphasized the importance of this concept heavily in *The Air Campaign*. Like Boyd, Warden adopted an idiosyncratic definition loosely connected to, but fundamentally different from, Clausewitz's. Center of gravity, he wrote, "describes that point where the enemy is most vulnerable and the point where an attack will have the best chance of being decisive." Unlike Boyd, and contrary to Clausewitz's more holistic view of war, Warden added, "Every level of warfare has a center, or centers, of gravity. If several centers of gravity are involved, force must be applied to all if the object is to be moved."[22]

The idea of a center of gravity being the point at which the enemy is most vulnerable is a significant departure from Clausewitz's concept, or even from Boyd's. Since Clausewitz argued that the center of gravity most frequently would be the enemy's army, he certainly did not imagine that to be the enemy's most vulnerable point. Boyd, in fact, explicitly picked up on this corollary to attack Clausewitz for advocating bloody supposedly decisive battles.[23] Warden did not address the contradiction between the Clausewitzian concept and his own in the work, although he was aware of the divergence. In a recent interview he noted that he probably would not have used that term if he had to write *The Air Campaign* again because of the confusion it introduced.[24]

Warden expanded on the concept in a lengthy section entitled, "Assaulting the Air Center of Gravity."[25] Even this title is informative—neither Clausewitz nor Boyd would likely have recognized an "air center of gravity" distinct from the overall center or centers of gravity of the enemy system as a whole. Warden explained, "The enemy's air center of gravity may lie in equipment (numbers of planes or missiles); in logistics (the quality and resilience of supply support); geography (location and number of operational and support facilities); in personnel (numbers and quality of pilots); or in command and control (importance and vulnerability)."[26] Of these categories, Warden believed that equipment and logistics might provide lucrative targets, geography was more a matter of focusing intelligently and being persistent in the choice of targets, and personnel probably did not offer good opportunities to find a center of gravity in most cases.[27]

The reasons for these evaluations lay in the combination of vulnerability and "criticality" of the issue under examination. Airplanes are useless without trained pilots, making personnel a critical target. But killing pilots or preventing them from developing expertise is inordinately hard, dangerous, and time-consuming. However critical that target might be, therefore, it is unlikely to furnish a useful center of gravity because it does not provide obvious vulnerabilities most of the time. Logistics, by contrast, are both critical and vulnerable. Airplanes cannot fly without fuel any more than without pilots. Because fuel is difficult to produce, store, and transport, supplying it to aircraft is relatively much more vulnerable than supplying them with pilots. The combination of the criticality of fuel with the vulnerability of the systems for producing and delivering it make it likely to be an excellent center of gravity in Warden's viewpoint. The production, transportation, storage, and maintenance of aircraft themselves offers similar likely vulnerabilities combined with the requisite criticality.

Elaborating on these issues recently, Warden explained that the issue of vulnerability was really secondary to the selection of centers of gravity to attack. Just about any target, he noted, can be successfully attacked if sufficient thought is put into the problem, and such considerations are tactical concerns that should not intrude excessively into the development of strategic plans. The real issue is that since militaries always have limited resources, the wise strategist must choose centers of gravity that are essential to the functioning of the enemy but whose destruction does not require an inordinate amount of effort for the planned return. We will consider this aspect of Warden's thought in greater detail below.[28]

In *The Air Campaign*, Warden paid particular attention to the opportunities to find centers of gravity in the enemy's command and control systems. "Clearly, command," he declared, "with its necessarily associated communications and intelligence gathering functions, is an obvious center of gravity, and has been from the earliest times: As the death of the king on the field of battle meant defeat for his forces, so the effective isolation of the command structure in modern war has led to the rapid defeat of dependent forces."[29] Finding the appropriate command and control targets to strike, Warden conceded, was difficult, but there are several ways of attacking a command and control center of gravity based on the nature of the function. In a manner similar to Boyd, Warden pointed out that for commanders to function, they had to be able to receive accurate information about the state of the war, make decisions, and pass those decisions on to subordinates to execute. Warden did not use the concept of the OODA loop explicitly, but the idea was intrinsic in his brief consideration of the nature of command.[30] "Consequently," he wrote, "command can be attacked in the following three spheres: the information sphere; the decision sphere; and the communications sphere. If any one of these can be sufficiently disturbed, the effectiveness of operations will begin to decrease dramatically."[31]

Warden emphasizes that the importance of attacks on the enemy depended directly on the degree of pressure being exerted by the attacker. An enemy forced to respond to a fast-paced and dangerous situation was much more vulnerable to attacks on his command and control structures, Warden wrote, than one engaged in a slow, methodical, and relatively stable campaign. "[A]bsent stress," he pointed out, "lower echelons of command need little guidance from higher echelons and probably could continue to function for some time without any guidance. In these circumstances, attacks on the command structure are not likely to produce immediately dramatic results," at least not in any short span of time.[32] In high-tempo operations, by contrast, "the need for information, decision, and communications goes up exponentially. Now, even a slight disturbance in the command process can be dangerous or even catastrophic." "Command," he concluded, "is a true center of gravity and worth attack in any circumstance in which it can be reached." [33]

Among the three elements of command, Warden argued that although striking the decision element—the leaders them-selves—would be the most effective, it is also the most difficult. Deliberately confusing the enemy through disinformation, thereby distorting his understanding of the battlefield, though less direct, is easier and can still produce significant results. Interestingly, Warden noted that "To date, no really good examples exist of successful theater attacks on just the communications part of the command system." He added, though, that the experience of the German commanders at Normandy was intriguing, von Rundstedt having declared, "high losses in wireless equipment by fighter bomber attack . . . were noticeable in making reporting difficult." In contrast, the Israelis successfully integrated all three aspects of attack on command structures during the 1982 Bekàa Valley raid: they sent unmanned drones to mislead the Syrians about the nature of the attack and to trick them into illuminating their SAM radars; they then attacked those radars, blinding the Syrian high command; finally, they jammed the voice and data communications between Syrian pilots and their ground-based directors. As a result, the Syrian response was uncoordinated, out of touch with reality, and completely ineffective.[34]

Warden synthesized these considerations into a more general view of the war as a whole, coming to a remarkable conclusion. He conjures an image of the opposing forces as two castles. He considered several possible cases based on which force was able to reach the battle's front line or the enemy's air bases (the categorization of air conflicts in accord with five possible such scenarios, in fact, was a major basis of the book). Considering the case that would ultimately best describe Operation Desert Storm, Warden explained that it "suggests besiegers surrounding a castle and attacking it at their leisure." In all cases, he explained that "extending the castle analogy, we can conceive three basic approaches to defeating the enemy. The *first* is a broad front approach where the object is to reduce every castle, either one by one or, if sufficient forces are available, by simultaneous attack. The *second* approach is to reduce one or two castles, ignore the remainder, plunge through the gap, and win by seizing the capital. The *third* approach is to figure out a way to avoid the castles entirely and go directly to the political center of gravity—the capital or the king." He concluded, "Assuming that all three approaches are physically practical, the third promises to be the quickest and cheapest, the second the next best, and the first the slowest and most costly."[35] Following a detailed consideration of the World War II "island-hopping" campaign in the Pacific, Warden declares, "the war against Japan illustrates the possibility of ignoring completely the line of 'castles' and going directly to the political center of gravity."[36]

Although Warden did not explicitly use the "enemy as a system" terminology and framework in *The Air Campaign* very much, a partial understanding of that concept underlay his discussion of the center of gravity. Attacking a center of gravity—a critical vulnerability, in Warden's usage—would allow the aggressor to shatter the enemy's system without having to face his fielded forces in direct combat. It is therefore the opposite of Clausewitz's concept of center of gravity, which called for attacking and destroying the enemy's strength.

The concept as delineated in *The Air Campaign* was not necessarily a call simply for strategic bombing, however. Warden's emphasis on the added value of placing the enemy under great strain (presumably by ground attack) while destroying his command-and-control system pointed up the interrelationship between air and ground operations not just in securing air superiority, but in destroying the enemy altogether. Warden did not point out the similar synergy that attacks on logistics or equipment production systems would achieve when combined with high-tempo ground operations, although the implications are obvious enough.

In this respect, *The Air Campaign* is moderately ground-breaking. Many of the concepts Warden describes reflected air power experiences in World War II, Korea, and Vietnam, just as many of his examples come from those campaigns. The synthesis of these examples, however, and the vision that led Warden to imagine the possible effects of even more sophisticated target selection led to an almost revolutionary image of war.

At the same time, Warden had not fully appreciated the revolution in air power wrought by the increase in the effectiveness and availability of precision guided munitions, the superiority of the American superfighters to their adversaries, and the ways in which these advances promised to transform air warfare fundamentally. He therefore continued to argue that victory in air warfare would likely go to the numerically superior side, and that the concentration of aircraft to generate local superiorities was essential to victory. This argument underlay his repeated assertions about the importance of seizing and holding the initiative in air combat and the search for air superiority. Considering that Warden was contemplating war against the Soviet Union, which had both overwhelming numerical superiority and advanced fighters whose full quality remained unknown, it is perhaps not surprising that his view of the mechanics of the search for air superiority remained so conventional.

Without the first Gulf War, there is no way to know how important *The Air Campaign* would have been. But Warden had an opportunity offered to not one military theorist in a thousand —he had the chance to put his ideas into almost immediate practice after Saddam Hussein invaded Kuwait on August 2, 1990.

The ideas Warden used to develop the basis for the air campaign plan actually used to attack Iraq in 1991 were not precisely those of *The Air Campaign*, however. After his National War College year, Warden went to an Air Force unit in Germany and then became General Michael Dugan's special assistant. He had done some experimenting with his concepts during the deployment of part of his wing to Turkey, but his assignment to Dugan's office was the critical turning point that allowed Warden to develop the concepts of *The Air Campaign* into a serious and sophisticated approach to winning war from the air.

Dugan welcomed Warden into his shop by sharing his fear that the Air Force had lost its bearings. Just as the Navy had suffered in the 1970s from its inability to develop an intellectual justification for its existence, so Dugan worried that the Air Force had "lost sight of what we're all about," according to

Warden. The service, he said, had fallen too much in love with equipment and "become a bunch of heavy equipment operators." He had read *The Air Campaign*, liked it, and asked if Warden had any ideas about how to use it to solve these problems.[37]

Warden began thinking about it and "was struck by the fact that we didn't have a good way to explain to anybody what the Air Force did." Everyone knew that the Air Force "blew up stuff," but "nobody had any particularly good way to explain what the impact of blowing that stuff up was, or why you were blowing up any particular stuff."[38] This sort of thinking, though at first glance almost trivial, can be enormously productive if pursued properly. Warden was doing nothing less than reconsidering the nature and purpose of aerial warfare, and the conclusions he came to were fundamental.

First he asked, "What does an Air Force do? Well, it does something to an enemy. What's an enemy? An enemy's a system." That concept is too complex, however; "it's meaningless." "So the next step," he continued, "is what are the components of the system? Then I realized that what was in *The Air Campaign*, centers of gravity, with a little different formulation," could produce a set of things that "could be put in an orderly fashion that could then give you a higher resolution picture of what a system was. And out of that flowed the five rings."[39]

The "five rings" proceeding from center to periphery as later codified in the planning for the Desert Storm air campaign and in an epilogue to *The Air Campaign* published after the war, were leadership, key industrial production, infrastructure, population, and fielded forces.[40] Warden believed that "that is an arrangement of the centers of gravity that you would find in any system, first thinking at a national level and then at any level below that; that it is an arrangement of the centers of gravity with their location within the five rings indicative of their probable importance to the system, to the enemy that you're trying to change."[41]

In the late 1980s, Warden advocated placing the greatest priority on attacking the leadership ring and the least on attacking the enemy's fielded forces. The attack on the leadership ring, moreover, was to be a sophisticated effort to deprive the enemy leaders of accurate information and the means of communicating with their subordinates. If it also proved possible to kill them or their staffs or disrupt their offices, so much the better. The organization of the enemy into a system of rings would greatly facilitate target selection, and Warden's prioritization of inner rings over outer rings naturally reinforced his targeting priorities.

As Warden and his subordinates were developing this theory, they also worked to test it against a real-world scenario. Since the military was still entirely focused on the Soviet threat, they looked to Europe for their model. Warden told his subordinates, therefore, to work up a plan for the attack against the fuel supply system for a Soviet corps in Germany, reasoning that fuel was an obvious center of gravity for any mechanized force. When his subordinates returned from conversations with people at the Defense Intelligence Agency, they were downcast. It seemed that the Soviets had amassed months' worth of fuel supplies in underground storage tanks. Efforts to destroy those tanks would take so long that the Red Army would be at the English Channel before they were completed.

Whereupon Warden instructed his staff to look at the problem differently. He told them to find the "five rings" within the fuel distribution system and to seek out a center of gravity that could be reasonably attacked and destroyed in a timely fashion. Renewed study of the problem revealed that the Soviets moved their fuel supplies to forward units with a fleet of tanker trucks, and that those trucks were loaded with fuel at a very limited number of specialized stations. Those stations could be readily found and destroyed, and their destruction would lead to the temporary paralysis of the movement of fuel. It also emerged that the Soviets did not maintain extra spare parts for these fueling stations, and that Soviet doctrine and techniques would have made it very difficult for neighboring corps to make up the loss resulting from that temporary paralysis. It was true that the Soviet corps would still have several days' worth of fuel supplies in its own logistics infrastructure, but Warden reasoned that a Soviet corps commander with his operational fuel supply system destroyed would not simply attack until he ran out of gas. The "five rings" analysis of the fuel supply had turned up a center of gravity that was both critical and destroyable, validating the theory. Warden's superiors were very impressed.[42]

The planning for Desert Storm developed further as Warden and his staff came to appreciate the revolution in air warfare brought about by PGMs and stealth aircraft, and to work that understanding into their planning concepts. The most serious problem World War II bombing planners had faced was that it took hundreds of aircraft and thousands of bombs to ensure the destruction of even one not very large target. As a result, the air war proceeded sequentially—the allies would bomb one factory at a time, allowing the Germans to work to rebuild or replace that factory's production between strikes. It was nearly impossible with such constraints to achieve systemic effects on the enemy.[43]

Stealth aircraft and precision weapons changed all that. Now U.S. airmen could pretty much count on using one aircraft and one bomb to destroy one target. As a result, Warden and his team could plan an air campaign that would hit tens or even hundreds of enemy targets simultaneously. If those targets were selected in accord with a solid understanding of the enemy as a system, it should be possible, they reasoned, to generate system-wide effects. They called this sort of attack "parallel war," and rightly believed that it represented a fundamental transformation in warfare.[44] We will see the implementation and significance of this approach in the development of the Desert Storm air campaign plan.

Parallel war offered the chance to do more than simply attain air superiority quickly, Warden and his colleagues believed. It created the possibility of using air power alone to achieve the political objectives of the war directly. To them, achieving the political objectives of any conflict involved reshaping the enemy's system. Air power could do that, they felt. Warden wrote, "the purpose of war ought to be to win the peace that follows and all planning and operations should be directly connected with the final objective. Although we pay lip service to this idea, in policy, military, and academic worlds, we easily get lost in a Clausewitzian world where defeat of the enemy military forces becomes an end in itself rather than merely one of a number of possible means to a higher end." Speaking retrospectively of the Iraq war planning, he argued that instead the goal of the war should be "to attack Iraq so as to change" the system formed by the Iraqi state and military "such that it would be compatible with the envisioned post war peace."[45] When the air campaign had achieved that aim, the war would have effectively been won.

The assertion that air power could, by itself, avoid fighting the enemy's fielded forces, strike directly at the enemy's centers of gravity, and win the war, is almost as old as military aircraft. Sir Hugh Trenchard, the fiery first head of the Royal Air Force, made it in the 1920s, and British political leaders had made it even before that. Major figures in air power theory like Billy Mitchell, Giulio Douhet, and Alexander de Seversky echoed it. In all cases, efforts to put it into practice had failed. The general explanation for that failure in the air power community had been either that the technology did not yet support the concept or, more commonly, that political constraints on the use of air power had prevented any of those attempts from being "a fair test." The war-winning claims of the parallel warfare enthusiasts were thus part of a long tradition of the yet-to-be fulfilled promise of air power from its very inception.

The novelty of Warden's argument lay in the approach to

targeting and the synergistic effects that would result from striking and destroying many critical targets simultaneously. Where writers like Douhet and de Seversky had advocated attacking the enemy population in order to destroy the enemy's will to continue fighting, Warden explicitly rejected the value of such attacks. While accepting the importance of attacking the economic targets popular with World War II aviators, he added a great deal of sophistication to the traditional methods of identifying appropriate targets. Above all, he developed a theory that promised to make efficient use of the radically new technologies then available that he and his colleagues felt made it possible for air power finally to make good on its ultimate promise.

In this regard, Warden's concept of air war was only to a limited extent part of the longer tradition of air power theory. Despite the similarity between his claims for his new concept and the claims of so many failed proponents of similar concepts before him, his ideas were different enough that they seemed as though they might escape the fate of their predecessors. A great deal would depend on exactly how they were implemented, of course, and his planning of the actual air campaign employed by allied forces against Saddam in 1991 provided a laboratory experiment by which they could be evaluated.

THEORY GOES TO WAR

All too often, military professionals or splenetic commentators dismiss theory as an irrelevant distraction from the real business of planning and conducting military operations. "Amateurs talk strategy, professionals talk logistics," a common refrain among the professional officer corps and part of the policy community, is another way of saying that it is the nuts-and-bolts "realities" of moving large numbers of people and equipment more than any airy theories that determine the outcome of wars. This dismissal of the role of theory has never been valid—theories of war have driven the planning and conduct of military operations since the mid-eighteenth century at least—but it is nowhere less valid than in the consideration of air power. From the first time a man put a bomb on a plane to drop on the enemy, the planning and conduct of air operations has been a thoroughly theoretical undertaking.

The importance of theory to air power flows from the fact that the critical question in air planning is, as Warden noted, "What should we bomb?" The ability of planes to fly over large portions of the battlespace and well into the enemy's rear makes the selection of the best answer to that question enormously difficult. The ground forces commander normally has a limited number of options. He can march on one or another of a small number of major enemy force concentrations, or on one or another of a small set of geographical objectives. The fact that few routes of advance will have enough transportation capacity to support a large army constrain his options even further. But the air power commander faces many fewer such constraints. He can attack the enemy's fielded forces, his political leadership, or an enormous number of economic or population targets, and any target that is within range of his aircraft can theoretically be struck. The planning for Desert Storm throws the importance of theory in air war into sharp relief, because we know what the senior air commander was planning to do before Warden persuaded him to adopt a targeting philosophy based on his new principles.

Important as Warden's theories were in shaping the Gulf War air campaign, however, Saddam's own decisions and actions were also crucial in setting the stage. When Saddam's forces invaded Kuwait on August 2, they took the vast majority of America's senior civilian and military leaders by surprise despite numerous warning signs. Although American intelligence systems detected the Iraqi military build-up and U.S. officials were aware of the various threats and demands Saddam was making of Kuwait, no one seriously believed that he intended to launch a war. It was a classic example of the "perfect" intelligence that tells you everything except what the enemy means to do.[46]

With his invasion, Saddam had seized the initiative. He had mobilized his army and occupied Kuwait, and now threatened Saudi Arabia. The Bush administration's failure to take the warnings seriously meant that the U.S. had no meaningful military presence in the area. Saudi Arabia could not defend itself against Iraq alone. Although American military power began flowing into the Arab kingdom within days of the invasion, arriving U.S. forces and the Saudis would continue to face enormous risks for weeks to come.

The commanders on the spot were well aware of the dangers. General H. Norman Schwarzkopf, the commander of U.S. Central Command, wanted to find a way to offer President Bush real military options if action were required quickly. Saddam held a large number of American and foreign hostages, for instance, and Schwarzkopf feared that he might be called upon to retaliate for their mistreatment and be unable to do so. He wanted an offensive plan quickly, but he also needed a plan to defend U.S. and allied forces and to prevent Saddam from continuing his invasion to overrun Saudi Arabia.

The problem of devising that plan fell to Lieutenant General Charles Horner, the CENTCOM Air Component Commander. From his base in Riyadh, Horner was acutely aware of the danger he and his command faced. He scrambled at the same time to find bases and establish the necessary logistical systems to support the flood of American aircraft entering the theater and to develop plans to blunt an Iraqi offensive should Saddam decide to launch one. His initial concepts focused on interdiction and close air support missions in the hope of reducing the Iraqi army through attrition, and he relegated any thoughts of deeper strikes to a very low priority in his thinking.

It is worth noting, in this regard, that the establishment of an adequate logistics system to support U.S. air forces in Saudi Arabia took weeks. Many of the airfields used were simply runways with hangars—they had no fuel storage or distribution facilities, no spare parts, no fuel supplies or ammunition, and not enough ground personnel to maintain the incoming aircraft. The transportation of all of those supplies and people took a considerable amount of time. This problem will generally hold whenever U.S. aircraft must operate from bases that are not already supplied to support them, and it means that there will normally be a significant delay between an event and the ability of U.S. air power to conduct large-scale operations. In Iraq in August 1990, this problem gave Horner nightmares and it helped make him less than receptive to the bright ideas of an upstart colonel from Washington who advised him strongly, among other things, to forget about the Iraqi army.

Warden learned about the Iraqi invasion while on a Caribbean cruise, from which he did not return until August 6. He immediately set his staff to developing a plan based on the principles they had been working on for the past few years. The result was a war plan he christened Instant Thunder. The name was an explicit attempt to exorcise the ghosts of the Vietnam air war, when gradual, escalating "strategic" bombing attacks under the codename "Rolling Thunder" had been used to "send messages" to the North Vietnamese leadership—and had accomplished nothing at a great cost in lives and treasure. Warden was sure that his quick and decisive plan would forever salve the Vietnam wounds of the Air Force.

He planned Instant Thunder to last for six days of intensive parallel bombing. He intended to strike command and control, leadership, air defense, and logistical targets not in Kuwait, but throughout Iraq. He established what he thought the political objectives of the war to be from Bush's August 8th speech: "(1) Iraqi withdrawal from Kuwait; (2) restoration of Kuwaiti sovereignty; (3) security and stability of the Persian Gulf; (4) protection of American lives." From these political objectives he deduced the following military objectives: "(1) force Iraqi withdrawal from Kuwait; (2) degrade Iraq's offensive capability; (3) secure oil facilities; (4) render Saddam ineffective as a leader."[47]

The initial Instant Thunder plan that Warden and his staff developed paid no direct attention at all to Saddam's force in Kuwait. Warden did not intend to bomb it or even necessarily to achieve air superiority over Kuwait. His plan was predicated on the assumption that once he had shattered the Iraqi system, Saddam would be compelled to pull his remaining forces out of Kuwait. Warden also hoped that he would have so destroyed the dictator's links with his people as to ensure his removal from power, thereby strengthening regional stability.

The question of who might replace Saddam received very limited consideration. Briefers assured Warden and his staff that Saddam was the major source of the Iraqi threat and that no one likely to replace him would fail to be an improvement. Warden and his team did not attempt to determine carefully what would follow in Iraq if their air campaign were as successful as they hoped. He later wrote, "Our view, with which [Schwarzkopf] agreed, was that it would be far better for Iraq if Saddam was no longer in power. However, as long as we had taken away from Saddam the tools (the system) he needed to be a regional superpower threat, his disposition was not of overwhelming importance."[48]

This lacuna is perfectly understandable. Warden and his staff were Air Force officers developing an air war plan, not strategists at the NSC developing an overall war plan. They did not have the regional expertise necessary to develop an overall war plan, and did not have a staff structure appropriate to developing that expertise.

The problem was that Warden was not just developing an

air campaign plan. He thought he was developing a plan for the entire war. In that sense, his failure to consider the real political consequences of the specifics of his war plan, testing his ideas not only against military reality but against diplomatic, political, and regional reality was unacceptable.

That failure flowed in part from one of the virtues of his theory. The basic presumption of the "five rings" theory is that "all organizations are put together in about the same way. Thus, every organization has a leadership function to give it direction and help it respond to change in its external and internal environments; every living entity has an energy conversion function . . . ; each has an infrastructure to hold it together; each has a population; and each has fielded forces to protect and project the organization."[49] This insight was critical in allowing Warden to develop a *generalized theory for the shattering of an enemy state.*

This generalized theory is not, in principle, incompatible with a specific focus on the particularities of a given case—indeed, *The Air Campaign* makes clear that Warden imagined just such a specificity to ensure that air operations achieved the political goal. In the case of the Gulf War, Warden believed that he had tied his military plans directly to the specific political goals the president had enunciated, moreover, and in a certain sense he had. In another profound sense, however, he did not.

Having established to his satisfaction the military goals of the war, Warden then developed them into a series of detailed and executable operational and tactical missions. Something similar should have occurred with the political goals that military campaign was theoretically supporting, but Warden paid those goals no further attention. Developing the political goals of a war is not the job of an Air Staff planner, of course. But then, neither is it his job to develop an *overall* war plan. If he once embarks on such an endeavor, then it is incumbent upon him to ensure, at least, that someone else is performing the parallel planning for the political side of the war.

Warden could not have done so, of course, and he soon found himself excluded even from direct participation in the military planning. The fault was not his, but that of an organization of the U.S. government that encourages military planners to develop their plans in isolation from political developments. Although Warden's plans ultimately were presented to senior military and political leaders and received their modifications and approval, presumably in accord with political directives among other things, the basic concept that shaped the air war remained unchanged, and its connection to the political aims of the Bush government was tenuous indeed. As we shall see, the mere process of requiring a close coordination between military and political planning would have pointed up a host of flawed assumptions that underlay both. An even greater danger lurking in this generalized approach to campaign planning is that the process of determining how to break the enemy-as-a-system apart into what Boyd would have called "noncooperative centers of gravity" is mesmerizing. It is possible to think about how to do that without really considering the political implications at all. Warden, let us emphasize, did not make this extreme error. But both his theory and the success of its application encouraged some of his successors to do so.

Warden's approach received an initially warm reception. Both Schwarzkopf and Chairman of the Joint Chiefs Colin Powell accepted many of the key ideas, although it is not clear that Schwarzkopf ever really understood what Warden was trying to do.[50] The reason for Schwarzkopf's enthusiasm was primarily that Warden was offering him the rapid offensive option he had been searching for to give the president in case Bush decided to retaliate for some further Iraqi provocation. Schwarzkopf had already briefed the president and the National Security

Advisor Brent Scowcroft on plans to deal with Iraq in the short-term, advising on August 4 that the main U.S. blows for the foreseeable weeks would have to come primarily from the air. He encountered opposition from then Secretary of Defense Dick Cheney, who declared, "The history of air campaigns suggests they are not terribly successful. . . . Why would this one be different?" Schwarzkopf answered, "I am not an advocate of air power alone. . . . But this is a target-rich environment. There is no cover in the desert. Their army has never operated under attack, and we have sophisticated munitions." The conversation then turned to the importance of inserting ground forces into Saudi Arabia quickly for the political purpose of showing resolve. Schwarzkopf consistently refused thereafter to contemplate Warden's ideas as an air-only strategy, however receptive he might have been to the overall concept of the air operations Warden developed.[51]

When Warden tried to brief Horner on his plan, however, the result was a disaster. Horner was a veteran of the Tactical Air Command (TAC), the Air Force community most committed to close integration with ground operations. Tactical Air Command had been instrumental in driving the Air Force to adhere to AirLand Battle, and many TAC officers had taken from Vietnam the critical importance of subordinating air operations to close air support and battlefield air interdiction missions. Horner was not likely to have been enthusiastic about Warden's plan at any time. He was much less so at the moment Warden briefed him, because he felt that Warden was ignoring the Sword of Damocles hanging over both their heads in the form of Saddam's army in Kuwait.

Horner was also furious because he felt that Warden's intervention in the planning process "smacked of Vietnam, when officials in Washington picked the targets." When presented with an advance copy of Warden's plan, Horner threw it against the wall of his office. When the briefer collected the slides and

handed them back to him, he threw it at the wall yet again.[52]
Warden had an uphill battle to get Horner even to listen to his
ideas.

Horner's basic opposition, however, stemmed from his
focus on the problem immediately in front of him. As he later
explained,

> The idea was that we were to deter an Iraqi invasion of
> Saudi Arabia, and if an invasion did come, we were pre-
> pared to defend. . . . Those were some of the worst nights
> of my life, because I had good information as to what the
> Iraqi threat was, and, quite frankly, we could not have
> issued speeding tickets to the tanks as they would have
> come rolling down the interstate highway on the east
> coast. It was an opportunity the Iraqis did not take, but
> every night we'd get more forces, and we'd sit down and
> get a game plan of what we'd do if we came under attack.[53]

The briefing revealed that Horner and Warden were talking
past one another. Both made valid points, but both missed
important issues as well. There can be no doubt that Horner
was, in a certain sense, excessively focused on the immediate
task at hand. He was so concerned with figuring out how to
fight a defensive air campaign that he was almost deaf to Warden's proposal to fight that defensive war offensively. How
would CENTCOM respond if an air campaign triggered an Iraqi
ground assault, he asked. "We could be looking out the window right now and see the Iraqi tanks come into Riyadh."[54]

Warden saw it differently. Had the Iraqis invaded and
CENTCOM then executed Warden's plan, it is by no means
clear that Saddam would simply have kept driving forward. If
Warden's plan worked, Saddam would quickly have lost control over his advancing forces, along with the wherewithal to
continue to supply them in a fast-paced advance. Would his

troops have rolled on regardless? It is possible, but unlikely. It is more likely that they would have slowed or halted the advance in an effort to stabilize their situation and regain contact with their superiors. "You are being overly pessimistic about those tanks," Warden declared. He did not think that the Iraqis could supply an assault deep into Saudi Arabia, and he did not believe the Iraqis "could go far in the face of American air superiority."[55] For Horner, of course, the fact that he could not have ensured that Saddam's army would grind to a halt made such a plan unacceptable. For Warden, it was a risk to take in the interest of bringing the war to a speedy close.

But if Horner did not see the virtues in Warden's revolutionary new way of thinking, he did point out one of the major flaws. Horner started criticizing the plan almost as soon as Warden started briefing it. Did Warden understand the logistical requirements for the air campaign and when they would be available in theater? What could the Air Force do by itself against Saddam's troops without the support of more American ground forces? Most importantly, "What would happen if the Iraqi regime did not collapse after a five or six day campaign and CENTAF had used up its logistic[al] base in theater?"[56]

The last criticism was the most important. Warden's theory had two critical components. One was the idea that striking the enemy in a certain way would induce paralysis and military incapacitation. The other was that those effects would lead the enemy to capitulate. Horner was asking what Warden's plan was if the enemy did not cooperate by surrendering despite the "success" of the air campaign. This critical question was immediately swallowed up by the trivialities, however, with Horner declaring, "If folks in Washington want to fight this war, tell them to come to the theater."[57] He ordered Warden back to Washington, followed shortly by the other staffers Warden had brought along with him, except for Lieutenant Colonel David Deptula, whom Horner kept on as part of his own planning cell.

In late August, Horner turned the task of developing CENTCOM's air campaign plan over to Brigadier General Buster Glosson, an Air Force officer serving as the Deputy Commander of the Navy's Middle East task force. Glosson was much more receptive to Warden's ideas when Deptula briefed him on August 21. Horner had warned Glosson that he did not want him to be influenced by the Warden plan, but Glosson kept his own counsel. He was intrigued by Instant Thunder, but was also concerned that it was incomplete and "did not explain how airpower should be used if the six days of bombing did not produce the victory that Warden promised. Central Command, Glosson told Deptula, needed an air campaign that would last for fifteen rounds, not two or three." He was also disturbed that the plan contained no provision for attacking the Republican Guard, the destruction of which was coming to be one of the major political objectives of the war.[58]

Glosson therefore accepted Instant Thunder and built a more thorough campaign plan around it. When he was done, the campaign consisted of four "phases" the first three of which the air power services would execute simultaneously: the core Instant Thunder "decapitation" plan; the suppression of enemy air defenses in what was coming to be called the Kuwaiti Theater of Operations (KTO); softening up the Iraqi military for the expected ground campaign to follow; and support of allied troops during that ground campaign.[59] On August 26, Glosson and Deptula finally won Horner over to the concept, although Horner continued to snarl about the name Instant Thunder.[60]

Glosson believed that air power alone could win the war. He told Powell that air strikes "would destroy Iraq's military capability, eliminate the Iraqi government's control, and generate internal strife. The result . . . would be to 'decapitate the Saddam regime.' If airpower failed to encourage Saddam Hussein's overthrow, Glosson believed it would limit an allied ground attack to a police action."[61] This view did not long remain a secret. When Glosson briefed Bush and Scowcroft on October 11, he "told the president that as a result of the air war Saddam Hussein would not be able to communicate effectively with his people or his military forces. Nor would he be able to reinforce his army in Kuwait. There would be disruption throughout Iraq." Bush took the hint, asking, "What if the coalition mounted an air campaign and then waited seven to ten days for the Iraqi government to give up or collapse? What would be wrong with that?"[62] The enthusiasm of Air Force Chief of Staff Michael Dugan for air power cost him his job—Cheney fired him following the publication of remarks suggesting that the Air Force could win a war by itself.[63]

The assertions on behalf of air power met immediate opposition from the two Army generals in overall charge of the operation, Powell and Schwarzkopf. Schwarzkopf adopted the reworked Instant Thunder plan more or less enthusiastically, but rejected the notion that it would suffice by itself to drive Saddam out of Kuwait. Powell resisted even more forcefully. When Bush asked Glosson if he thought the air campaign could succeed by itself, Powell interjected before Glosson could respond: "I have to tell you, Mr. President, that it will not meet your objectives. I cannot assure you that Iraqi ground forces will be out of Kuwait, just because we do an air campaign."[64]

The basis of Powell's criticism is not entirely clear. It appears that he was as much concerned with the possibility that Bush might seize upon airpower promises to launch a war that Powell opposed as he was with the fear that the plan might not work. Schwarzkopf told Glosson, "Buster, the chairman is afraid that if the brief goes to the president like this, the president will execute the air campaign" and advised him not to be "too enthusiastic" in presenting the plan to Bush.[65] At all events, by September Warden had succeeded in getting the leadership to adopt the central concepts of his targeting plan instead of the more gradual "roll-back" programs advocated by the Navy and initially by Horner that would have focused on destroying the Iraqi air defense network before doing anything else. But he had failed to convince any senior decision-maker except Glosson that air power could do the job by itself. Instant Thunder was therefore rolled into a plan to prepare for a massive ground assault. The stage was also set thereby for the dueling interpretations of "what won the Gulf War" that began the moment the shooting stopped and have yet to end.

WHAT WON THE GULF WAR

The air campaign against Iraq began on January 17, 1991 and continued unsupported by large-scale ground action for thirty-eight days. The ground war began on February 24 and lasted for one hundred hours. Both the air and the ground campaigns were unprecedentedly successful, devastating Iraq's military and state structures with a tiny number of U.S. casualties. With a success like this for all parts of the military, with so much praise to go around, it is in one sense surprising how much inter-service bitterness resulted from attempts to interpret the significance of the war.

In another sense, the debate that arose was perfectly natural. The Gulf War reinvigorated those in the air power community who believed that air power could achieve strategic effects directly without the employment of ground forces. Throughout the 1970s and 1980s this sort of thinking had largely been marginalized within the service as the TAC community drove the Air Force, apart from the nuclear deterrent force, to accept a subordinate role in the Army's AirLand Battle doctrine. The Gulf War seemed to the "true believers" to have shown that they were right all along.

The culture of defense budget cutting that began to follow the Iraq war immediately, since victory in the desert coincided so closely with the fall of the Soviet Union and the end of the

Cold War, meant that the debate had acquired new urgency. An Air Force that could argue effectively that air power could win by itself could expect to fare well in the ensuing budget battles. The Army and Marines had a similar interest in proving that ground forces remained essential. The end of the Cold War, finally, meant that all of the service doctrines and programs had lost their obvious justification. The service that could claim to have won what looked like the first "post-Cold War" war would be well positioned in the years to come.

A detailed consideration of all of the debates, let alone of the military operations that gave rise to them, is beyond the scope of this inquiry, but certain salient facts bear highlighting. First, the air campaign achieved part of its objective. It struck the critical nodes of Iraq's command, control, communications, and logistics system, and took down the electrical power grid. It deprived Saddam of the ability to maneuver a large portion of his army and completely neutralized the Iraqi air force. It severely attrited Iraq's fielded combat forces, including portions of the Republican Guard, and so demoralized the rank-and-file of the regular Iraqi army units that they deserted in droves rather than fight oncoming coalition forces. It deprived the Iraqi army of the ability to maneuver large forces over operationally significant distances and thereby prevented Saddam from assembling a sizeable coherent force to react to the ground offensive.

But the air campaign failed in a number of important initial objectives. It did not, by itself, convince Saddam to withdraw from Kuwait as Warden and Glosson had confidently expected it to. Even as he lost communications with a large portion of his army and learned of its spreading collapse, Saddam held firm in his resolve to cross swords with the Americans directly rather than surrendering. In this regard, Instant Thunder was no more successful in its overall objective than any previous strategic bombing campaign.

The air campaign also failed to destroy the Republican

Guard. It mauled certain Guard units very badly and significantly reduced the logistical support and maneuverability of many others; nonetheless, when the ground campaign began, several Republican Guard divisions were still able to maneuver, deploy, and engage coalition ground units in purposeful combat. These units had evidently maintained sufficient communications and situational awareness to reorient themselves in response to the U.S. flank attack, and to attempt to withdraw from Kuwait as the situation to their front collapsed. In Boyd's terms, the air campaign had been unable to destroy that *schwerpunkt* within the Iraqi military by which the Republican Guard troops continued to orient themselves. A significant number of those troops had also managed to maintain sufficient logistics to have fuel and ammunition for their tanks and food and water for their soldiers and so they were combat-capable when the ground war began.

The successes of the air campaign are not sufficient, therefore, to explain the successes of the ground war, which were as staggering in their lopsidedness as the air combat had been. Iraqi forces armed with some of the best military equipment in the world, including Soviet T-72 tanks, were repeatedly destroyed by smaller American forces in minutes without inflicting any casualties. Republican Guard divisions that had survived repeated air strikes crumbled helplessly before advancing U.S. troops. The air campaign might explain why Saddam could not maneuver large forces enough to amass a large defensive reserve, or why those forces could not defeat fresh, fully supplied American soldiers, but it does not explain why they could not hold their ground even for minutes or inflict virtually any casualties.

The success of the coalition ground offensive was not primarily due to any brilliance in the ground campaign plan either. The development of that plan had been flawed from the start, when it initially called for an unimaginative advance through the strongest Iraqi defense belts along the Kuwaiti–Saudi border. Schwarzkopf then asked for and received additional troops and developed the concept of the "left hook," which brought the bulk of the U.S. forces in an arc from the west swinging around the Iraqi defensive positions and directly into the rear of the Iraqi army in Kuwait. This plan was intelligent and sensible, and facilitated subsequent success, but it also does not explain the overall outcome.

A number of Republican Guard divisions were able to reposition themselves to meet this attack, and, indeed, met it in well-prepared defensive positions. They were nevertheless destroyed almost effortlessly by the advancing ground forces. When the Marines drove into the Iraqi defensive belts in Kuwait in what was intended to be a supporting attack, they also found no difficulty in crushing those prepared positions. Nothing in the ground plan or the air campaign explains why the Iraqi ground forces were so hopelessly overmatched at the level of individual soldiers, tanks, and small units.

The reasons for that overmatch lie, instead, in the Army's transformation begun in the 1970s. The combination of professionalism and skill in the all-volunteer force, the improved training, which included rotations through the National Training Center in the high California desert, and the fielding of the M1 and Bradley team of ground combat vehicles all left even the best Iraqi troops helpless. Trained M1 gunners hit their targets the first time they fired nearly every time. The depleted uranium main gun rounds destroyed virtually every enemy tank they hit. It is worth noting here that the depleted uranium rounds used in combat are much more accurate than the dummies used in training—American tankers had developed more skill while training than they actually needed in war. Skilled and professional M1 loaders maintained a higher rate of fire than the automatic loaders in Iraqi tanks. U.S. small units extensively trained in armored warfare needed very little direction even in surprise engagements—everyone knew what he was supposed to do without being told. As a result, in the vast majority of engagements U.S. troops got the first shots in, killed everything they shot at, and reloaded and shot again faster than their enemies. The M1's superb armor protection, moreover, meant that even the few Iraqi tanks that managed to fire were frequently unable even to damage the American tanks, let alone destroy them. The combination of technology, training, professionalism, and small-unit doctrine gave U.S. ground forces uncontestable overmatch over even the elite Iraqi armored forces. Army hyperbole to match the Air Force's exaggerated claims runs that the U.S. troops were so much better man-for-man than the Iraqis that they could have swapped equipment and still won. The 1990s saw as much enthusiasm in the Army for dismissing the role of the air campaign as it did in the Air Force for belittling the importance of the land war.

The real significance of the Gulf War is quite different from either of these emotional and politically-charged interpretations. Warden proved that the basic theory he set out in *The Air Campaign*, as well as the critical concepts Boyd had developed earlier, really works. It is possible using the advanced technology now available and sufficient understanding of the enemy as a system to strike critical vulnerabilities, thereby enormously degrading the foe's ability to maintain control over his troops and over his country. The questions Horner and others asked were fundamental, however: What happens if the enemy does not surrender in response to such an attack? The answer is that his system attempts to recover from the shock.

The thirty-eight days of the pure air campaign allowed the Iraqis time to develop responses to the disaggregation of their forces. At the soldier's level, these responses included such innovations as using cluster bomb cases to reinforce bomb shelters. At higher levels it involved creative ways to restore basic communications, movement, and logistics to critical units.

Iraqi leaders used cellphones, which were much more difficult to locate, track, decrypt, or jam than traditional military radios, and sometimes human couriers to overcome the loss of their communications systems. They took advantage of the fact that bombers cannot bomb every line of communications all the time to sneak fuel and supplies to vital units. In this way, they avoided the complete collapse of their military that Warden and Boyd counted on to force Saddam to surrender—or to encourage his entourage or population to rise up against him.

The continuation of the air campaign did prevent Saddam from reconstituting an effective fighting force for any large-scale campaign, however, and the ground attack put an end to any possibility of such a reconstitution. The real key to success in Operation Desert Storm, therefore, was that a well-prepared ground offensive was launched in a timely manner to take full advantage of the disruption and disaggregation caused by the well-planned and skillfully conducted air campaign.

Boyd would have had no problem with such an evaluation, since he never made a claim for an airpower—pure solution. Warden and Glosson, however, had sought such a solution, and they and their supporters eagerly claimed in the war's aftermath that they had achieved it. By making such a claim in the face of substantial evidence to the contrary, they repeated the errors of previous airpower enthusiasts, who had claimed following World War II, for instance, that the Germans would have had to surrender in a matter of months because of air assault even had the allies not pushed on to Berlin. Warden, in fact, made precisely that argument in *The Air Campaign*. The repetition of the assertion that if only the air campaign had been given more time, resources, and priority, ground combat would have been unnecessary thus threw the development of U.S. military theory off on a tangent. The support and refutation of that assertion became one of the central aspects of a debate that increasingly veered away from a true understanding of the virtues of the airpower theory when combined with an appropriate ground campaign. The Gulf War was thus a turning point in the development of the American military in both a positive and a negative way.

The New World Order and the Revolution in Military Affairs

I N 1991, the U.S. went almost overnight from facing a massive threat in many theaters, including a direct threat to the U.S. homeland, to facing no threats at all. Or so it seemed. By contrast with the Warsaw Pact, the problems of Iraq, Iran, North Korea, etc., seemed trivial. The absence of a clear ideological challenge made the situation even more ambiguous, since the ideology of the Cold War had provided a simple compass by which to set national security policy for nearly half a century. It was necessary to develop not simply a new national security strategy, but an entirely new basis for thinking about national security.

Both the first Bush presidency and Congressional critics, as well as outside analysts, made various efforts to develop such a basis, as we shall see. All, however, agreed upon one critical assumption—whatever the requirements of a post-Cold War national security strategy might be, the nation would be able to benefit from a significant "peace dividend" in the form of substantially reduced defense budgets and smaller armed forces.

The context within which the military thought about strategy, force structure, and the continuation of its transformation also shifted very rapidly. The collapse of the U.S.S.R. deprived the military of its obvious adversary and the lynchpin around which it had been organized, trained, and equipped. The promised significant reduction of defense resources ended the long era of military build-up that had begun in 1979 and placed new emphasis on inter-service rivalry for the limited resources that were now available.

The Gulf War played a much smaller role in the initial military and political reaction to the changed circumstances for two reasons. First, the Soviet Union began its obvious collapse in 1990 or even 1989, well before Saddam invaded Kuwait. Planned reductions in the defense budget were already underway, therefore, as U.S. troops streamed into Saudi Arabia. Second, the rapid victory in Desert Storm seemed to have defanged Saddam, thereby only reinforcing the notion that the U.S. did not face any meaningful threats.

Over the course of the 1990s, however, one salient fact emerged in contrast. The efforts of the Army and the Navy to develop strategies tightly tied to the Soviet Union had succeeded all too well, leaving those services adrift in the wake of the U.S.S.R.'s collapse. The development and implementation of Warden's concepts in Iraq, however, promised to make airpower in general and the Air Force in particular much more obviously relevant and important in the new world order that President Bush proclaimed.

IN SEARCH OF A NEW GRAND STRATEGY, 1989–1993

As the collapse of Soviet power proceeded in 1990 and 1991, two main visions began to develop within Washington about how to adapt American grand strategy to the new reality. The first flowed from independent efforts by the Undersecretary of Defense for Policy Paul Wolfowitz and the Chairman of the Joint Chiefs of Staff Colin Powell to determine the appropriate size for U.S. armed forces in the post-Cold War world. According to Powell, his own effort was initially based more on hunches and educated guesses than on careful strategic reasoning, and it was motivated primarily by the desire to ensure that the armed forces controlled their own reduction program rather than having Congress force one down their throats. The Wolfowitz program was built upon a more thoughtful strategic calculus that considered what America's role in the world should be after the Soviets' fall. The end result, which the Bush administration called the Base Force, used the Wolfowitz logic to support the Powell plan.

The basic strategic assumption underlying the Base Force plan was that the United States must maintain an active role in the world as the only remaining superpower in order to shape the future development of the international system. Supporting the program against its growing number of critics, then Secretary of Defense Cheney argued that the U.S. had acquired a great deal of "strategic depth," both geographically and temporally, with the fall of the Soviet Union. The borders of the U.S.S.R., for the moment renamed the Commonwealth of Independent States, had moved hundreds of miles to the East, leaving behind the newly independent states of the Baltics, Caucasus, and even Ukraine and Belarus. The remnant Russian armed forces, moreover, were so severely weakened by the collapse of the authoritarian system that had sustained them as to pose no real conventional threat even to their neighbors, let alone to Western Europe. With the end of communism and Boris Yeltsin's rise to power, finally, even the still-formidable Russian nuclear arsenal seemed much less a matter of immediate concern. The U.S. would have ample warning, probably as much as a decade, of any Russian attempts to rebuild a serious threat to American interests.

Cheney believed that the U.S. could take advantage of this interval to reap a significant peace dividend, to be sure, but he also felt that America should seize the opportunity to handle such smaller threats and instabilities around the world as had the potential to destabilize the peaceful new world order that seemed to beckon. He argued that the U.S. should not wait for obvious threats to appear and attack, but should remain engaged in vital regions around the world to prevent those threats from even arising. He argued that it was necessary to maintain powerful American armed forces to underwrite this international shaping, but pointed out that the maintenance of such forces would prove far cheaper than fighting the wars that would likely result from American neglect and isolationism.

Cheney therefore strongly supported the Base Force structure that Colin Powell had worked out, ostensibly designed to handle two large-scale conflicts (then called Major Regional Conflicts, or MRCs) at the same time. Cheney, Wolfowitz, Powell, and others in the administration consistently refused to specify any two particular conflicts against which the force had been arrayed. They did not feel that America's armed forces should focus on the threat of the moment, but that instead the U.S. should maintain the capabilities needed to underwrite their strategy of shaping and engagement.

One problem emerged almost immediately, however, as Powell and other military leaders were forced to admit that even the force structure they had designed could not really handle two MRCs simultaneously, at least not if one was on the scale of Desert Storm and the other on the scale of anticipated conflict in Korea. Under the Base Force concept, the Army would be reduced from 18 active and 10 reserve divisions to 12 active and 6 reserve divisions; the Navy would fall from 508 ships to 411; the Air Force would drop from 24 active and 12 reserve wings to 15 active and 11 reserve wings.[1] A force of that size would have been hard-pressed to maintain the 7⅔ divisions and hundreds of aircraft used in Operation Desert Storm and undertake significant combat operations elsewhere at the same time.

Any attempt to fight two such simultaneous or even nearly simultaneous conflicts, moreover, would have required a massive shifting of various critical enabling elements in all of the services from one theater to another. As the Base Force concept was wargamed and evaluated, however, it became clear that the U.S. did not have the strategic air- and sealift required to make such shifts efficiently. Pressed in 1992 to explain whether or not the armed forces could simultaneously wage a Desert Storm-type war in the Persian Gulf and a conflict on the Korean peninsula, Powell responded, "Yes, but at the breaking point." Representative Ike Skelton asked him to explain what he meant. Powell answered that if conflict in Korea and Iraq "were both emergencies that did not give us the opportunity to fully mobilize . . . all of our Reserve components, to send 7⅔ divisions to Desert Shield/Desert Storm, to provide a large air component to Korea and ground forces to Korea and Marine forces to Korea would strip us of all active forces and would place an immediate demand on the total reserve component to get mobilized as quickly as possible." He added, "at that point, we would no longer have the capability to deal with anything else that might happen elsewhere in the world." [2]

Like the apparently free-spending Reagan defense program, therefore, the Base Force, which seemed excessive to many critics, also contained significant elements of risk in the opinions of its advocates. A variety of factors mitigated those risks, to be sure, and we will explore them in more detail below. But it is open to question whether even the Base Force could reliably have supported a two-MRC strategy. This point would become important in the subsequent debates in the 1990s.

The Bush administration's defense concepts came under attack almost immediately, however, on the grounds that they did not make sufficient cuts in military expenditures. Some critics simply called for a fundamental reorientation of U.S. policy away from defense spending and foreign policy and toward domestic priorities they felt had been neglected. They wanted, to use Lloyd George's phrase of the post-World War I era, to make America a land fit for heroes to live in.[3]

Others launched more specific attacks against the way the administration had developed its program. Representative Les Aspin, the chairman of the House Armed Services Committee, led this group. Aspin seized upon the apparent vagueness of the threats against which the Bush grand strategy sought to defend the U.S. At a series of committee hearings, he was unable to force administration representatives, either military or civilian, to describe the specific scenarios they had used to devise the force. The administration insisted that the U.S. military should not enter the new era sized to face particular threats that might be fleeting, while ignoring apparently benign situations that might suddenly erupt into war, as had happened in Kuwait in 1990. Aspin was not convinced. He began to argue for a complete re-evaluation of U.S. grand strategy and the American military posture, and to demand what he called a "bottom-up review."

The ideas behind the bottom-up review were two-fold. First, that the administration should not start its evaluation of U.S. military needs by looking at the current force structure and seeking to reduce it, but should instead build up a force structure appropriate to the new situation starting from scratch. Second, that the basis for designing that new force structure should be a clear and specific identification of threats to American interests. Aspin was confident that any such calculus would show that the administration's proposed defense program was excessive and inappropriate to the current situation.

The administration's representatives had a difficult time in this argument. The sophisticated reasoning that underlay their strategic vision seemed to Aspin and his allies to be vagueness concealing an unwillingness to make the necessary reductions in defense. Meanwhile, the administration officials arguing with him thought he was missing the point. In truth, neither side was communicating with the other since both were proceeding from different and mutually exclusive points of departure.

If Aspin was right and U.S. forces should be sized and structured to meet visible threats, then he was also right that the armed forces the Bush administration proposed were too large. If Powell, Cheney, Wolfowitz, and company were right and the American military should be designed to engage with and shape the international order, as well to be prepared to meet future threats that might develop, then the armed forces were probably too small.

An important part of the discussion hinged on a disagreement about how rapidly the U.S. could or should respond to changing circumstances in the international arena. Aspin, along with an unlikely ally in the normally hawkish Senator Sam Nunn, argued that America could and would respond to any developing threat in time to be able to defeat it. The administration believed that such a stance placed too much pressure on the U.S. to identify changing threats instantly and instantly respond to them. It also denied America the ability to deter those threats, nip them in the bud, or otherwise prevent them from arising in the first place. The conflict was irreducible and neither side was able to convince the other.

The Bush administration nevertheless managed to get is program through Congress, despite Aspin's opposition, and the Base Force became the basis for the reduction of U.S. military power after the end of the Cold War—but only briefly.

Bill Clinton's election in 1992 changed all that. Clinton had run for office with the slogan, "It's the economy, stupid," and he promised to "focus like a laser beam" on the economy once elected. The selection of Les Aspin to be his secretary of defense gave the congressman the unexpected chance to put his own program into immediate practice.

The Bottom-Up Review (BUR) of 1993 proceeded more or

less as Aspin had promised. It considered and evaluated specific threats—post-Desert Storm Iraq and North Korea particularly, and defined a force supposedly to respond to those threats. Aspin went even further in the BUR in attacking the Base Force than he had as a congressman, moreover, by attempting to abandon the two-MRC force-sizing construct that the Bush administration had used. Instead, he floated a concept called "win-hold-win," in which U.S. airpower would hold one adversary at bay while the ground forces finished another, and then the ground forces would shift to mop-up whatever the Air Force and Navy had been unable to destroy in the second theater. Critics immediately dubbed this idea "win-lose-lose" and "win-hold-oops," and Aspin formally abandoned it, although he did not actually alter the proposed force structure in any significant way after having done so.

Aspin therefore proposed to bring the American armed forces down to 10 active and 5 reserve Army divisions, 346 ships in the Navy, and 13 active and 7 reserve Air Force fighter wings.[4] This was the configuration that actually defined U.S. armed forces in the 1990s. By 1996, the Army had 10 active and 8 reserve divisions (cutting the National Guard combat brigades proved to be politically too daunting); the Navy had 348 ships; and the Air Force had about 13 active and 7 reserve fighter wings.[5] Aspin had won the argument.

It was evident from the beginning, however, that U.S. forces could not contemplate the prospect of two nearly simultaneous MRCs with any degree of equanimity. The BUR estimated that one such conflict would require 4–5 Army divisions, 10 Air Force wings, and 100 Air Force bombers—two such conflicts, fought simultaneously and with little warning, would therefore have required 8–10 active Army divisions, 20 Air Force wings, and 200 Air Force bombers. Although the Army theoretically could have handled its part of such a commitment by deploying every soldier in the active force (something that would be, in practice, virtually impossible), the Air Force would have had to deploy immediately not only all of its active wings, but all of its reserve wings as well—and it did not have enough strategic bombers under any calculation. The Air Force would then enter the conflict with no reserve whatsoever, while the Army would have to rely on slow-mobilizing Guard and Reserve forces should anything go wrong. The margin of error was razor-thin. When the General Accounting Office reviewed the proposal, moreover, it pointed out that the air- and sealift forces essential for swinging troops rapidly from one theater to another did not exist in sufficient quantity in 1993, and would not be fielded until 2000 at least, if then. The BUR did not provide a meaningful two-major regional conflict capability.

The concept of a two-MRC strategic capability has come under attack virtually from the moment the Bush administration enunciated it. Some critics have derided it as an arbitrary standard—why two MRCs, they ask? Why not one or seven or twenty? Others argued that contingencies were too complex and variable to be encapsulated in an "MRC" standard, or that the U.S. should be preparing to conduct peacekeeping and stabilization missions rather than major wars. Since the armed forces had never, since the end of the Cold War, actually been maintained at a two-MRC standard, they argued, it seemed sometimes to be a moot argument.

The basic grand strategic concept, however, is real, valid, and important. The United States has for more than a century been a global power with interests around the world. Those interests have brought America into contact with a wide variety of powers, some of which have been and are capable of fighting major regional wars. During the Cold War, the U.S. faced an enemy in the Soviet Union that also had global interests and the capability to pursue them. The Soviets could attack America's allies simultaneously in Europe and in Asia, and the Navy's argument about the need to be able to respond in all theaters was well-founded. In the post-Cold War world, the argument for a capacity to wage war in multiple theaters simultaneously has seemed less urgent, since there is not one single directing hand that can move forces against America simultaneously around the globe as there once had been. America's potential adversaries, moreover, have not generally coordinated their actions or formed alliances to take advantage of the U.S. incapacity to be everywhere at once, with one or two exceptions. Looked at purely from the perspective of threats, therefore, the two-MRC standard seems unnecessary, which is one of the reasons why Aspin tried to abandon it explicitly and did abandon it implicitly with an inadequate force structure.

When looking at the world from the standpoint of the president and his key advisors, however, a different picture emerges. If the U.S. maintains a military capable of fighting and winning only one major conflict at a time, then the president is likely to find himself in an uncomfortable position during any crisis. Is the rest of the world safe and stable enough, he must ask, to commit the only meaningful response force I have to this one situation? Can I be sure that no other potential foe will take advantage of America's preoccupation and the absence of reserve forces to challenge us? There need be no prior coordination between enemies—an enemy in one region, observing the bulk of the U.S. military drawn around the globe away from it, might spontaneously decide to act aggressively in the hopes of achieving success. Something like that happened in 1994, as we shall see, and again in 2003, when crises in Iraq and North Korea complemented one another dangerously for overstretched U.S. forces. The reason to maintain the capability to fight two major regional wars, therefore, is to preserve the freedom to contemplate one of these wars with equanimity. Aspin's effective rejection of this approach thus threatened to constrain American responses to emerging crises and to drive the U.S. toward self-deterrence.

Aspin did not think that he was constraining potential American responses, however, because he would have rejected the analysis of the inadequacy of his proposed force structure offered above.[6] Focused entirely on the threat of unprovoked and sudden aggression against a U.S. ally, Aspin developed a template for such a war. Conflict would begin with an enemy attack, so the first phase of the U.S. response would focus on halting that attack. Once the attack was halted, U.S. forces would proceed with phase two, building "up U.S. combat power in the theater while reducing the enemy's." When the force ratios were right, American troops would move to phase three, "decisively defeat the enemy." After that victory had been accomplished, those forces needed in other theaters would depart, while remnants would remain to "provide for post-war stability."[7]

The key phase in this scenario is the first one, the "halt phase." If U.S. forces, in conjunction with American allies on whom "primary responsibility for the initial defense of their territory, rests, of course," could stop the enemy attack, then the U.S. military could gradually build up the counter-attack force, taking the necessary time to prepare a crushing blow. If the "halt phase" failed, however, then the U.S. might not even have the necessary bases into which to send the reinforcements needed for the counter-attack phase.

Aspin believed that American air power would suffice to handle the halt phase with virtually no assistance from the ground forces. "The requirement to halt regional invasions early," he said in 1993, "looked very much like an insoluble problem until very recently." "Two high-tech responses operating synergistically," he continued, "have combined to give us a much better chance: ... smart anti-tank munitions and electronic battlefield surveillance." "For the first time," he concluded, "it appears possible that air and missile forces will be able to kill large numbers of armored vehicles quickly from the air, land and sea—and that's the key. For the first time, highly deployable early arriving forces will be able to kill armor quickly and in large numbers. This would be a real revolution, and it looks like we can do it while minimizing U.S. losses."[8]

Aspin's "halt phase" differed fundamentally from the air power concepts John Warden and John Boyd had developed. It did not rely on understanding the enemy as a system at all, or on analyzing the enemy force for centers of gravity. It was instead old-fashioned attrition warfare based on the assumption that U.S. air power was now both invulnerable and unprecedentedly lethal. Aspin clearly imagined that American planes and cruise missiles would attack the leading edge of the enemy's invasion force, using advanced sensors to locate the vehicles and precision-guided munitions to destroy them. In a sense, he was calling for close air support missions in support of no ground forces. The emphasis on attacking the enemy's fielded forces was the exact opposite of what Warden and even Boyd had advocated.

Aspin's approach was nevertheless extremely attractive to the Air Force for several reasons. First, it put air power at the center of a campaign and identified it as the supported rather than supporting force. This distinction is important in American military affairs, because the supported force is the one that develops the plans, sets priorities, and makes the critical decisions that shape the campaign; the supporting force goes along. Elements of the Air Force had long argued that it was time to stop seeing air power as supporting ground forces but instead to value it as a war-winning force in its own right. Aspin seemed to be accepting that argument with the "halt phase" concept.

Second, it helped unite the disparate Air Force subcommunities. Strategic bombing enthusiasts were pleased because "halt phase" put the Air Force in charge of a war. Tactical Air Command veterans could be pleased because the destruction of the enemy's fielded forces was their traditional mission.

A number of air power enthusiasts adopted the concept rapidly for their own and tried to argue that "halt phase" should lead to a shift of budgetary priorities to the Air Force as well, as we shall see. It was, after all, a short step to argue that if the Air Force could win the halt phase, the rest of the war would be relatively insignificant by comparison. By introducing this concept in 1993, Aspin substantially structured the debate on roles and missions for the next five years and more.

The search for a new grand strategy following the Soviet Union's fall and Desert Storm overlooked a number of critical factors, chief among them the nature of the new threats the U.S. might expect to face. Despite Aspin's call for a "bottom-up review" that would take nothing in the old force structure for granted, even his strategy was not developed in that way. The U.S. armed forces that emerged from these various reviews were fundamentally simply smaller versions of those that had been maintained to fight the Soviets. No one seriously questioned the validity of such an approach.

But there was a sharp contrast between the expected battle in the Fulda Gap and the Desert Storm look-alikes that served as scenarios for those who were redesigning U.S. forces. The Reagan years had seen a shift away from the focus on winning the first battle to a return to the idea of winning a protracted war. Reagan's emphasis on building up the reserves emphasized his belief that a war with the Soviet Union would probably turn into a war of national mobilization. The front-line forces would serve their purpose if they held off the initial attack long enough for that mobilization, first of reserves, then of conscripts, to take effect. No one expected those active forces to win the war by themselves unsupported.

The dawning post-Cold War era demanded forces that could do precisely that. Desert Storm became the exemplar of the "come-as-you-are" war, the war that breaks out with little notice, lasts a short time, and ends with a decisive U.S. triumph. It did not prove possible, in fact, to introduce National Guard combat units into the Desert Storm order of battle despite six months of preparation. In the shorter-notice wars that most people expected to be the norm in the future, it was unlikely in the extreme that Guard or Reserve combat forces would see action.[9]

The comparison between the forces needed to combat the Soviet Union and those needed in the new era was, therefore, a comparison of apples with oranges. It was quite possible that the *active* forces required to fight two simultaneous short-notice wars would not be much smaller than the *active* forces needed to hold the Soviet Union at bay. The simple and universal assumption that the collapse of the U.S.S.R. inevitably meant that the active force should shrink significantly was not necessarily valid.

At the same time, the debate over a new grand strategy and force structure also overlooked a series of critical assumptions that had underlay the Cold War military. First, it ignored the significant risk that Reagan and his advisors believed they were accepting by holding the size of the Active Army constant. Just because the Army was a given size when the Soviet Union fell did not mean that it was, in fact, adequate for its assigned missions and it did not necessarily follow, therefore, that it should be cut dramatically in the new era. Aspin's proposals for the cuts in Air Force were even more illogical, considering the dramatically *increased* burden he proposed to place on that service through the "halt phase" concept.

Second, the debate largely ignored the problem of strategic lift. Moving troops to Europe was a well-understood challenge in 1990. For years, the U.S. armed forces had practiced just such a maneuver in exercises called REFORGERs (which stood for Return of Forces to Germany). There may or may not have been quite enough strategic lift to conduct that operation, but at least its parameters and demands were well enough understood that the air and maritime services knew what they could expect.

The post-U.S.S.R. problem of rapidly deploying troops to an unknown part of the world, where port facilities might be weak or even under attack, where "host nation support" had to be arranged from scratch in great danger (as had been the case in Saudi Arabia in 1990), was a problem of an entirely different order. But the "halt phase" then required an additional massive movement of forces from one theater to another following the defeat of the first adversary. Although Aspin and others made pious demands for an increase in strategic lift, no one took the problem seriously enough actually to solve it or even think it all the way through.

Third, the debate ignored a series of trade-offs that the Army of the 1970s had accepted to support the goal of winning the first battle. When Creighton Abrams placed the bulk of certain critical combat service support elements into the Reserves in order to maximize active duty combat strength, he did so in the assumption that troops in Europe could benefit from economies of scale in logistics. Several corps lined up shoulder to shoulder can get by with many fewer support elements than the same number of corps operating independently in far-flung theaters around the globe. The same is true at every level of war.

Although the Navy had contemplated the problem of fighting a multi-front war in the 1970s and especially the 1980s, the Army really had not. Its leaders expected to fight in Europe and only in Europe, with the possible exception of relatively minor diversions to the Persian Gulf, but only if circumstances in Europe allowed. The shift to a notion of fighting multiple regional wars simultaneously should have underlined the inadequacy of this assumption about the number of support troops needed. This problem naturally had implications for the ultimate size of the Army and possibly for the question of the balance between the active Army and the Guard and Reserve. The matter did not come up in serious discussions, however, setting the Army up for a host of substantial problems in the 1990s and beyond.

The search for a new grand strategy and force structure, therefore, was half-hearted and incomplete. Far from exorcising the various contradictions and risks that had crept into the late-Cold War force, it mostly accepted those contradictions and risks and layered new ones on top of them. The one thing everyone could agree upon was that the armed forces needed to be substantially smaller than they had been, and that, for political reasons if nothing else, the cuts had to be reasonably equitable among the various services. To a considerable degree, the arguments about capabilities-based or threat-based planning, about one-MRC or two-MRC capabilities, and about "halt phase" and the concomitant roles and missions debate really served more important arguments about the military budget. At no time did U.S. military planners objectively attempt to determine the military America would really need and try to build support for it. The U.S. military in the 1990s was therefore placed increasingly in a dangerous situation as it became clear that it was neither sized nor shaped adequately for the grand strategic tasks it was being called upon to fulfill, and as the increasing tensions over falling budgets created in all services a *"sauve qui peut"* mindset. It was not an auspicious beginning for the military designed to police the new world order.

A TALE OF TWO SERVICES

The Army and the Air Force reacted to the Gulf War and the end of the Soviet Union in opposite ways. Many in the Air Force embraced Desert Storm as the vindication of Air Force doctrine, of the centrality of the Air Force in warfare, and even of the decades-long tradition of promises by air power enthusiasts. Arguments in the Air Force's theoretical journals centered on how to make the other services and the nation realize the "lessons" of Desert Storm by placing air power at the center of America's military priorities and effort in the future.

The Army learned a different lesson. Army leaders saw Desert Storm as likely to be the last major ground conflict of its kind, and rejected the idea of building future force structure to fight similar wars in the future. Army thinkers and leaders focused instead on two main trends they discerned in the post-Cold War world: the advance of technology and the fragmentation of the international order. Far from arguing that Desert Storm had vindicated AirLand Battle doctrine, the Army abandoned it almost completely in its doctrinal revision of 1993. Pride of place went instead to "operations other than war" (OOTW), including peacekeeping and humanitarian missions.

At the same time, the Army Chief of Staff Gordon Sullivan argued that advances in technology would transform the way the Army fought in the future. He became preoccupied in particular by advances in communications technology, but he initially advocated a broad-based approach to Army transformation. The services went in different directions for much of the 1990s, and each continued to seize upon the unusual military operations of that decade to "prove" the validity of its own approach.

Air Power Takes Flight

Most Air Force commentators following Desert Storm did not focus on the revolutionary new aspects of Warden's theories, or the transformation of "strategic" bombing that resulted, but instead on the simple assertion that the Gulf War placed air power at the center of any future conflict. Secretary of the Air Force Donald Rice declared in 1992, "Air power—of the Air Force, Navy, Army, and Marine Corps—has emerged as a dominant form of military might. The term *air campaign* is fixed in the lexicon, and warfare has entered a new era." He continued that in the Gulf War, "Air power did exactly what air power visionaries said it could"[10] Air power had finally lived up to its decades-old promise: "We can plan a strategic campaign and carry it out. We can go around and over the enemy, strike critical nodes precisely, and paralyze him with strategic and tactical assets. We see his every move and block it." He noted that "air power had an almost mystical effect on some Iraqi soldiers," and generated desertion rates that were testimony to the impossibility of facing precision air attack.[11]

Warden wasted no time in claiming a unique place for air power as demonstrated by the Gulf War. He argued, "The loss of air superiority put Iraq completely under the power of the coalition; what would be destroyed and what would survive was up to the coalition, and Iraq could do nothing. It lay as defenseless as if occupied by a million men. For practical purposes, it had in fact become a state occupied—from the air." The lessons of the war were therefore clear: "Coalition air operations are the first example in history of a pure strategic and operational air campaign designed to be the primary instrument in achieving the political and military objectives of war." He even coined a new term to describe the new sort of warfare epitomized by Instant Thunder: "The Gulf conflict was also the first example of 'hyperwar'—one that capitalizes on high technology, unprecedented accuracy, operational and strategic surprise through stealth, and the ability to bring all of an enemy's key operational and strategic nodes under near-simultaneous attack." He concluded, "The world has just witnessed a new kind of warfare—hyperwar. It has seen air power become dominant. It has seen unequivocally how defenseless a state becomes when it loses control of the air. . . . It has seen the awesome power of the air offensive—and the near impossibility of defending against it. It has seen a demonstration of strategic attack theory. . . . We have moved from the age of the horse and the sail through the age of the battleship and the tank to the age of the airplane."[12]

Others were also quick to pick up on the implications of the apparent air power victory for the development of the U.S. military. One Air Force lieutenant colonel declared immediately after the war, "Contrary to the underlying assumptions found in much of the U.S. military's current doctrine, air power dominated the conduct of Operation Desert Storm. As a result, perhaps the most important lessons the U.S. military could learn from Desert Storm is that it needs to change its doctrine to recognize the reality that air power can dominate modern conventional war. . . . Surface forces are still very important, but campaign success now depends on superiority in the air more than it does on surface superiority."[13]

Proponents of the air power orthodoxy naturally chafed under the requirement to assert the primacy of "jointness" in military planning and operations. The emphasis on jointness, the coordinated operation of multiple services, increased dramatically in the 1980s, culminating in the Goldwater–Nichols amendment of 1986. This law had a variety of complicated consequences, including the removal of the Joint Chiefs of Staff from the chain of command and a significant increase in the power of regional commanders-in-chief (like CENTCOM commander Schwarzkopf). It also ensured that success for senior officers lay in showing their political and military superiors that they had embraced the importance of jointness and were not simply advocates for their own services.

To the air power visionaries, this emphasis was misguided. As one pointed out in 1992, "jointness in the operational context is not a useful measure of military effectiveness." No enemy, he declared, had ever died from jointness. Jointness is simply a measure of efficiency in budgetary allocations, but "it is not a substitute for effectiveness. Further, jointness is not a substitute for high levels of competence in a particular medium of warfare, but rests on an appropriate degree of integration of these highly developed specialized competencies."[14]

Another observer lamented, "One would think that the Gulf war, the most decisive air war in history, would sweep away the doubts and uncertainties regarding the potentialities of air power. Unfortunately, that may not be the case. Some leading airmen are still reluctant to draw lessons regarding the role of air power in future wars."[15]

Such views rested heavily on a particular interpretation of the Gulf War that has since been shown to be problematic. One observer described the air war and concluded, "The result . . . was that when the ground offensive began in mid-February, it met minimal resistance and quickly swept forward from Saudi Arabia all the way to the Euphrates River, accepting the surrender of tens of thousands of hungry, demoralized Iraqi soldiers. The magnitude of the aerial victory in the overall campaign was revealed by the almost unbelievably low casualty rate suffered by coalition surface forces."[16]

Another observer was even more direct: "the final ground offensive of Operation Desert Storm was not offensive at all but an almost unopposed advance. Heavily protected American M1 tanks got through unscathed, but so did lightly armored troop carriers, the jeeps of the French foreign legion, and even the rented cars of adventurous journalists. Air power had finally done it."[17] The so-called Battle of Khafji was a frequently cited example of the impossibility of an enemy conducting ground operations in the face of U.S. airpower. Elements of two Iraqi corps (sometimes portrayed by airpower enthusiasts as two entire corps) advanced over the Saudi border some days before the beginning of the ground offensive, apparently hoping to precipitate that attack. U.S. airpower attacked the exposed forces, driving them to take cover in the village of Khafji, from which they subsequently withdrew with crippling losses. Airpower visionaries seized particularly on this battle to "prove" that air-power could stop ground assaults by itself.[18]

Confronting the obviously transformed international security environment of the 1990s, airpower enthusiasts claimed both that future wars were likely to be against relatively advanced conventional enemies and also that airpower would be effective against terrorists and unconventional foes. A handful of more cautious observers warned that airpower was not likely, in fact, to be as effective at the low end of the spectrum of conflict, or even at the high end in certain climes and in certain locales. But few visionaries doubted that the transformative events of 1991 would carry over into any and all missions that the U.S. armed forces might face for the foreseeable future.

The obvious problem with this enthusiasm was that it was mostly based on a misreading of the actual events of the Gulf War. It is now clear that the ground advance into Iraq was not an unopposed movement consisting mainly of Iraqis demoralized by air strikes surrendering to advancing forces. In certain pitched battles, notably 73 Easting, Republican Guard troops demonstrated skill in deployment, setting up an armored ambush, and determination in the struggle—Iraqi infantry on several occasions attempted to engage M1s from the rear with their hand-held machine guns, only to be mowed down by advancing Bradleys. The argument that the ease of the ground advance proved the devastating effectiveness of the air campaign was tautological and unsupported by the facts.

This misperception did not result simply from the airpower enthusiasts seeing what they wanted to see. The Army's incompetent handling of the media in Desert Storm ensured that the story of the ground fight got out only very slowly and piecemeal. It took a number of years for the true story of that advance to emerge, and by then the image of a pure airpower victory had firmly established itself in the public as well as the military mind.

The exaggeration of the effects of airpower in Desert Storm

was nevertheless important. It led to the repeated assertion that airpower could win future wars by itself, that the Air Force should receive the lion's share of defense budgets, that ground forces could safely be cut or even eliminated—relegated, at the very least, to mopping-up duties in the wake of the inevitable airpower victory. The important synergies between the ground operations and the air war, including the fact that the presence of a large coalition army forced the Iraqis to keep their troops concentrated and in relatively exposed positions, were lost in this view. Warden's warning from *The Air Campaign* that air attack on centers of gravity was likely to be most effective when the enemy faced a high-tempo and large-scale threat was also lost.

The airpower triumphalism also glossed over the failure of the air campaign to destroy the Republican Guard which allowed Saddam to crush the Kurdish and Shi'ite uprisings that followed the war, thereby helping him stay in power. It is quite true that Bush and Powell deliberately ended the war quickly rather than pursue that objective, but it is also true that Warden and others in the fall of 1990 confidently predicted that Instant Thunder as originally planned and subsequently executed would lead to the collapse of Saddam's regime. In the aftermath of the war, they did not consider the possibility that the failure to achieve this goal might have reflected any more fundamental flaw in the theory.

Above all, the tense budget battles that had begun swirling around the Pentagon even before Desert Storm had the effect, in Boyd's terms, of turning the military in on itself instead of allowing it to focus on potential enemies. Air Force officers at all levels were at least as interested in preserving their service from budget cuts by deflecting those cuts onto their sister services as they were in developing the new airpower theory to its fullest potential. The evidence of this focus is in the legion of articles they produced, all having the common and simplistic thesis that the most important lesson to learn from Desert

Storm is that airpower had become the dominant means of war. An opportunity to learn from victory was turned into an opportunity to fight off rivals for defense budget funds in a time of falling budgets.

Ignoring the Last War

If the Air Force community largely took the Gulf War as evidence to stay the course, the Army moved rapidly to change course entirely. Inklings of this change predated Desert Storm —in 1990, General Gordon Sullivan, soon to become Army Chief of Staff, declared that the fall of the Soviet Union would lead to an increase in the importance of low-intensity conflicts, and that "the next thirty to sixty years will witness a revolution in land warfare as dramatic as the changes that followed the battles of Crécy and France (1940)." He continued, "Technologies that will feed this revolution-directed energy, high-velocity kinetic energy, new propulsion technologies, advanced sensors, and high-speed microprocessors—will soon reach the point where doctrinal integration, not technological breakthroughs, will pace further advances."[19]

In 1993, as Chief of Staff, Sullivan co-authored a lengthy paper arguing that two fundamental shifts were affecting the U.S. military: a shift away from the traditional definition of war and the use of military force, and a revolution in the nature of war brought on by a "military-technical revolution." The first shift reflected the collapse of America's principal threat and the emergence of a world order in which failing states and international chaos seemed to pose greater threats than any state's military. Sullivan quoted the historian Michael Howard:

> It is quite possible that war in the sense of major, organized armed conflict between highly developed societies may not recur. . . . Nevertheless violence will continue to

erupt within developed societies as well as underdeveloped, creating situations of local armed conflict often indistinguishable from traditional war.[20]

Sullivan argued that the Army and the nation would have to start paying much greater attention to "operations other than war" and to redefine its notion of how military force should be used.

Part of the impetus for this focus came from the fact that the Army found itself plunged almost immediately into a series of "operations other than war" that rapidly came to preoccupy its leaders. Immediately following the Gulf War, the Army began Operation Provide Comfort to relieve humanitarian crises in the Kurdish areas of Iraq. In early 1993, U.S. forces deployed to Somalia in support of Operation Restore Hope, a humanitarian relief effort aimed at stemming the effects of a politically-managed famine. The year 1994 saw a large American force enter Haiti in Operation Uphold Democracy and a small force deployed to Rwanda. All the time, the Army had its eye on the steadily deteriorating situation in the Balkans, which culminated in the deployment of a large U.S. contingent to Bosnia in 1995 in support of the Dayton Accords. In this context, it was only natural that the Army should focus its attention increasingly on humanitarian and peacekeeping missions to the exclusion of a focus on warfighting, and Sullivan alluded to both Somalia and the possibility of U.S. intervention in Bosnia in his 1993 paper.[21]

Sullivan's assertion that the Army would gradually be drawn into more and more OOTW missions was more a recognition of reality and an attempt to shape the planning and conduct of those missions than any enthusiastic embracing of them. He pointedly noted, "leaders and strategists must recognize the requirements essential to success whenever military force is employed: identifying clear, achievable political aims; planning and employing strategic measures for achieving those political aims; raising and sustaining adequate means to implement the strategic measures; and ensuring the support of the nation (or coalition)." He warned that both political and military leaders would be uncomfortable with OOTW, "for they find it is difficult—albeit no less important—to identify clear, achievable strategic aims. There is an emotional temptation to want to 'do something' without first clearly understanding what political purpose that 'something' is supposed to accomplish."[22]

The emphasis on having clear political objectives, providing adequate forces, and maintaining the support of the people are all lessons of Vietnam. They reflected an updating of the Weinberger Doctrine and the Powell Doctrine for an era in which Army involvement in OOTW was becoming obvious and unavoidable. Sullivan did not attempt to resist that involvement—he saw it as an inevitable development of the international system. He sought instead to shape it in ways that would minimize the Army's exposure if things went badly.

Sullivan's acceptance of the idea of OOTW rapidly turned into formal Army acceptance of the idea as well during the revision of the Army's capstone doctrinal manual, FM 100–5 (now renumbered FM 3–0), in 1993. The new manual tacitly abandoned AirLand Battle by failing to use the term and incorporating the key "tenets" of AirLand Battle doctrine only as part of a long laundry list of "foundations of Army operations."[23] It was telling that the first section of the chapter on "fundamentals of Army operations" entitled "the range of military operations" began with "operations other than war" and only then considered "war."[24] The manual included for the first time an entire chapter on OOTW.[25]

Sullivan did not confine his focus to current Army operations, however. He also firmly believed that a fundamental change in the nature of warfare was underway, and he sketched the basic outlines of this change in detail with all the zeal of a visionary. The "military-technical revolution," he explained, would "have a dramatic effect on the Army and land warfare through five dominant trends: lethality and dispersion; volume and precision of fire; integrative technology; mass and effects, and invisibility and detectability."[26]

Sullivan argued that technology was transforming war by increasing the lethality of modern armies not geometrically, but exponentially. New systems allowed ground forces to engage their enemies "over-the-horizon" with phenomenal precision and deadly effect. As a result, it was possible to disperse modern armies much more widely than in the past, since the range of their weapons obviated the need to keep the shooters massed. The buzz-phrase "mass effects, not forces" would come to define the Army's thinking in the 1990s. At the same time, the increasing lethality of the enemy's weapons systems made massing forces an inherently bad idea—large concentrations of troops simply offered too lucrative a target.

The lethality of modern forces accompanied by their greater dispersion on the battlefield meant that much smaller units could produce potentially decisive effects. Sullivan argued, thus, that "these trends indicate, and the Gulf War as well as Operation Just Cause corroborate, that as the size of the unit decreases, there can be a corresponding increase in the effects it is able to produce if it is equipped with the right technology used by high-quality, well-trained and well-led troops employing proper doctrine." He continued, "smaller or fewer units will be able to produce decisive effects because of the vast array of weaponry that they have at their disposal and the speed with which they will be able to acquire targets, maneuver, employ fires, and relocate." In an amazingly prescient passage, he concluded,

Think of the maneuver possibilities that could be generated for ground or air commanders by very dispersed special operations forces or of the potentially decisive effects these very small forces—integrated into the forces of all services—have when equipped with secure satellite communications, laser designators, and position guidance systems. Small teams in the right place, at the right time, and linked in with the right systems have the potential to produce, or at least contribute to, decisive results.[27]

Sullivan might have been predicting the U.S. war in Afghanistan that occurred eight and a half years later.

A key to the revolution in military affairs that Sullivan saw lay in "integrative technology," which he wrote "will introduce a level of precision to the overall force, not just to individual and massed fires, that has been impossible up to this point in the history of land combat. In the twenty-first century, the systems of land forces will become an integrated circuit that is, in turn, part of a network of combined land/air/sea/space forces. With this integration network will come improved precision at the point of battle."[28] He added, "Extensive, near-real time communications among a number of intelligence gathering systems, maneuver systems, fire systems, and logistical support systems provide the ground commander with a potentially revolutionary opportunity and with monumental challenges." He continued,

The opportunity is the integration of the reconnaissance and intelligence gathering systems (technological and human) with command and control, fire delivery, and maneuver nodes. Once all are linked digitally to logistical support centers, these task forces will become combined arms task forces qualitatively different from the ones we now have. The degree of situational awareness that a commander will have under these conditions will be orders of magnitude better than he has now. It would not be too bold to claim that his perception of the battlefield will change.[29]

He concluded, "The digitization of the battlefield is a major leap-ahead in the conduct of warfare, but not a break from the past."

For Sullivan warned that the changing technology would not transform human nature, and war would therefore remain a hybrid of science and art. He noted that two myths had accompanied every previous change in the nature of communications and intelligence technology: "first, that some extraordinary technological advance yet to take place would result in the land commander['s] acquisition of 'perfect, real-time' information upon which to base his decisions and direct his subordinates; second, that greater centralization in decision making would yield greater combat effectiveness at the point of battle." Sullivan rejected both of these beliefs, even in the context of the revolutionary changes he foresaw:

Realities on the battlefield, however, proved otherwise. The very nature of war consists of fear, fog, danger, uncertainty, deception, and friction—these are not conditions that can ever generate "perfect information." Reports that a commander receives are often incomplete and incorrect. An enemy commander strives to deceive his adversary, hiding what he does as best he can; what one sees on the battlefield, therefore, must be interpreted. Interpretation faces the same impairments that we noted above in connection with obtaining information. Certainly, advanced technologies, multiple collection methods, and other means can increase the reliability of information and aid in decision making. The realities of what goes on in combat, however, will frustrate forever those searching for "perfect, real-time" information. To hope for technology that will be capable of gathering and using such information to feed a centralized military decision-making system is to hope in vain.

The major challenge facing visionaries working for the revolution in land warfare, therefore, lay more in the training and developing of leaders and soldiers than in the technology. Sullivan clearly believed that the technological problems would be overcome, but he feared that they would lead to inadequate solutions without the creation of the proper human material and human organizations. As Army Chief of Staff, Sullivan worked hard to put the Army on course to developing both the technology and the human capital necessary to bring about and sustain the revolution in warfare he foresaw.

The vision of warfare Sullivan was pursuing was similar to and different from that propounded by Warden and the other airpower enthusiasts. According to Sullivan, land forces would "be capable—operating as part of a joint force—of detecting the enemy at extended, over-the-horizon distances while remaining invisible to that enemy; delivering fires—also over the horizon—to facilitate maneuver; thus destroying the enemy force and disintegrating his cohesion throughout the depth of the theater or battlefield."[30] This notion of essentially disaggregating the enemy-as-a-system is similar to Warden's vision, although couched in different terms. It is equally a vision of removing the Army from the business of close combat and transforming it into a force capable of essentially shattering the enemy at long range. It appears that Sullivan even imagined that these new technologies would carry over into OOTW, as some of the airpower enthusiasts also argued.[31]

In this sense, Sullivan set the Army on a course to its own political destruction. He did not emphasize missions unique to land power, such as controlling terrain, intermingling with populations, forcing the enemy to concentrate his troops, etc., but instead focused on tasks many of which air power could perform as well or better. If the airpower services could attack critical nodes throughout the theater and thereby disaggregate the enemy system, did the nation need to spend billions to upgrade the Army so that it could do the same things? If the objective was to remove the Army from close combat so as to reduce U.S. casualties and speed deployability, would it not be better to do without ground forces entirely? Sullivan did not foresee or answer these potential challenges, which, to be fair, only a handful of theorists and airpower visionaries were making at the time he co-authored this pamphlet. By focusing so heavily on the missions the Army shared with the other services, however, Sullivan did create important vulnerabilities for the service at the beginning of a desperate fight for limited resources.

Both the Army's and the airpower visionaries' discussions of the revolution in military affairs suffered from an even more fundamental problem, however. They both addressed changes in warfare in the abstract without considering the geostrategic realities the U.S. faced in the post-Cold War world. This problem even bedeviled Sullivan's pamphlet despite its focus on OOTW—that section was almost completely disconnected from the revolution in military affairs (RMAs) section and no real effort was made to harmonize the two.

Revolutions in Military Affairs have rarely come about as the result of astrategic reasoning about technological or other military capabilities. Changes in warfare during the French Revolution and Napoleonic period, for instance, were aimed at allowing France to defeat much more powerful coalitions—and then at allowing the survivors of defeated coalitions to defeat the seemingly invincible Napoleon. When Helmuth von Moltke the Elder, a true RMA visionary who has not received the credit he deserves for the intellectual transformation of warfare in the nineteenth century, fought to integrate railroads into military planning and deployment, he did so in order to solve the crushing geostrategic problem Prussia faced: how to fight when outnumbered on three widely separated fronts. The near-contemporaneous integration of railroads and rifles into U.S. Civil War armies likewise occurred in the face of clear strategic necessity.

The development of German blitzkrieg techniques in the Interwar Years focused on allowing a Germany badly weakened by the Versailles treaty to defeat first Poland and, ultimately, France in a future war, once again circumventing Germany's terrible geostrategic position. The development of Soviet operational art in the same period was likewise an effort to solve what the Soviets believed was the fundamental problem of warfare at that time—how to prevent ground campaigns from crystallizing into trench warfare.

The mating of thermonuclear warheads to ICBMs in the 1950s, the event that caused the Soviets to coin the term "revolution in military affairs" in the first place, was likewise a response to a geostrategic need—in that case, how to threaten the continental United States without having to develop truly intercontinental bombers and necessary escort fighters with ranges in the thousands of miles and then defeat the awesome American Air Force over its own territory. And, as we have seen, the developments of the 1960s and 1970s that led to the first modern U.S. military transformation took place in response to the perception of an overwhelming Soviet threat.

Neither Warden's nor Sullivan's visions were developed to counter any particular threat or solve any specific geostrategic problem. They were both attempts to extrapolate from recent technological developments in ways designed to ensure that the U.S. military would become and remain invulnerable for the foreseeable future against any challenger in any theater. They were generic thoughts about how to transform war itself, rather than responses to particular needs.

This free-thinking was possible because after 1991 it did not appear that the U.S. military faced any particularly worrisome threat at all. This situation was unprecedented in recent American history. Even in the interwar years, the U.S. Navy saw a significant potential threat in Japan, while the Army was well aware of its inability to hold its own against European land forces. For all the seeming unlikelihood of U.S. involvement in such wars, that period did not compare with the relative security America seemed to enjoy following Desert Storm. The Soviet Union was gone, and the Russian armed forces rapidly collapsed. China seemed internally focused in the wake of the Tiananmen Square debacle, and the limited challenge it posed to Taiwan seemed easily countered. North Korea remained a concern, to be sure, but was there any doubt that the U.S. military that had so shredded Iraq would prevail against Kim Il Sung's fanatical but starving hordes? The U.S. had never in its history enjoyed such an apparently total freedom from threats. The tendency of military theorists to let their imaginations roam freely into fantasies of transformed future warfare was, therefore, natural. It remained to be seen whether it could produce a military posture that would survive intense budgetary pressure and that was appropriate for the world as it developed over the course of the succeeding years.

CHAPTER FIVE

Peace, War, and In-Between

THE DECADE BETWEEN 1991 and 2001 presented the
U.S. military with a series of contradictions.

On the one hand, it was a period widely seen as being a
"strategic pause," an epoch in which U.S. military predominance was so great that no challenges to it could be foreseen. In
this respect, politicians and pundits saw it as a time to reduce
and constrain the defense budget and to reorient spending priorities to domestic programs. A considerable number of military officers, in turn, argued that it was a time to "transform"
the U.S. military to prepare it for the challenges that they foresaw in the decades to come.

On the other hand, the 1990s was a decade of almost unprecedented activity for the armed forces. From 1991 on, the
air power services enforced "no-fly" zones in northern and
southern Iraq in support of U.N. inspections. In 1992 American troops deployed to Somalia; in 1994 they went to Haiti. In
1995, American aircraft conducted a brief attack on Bosnian
Serb positions in Bosnia–Herzegovina, and U.S. ground forces
entered that war-torn land as peacekeepers—from which they
only withdrew in 2005, turning the mission over to European
forces. On a number of occasions throughout this period,

American cruise missiles and aircraft attacked sites within Iraq to punish Saddam Hussein for violations of the inspections agreements, culminating in a large-scale attack dubbed Operation Desert Fox in 1998. In 1999, the Air Force and Navy conducted a massive bombing campaign against Serbia, followed by a large-scale deployment of U.S. ground forces to enforce the peace in Kosovo—where they still are. The military was busy in a host of missions ranging from humanitarian relief to massive air assault.

This unprecedented "peacetime" activity placed a great strain on the military in this period, and brought into question its ability to meet its obligations to support the current national security strategy. A crisis in Army readiness that emerged at the end of the decade seemed to underline this problem. But the military leadership in all services split its attention between these ongoing operations and a military transformation agenda focused on exploiting current advantages and new technologies to maintain U.S. predominance indefinitely into the future.

Engagement and Enlargement

The Clinton administration attempted to give coherence and clarity to its vision of the new world order in the national security strategy of July 1994.[1] It identified three primary goals: "To credibly sustain our security with military forces that are ready to fight; to bolster America's economic revitalization; [and] to promote democracy abroad."[2] This statement of goals was a fairly dramatic departure from the objectives outlined in the prior administration's "regional defense strategy" of 1993, which included "to deter or defeat attack from whatever source . . . to strengthen and extend the system of defense arrangements that binds democratic and like-minded nations together in common defense against aggression . . . to preclude any hostile power from dominating a region critical to our interests . . . [and] to help preclude conflict by reducing sources of regional instability and to limit violence should conflict occur." [3]

The prioritization of "bolstering America's economic revitalization" suggested continued lean years for the defense budget, while "credibly sustaining our security with military forces that are ready to fight" was a far cry from precluding hostile powers from gaining ascendancy in critical regions. The increased focus on spreading democracy was both novel and somewhat confusing.

Clinton's national security strategy declared, "All of America's strategic interests . . . are served by enlarging the community of democratic and free market nations. . . . The core of our strategy is to help democracy and markets expand and survive in other places where we have the strongest security concerns and where we can make the greatest difference." The strategy noted, "This is not a democratic crusade; it is a pragmatic commitment to see freedom take hold where that will help us most. Thus, we must target our effort to assist states that affect our strategic interests, such as those with large economies, critical locations, nuclear weapons, or the potential to generate refugee flows into our own nation or into key friends and allies." [4] This is language not all that far removed from the language found in the most recent national security strategy, with one major difference.

In the 1990s, it seemed that democracy was spreading across the globe spontaneously, and the U.S. could limit itself to supporting a movement that was progressing under its own steam anyway. The focus of attention was naturally on Russia and the newly-independent states of the former Soviet Union, but the Clinton National Security Strategy (NSS) proudly pointed also to South Africa, Cambodia, and El Salvador as examples of the spreading wave of democracy and free markets. The Clinton NSS also made much of the administration's commitment to combating the proliferation of weapons of mass destruction and fighting terrorism. Clinton saw the problem of non-proliferation primarily as an issue of international law and multilateral cooperation, not as a task falling on the United States in direct defense of its own vital interests. And he saw the problem of terrorism as, on the one hand, a problem of deterring state sponsors of terrorism and, on the other, a law-enforcement task of hunting down and bringing to trial individual terrorists and groups. The 1994 NSS embodied a few particular statements that defined the shape of the armed forces and their probable employment. It enshrined, for example, the commitment to a military able to "defeat aggression in two nearly simultaneous major regional conflicts." It offered a concise and lucid definition of this standard, Aspin's failed attempts to jettison it notwithstanding:

As a nation with global interests, it is important that the United States maintain forces with aggregate capabilities on this scale. Obviously, we seek to avoid a situation in which an aggressor in one region might be tempted to take advantage when U.S. forces are heavily committed elsewhere. More basically, maintaining a "two war" force helps ensure that the United States will have sufficient military capabilities to deter or defeat aggression by a coalition of hostile powers or by a larger, more capable adversary than we foresee today.[5]

In addition, the NSS called for forces capable of "providing a credible overseas presence," "countering weapons of mass destruction," "contributing to multilateral peace operations," and "supporting counterterrorism efforts and other national security objectives" including "counterterrorism and punitive attacks, noncombatant evacuation, counter-narcotics operations, nation assistance, and humanitarian and disaster relief operations."[6]

This laundry list of tasks the armed forces were expected to perform was impressive. It was, in fact, too impressive for the force structure the Clinton administration was prepared to pay for. Aspin's Bottom-Up Review, as we have seen, produced a military minimally capable at best of supporting the two-MRC standard. It certainly was not capable of maintaining that standard while also conducting or being ready to conduct the additional missions the National Security Strategy laid out.

The military implicitly accepted this reality in the National Military Strategy released in 1995: "We will quickly generate combat power in wartime," it declared. "Active forces engaged overseas in lower priority missions may be recalled, reorganized, retrained, and redeployed." Noting optimistically that U.S. forces would withdraw from OOTW situations when they had been "stabilized and other organizations are prepared to assume responsibility for relief or security," it added, "In times of crisis, we will need to accelerate this process." As a result, "Activities not involving critical U.S. interests will be turned over to the United Nations or other responsible regional security organizations while we attend to higher priority taskings."[7]

It is not at all clear that the Clinton administration meant to view OOTW and the other non-combat missions it described as lesser included tasks subordinated to the need to be prepared to fight MRCs. On the contrary, according to the NSS, the list of requirements a crisis must meet to justify sending U.S. military forces makes such a reading unlikely. Largely adopting the Weinberger–Powell doctrine, the NSS declared that U.S. forces would only be deployed in support of important interests. Clinton intended to deploy American forces only when allied troops were not available for the job, when he had exhausted non-military means of resolving the problem, obtained a "reasonable assurance of support from the American people and their elected representatives," established clear milestones for success, and developed an exit strategy.[8] Missions meeting all of these criteria are clearly not missions that the administration should happily see jettisoned in the event of a major crisis elsewhere in the world. The gap between the language of the NSS and that of the National Military Strategy reflected the gap between capabilities and expected missions within the armed forces themselves. That gap in turn arose partly from budgetary pressures, but substantially from a failure to consider the nature of the stresses that long-term peacekeeping and OOTW missions would place on the armed forces of the 1990s, as we shall see.

For a brief time in 1994, it appeared that the Clinton administration would face an early test of the two-MRC capability in defense of its stated goal of fighting the proliferation of WMD. Two non-proliferation crises came together when North Korea announced in May that it would remove the fuel rods from its Yongbyon nuclear reactor without permitting the International Atomic Energy Agency (IAEA) to oversee the process. This action would make it impossible for the IAEA to certify that North Korea did not divert any of the spent fuel rods to the production of nuclear weapons, thereby violating its commitments under the Non-Proliferation Treaty. Then, in October, Saddam Hussein concentrated 80,000 troops and nearly 1,000 tanks along the Kuwaiti border in response to a U.N. commission's decision to "rectify" that border to Iraq's disadvantage. Saddam's action occurred within the larger context of a deliberate and systematic Iraqi effort to prevent UNSCOM from verifying Iraq's dismantling of its own WMD programs. And in September, 20,000 U.S. troops had gone ashore in Haiti as part of a peacekeeping operation.[9]

This crisis revealed worrisome problems with the force structure established by the Bottom-Up Review (BUR), and with the military concepts that underlay the "halt phase." In response to the Iraqi build-up, the U.S. military mobilized more than 200,000 servicemen and began deploying them to

Kuwait. But the prospect of a war with North Korea was even more daunting. Considering the possibility of an air attack on the Yongbyon reactor, which was militarily quite feasible, the Chairman of the Joint Chiefs of Staff General John Shalikashvili and the Secretary of Defense William J. Perry "concluded that such an attack was very likely to incite the North Koreans to launch a military attack on South Korea. Even though the North Koreans would surely lose this second Korean War, they could cause hundreds of thousands, perhaps millions of casualties before being defeated. Therefore, I decided against recommending this option to the president at that time." Detailed estimates predicted that 52,000 Americans and 490,000 South Koreans would die in the first ninety days of combat.[10]

"Halt phase" doctrine did not prove sufficiently reassuring in either crisis. In both cases, the U.S. did not have enough strike aircraft already in the theater to stop an enemy advance from the very beginning. There would certainly be a period of days and probably weeks in which U.S. airpower forces scrambled to concentrate in the theater while the enemy advanced. There was little doubt that U.S. airpower, once built up, would be able to smash the Korean or Iraqi advances, and prepare the groundwork for land forces to finish them off, but political leaders had to be concerned with what would happen before the halt. Would North Korean troops be able to take or destroy Seoul? Would the Iraqis be able once again to overrun Kuwait and destroy the oil infrastructure only just being rebuilt? How many civilians would be killed? There was also the danger that U.S. war planes, hurled at the enemy without having time to be fully assembled into reasonable packages, perhaps even before they had been able to achieve air superiority, would take significant losses of their own. The political and detailed military planning complexities of "halt phase" were much greater than the simple charts and diagrams of its proponents had suggested.

Aircraft can assemble much more rapidly in a theater than

ground forces, to be sure, and a "halt phase" approach would have brought U.S. power to bear on the enemy much more quickly than land forces could. But even air forces take time to move—not the planes themselves, but all the infrastructure that is needed to support prolonged high-intensity air campaigns, without which the planes are largely useless. That time permits the enemy to take actions that may be unacceptable. Halt phase enthusiasts tended to focus exclusively on the outcome of the operation—the U.S. would inevitably win. They tended to ignore the detailed course of the operation—what would happen before the victory—and especially the political costs and consequences of the course they favored.[11]

In addition to questions about the "halt phase" in 1994, the issue of the size of the military came sharply into relief. Could the U.S. have sustained a 200,000-strong force in Iraq while fighting North Korea? Could it have done so while supporting 20,000 troops in Haiti? Although the overall force strengths in the Army and the Marines (about 715,000 in the active components of both services) seem to support such a notion, reality was quite different. A substantial portion of the Army, and a smaller proportion of the Marine Corps, is committed at all times to the maintenance of the "institutional" force, including all of the training, procurement, doctrinal development, and educational programs essential to the survival of the institution. Soldiers can be ripped out of training and other programs, of course, although at terrible cost to the long-term well-being of the service, but it takes time to identify them, reassign them, and move them into combat units deploying to a far-off theater. The resulting personnel turbulence also degrades the combat effectiveness of those units. The three potential deployments of 1994, therefore, would have strained the landpower services to and beyond their breaking points, even assuming a fairly benign scenario in the most dangerous one—North Korea.

Finding the Target

The crises of 1994 should, therefore, have sent up alarming warning signals about the ability of the Bottom-Up Review force to meet the two-MRC requirement, and about the strain peacekeeping operations would impose on that ability. It did not do so. Instead, the Clinton administration brokered a deal with the North Koreans that largely allowed them to continue to pursue the development of nuclear weapons technology, and increasingly adopted an approach to Saddam Hussein that relied heavily on sea-launched cruise missiles to send messages. In sum, Clinton learned that he could not really contemplate war on the Korean peninsula and so had to negotiate with Pyongyang from a position of weakness, and he learned that he could not afford to allow Saddam to spook him into costly mobilizations. The underlying problems with the BUR force structure and concepts went unexplored.

War and Peacekeeping in the Balkans

The peacekeeping deployment to Haiti proved short-lived. By 1995, the U.S. had withdrawn most of its forces in an effort to turn the crisis over to international organizations. But in that year the long-simmering crisis in the Balkans boiled over, and the Clinton administration found itself drawn into both significant military operations and long-term peacekeeping commitments.

The collapse of Yugoslavia and the origins of the Balkan conflicts that followed are now so well known as not to require recounting. The Bush administration steadfastly resisted direct U.S. involvement in those conflicts, a decision that, in retrospect, allowed those conflicts to deepen and permitted the needless deaths of many people. Clinton at first continued Bush's hands-off policy, hoping that the European community and the U.N. would take the lead in solving what was clearly a European problem. In the wake of the "Blackhawk Down" disaster in Mogadishu in 1993, moreover, Clinton was extremely reluctant to deploy American ground forces in support of peacekeeping operations in the Balkans.

By 1995, however, the situation in Bosnia–Herzegovina, the focus at that time of the Yugoslavian civil wars, was becoming unacceptable. The U.N. and other non-governmental organizations (NGOs) had a significant presence in the region attempting to stave off the worst of the humanitarian disasters. The tides of war threatened to envelop these people in the conflict, and Clinton found himself gradually drawn into the crisis. In the summer of 1995, he and his advisors decided that if, as seemed likely, the U.S. would be called upon to use force to extract U.N. and European personnel from a deteriorating situation, it would be better to use that force to impose a peace settlement. He therefore turned to the military for a campaign plan that would compel the Bosnian Serbs—who were regarded as the aggressors and the principal obstacles to peace in the region—to negotiate an acceptable deal.

The Bosnia crisis presented the military with a series of daunting challenges. First, it was not a U.S. operation, nor even a NATO operation, but a joint U.S.–NATO–U.N. operation. British and French aircraft flew a substantial number of the sorties and were involved in the planning of the operation in a way that greatly complicated the planning process. The direct involvement of the U.N. in the planning process made it even more complex and intractable. The problem developed from both sides—the U.S. had no doctrine for planning and conducting air operations in support of U.N. forces, and the U.N. had no doctrine for using airpower in support of peacekeeping missions at all. The campaign would be an ad hoc effort on all sides from start to finish.

Second, the military means were tightly circumscribed from the beginning. Clinton refused to contemplate using U.S. ground forces in the combat phase of the operation and determined to restrict that phase to airpower alone. This decision posed a direct challenge to the U.S. airpower community, because it required that community to develop and execute a pure air campaign designed to achieve extremely precise and limited objectives. One objective was to protect the U.N. and NGO personnel on the ground. Another was to defend the "safe havens" in which Bosnian Muslims and Croats had concentrated under the pressure of Bosnian Serb forces. But the overriding objective was to coerce the Bosnian Serbs into negotiating on unfavorable terms. Throughout the operation, avoiding any collateral damage and keeping allied casualties as close as possible to *zero* were critical priorities as well. The restrictions imposed on Operation Deliberate Force, as it came to be known, made the political "interference" of the Vietnam air war pale in comparison.

The U.S. military was not caught entirely off guard by the decision to coerce the Bosnian Serbs with airpower in 1995. Since 1993, planning cells in European Command (EUCOM) had been working on plans for a possible air operation in Bosnia, and those plans had been continually refined and expanded as the crisis grew. European Command planners were very worried about the Bosnian Serbs' "integrated air defense system" (IADS), which they feared could pose a significant challenge to allied air superiority. They knew that the Bosnian Serbs relied on intelligence sent from the Yugoslav air defense system, and that they could not attack Yugoslavia itself. They also knew that they could not expect to be allowed simply to strike military targets in Bosnia at will—from the beginning, the planners understood that they would have to fight a carefully controlled, even micro-managed air campaign that was the antithesis of Instant Thunder.

They nevertheless used a number of the basic concepts that Warden had employed originally in the Instant Thunder plan. They first worked to identify the Bosnian Serbs' "center of gravity," which they believed was a historical fear of being dominated by the other ethnicities in the region. They felt that if they could reduce the combat capabilities of the Bosnian Serb army sufficiently to expose the Bosnian Serbs to potential defeat at the hands of their enemies, then they would negotiate rather than accept such a risk.

This plan took shrewd advantage not only of the history of ethnic conflict in the region, but also of the recent history of the Yugoslavian civil war. Not long before the allied air attacks began, elements of the Croatian army had driven into Bosnian Serb territory, routing the Bosnian Serb army. By weakening that army while the memory of that defeat was still fresh, the EUCOM planners were right to expect the Bosnian Serbs to negotiate. This was an excellent example of choosing a complex "center of gravity" that did not lie in the military realm at all and translating it into a series of objectives that could be struck by air power.

The decision to weaken the Bosnian Serb army did not translate immediately into a series of obvious military targets, however. That army was widely dispersed throughout Bosnia, and the heavy artillery pieces that constituted its most important equipment were also dispersed and hidden. Going after each and every one would be costly and time-consuming—and might not work, given the terrain and weather of the region that reduced the effectiveness of precision-guided munitions. So the EUCOM planners conducted a Warden-like evaluation of their chosen "center of gravity" to find its own "center of gravity." In this case, they realized that the Bosnian Serbs relied upon their ability to shift a relatively small number of key people and equipment rapidly around the theater to support their operations. Disruption of their communications net would badly degrade this ability. They also realized that although the artillery pieces themselves were dispersed, their main ammunition storage facilities were not. By striking those facilities, the allies could make the artillery itself irrelevant.

The air campaign thus begun at the end of August quickly achieved its objectives. Within two weeks, the Bosnian Serb leadership had agreed to negotiations. This agreement would later lead to the Dayton Accords that divided Bosnia along ethnic lines and paved the way for the introduction of U.S. and allied peacekeepers. The highly restricted surgical bombing campaign had not destroyed the Bosnian Serb state or army as a system, and had not destroyed the Bosnian Serbs' ability to continue fighting. It had degraded the immediate effectiveness of the Bosnian Serb forces to such a point that the leadership decided to make peace rather than risk the consequences of continued resistance.

The Bosnian Serbs found it easier to make this decision because the bombing attacks of early September coincided with the launching of a ground offensive by the Bosnian Muslim and Croatian forces. European Command did not coordinate its air campaign with that offensive—indeed, it worked hard to distance itself from the Muslim and Croatian attacks, but to the Bosnian Serbs it probably looked like a combined effort to destroy them. As a result, the Bosnian Serb army "was severely pressed from the western offensive, was being hurt by the bombing, and was unable to exercise effective [command and control] over its forces." The Air Force's detailed study of the campaign concluded, "thus, ground and air forces achieved de facto synergies with each other's operations that undoubtedly propelled both toward achievement of their respective objectives."[12]

The same Air Force study came to two other important conclusions on the basis of this operation. First, although "some modern airpower advocates, such as Col[onel] Phillip Meilinger, have gone so far as to equate air superiority with victory," the equation was invalid in Bosnia: "NATO unequivocally achieved air superiority almost immediately on 30 August, yet overall success remained in question even after the final bomb fell on 14 September. The nature of the operation did not lend itself to final solution through the application of airpower although such application absolutely facilitated success." [13]

Second, the report noted that American airpower enthusiasts had spent too much time thinking about the enemy's centers of gravity, and not enough time thinking about their own. Although the EUCOM planners "determined that the 'historic Bosnian Serb fear of domination' was the COG to attack, it was equally important to defend the Bosnian-government COG—the city of Sarajevo. . . . Thus, protection of the 'friendly' COG was every bit as important to the overall success of the operation as was attack of the 'enemy' COG. Current doctrine," it concluded, "is virtually silent about the issue of defending friendly COGs." [14]

This nuanced view of the significance of the air campaign was both refreshing and important. Once again, a critical element of Warden's initial theory was validated—the effectiveness of an air campaign varies directly with the amount of pressure the enemy feels from ground forces. The presence of indigenous forces to press the Bosnian Serbs meant that the absence of U.S. ground forces was not fatal. The good fortune that led the Bosnian Muslim/Croat armies to attack when Deliberate Force was underway created "unintended synergies" that certainly helped turn the tide within the Bosnian Serb leadership toward negotiation rather than further resistance. It is not at all clear that the air campaign over Bosnia in 1995 would have had anything like the same result without the credible threat of that ground attack.

This was not, however, the lesson that some in the airpower community drew from Operation Deliberate Force. Richard Hallion, author of one of the definitive airpower treatises on the Gulf War, declared, "One of the great things that people should have learned from this is that there are times when air power—not backed up by ground troops—can make a difference." [15] Lieutenant General Michael Ryan, the commander of the air campaign, declared that "Deliberate Force testifies to the capability of airpower 'to coerce compliance with international mandates.'" Against an intransigent Serb leadership, airpower had shown little effectiveness in small doses, Ryan said, but "when it was finally used in very deliberate . . . but sustained way, I think it . . . was the most decisive element of bringing the warring factions to the table and to the successes that were achieved at [Dayton] and eventually signed in Paris."[16] Another commentator declared that Deliberate Force is "the prime modern example of how judicious use of airpower, coupled with hard-nosed diplomacy, can stop a ground force in its tracks and bring the worst of enemies to the bargaining table."[17] An article in an aviation community journal was entitled simply, "Air Power Vindicated."[18]

"ONE OF HISTORY'S MOST IMPRESSIVE AIR CAMPAIGNS"

The war in Kosovo and Serbia of 1999 was in many respects a continuation of the Bosnian crisis of 1995. Serbia's president, Slobodan Milosevic, launched an offensive in the predominantly Albanian province of Kosovo in 1998 designed to drive out the Kosovar Albanians and "cleanse" the area for Serb settlement and reconquest. His offensive was in part a response to aggressive actions by Kosovar separatists emboldened by events in Bosnia, and this offensive was clearly designed to regain his prestige within Serbia and the region and redress the defeat of 1995 in an even more important location.

Once again, the Clinton administration refused adamantly to contemplate deploying U.S. ground forces into the theater and made the mistake, again, of publicly announcing this decision. In contrast to the situation in 1995, however, there was no meaningful ground threat to Milosevic without the introduction of U.S. or European forces: the Kosovo Liberation Army

(KLA), comprised of Kosovar separatists, was unable to stand up to the better equipped and disciplined regular Serbian forces, and Milosevic knew that no other regional power would involve itself in his struggle. As a result, the U.S. and NATO once again began a pure air campaign, but this time there was no indigenous ground force to create an "unintended synergy."

The absence of such a threat to the Serbian regime greatly complicated the efforts of air planners to develop their notions of the enemy's centers of gravity. The unrealistic political assumptions of the senior military and civilian leaders also played a key role. It seems clear that most senior officials thought that a brief demonstration of force would suffice to persuade Milosevic back to the table, as it had in 1995. General Wesley Clark, the EUCOM commander who oversaw the operation, apparently declared that he thought there was a 40 percent chance that Milosevic would fold within a few days of the beginning of bombing.

As a result, the allies did not concentrate sufficient air power within the theater before the campaign began, and did not undertake a meaningful air campaign at the outset of hostilities. Initial operations, instead, were unfocused and sporadic. One Air Force officer, derisively comparing the initial air war over Kosovo to the Instant Thunder plan of 1991, called it Operation "Constant Drizzle."[19] When it became apparent that Milosevic would not fold in the absence of a ground threat, the allies had to scramble to get additional air power into the theater and to find targets to hit.

As a result of this incomplete planning and preparation, the Kosovo air campaign was virtually the inverse of the approach Warden had pioneered in Iraq. Coalition forces started by trying to attack Serb fielded forces—Warden's outermost ring—and gradually worked their way into the inner rings—critical infrastructure, command and control nodes, and finally, just at the end of the campaign, the leadership itself. The low intensity of most of the bombing period precluded any "shock" effect on the Serbian system, and the failure to attack or even identify the central nodes of that system from the beginning meant that the allies never induced disaggregation or paralysis.

Amazingly, Operation Allied Force never achieved real air superiority, either, in the sense that it completely suppressed the Serb IADS. The Serbs had learned both from Desert Storm and from Deliberate Force that a standard Soviet-style IADS was helpless in the face of a U.S. air power system designed specifically to defeat such a system. So the Serbs dispersed their radars and SAMs, including man-portable SAMs. They used their radars sparingly, if at all, and established a complex system of visual observers to provide early warning. The terrain of the Balkans helped a great deal—there were very few ways for allied aircraft to approach their targets, and the Serbs took to placing both observes and weapons systems along the routes they saw the allied aircraft taking. This procedure was probably what allowed them to shoot down an F-117 stealth fighter. The allies tried for a time to destroy the Serb IADS by attacking individual SAM sites, but found that approach far too cumbersome and slow.

The result of the allied failure to suppress the Serb IADS completely was that the majority of bombing runs took place from high altitudes, beyond the range of Serb gunners and missileers, with concomitant decreases in the efficiency and, in some cases, effectiveness of the strikes themselves. This failure also required that strike aircraft be accompanied by suites of aircraft able to locate and attack SAM sites and jam their radars.

The absence of a ground threat also badly degraded allied air power's ability even to attrit the Serb fielded forces in a traditional manner. The Serbs concealed most of their tanks and heavy artillery in widely dispersed locations. They then set up a series of ingenious decoys designed to draw the fire of allied aircrews. These decoys worked remarkably well, and led to wildly inflated estimates of the damage the air campaign was doing to the Serb army. Had the Serbs feared an imminent invasion, they would have been forced to concentrate actual soldiers and equipment along strategic avenues of advance, thus providing lucrative targets. The one occasion on which the allies did destroy a significant Serb ground force resulted from an ill-advised concentration of Serb units to attack a KLA force near Mt. Pastrik on June 7, two days before Milosevic's capitulation. The absence of even "unintended synergy" with ground forces protracted the air campaign and made it much less effective than it would otherwise have been.

The failures to suppress the Serb air defense system and to disaggregate or even attrit the Serbian army led to serious failures at the political level. Shortly after the air campaign began, Milosevic ordered his troops to launch an "ethnic cleansing" campaign to drive the Kosovar Albanians out of Kosovo entirely. Small teams of twenty or so Serb soldiers on a single truck would ride into a village and destroy it. Allied air power and intelligence were not effective enough to identify these tiny concentrations of force and attack them, and the failure to disrupt Milosevic's command and control of his forces allowed them to continue a purposeful military campaign even during the height of the bombing. Milosevic's forces where thus able to drive hundreds of thousands of Kosovars out of their homes and effectively accomplish a significant portion of his political objective, greatly complicating post-war efforts to achieve the political goals of the coalition.

It is impossible to know for sure why Milosevic finally capitulated. A series of events converged, all of which probably contributed to the decision. His indictment as a war criminal in the Hague and his abandonment by his erstwhile Russian allies were factors. The shift of allied bombing attacks to targets central to the maintenance of the regime may have led some of his inner circle to press for peace. The fact that Clinton and his allies seemed to be moving reluctantly toward the conclusion that they would have to insert ground forces into Serbia, and that General Wesley Clark was both pushing and preparing for such a contingency, may also have played a role. Or Milosevic may have felt that he had laid the groundwork for his own success following the peace by driving the Kosovars out of Kosovo. It seems clear, however, that the air campaign by itself had not achieved the desired political and military ends, and that the determination to fight an air-only campaign rendered air power itself significantly less effective than it had been in the previous crises.

The reaction to Operation Allied Force was extremely complicated and important to the future development of the American military. Responsible observers even within the airpower community recognized that it was, at best, an ugly victory, and noted the problems that arose from the lack of synergy with ground forces.[20] They tended to lay the blame on the lack of clear political direction and on the unreasonable expectations of political leaders about how the war would go.

There is a considerable amount of truth in this view—the EUCOM Air Component Commander, General Michael Short, was extremely frustrated with the way the campaign unfolded and his relationship with Clark was very tense. Even Clark, however, felt that the air campaign was inadequate and excessively hindered by political restrictions.

But there is another respect in which the attempt to heap the blame for Allied Force's failures on unreasonable politicians is not appropriate. Ever since Desert Storm, airpower enthusiasts had been arguing that airpower could win conflicts by itself without any ground element. Some had seized on Deliberate Force to argue that this was true even in OOTW. The Clinton administration, badly burned by its experience in Somalia, did not invent the notion of relying on airpower but rather seized upon the promises of some of the more radical airpower enthusiasts. In this sense, the airpower community was itself partially to blame for the unreasonable expectations that led to mistakes at the beginning of Allied Force. It has been a problem from the very inception of airpower that the more extreme advocates have made claims and promises far beyond the abilities of machines and men to achieve, leading to inevitable disappointments. The repeated assertions that Desert Storm and then Deliberate Force had finally "vindicated" generations of airpower visionaries only added to this problem.

Unfortunately, the exaggerated claims continued after Kosovo. One commentator proclaimed as an "indisputable fact" that "for the first time in history, the application of airpower alone forced the wholesale withdrawal of a military force from a disputed piece of real estate."[21] Air Force Chief of Staff Michael Ryan agreed: in Allied Force, "a very well-run air operation . . . brought a cessation of hostilities and the withdrawal of the Serbian forces from Kosovo. 'That fact,' he added, 'can't be rewritten, no matter how hard the pundits try to rewrite it.'"[22] An article in the *Los Angeles Times* declared, "If the peace agreement with Yugoslav President Slobodan Milosevic holds, the United States and its allies will have accomplished what some military experts had predicted was impossible: a victory achieved with air power alone."[23] Even President Clinton said that Allied Force "proved that a sustained air campaign, under the right conditions, can stop an army on the ground," and the Chairman of the Joint Chiefs of Staff Henry Shelton called it "an overwhelming success."[24]

Considering the clear limitation on the effectiveness of the operation imposed by a flawed planning process, unreasonable expectations of easy and quick success, and the absence of a meaningful ground threat until the very end of the campaign, these accolades were both excessive and dangerous. They continued to stoke the growing expectation that airpower alone could defeat any enemy, and added fuel to the struggle between the Air Force and the other services in the ongoing defense budget battles.

The Air Force leadership was, in fact, shameless in its use of Kosovo to defend specific modernization programs, particularly the F-22 (under attack in Congress then as now).[25] *Air Force Magazine* declared, "Hand in hand with the military lesson learned is its hardware counterpart: The Air Force has to have the F-22. 'Sure, we did OK against some MiG-29s that came out,' [Air Force Chief of Staff] Ryan allowed, 'but if you look at system vs. system, we need the next generation of air superiority to clean them out.'"[26] In an article entitled, "Are We Ready To Lose the Next Air War?," published five weeks after Milosevic's capitulation, the Acting Air Force Secretary F. Whitten Peters declared, "Operation Allied Force in the skies over Kosovo illustrated that air superiority is the foundation for victory on land, at sea and in the air. As we rapidly deploy decisive combat forces from the United States to the scene of hostilities, fighter jets will be the first to arrive. They will help us deter an adversary from attacking and, if deterrence fails, to fight on the ground and in the air, and win. The F-22 will guarantee success in these vital missions for decades to come."[27] The implication that Kosovo proved the need for the F-22 was both clear and totally unsupported by the events of that campaign. Once again, the exaggerations of some radical airpower enthusiasts and the politicization of the process of learning lessons from Kosovo distorted the real lessons badly.

One of those lessons should have been that the Bottom-Up Review force structure was inadequate and unable to support the missions assigned to it. Operation Allied Force badly overstretched the Air Force. Failures to stockpile munitions adequately led to critical shortages—one month into the campaign there were only 690 JDAMs (precision-guided bombs) in the arsenal.[28] The air campaign ultimately required the deployment of more than 730 U.S. aircraft, including 323 strike aircraft—

about one-third of the total number of strike aircraft in the active Air Force at the time.[29] The need for so-called "low-density/ high-demand" aircraft like AWACS, reconnaissance and targeting platforms, B-2 bombers, and electronic warfare aircraft used to jam Serbian air defense radars stripped such aircraft from other theaters and required the termination of training in some of those systems for the duration of the conflict. The campaign required the diversion of an aircraft carrier from the Mediterranean and another from the Pacific, leaving Pacific Command temporarily without any aircraft carriers for the first time since the Second World War. The strain on tankers and airlift was also critical. The Air Force was forced to mobilize more than 30,000 reservists, and to cancel the enforcement of one of the Iraqi "no-fly" zones. And all this for a "small scale contingency."[30]

It was very disturbing that an operation such as Allied Force should have so stretched the Air Force's resources. Milosevic's Serbia was in no way a dangerous adversary, and the conflict was primarily an attempt to use airpower to impose a peace-keeping mission—it was not even a "minor regional conflict" in the sense in which the term MRC was usually used. The Bottom-Up Review had assumed that forces capable of conducting two nearly simultaneous MRCs would be easily capable of fulfilling such "smaller" missions, but Kosovo called that assumption into question. The Air Force would have been extremely hard pressed to take on any contingency elsewhere in the world during Allied Force, partly because of the strain on aircrews and attack aircraft, but mainly because of restrictions in the munitions inventory and in "high-demand/low-density" airframes and systems.

There was no lack of commentators calling attention to this problem at the time and subsequently, but the Clinton administration was apparently not interested in learning that particular lesson. The myth was reinforced that the U.S. military as structured in 1999 could fight and win two nearly-simultaneous

MRCs and handle the necessary peacekeeping missions, despite the clear problems Allied Force made visible. As with the notion that airpower had won and could win "wars" all by itself without any assistance from the ground, the conviction that a military designed to meet an arbitrary budget ceiling could necessarily manage the tasks assigned to it also persisted despite substantial evidence to the contrary. In both cases, learning the real lessons of the conflicts of the 1990s was simply too hard to do.

CHAPTER SIX

Transformation in a Strategic Pause

IN THE 1990s the armed forces spent much more time and effort talking about and claiming to be engaged in transformation than the military had in the 1960s and 1970s, but with far less result. There were so many articles, conferences, books, and speeches about transformation and the new revolution in military affairs that the terms themselves became meaningless and almost ridiculous. A letter to the editor of *Parameters*, the Army's professional journal, in the late 1990s offered a method for selecting random phrases from six columns to form sentences that sounded like they might have come from military writings about transformation without meaning anything. Experimenting with this method produced results as humorous as they were frighteningly realistic. It seemed impossible to find any military literature in the period that was not studded with words like "dominant," "precise," "agile," "focused," "synergistic," "system of systems," and "the power of information."

The differences between the transformation of the 1970s and the "transformation" of the 1990s went beyond verbiage, however. In the 1970s, as we have seen, the military saw a series of clear and imminent threats to which it had to respond. It reacted to obvious challenges from particular enemies and to problems it expected to face in certain theaters (like the Persian Gulf). It considered a number of particular technical, doctrinal, organizational, and personnel challenges as well. How could U.S. forces defeat numerically superior Warsaw Pact troops? How could the armed forces transition from a draftee to a volunteer force? How could current U.S. aircraft or tanks be improved to compete with their Soviet counterparts? These and other obvious and straightforward questions formed the basis for a massive transformation of the military.

Although responding to each of these challenges was difficult, it was much easier than attempting a transformation in the absence of any clear meaningful threats. In this regard, the intellectual problem facing military leaders in the 1990s was much more daunting than the one that was overcome in the 1970s. Even so, with a handful of exceptions, the political and military leadership in the 1990s made little serious effort to determine whether there were any clear problems that the military had to solve, or obvious threats that might emerge against which forces could be tailored.

There is virtually no example in history of a revolution in military affairs conducted successfully in such a strategic vacuum. Without considering potential enemies or, at least, likely specific military problems that must be solved, it is extremely unlikely that a military can choose a transformation path successfully. The lack of any meaningful threat, moreover, removes the urgency that provides the necessary pressure to choose well and to support the effort properly. Transformation becomes both an intellectual and a budgetary luxury.

This is exactly the problem that bedeviled the U.S. military in the 1990s. A number of senior leaders were taken by the theory that the world was moving from the "industrial" into the "information" age, and that militaries that did not "transform" to respond to this transition would be left hopelessly behind. This ideology provided nearly the only intellectually coherent basis for transformation. Budgetary considerations, as we have seen, were generally much more powerful. The "peace dividends" that had already ravaged the services also put them at each other's throats for limited defense dollars. Worst of all, the focus on inter-service rivalry for inadequate defense budgets led to regression in the quality of airpower theory, and to the introduction of enormous confusion into the Army's understanding of land warfare. Although the transformation efforts of the 1990s did produce certain advances in particular capabilities, therefore, they represented a fundamentally wrong turn in the history of U.S. military development, and laid the groundwork for the major problems America encountered in the wake of September 11.

ARMY TRANSFORMATION IN THE 1990S

The Army has been the target of transformation enthusiasts since the end of the Gulf War. Repeatedly, advocates of airpower or simply of defense cuts have argued that the Army never adapted its "Cold War" force structure to the new international realities and was unwilling to change its way of thinking about war to accord with the information age. Ironically, the Army was the service that moved most quickly to adopt an entirely new paradigm for thinking about war, and that attempted to make the most changes in its way of organizing, equipping, training, and preparing for combat. The problem was not that the Army was insufficiently "transformational." The problem was its critics, who were so opposed to landpower to begin with that the Army could have done nothing to persuade them of its relevance, whatever changes it made.

As we have seen, Army Chief of Staff General Gordon Sullivan began a significant effort to transform the Army in the immediate wake of the Gulf War. That effort rested on a lengthy set of a assumptions, of which the most important were: that the world was moving from the "industrial age" to the "information age," as Alvin Toffler had claimed in his book, *The Third Wave*; that the U.S. faced no easily discernable threats at the moment or in the future; that OOTW would be a major part of the Army's mission for decades to come; and that the Army needed to be more readily deployable in order to stay relevant in come-as-you-are wars.

In the early 1980s, Toffler had applied a neo-Marxist historical view to argue that human civilization had proceeded from the "agrarian" to the "industrial age," and was then moving into the "information age," an era dominated by revolutionary changes in economic structures resulting from computerization.[1] Toffler argued, for instance, that computerization allowed the consumer to participate directly in production, thus becoming a "prosumer"—a clear riff on the Marxist notion of transforming the relationship between the proletarian and the means of production. The prominence of the Marxist influence in this vision lent irony to the enthusiasm with which Cold Warriors like Sullivan embraced it.

But Sullivan did not notice or care about the Marxism of *The Third Wave*—he cared about the trend toward the dominance of information systems that Toffler described. He began by reinterpreting recent military history in light of Toffler's theory:

> In our most recent major conflict, Operation Desert Storm, Iraq lost the war before it even began. This was a war of information, intelligence, electronic warfare, command and control, and counter-intelligence. The Iraqi forces were totally overwhelmed by the superiority of our technology. Desert Storm proved for the first time that modern wars will be won through the effective use of command, control, communications, computers and intelligence . . . technology.[2]

In another article, he laid out the third-wave theory directly:

> Today, we are at the threshold of a new era, and we must proceed into it decisively. The industrial age is being superseded by the information age—the third wave— hard on the heels of the agrarian and industrial eras. Our present Army is well configured to fight and win in the late industrial age, and we can handle agrarian-age foes as well. We have begun to move into third-wave warfare, to evolve a new force for a new century—Force XXI. Force XXI will synthesize the science of computer technology, the art of integrating doctrine and organization, and the optimization of our quality people. The goal is to create new formations that operate at even greater performance levels in speed, space and time. Force XXI . . . will use command and control technology to leverage the power of the information age.[3]

To support these insights, the Army promised in 1994 to field a "digitized" (one might almost say "Tofflerized") brigade by 1996 and a "digitized" division by 1998.[4]

The validity of the "third wave" theory is open to debate. Some continue to believe in it; some never accepted it; others were disenchanted following the technology bust of the late 1990s. The revisionist interpretation of the Gulf War, however, cannot be supported by the facts. In the most exemplary engagement of that war—73 Easting, to which Sullivan and other Army leaders frequently referred—information technology played virtually no role. The tactical commander at that battle, then-Captain H. R. McMaster, had poor situational awareness. He did not know that he was driving into an Iraqi mechanized ambush. Indeed, he did not even have a decent map of the area and was unaware that he was driving across the desert parallel to a road. Once the shooting began, he played little role in commanding or controlling the developing action. As he himself has repeatedly explained, the excellent training of the soldiers enabled them to operate on their own without waiting to receive instructions from him. And although technology was important, it was the technology of Chobham armor, stabilized weapons, and depleted-uranium rounds—not the technology of the infoworld. To see in this or any of the other ground battles of the Gulf War evidence that the war was won, as Sullivan claimed, by superior information technology, is sheer fantasy.

The truth is simply that the Army leadership of the early 1990s was captured by an idea. This is not that unusual a phenomenon. Robert McNamara brought with him into the Pentagon a belief in the value of "systems analysis" that still dominates portions of the lengthy corridors in the building. The Army of the mid-nineteenth century was so taken with a misreading of Napoleonic history that its officers were frequently portrayed with one hand tucked into the breasts of their service jackets (whose cut was spectacularly ill-suited for the gesture), in imitation of the classic Napoleonic pose. Intellectual fads are no less prevalent or influential in the military than they are anywhere else in American society. Such fads can take root and germinate much more rapidly, however, in the absence of a clear threat against which the Army must be prepared. And the Army of the 1990s simply had no idea about what contingencies it would have to be ready for.

Sullivan made this confusion clear in an article published near the end of his tenure:

> We must have an idea of what the world will look like in the next century, and we must have a vision of America's Army-trained and ready, a strategic force, serving the nation at home and abroad, capable of decisive victory,

today and in the 21st Century. . . . Much of what lies ahead is difficult to define precisely. We cannot know with absolute certainty what the mission will be or who the enemy will be, but we do know that our nation will expect us to deliver victory—decisive victory—at whatever task the Army is called on to perform.[5]

An Army publication of August 1994 designed to think deep thoughts about Army transformation made this strategic uncertainty crystal clear:

Most of the conflicts involving the U.S. Army will be OOTW or low-intensity conflicts, as few states will risk open war with the U.S. However, the specter of open war against foes fielding advanced, armor-mech-based armies must be considered. At this point, we can identify regions —*not specific countries*—where the conditions to facilitate or cause high-intensity conflict or overt military challenges to U.S. interests exist.[6]

Although completely uncertain about whom they might be fighting, the authors of this pamphlet were very certain that any future war would require "*spectrum supremacy*—a key element of information operations. While control of the entire electromagnetic spectrum is impossible, key portions must be commanded most of the time."[7] How is it possible to know for certain what the nature of war will be without having any idea of where or when it might be fought? Tofflerism, with its Marxist historical determinism that promised accurate prediction of the future, went deep into the Army's intellectual core quickly.

As before, the constant repetition of the importance of OOTW in future conflicts did not lead to any particularly deep thoughts about how to conduct such operations. Most Army transformation literature treated them as lesser included missions and saw the third wave as a rising tide that would float all of the Army's boats. The Army's leaders were somewhat more specific about the need to make the force more rapidly deployable, although here, too, they were hard-pressed to find meaningful answers.

Thus the Army's Deputy Chief of Staff for Operations and Plans (DCSOPS—one of the most powerful officers on the Army staff) argued that the Army needed to develop the ability to move

- A light brigade anywhere in the world within four days.

- A light division anywhere in the world within twelve days.

- A heavy brigade (prepositioned afloat) anywhere in the world within fifteen days.

- Two heavy divisions from the continental United States anywhere in the world within thirty days.

- A five-division corps with support anywhere in the world within seventy-five days.[8]

These were laudable and, indeed, important goals, but the DCSOPS could suggest no way of achieving them other than having the Air Force and the Navy buy a lot more strategic lift—something neither service was keen to do, particularly in the midst of a dramatic budget draw-down. Enmeshed in its own budget fight, however, and committed to a Tofflerite vision of future warfare, the Army could not afford to think seriously about finding its own ways of solving this problem either. There just was not enough "transformation" funding both to digitize the force and to explore ways of making it more readily deployable. As a result, the problem was not even moving in the general direction of a solution in the 1990s.

The outcome of these reflections and deliberations was the

Force XXI project, firmly established in 1994. This project was focused entirely on "digitizing" the Army by adding computerization and communications systems that would link the most senior general to the most junior lieutenant (or, perhaps, private, depending on the vision). The goals of this effort were to allow the Army as a system to gather and disseminate an enormous amount of information, thereby letting all Army leaders develop the best possible understanding of the "battlespace" (a new term coined to bring "battlefield" into the twenty-first century). The Army's leaders would then use this superb understanding of the battlespace to make their plans and then would use the excellent communications at their disposal to make sure that all of their subordinates fully understood their intentions and the context within which they had been developed. In concrete terms, this meant welding laptop computers into M1 tank turrets and developing "vest-pocket" computers for infantrymen to wear, as well as an enormous effort expended on building a battlefield intranet to allow all of these systems to talk to one another seamlessly.

There was a certain amount of discussion about using the new information technology to "flatten the Army hierarchy" by empowering subordinates to make their own decisions based on the improved situational awareness they would possess— possibly to the extent of removing some echelons of command. Colonel Doug MacGregor, a veteran of the Gulf War (where he was the squadron executive officer accompanying Captain McMaster at 73 Easting), took up this theme emphatically in his 1997 book, *Breaking the Phalanx*.

MacGregor used historical examples and examples taken from the business world to argue that the expanded use of information technology would allow the Army to eliminate both corps and division headquarters. The goal was to create brigade-sized units, which MacGregor called groups, with a series of specific advantages aimed in part at solving current problems and in part at leading the way toward future-oriented transformation.

The groups would be able to deploy and sustain themselves without additional resources drawn from higher headquarters. This capability would have been a dramatic change from the status quo, since 1990s brigades required significant augmentation from support troops maintained at division and corps headquarters. As a result, it was extremely difficult to deploy a single brigade from a division without dramatically degrading the capabilities of the other two brigades that were not deploying. The ongoing peacekeeping operation in Bosnia was making this problem apparent as MacGregor was writing; the deployment to Kosovo following Operation Allied Force only reinforced its importance.

MacGregor's groups were also designed to operate more effectively in a joint environment, since their command and staff structures would include joint representation and the ability to communicate effectively with units from other services—a great increase in capability over brigades of the 1990s. The groups would also combine arms—infantry, armor, aviation, artillery, etc.—more effectively than 1990s brigades. Critics complained that the groups looked a lot like armored cavalry regiments (ACRs), which also incorporated all arms much more effectively than regular mechanized or light infantry brigades at the time. MacGregor and his defenders pointed out both the differences between the groups and ACRs, which were substantial, and the advantages ACRs had demonstrated in the Gulf War as combat formations.

Above all, MacGregor believed that eliminating division and corps headquarters would allow the Army to become much more responsive. Allowing a Joint Task Force (JTF) Commander, like Schwarzkopf in the Gulf War, and his staff to control combat groups directly, MacGregor believed, would eliminate two layers of command that generally slowed down decision-making. In its own way, *Breaking the Phalanx* was an attempt to reduce the internal friction within the Army that Boyd had identified as a major factor preventing a force from "getting inside the enemy's decision cycle."

MacGregror's ideas did not gain traction within the Army leadership, although the opposition never really mustered meaningful arguments against them. The reaction seems to have been more emotional—the prospect of disestablishing the Army's divisions struck at fundamental service traditions, the promotion system, and the entire way the Army thought about itself. Despite official publications calling for precisely the capabilities MacGregor had described, it appears that his outsider status and the prospect of shattering the Army's self-image prevented an objective evaluation of his proposals.

Even without the flattened hierarchy and other advantages MacGregor proposed, however, the idea of digitally linking all of the soldiers and commanders on the battlefield, allowing them to share information and to develop a common picture of the engagement, is in principle an excellent one. It is certainly easy to imagine that an army that achieves that goal will have gained a significant advantage over an army that does not. The development of such a system faces a number of inherently daunting challenges beyond the mere technical, of course. In particular, it is also easy to imagine the senior commander's head exploding from the sheer volume of information with which he could potentially be flooded. Giving the senior commander the ability to see the battle through the eyes of a private runs a variety of serious risks of another sort, including increasing the danger of micromanaging and distracting the senior commander from his primary task of managing the battle overall. Most brigade commanders, for example, are certain that they could maneuver a platoon better than any lieutenant. Without a fundamental change in the Army's training and education programs (which the authors of this transformation vision repeatedly insisted upon, to be sure), these dangers were not small.

Intriguing as it was, however, it was very far from being clear that the digitization of the Army should have been the priority transformation program of the 1990s. The leaders of that program never identified any specific problem that such a transformation would solve, still less any particular enemy it might help defeat then or in the future. They did not generally place the digitization concept within any meaningful vision of U.S. strategy or grand strategy, or even within the context of joint warfighting. The historical references used to support the importance of the concept were either facile or just plain wrong, and the Redland vs. Blueland nature of the experimental exercises were reminiscent of the British experiments with mechanization of the 1920s—experiments that led nowhere because of their total failure to mesh with national military strategy or solve any visible strategic problem Britain was likely to face.

It is worth pointing out still another problem with the exercises conducted in the 1990s: they all posited a transformed force defeating an untransformed foe. In no case did the experiments attempt to pit two digitized forces against one another on the assumption that the capabilities to field such transformed forces would spread beyond the U.S. and its allies.

This is an important point. The nature of revolutions in military affairs is that they spread over time to all of the major powers of the world. One has only to consider the rapid spread of gunpowder, rifles, railroads, tanks, airplanes, and ICBMs to realize that the originator of such a revolution can count on a certain limited period of monopoly of the technology, but, if the technology really does lead to a fundamental change in the nature of warfare, other major powers will inevitably, usually fairly rapidly, copy it.

The revolution in warfare occasioned by the use of railroads is perhaps the most apposite to the information revolution, since, like the "third wave," it required an enormous investment in infrastructure as well as a transformation in doctrine, organization, and planning procedures in order to use. The Prussians led the way in Europe toward the fielding of a railroad army, beginning aggressively in the 1840s. But their advantage was brief. By the 1850s, all of the major continental powers were building up their own railroad nets and general staff planning cells to make use of them. In 1866 and 1870 the Prussians made use of their initial lead in the technology to defeat Austria and France respectively, but by the 1880s, the German general staff no longer believed that it had any significant advantage in railroad mobilization capabilities over its likely enemies. In a similar fashion, the extensive use of the internet by al Qaeda and China's aggressive efforts to hack into U.S. computer systems highlight the determination with which enemies and potential enemies today seek to exploit the same technologies that now give American military forces their advantage in "information warfare."

If it is true that digitization will transform warfare, then it is equally true that other states will seek to develop similar capabilities over time. Techniques developed to use a digitized force against a non-digitized enemy will probably not succeed against a digitized enemy. This is not to say that the Army should not have conducted experiments to test the value of digitizing in the first place (assuming that they were conducted and evaluated honestly enough to make them a meaningful test of the proposition). But those experiments should have evolved rapidly to include thinking about how enemies might respond and what counter-responses might be necessary. Instead, the Army moved in the direction of trying to develop a system that could never be copied and that would provide an indefinite (and nearly infinite) advantage over all foes far into the future. This approach misread the history and dynamics of military transformation very badly, and led to a failure to think the "information" transformation through to its conclusions.

★   ★   ★

THE TRANSFORMATION MOVEMENT
GATHERS STEAM

As the Army moved along its chosen course toward transforming for the "information revolution," senior military leaders
and defense analysts were applying similar principles to the military as a whole. In the mid-1990s a growing number of official
and unofficial defense studies argued that an information Revolution in Military Affairs was underway, that the U.S. could
derive nearly infinite advantages from pursuing it, and that the
failure to "respond" would leave American forces increasingly
vulnerable over time. Once again, although some of these studies
used simplistic scenarios to "prove" their thesis, none asserted
that any particular state had or was developing the capabilities
needed to threaten the U.S. with "information age" warfare.
Advocates of this RMA vision asserted, instead, that the development of such threats was both inevitable and fairly imminent, thus adding a sense of urgency to their demands for the
reprogramming of defense funds and the massive reorganization of the U.S. military.

Dominant Battlefield Awareness

One of the earliest of these studies was *Dominant Battlespace
Knowledge*.[9] This edited volume, published in 1995 by the
National Defense University Press and with an introduction by
the Vice Chairman of the Joint Chiefs of Staff Admiral Bill
Owens, lent a semi-official gloss to the concept that was its title
and its subject. Ostensibly a project to evaluate the utility of
"dominant battlespace knowledge" (DBK), the volume was, in
fact, a polemical call for the immediate development of such a
capability.

Dominant Battlespace Knowledge offered no clear definition of the concept it proposed to describe. The closest the volume came to such a definition was in Admiral Owens's introduction:

> What is happening, driven in part by broad conceptual architectures, in part by serendipity, is the creation of a new *system of systems*. Merging our increasing capacity to gather real-time, all-weather information continuously with our increasing capacity to process and make sense of this voluminous data builds the realm of dominant battlespace knowledge (DBK). Dominant Battlespace Knowledge involves everything from automated target recognition to knowledge of an opponent's operational scheme and the networks relied on to pursue that scheme. The result will be an increasing gap between U.S. military forces and any opponent in awareness and understanding of everything of military significance in any arena in which we may be engaged.[10]

The lack of a clear definition bedeviled the rest of the work, for although a number of contributors noted that DBK did not require "perfect" intelligence, none of them explained how "near-perfect" it had to be.

Although the basic impetus for DBK came from the contributors' belief that an RMA was unstoppably underway, a number of them offered another point of departure to support their case. The U.S. defense budget was simply too small, they argued, to sustain a military able to accomplish the national security strategy at an acceptable level of risk in the traditional way. Proceeding from the assumption that constrained defense budgets would be the norm indefinitely into the future, they argued that the military could only fulfill its purpose if it operated more efficiently. Dominant Battlespace Knowledge, they argued, was the key to that efficiency.

The model for such an increase in efficiency through the use of information technology came from business. The changes in the way large corporations organized themselves and functioned in response to growing computerization and improved communications offered an example, they believed, that the military should follow. One contributor went so far as to coin the term "just-in-time war" modeled on the "just-in-time" principle then in vogue in which businesses relied on perfect knowledge of their stocks and customer demands and the ability to produce products quickly on request to keep inventories to an absolute minimum. The near-perfect intelligence and computerized decision-making aids that made DBK possible, they argued, would allow small forces to fight efficiently, eliminate the need for inefficient reserves, and obviate the necessity to maintain large and expensive stockpiles of equipment and ammunition.

Above all, however, DBK would provide certain victory in any future war. U.S. forces would acquire vast amounts of information from ground- and air-based sensors of all varieties, "fuse" this information using sophisticated computerized decision-making aids that could determine which of the blips appearing on the radar were targets and transmit that information immediately to weapons of all kinds that could destroy them. The computers would be able to determine automatically, in fact, which weapons were best suited by location and specifications to attack which targets. Targeting would therefore become almost completely efficient, still further reducing the number of forces required for defeating a given enemy.

In some cases, the arguments advanced were naïve and simplistic:

The October 1994 feint by Iraqi divisions toward the Kuwait border involved about 1,700 armored vehicles. What could we do with air power if we had the right munitions and knowledge of the location of the armored vehicles? With enough warning time to deploy 200 U.S. aircraft to the theater — combined land and sea based — and four antiarmor munitions per aircraft, at two sorties per day, and Pk [probability of kill] of .5, *then up to 800 armored vehicles could have been killed on day one of the attack.*[11]

The author did not consider the possibility that there might be other targets that U.S. aircraft might need to attack—enemy air defenses, for instance—or that the locations of all of the tanks might not be perfectly known (granted, an assumption of DBK), or that the enemy might disperse his vehicles so that each aircraft could not use all four of its bombs, or the enemy might take any sort of other counter-measures. Other portions of the argument were more sophisticated, including an admission that DBK was not likely to be available or effective in insurgencies. The task of distinguishing friend from foe by remote sensors in such situations, one contributor admitted, was probably beyond the ability of any foreseeable technology.[12]

Dominant Battlespace Knowledge was unrealistic about the ability of military organizations to reorganize rapidly as well. To take full advantage of the technology and the capability it offered, the authors argued, would require a wholesale transformation of military and service culture and organization. Like MacGregor, they saw the military's hierarchical command and control structure as a hindrance to the efficiency DBK promised, but unlike him, they proposed to create instead a "networked" organization in which both information and orders flowed horizontally as well as vertically, and in which subordinate humans and even weapons systems were empowered to act autonomously—and they thought that such an organization was achievable by 2008, twelve years after the publication of the book.

It is astonishing that senior officers and experienced defense analysts could imagine that the U.S. military could completely transform its operating culture, along with its organization, a little more than a decade after first announcing an idea. Even assuming that the military had adopted the ideas in DBK instantly and completely in 1996, in 2008, all commanders from battalion up, all ship-, squadron-, and wing-commanders would still be officers whose understanding of their profession and service had been formed in the pre-RMA military. The likelihood that all, or even a substantial fraction of them, could have completely changed their understanding of how the military should function within a decade was nil. This failure to take the human dimension into account was one fatal flaw in the Dominant Battlespace Knowledge proposal.

Another more fundamental flaw was that DBK saw war as not merely a targeting drill, but a targeting drill aimed at attriting the enemy's fielded forces. The whole thrust of the work was that DBK would allow the U.S. to locate, identify, target, and destroy all of the enemy's weapons systems throughout the battlespace. When enough had been destroyed, the authors argued, then the war would be over—whatever the political objectives of either side might have been. The consideration of political objectives, in fact, played virtually no role in the DBK discussion. Once again, DBK was an effort to template all future conflict and find a single concept of operations that would serve all possible contingencies (apart, perhaps, from insurgency). It did so by equating victory with the destruction of the enemy's fielded forces.

This equation allowed the authors of DBK to argue for a numerical approach to planning and to victory:

In a military setting timely responsiveness would be measured by decision cycle time, time lost awaiting decisions, percent deliveries on time, etc. Efficiency is measured by cost per kill, kill probability per weapon, the number of sorties per day, etc. Knowledge transfer is analogous to information availability and intelligence and is measured by the ability to connect sensors and weapons, to interlink reconnaissance systems, and to check against faulty data.[13]

Such measurements are meaningful for Department of Defense bean-counters concerned with keeping defense budgets down, and with McNamara-era systems analysts eager to find precise measurements of the progress of a war. They are not, however, indicators of progress toward victory, which is "measured" in the will of the enemy to continue to resist, in the will of one's own people, soldiers, and government to continue to fight, and in a variety of other tangible and intangible (and therefore unmeasurable) elements.

Dominant Battlespace Knowledge nevertheless helped ingrain into U.S. defense thinking the notion that the "information RMA" was well underway and would progress inevitably, whatever the U.S. did. Admiral Owens wrote,

This new system-of-systems capability is at the heart of the American revolution in military affairs (RMA). . . . This transition is inevitable, but the speed at which we complete it depends on recognition of what is emerging and on our defense planning and programming decisions over the next several years. If we decide to accelerate the transition, it can be completed early in the next century. We could therefore be on the other side of this new revolution in military affairs years, perhaps decades, before any other nation. This is important for many reasons; one of the most significant is that completing the revolution offers us the opportunity to shape the international environment, rather than simply react to it.[14]

There is a subtle but important misreading of military history in this assertion. At root, such an argument assumes that RMAS result from naturally-occurring changes in basic technology, that they progress inevitably and inexorably, and that they are effectively independent of the decisions that individual military and political leaders make. Those decisions might make the RMA come sooner or later in one country or another, but they can neither change the nature of the RMA nor prevent it from occurring.

The evidence against this notion is overwhelming. The Chinese had gunpowder for centuries before it transformed the way their armies fought. The same technology—rapid-firing artillery and machine guns—that transformed warfare on the Western Front in World War I had not transformed it fundamentally in the Russo-Japanese War (where open flanks allowed maneuver to continue), on the Eastern Front (where the Germans made several advances of hundreds of miles), nor did it transform the Russo-Polish or Russian Civil Wars that followed (in which rapid and deep advances were also common), despite the possession by all sides of similar technology. It is even questionable how much the "nuclear revolution" transformed warfare, since nuclear weapons have never been used (the Hiroshima and Nagasaki bombs were atomic), and conventional warfare during the Cold War proceeded along a continuous and recognizable developmental path of its own, even under the nuclear shadow. This technology-based RMA model also ignores the transformation in warfare during the French Revolution and Napoleonic eras in which technological change played virtually no role at all.

It turns out that individual decision-makers have a great deal to do with whether or not an RMA comes about. The British, French, Germans, and Russians all built tanks after World War I (all but the Russians, in fact, built and used them during the war). The ways in which the British and French prepared to use them during the Interwar Years were far from revolutionary, but the ideas of von Seeckt, Guderian, Tukhachevski, Triandafillov, and others led to military transformation in Germany and the Soviet Union. The technological capabilities embodied in DBK can be used in a revolutionary fashion, perhaps, but they can also be used simply to support traditional ways of waging war. It was far from inevitable in the mid-1990s, as it is still far from inevitable, that if the U.S. does not pioneer a particular way of using these capabilities, someone else will. Nor is it clear that pioneering such a revolutionary approach will lead to ultimate success—the British, after all, invented the tank, but they not only failed to develop an appropriate doctrine for using it, they could not even build a combat-worthy tank by World War II. British armored forces in Normandy and elsewhere rode American Shermans.

But the RMA bug had infected the armed forces, the Clinton administration, and Congress. Its attractiveness ranged from the promise of quick, decisive, and bloodless (from the U.S. perspective) wars to the prospect of even lower defense budgets buying revolutionary, dominant military power. A similarly attractive image of war emerged from an intellectual successor to Warden's ideas—"Shock and Awe."

Shock and Awe

In 1996, Harlan Ullman and James P. Wade published a study called *Shock and Awe: Achieving Rapid Dominance* that attempted to lay out a new paradigm for U.S. defense planning.[15] Like the authors of Dominant Battlespace Knowledge, Ullman and Wade proceeded from the assumptions that the U.S. was in an era of constrained defense resources, that it faced a decade or more without the likelihood of a serious threat developing and could therefore safely transform itself, and that information technology was revolutionizing warfare. Ullman and Wade also argued that the military would increasingly be called upon to undertake OOTW missions, and that any paradigm for future war had to support such operations.

The core argument in *Shock and Awe* was a simplification of Warden's concepts. Ullman and Wade advocated using military force to achieve direct effects on the enemy's leadership rather than to attrit the enemy's fielded forces. They naturally preferred to use long range air- and seapower, although they acknowledged (as Warden had in *The Air Campaign*) that ground forces could play a role, if only in "mopping up" operations.

But Ullman and Wade diverged from Warden on a number of key points. First, their analysis did not make explicit use of the centers of gravity framework that Warden developed. As a result, they offered no detailed consideration about how to select what critical targets to hit and destroy, and their targeting advice was often reduced to exhortations to hit things the enemy cared about and hit them hard. Second, their emphasis was not so much on disaggregating the enemy-as-a-system as on using a variety of means, both kinetic and information operations, to blind the enemy and allow him to "see" only what U.S. forces chose.

Ullman and Wade described "Shock and Awe" as the critical capability that would allow U.S. forces to achieve "Rapid Dominance"—the key to future victories. Rapid dominance required four core competencies in the armed forces: "knowledge of self, adversary, and environment; rapidity; brilliance in execution; and control of the environment." The standard for each of these competencies was high: "Knowledge means more than dominant battlefield awareness. It means understanding the adversary's mind and anticipating his reactions. It means targeting those things that will produce the intended *Shock and Awe*. And, it means having feedback and good, timely battle assessment to enable knowledge to be used dynamically as well as to know how our forces will react."

The measure of success in the other areas was also strict: "Rapidity means moving and acting as quickly as necessary and always on a timely basis. Rapidity can be instant or as required." As for brilliance, it meant "achieving the highest standards of operational competence and, through a superiority of knowledge, maintaining the ability to impose *Shock and Awe* through continuously surprising and psychologically and physically breaking the adversary's will to resist." "Control of the environment," finally, included "complete signature control on the entire battle area out to hundreds of miles. We would control our signatures as well as what we wanted the adversary to see or hear and what we do not want the enemy to know. . . . Small units would be able to call in 'fires' for 360 degrees on a nearly instant basis."[16] Like the authors of DBK, Ullman and Wade were far too sanguine about the ability to achieve these standards in the near future—or at all.

Shock and Awe and DBK suffered from a major technical problem. Many theorists in the 1990s measured the information revolution incorrectly. They focused on the extremely rapid improvements in computer hardware and extrapolated based on that rapidity. They tended not to notice that improvements in software were much slower and less predictable. It turns out, in fact, that making computer components with particular technical characteristics is fairly easy, but designing computer programs to make those computers do what people want them to do is much harder. One of the contributors to DBK alluded to this fact, but most of the information RMA advocates took for granted that the improvement of the technical specifications of computer and communications systems would carry over quickly into improvements in their functional capabilities.

This mistake was one of several fatal errors in these theories. Both DBK and Shock and Awe relied completely on the development of computerized decision aids to handle the enormous amount of information that the floods of sensors they wanted to deploy would generate. Without those decision aids, human commanders would simply be overwhelmed by the data and even less able to operate with the information RMA systems than they had been without them.

None of these studies, furthermore, considered the *certainty* that the software itself would generate fog and errors of its own. As we have seen since the first experiments in cybernetics, the more programmers try to make computers think like people, the more unpredictable and erratic the computers become. And software code itself is not objective or scientific—it is the creative effort of teams of humans, and it contains assumptions, sometimes true, sometimes false, and legacy ways of looking at the world just as any logic system does. The fact that computers can now generate their own software in certain cases only pushes this problem back a step, since the basic assumptions on which they make decisions still flow from the human authors of the software-writing code. The impossibility of creating perfect software will inevitably combine with errors generated by sensors operating in the real world—and with deliberate attempts by the enemy to mislead those sensors—to induce fog and friction of a new variety. This is a problem for the long term, however, since in the short-term it seems extremely unlikely that anyone will be able to write the code necessary for the complex and subtle decisions that the authors of *Dominant Battlespace Knowledge* and *Shock and Awe* required of their expert systems.

Although *Shock and Awe* focused heavily on the need to adapt the information revolution for OOTW, it offered few meaningful suggestions for how to do so. The most specific recommendation ran as follows:

In OOTW, the Rapid Dominance JTF [Joint Task Force] might function as follows. First, the ability to deploy dominant force rapidly to attack or threaten to attack appropriate targets could be brought to bear without involving manpower-intense or manned sensors and weapons. Second, once deployed, since self-defense is likely to be required against small arms, mines, and shoulder carried or mortar weapons, certainly some form of "armor" or protective vehicles and shelters would be necessary. However, through the UAVs, C4I, and virtual reality systems, as well as through signature management and other Shock and Awe weapons including High Powered Microwave (HPM) and "stun-like" systems, this force would have more than dominant battlefield awareness.[17]

This example treats OOTW as a form of small-scale combat waged with tight political constraints, rather than the very different form of operation it actually is. At no point did Ullman and Wade make clear how the U.S. could use Shock and Awe in OOTW situations apart from Decisive Force-type missions. They seemed, in fact, to confuse those missions, which were combat operations designed to set the stage for OOTW, for the OOTW mission itself, which followed the air campaign.

This implicit assumption may have reflected the fact that many military officers and a certain number of military historians believe that "real" war is unlimited, or total, while war fought under significant political restrictions is really an "operation other than war" that should be avoided.[18] This principle is encapsulated in the Weinberger and Powell doctrines that call for the application of overwhelming force if any force is to be used at all. Ullman and Wade specifically reject this approach to war, arguing that the U.S. cannot afford to maintain the capability to confront the enemy with overwhelming power in force-on-force engagements, but they seemed unable, even with the OOTW part of the Bosnia mission occurring as they wrote, to see OOTW as anything other than a struggle between armed forces. For all of its flaws, however, Shock and Awe and many of its embedded concepts appealed strongly to important sections of the military and policy community, and even influenced the planning and course of subsequent military operations, as we shall see.

Halt Phase

The community of airpower enthusiasts had split in the wake of the Gulf War, although few in the defense community took notice of the cleavage. Some, like Ullman and Wade, adopted an approach based on Warden's ideas of attacking the enemy-as-a-system. Others, like Les Aspin, focused instead on the use of advanced targeting and precision technologies to attack the enemy's fielded forces. As Ullman and Wade were "updating" (really watering-down) Warden's theories for the 1990s, a number of "halt phase" enthusiasts were carrying Aspin's concepts forward as well.

One the most articulate exponents of this vision was retired Air Force Major General Charles Link, who laid out his notion of "halt phase" in a series of debates with landpower defenders Army Major General Robert H. Scales and retired Marine Lieutenant General Paul Van Riper. Link's argument was based explicitly on the Korean scenario and particularly on a problem he had noticed with the way the military modeled that scenario. Relying on outdated notions of how aircraft would be used in modern war, Link argued, the military's simulators drastically underestimated the effectiveness of airpower in attriting a North Korean attack. He blamed this underestimation, in part, on a naïve understanding of "jointness" that emphasized the importance of having all services take part in operations. True jointness, he argued, meant using the service that was best for the job, and for the task of stopping a North Korean invasion, that service was definitely the Air Force.

When he had adjusted the military simulators to reflect "real-world" capabilities, Link found that airpower alone would so reduce the combat power of the North Koreans that they would not even be able to reach Seoul before collapsing. He put the matter bluntly:

> I suggest that the crux of the issue is whether modern aerospace forces—the forces we have today and will have in 2006—actually can constrain or deny land forces freedom of action. I suggest they can. More important, can modern aerospace forces attrit moving enemy forces faster than those forces can accumulate mass on the objective? Once again, I tell you they can. If our aerospace forces can accomplish these goals, should we not choose to go for it?[19]

Link declared that the point at which the enemy was halted was the critical turning point in the operation: "At that point, the North Koreans are halted short of their objective."[20] The U.S. could then decide whether to begin a ground counterattack, to impose sanctions on the enemy to force his final capitulation or simply proceed with "dismantling him with aerospace power." There would be no urgency about choosing any of these options, moreover: "If you buy the capability to do two simultaneous halts, you should not care when the second one starts because once you have accomplished the second halt, you can schedule the counteroffensives at your convenience."[21]

The lack of political perspective and even of military reality in this image is breathtaking. One could argue that after the failure of the Schlieffen Plan in 1914, the French and British had succeeded in halting the Germans short of their objectives, and could then schedule the counter-offensive more or less at their leisure. It did not appear so to French leaders who had to contemplate German occupation of their territory, and invaded

U.S. allies are also likely to take a dim view of a long delay between halting the enemy and driving him out of their states. Although Link assured his listeners that the period following the halt was not a stalemate, one has to admit that it might look very much like a stalemate to regional leaders who do not see the U.S. forces necessary to repulse an invader who has merely been stopped.

Another problem is that, especially in the Korean case, the margin of error is extremely narrow. What if U.S. forces do not arrive in the theater in time to halt the North Koreans before they get to Seoul? If North Korean troops actually took all or part of the South Korean capital and then dug in there, it is not at all clear that Link's strategy of pounding on them from the air would be effective. It is at least possible that such an eventuality would lead to the collapse of the South Koreans' will to continue the fight, leading, perhaps, to some more or less unacceptable compromise solution.

If Link had been advocating developing this capability in tandem with the ability to stop a North Korean advance immediately with ground forces, or in the context of a rapid ground forces build-up, it would be unobjectionable. Obviously, the U.S. should be able to inflict as much harm on an invading force as possible from the earliest moment. But the whole thrust of the presentation was to emphasize the *immorality* of not pursuing "halt phase" to the *exclusion* of ground preparations. Link repeatedly emphasized that the ability to defeat the enemy without putting soldiers in harm's way was tantamount to a moral imperative to do so. He even concluded one of his briefs with a slide that read: "Think about it . . . like a father . . . like a grandfather."

"Halt phase" was a throwback to an attrition-based model of airpower—pure warfare. It focused on attacking the enemy's fielded forces without the aid of friendly ground troops to force them to concentrate or even to move, it posited American capabilities to deploy large numbers of aircraft and their supporting structures to a theater nearly instantly, to fly them at high sortie rates indefinitely, and to supply them with infinite numbers of advanced munitions. It rejected the wisdom of Warden's understanding of airpower's capabilities in favor of an argument that could succeed in the budget battles of the day. Above all, it created a tension within developing airpower theory that few commentators noticed or addressed.

New Defense Reviews

1996 and 1997 saw a considerable amount of intellectual effort expended in re-considering the roles, missions, and, above all, future visions of the services and of the military as a whole. The process was begun by the report of the Commission on Roles and Missions (CORM) in 1995, although that report focused mainly on bureaucratic improvements within the Pentagon and addressed the larger questions of strategy and operational technique only obliquely.[22] Perhaps the most lasting contribution of the CORM was to recommend the institution of a "Quadrennial Strategy Review" at the beginning of each presidential term to assess the capabilities and needs of the armed forces on a regular basis. This proposal ultimately took shape as the Quadrennial Defense Review (QDR) of 1997.

In part as a preparation for that review, the Department of Defense produced *Joint Vision 2010* in 1996, which established the basic requirements that the Pentagon as a whole believed that the military needed to develop. *Joint Vision 2010* led, in turn, to a series of service-specific "visions," including *Army Vision 2010* and *Global Engagement: A Vision of the 21st Century Air Force*.[23] (The Air Force has always had the edge on the Army in flashy names and packaging for its intellectual products, and the few times the Army has tried to contest that edge, as with Maxwell Taylor's "Pentomic Division," have generally been disastrous.)

All three of these vision statements were glossy products full of pictures and graphics and a small number of vague and general words. Reflecting the intense competition for resources and the need felt by all Department of Defense agencies to make themselves appealing to Congress and the public, far too much effort went into the packaging and far too little into the product itself. The need to produce a document that all four services could agree on, in the case of JV2010, or that all of the components of the Army or Air Force could accept, in the case of the service visions, necessarily led to even greater vagueness.

The key to all three visions appeared on the first page of JV2010:

This vision of future warfighting embodies the improved intelligence and command and control available in the information age and goes on to develop four operational concepts: dominant maneuver, precision engagement, full dimensional protection, and focused logistics.

The stated goal of JV2010 was to produce armed forces that would possess "full spectrum dominance," by which was meant the ability to win in every type of conflict from intercontinental war to peacekeeping. The tag-line was: "persuasive in peace, decisive in war, preeminent in any form of conflict." [24]

Once again, the theme of efficiency was prominent in JV2010:

The American people will continue to expect us to win in any engagement, but they will also expect us to be more efficient in protecting lives and resources while accomplishing the mission successfully. . . . Risks and expenditures will be even more closely scrutinized than they are at present.[25]

Whereas this admonition led to calls for increased use of technology in DBK and *Shock and Awe*, JV2010 simply concluded with a pious admonition to the services to be more "joint," equating increased jointness with increased efficiency.

Joint Vision 2010 accepted all of the major assumptions of the transformation theories advanced to date. Its authors professed to have no idea about which enemies the U.S. might face, although they identified the ways in which those nameless enemies might attack American forces. It also accepted the inevitability of the information RMA:

> This era will be one of accelerating technological change. Critical advances will have enormous impact on all military forces. Successful adaptation of new and improved technologies may provide great increases in specific capabilities. Conversely, failure to understand and adapt could lead today's militaries into premature obsolescence and greatly increase the risks that such forces will be incapable of effective operations against forces with high technology.

Joint Vision 2010 then made perfectly clear what technology it had in mind: "Long-range precision capability, combined with a wide range of delivery systems, is emerging as a key factor in future warfare. Technological advances will continue the trend toward improved precision."[26] The adaptation of these new technologies would result in cost savings, increased efficiency, and more combat power vested in fewer forces.

Joint Vision 2010 also accepted the concept of "dominant battlespace awareness" (a de facto synonym for "dominant battlespace knowledge" with differences in shades of meaning of interest only to the initiated), although it denied that it would be possible to "eliminate the fog of war" and did not claim that it would produce perfect or near-perfect intelligence. Even so, "the combination of these technology trends will provide an order of magnitude improvement in lethality." *Joint Vision 2010* accepted the premium that Ullman and Wade placed on speed, including both rapidity of deployment to the theater and a high tempo of operations within the theater. Only speed, they and JV2010 argued, would offset the likelihood that enemies would obtain increasingly precise and lethal systems of their own. As before, U.S. military capabilities were said to require "information superiority: the capability to collect, process, and disseminate an uninterrupted flow of information while exploiting or denying an adversary's ability to do the same."[27]

Ullman and Wade's concepts received the imprimatur of the Joint Staff in the form of JV2010's concept of "dominant maneuver," which was defined in a manner very similar to the "Rapid Dominance" of *Shock and Awe*.[28] In truth, JV2010 was little more than *Shock and Awe* watered down so as not to offend joint—mainly Army—sensibilities. Phrases about the fog of war and the necessity for ground forces were tossed off to placate Army constituencies, but the thrust of the document was very close to the nearly airpower-pure doctrines of DBK and *Shock and Awe*.

The Air Force naturally accepted that thrust happily in *Global Engagement*, and did not bother to placate Army constituencies in its own vision statement. It thus claimed that "In the twenty-first century, it will be possible to find, fix or track and target anything that moves on the surface of the earth. This emerging reality will change the conduct of warfare and the role of air and space power."[29] Reaching back to Warden's arguments, *Global Engagement* re-inserted an old claim back into the argument as well: "With Air and Space Superiority, the Joint Force can dominate enemy operations in all dimensions—land, sea, air and space." The Air Force naturally embraced the concept of "dominant battlespace awareness" eagerly as well. Its vision made no effort to distinguish between "halt phase" and "shock and awe" as preferred approaches to the use of airpower.

Army Vision 2010 was an attempt to respond directly to the challenge airpower enthusiasts posed to the relevance of ground forces. That attempt was seriously constrained, however, by the Army's need to develop its vision within the confines of JV2010 —which effectively already accepted the airpower enthusiasts' arguments and which the Army leadership had signed off on.

Army Vision 2010 thus placed the argument up front:

> With the end of the Cold War, a prominent theory arose that there would no longer be a need for large land forces, that power projection and national military strategy could primarily be carried out through precision strikes using technologically advanced air and naval forces. This "standoff" approach would reduce the level of U.S. involvement and commitment and thus the requirement for large land forces. Reality proved that theory to be invalid.

The Army also offered a statement of its unique contribution to U.S. military capabilities:

> The power to deny or to destroy is possessed by each of the military Services. The contribution of land forces to the joint warfight is the power to exercise direct, continuing, and comprehensive control over land, its resources, and its peoples. It is this direct, continuing, and comprehensive control over land, resources, and people that allows land power to make permanent the otherwise transitory advantages achieved by air and naval forces.

Army Vision 2010 went on to make a cogent defense of the Army's essential contribution to OOTW and, in fact, to every sort of military operation short of major theater war. It failed, however, to make the case for the Army's role in large-scale conflict, falling back on assertions about the need to be able to "dominate" terrain that were unlikely to convince anyone who did not already accept the Army's viewpoint. The thinness of the document and the absence of any detailed historical examples made it unlikely to persuade airpower partisans to change their minds.

The need both to accept the premises of JV2010 and to defend Force XXI, moreover, drove the Army toward a definition of its future combat capabilities that seemed redundant. Describing the Army's role in "dominant maneuver," *Army Vision 2010* declared,

> Decisive operations force the enemy to decide to give in to our will. They are inextricably linked to shaping the battlespace and precision engagement in that decisive operations are vastly enhanced by the precision fires, precise information, and precise detection capabilities inherent to precision engagement.

The Army declared that "shaping the battlespace is far more than precision strike which, as a lone function, is nothing more than twenty-first century attrition warfare." But it went on to argue that

> Shaping the battlespace will be facilitated primarily by sharing "real time" information among all Services, allies, and coalition partners. This process will be accomplished by effectively exploiting information age technologies that permit: isolating, tagging, and tracking of the most fleeting enemy forces and targets with preci-

sion; processing and fusing multiple sources of information from all involved components; and employing the proper force, munitions, or energy before the target is lost. Immediate and accurate battle damage assessment will facilitate re-engagement. As future joint forces combine processes to make virtually any enemy force or target accessible, other technologies will enhance the intelligence and precision of the weapons used to engage them.

This was a key statement that was necessary both to show the Army's acceptance of JV2010 and to defend Force XXI. But which of those functions could the Army perform better than the airpower services? The Air Force already claimed that it could "find, fix or track and target anything that moves on the surface of the earth." If it could do that with airplanes, both manned and unmanned, from safe distances and bases the enemy could not attack, why should the U.S. spend needless money and risk the lives of American soldiers unnecessarily? The Army's attempts to answer that question were inadequate.

Not surprisingly, the major defense-wide reviews of the U.S. military posture in 1997 both effectively accepted the airpower arguments and rejected the Army's defense of its own role in major war.

THE RMA IN NATIONAL MILITARY STRATEGY, 1997

The defense-wide, Congressionally-mandated QDR took place in early 1997 on the basis of the joint and service visions. It adopted the revolution in military affairs principles laid out generally in those documents, but the QDR took much more seriously the task of reconciling transformation to meet future threats with the current needs of the armed forces, and certain of its recommendations reflected confusion about precisely which vision of airpower it embraced.

233

The QDR proceeded, as did all defense planning documents of this period, from the assumption that the defense budget would remain stable or even fall for the foreseeable future. From the outset, therefore, it was not a real strategic review in the sense that the total cost of the defense program was mandated from the start. Nor was there an honest effort to evaluate whether a military structure costing the estimated $250 billion per year that the QDR anticipated could actually sustain the missions and capabilities the strategy called for.

Accepting that limitation on available defense funds, the QDR considered three scenarios for spending them. One was to ignore the future and focus solely on present threats; another was to ignore the present and focus exclusively on future threats; the third was to balance present requirements with future needs. The QDR naturally adopted the third approach and rejected the two strawmen.

The QDR proceeded from yet another assumption: U.S. forces as constituted in 1997 were capable of conducting the national security strategy, including both meeting the two-war standard and conducting smaller-scale operations at the same time. It declared, "a force of the size and structure close to the current force was necessary to meet the requirement . . . of being able to win two, nearly simultaneous, major theater wars in concert with regional allies."[30] The example of 1994 apparently made little impact on those evaluating U.S. force structure two and a half years later, possibly because they relied on modeling and wargaming to persuade themselves that what they wanted to believe was, in fact, true.

But the authors of the QDR did not believe that the U.S. could afford even to maintain that level of force and still modernize. They pointed out that modernization accounts had fallen faster since the end of the Cold War than the defense budget as a whole, and warned that the U.S. would not be able to participate in the ongoing RMA if this trend were not reversed. The QDR therefore recommended actually cutting overall U.S. force structure by a total of 60,000 active duty, 55,000 reserve, and 80,000 civilian personnel. It proposed making these cuts primarily by slashing "overhead" in head-quarters and support structures while keeping the same number of units available in the Active Army. It did propose to move one Air Force wing from the active component to the reserve, and to reduce the number of Navy surface combatants from a programmed 131 to 116.

The QDR acknowledged that these cuts would not be enough to make modernization possible at a sufficient pace, and therefore proposed to institute a "Revolution in Business Affairs" in the Department of Defense. The efficiencies that would result from this change in business practices would also be used to fund modernization. The QDR itself was fairly vague about what the revolution might look like, although it clearly involved outsourcing, increased use of off-the-shelf and dual-use technologies, and facilitating greater competition in the defense procurement processes. The QDR also called for two more rounds of base closings, noting that Department of Defense infrastructure had fallen at a slower rate than both the force size and the budget since the end of the Cold War. Taken together, the cuts in force strength, improvement in business efficiency, and base closings would, the QDR promised, allow the U.S. to stay on the cutting edge of military transformation and handle all ongoing and likely future threats at an acceptable level of risk without increasing the defense budget.

The QDR thereby only widened the disconnect between U.S. strategy and U.S. force structure. It maintained the criti-cality of being able to fight two nearly-simultaneous major the-ater wars, the force-sizing construct that had created the armed forces of 1997, but acknowledged that the military would have to undertake an increasing number of smaller-scale contingen-cies (like Bosnia or the Iraqi no-fly zones) over a long period of time. We have already seen how questionable was the notion that the military really could have fought both Iraq and North Korea in 1994 with acceptable levels of risk. That task would certainly not become easier with the deployment of an Army division in Bosnia after 1995, and part of another in Kosovo after 1999. And if the second contingency did not involve Iraq or North Korea, then the forces already stationed in those theaters would have either to abandon their critical deterrence missions or compromise the ability of the armed forces to meet regional aggressors elsewhere still further. And even as the QDR implicitly acknowledged that the military's requirements were growing, it proposed to reduce the size of the military in order to pay for adaptation to the inevitable information RMA. The QDR therefore deepened the trend already underway toward shortchanging the military's ability to meet current and medium-term challenges in order to defend transformation.

The QDR pleased very few observers. A handful opposed it because of the proposal to reduce the size of the military. A larger segment opposed it because it sustained the two-war force-sizing standard. This latter complaint formed the departure point for the National Defense Panel (NDP), a Congressionally-mandated review of the QDR undertaken later in 1997.

The NDP declared at the outset:

> Defense choices invariably entail risk; the only question is where we take the risk. A significant share of today's Defense Department's resources is focused on the unlikely contingency that two major wars will occur at almost the same time. The Panel views this two-military-theater-of-war construct as, in reality, a force-sizing function. We are concerned that, for some, this has become a means of justifying current forces. This approach focuses significant resources on a low-probability scenario, which consumes funds that could be used to reduce risk to our

long-term security. The Panel believes priority must go to the future. We recognize that, in the near term, the United States cannot ignore the threats posed by Iran and Iraq in the Persian Gulf and North Korea in Northeast Asia. However, our current forces, with the support of allies, should be capable of dealing with both contingencies.[31]

Two major assumptions underlay this bold assertion. First, that the threat of multiple nearly-simultaneous conflicts was sufficiently remote that there was little need to prepare for it. Second, that the progression of the information revolution was sufficiently inevitable that preparing for it must take priority.

The argument over whether or not to prepare for a two-war contingency, and the related argument about how much force such a contingency would require, was a natural and inevitable part of the strategic landscape in 1997. It needed only a little imagination to see that if the U.S. clearly did not have the ability to fight two wars, that fact in itself might lead to the unprecedented, possibly accidental, cooperation between two adversaries that seemed otherwise so unlikely. And the defensiveness of the services and of Department of Defense in general made the notion that this standard was being used primarily to ward off change or budgetary reductions more plausible than it might otherwise have been. In truth, the casualness with which the NDP consigned the danger of a multi-theater war to extremes of improbability was disturbing and unfounded, but it was understandable.

The absolute conviction with which the NDP declared that a military information revolution was on the way, however, was less justifiable. It probably resulted in part from the fact that the military had repeated this assertion over and over again until it became embedded in the thinking of just about all defense analysts. The continuing technological revolution within the business community appeared to strengthen this conviction, as the repeated references to the need for the military to adopt revolutionary new business practices emphasized. Nevertheless, when the NDP announced, "It is clear, however, that in the 2010–2020 time frame our military forces will need capabilities very different from those they currently possess. We are on the cusp of a military revolution stimulated by rapid advances in information and information-related technologies," it treated these assertions as axiomatic and requiring no proof when, in fact, they were no less arguable than the dangers of a two-war contingency.

To its credit, the NDP noted that its proposed transformation program would require an additional $5–10 billion per year, and that it would be preferable simply to add something like that amount to the defense budget. It acknowledged that such an increase was unlikely, however, and therefore proposed reducing the size of current forces, scrapping the two-war standard, canceling certain weapons systems, and channeling the money thus saved into transformation.

In particular, the NDP proposed a new approach to transformation. Rather than upgrading so-called "legacy" systems until improved versions or new systems came on-line, the NDP suggested terminating those upgrade programs and, in effect, leaping-ahead to next generation technology. Instead of improving the M1 tank, therefore, the NDP proposed developing "the twenty-first century tank to be a unique vehicle relying on speed, agility, and hyper-velocity gun technology for operational effectiveness (the Panel's view is that 30–35 tons is the appropriate weight range)."[32] This recommendation flowed from the Panel's belief in the urgent need for the land forces to "Become more expeditionary: fast, shock-exploiting forces, with greater urban operations capability" and to "Reduce systems that are difficult to move and support; shift to lighter, more agile automated systems." In other words, the NDP advocated relying entirely on the information revolution to protect future "armored" vehicles in order to ensure their rapid deployability to a theater. Speed had become all.

The NDP made similar proposals for the Navy. It advocated designing and building smaller, stealthier ships, shifting to smaller carriers operating vertical/short-take off and landing (V/STOL) aircraft, building sea-bases to facilitate rapid deployment, and restarting the "arsenal ship" program to build a stealthy ship capable of launching volleys of precision-guided munitions safely from hundreds of miles off an enemy's shore. All of the armed services were to be restructured to support a vision of precision attack from stand-off distances, the core of the RMA the NDP saw inevitably developing.

ARMY TRANSFORMATION CHANGES COURSE

If the NDP mostly pleased the Air Force and, to a lesser extent, the Navy, it challenged the Army yet again. It was no longer enough for the Army to digitize and take its proper place in the information revolution. Now the NDP demanded that the Army focus on becoming lighter, more deployable, and more strategically agile. This pressure combined with the experience of Operation Allied Force to convince the new Army leadership at the end of the decade to change the focus of transformation fundamentally. The change was primarily the work of the new Army Chief of Staff, General Eric Shinseki.

Whereas Sullivan's successor as Chief of Staff, General Dennis Reimer, had been closely involved with the development of Force XXI as Commander of U.S. Army Forces Command,[33] Shinseki had spent the time before taking the reins of the Army in a real world operation, commanding the "International Force" (IFOR) of U.N. troops in Bosnia. He was thus both much less intellectually invested in Force XXI and much more concerned with the Army's ability to execute current missions and those that he could see were likely in the immediate future.

Even before Allied Force he had decided that Sullivan and Reimer had focused too heavily on digitization at the expense of deployability. If the Army could not get to the theater in a timely fashion, he reasoned, it hardly mattered how well inter-netted its troops and systems were. The debacle of Task Force Hawk during Allied Force powerfully reinforced his sense of urgency in tackling this problem.

The tragedy occurred in the midst of the Kosovo air cam-paign, when General Wesley Clark began arguing for the deploy-ment of ground forces, or at least for the preparations for such a deployment. He was unsuccessful in that endeavor, but he did manage to persuade a reluctant president to allow him to shift twenty-four Apache attack helicopters from bases in Germany to a base in Albania from which they could support operations in Kosovo. Since the Apache was specifically designed to find and kill enemy tanks, it seemed in one sense to be an ideal system to use in the struggle to attrit the Serbian army.

The Army had never intended for the Apache to deploy or operate by itself, however. Army doctrine explicitly called for the integration of Apaches into a complex air-ground team and eschewed long-range independent Apache strikes as high risk undertakings that could only be justified by the prospect of gain-ing a major advantage over the enemy. In addition, the bases from which Clark wished to launch the Apaches were in principle vulnerable to Serb cross-border raids. The Army insisted, there-fore, on providing ground forces to secure them, including a mechanized company, light infantry, counter-battery radar sys-tems designed to locate enemy artillery systems, and Multiple-Launch Rocket System units to provide immediate fire support should the Apaches come under attack. In all, the deployment came to over 5,000 soldiers—essentially a reinforced brigade in size, although not in ground combat power.

The Army had made no preparations to form or deploy such an ad hoc collection of individual pieces, and there was no infrastructure in place in the theater to receive or support them. As a result, the units' movement required a massive airlift effort, a significant base-construction effort—and far too much time. To cap it all off, when the units finally arrived and settled in, they quickly lost two Apaches to training accidents, one of which claimed the lives of the helicopter crew.[34]

The deployment of Task Force Hawk was thus a catastrophe for the Army. The helicopters were never used in combat, and although the counter-battery radars ended up playing an important role in the air campaign, that probably did not justify the enormous time and expense required to get the task force to Albania. The fact that a handful of retired Army officers later claimed somewhat desperately that Task Force Hawk had, in effect, won the conflict, showed only the bitterness of the interservice rivalry and budget competition in the late 1990s and the Army's fear of seeming completely irrelevant.[35]

Rather than attempting to find something positive in the Task Force Hawk experience, Shinseki seized upon the debacle to argue that the Army must transform itself fundamentally in order to remain relevant. Its light units must become heavier, he argued, while the heavier units became lighter. By that he meant that the Army suffered from a significant deployability problem. It could move light infantry units at little notice with a small amount of airlift to anywhere in the world. When they arrived, however, those units would have no armor protection at all, limited vehicular mobility, and inadequate firepower to defend themselves against all but the most lightly-armed foes. Heavy mechanized forces, by contrast, arrived with superb armor protection and mobility within the theater and had enormous organic firepower, but they required a phenomenal amount of air and sealift to move. Because of the M1's great weight, for example, even the vast C-5 airlifter could carry only one at a time. Shinseki argued that this problem made the Army irrelevant in the modern world—it simply could not get militarily useful forces to the combat zone in time to make a difference.

Shinseki therefore dedicated himself from the very beginning of his tenure to reorienting Army transformation. He felt a great deal of urgency in his efforts, because he noted that previous attempts at transformation had faltered when their originators left office. He was determined to ensure that his vision would be so firmly rooted when he left that it could survive the transition.[36]

Shinseki began by laying out a clear path to the future Army, which, he argued, needed to develop and maintain three forces simultaneously—the legacy force, the interim force, and the objective force. The legacy force consisted of current Army systems like the M1 and the Bradley. Under Shinseki's vision of transformation, these systems would continue to play an important role within the Army for two decades or more, and they were critical to underwriting the Army's "non-negotiable contract with the American people" of "fighting and winning the nation's wars" in the near term.

But a number of recent events had persuaded the Chief that the Army needed to develop a second force quickly that would be able to make good obvious shortcomings in its current force structure that prevented it from accomplishing critical missions in the near term. This interim force would have to be rapidly deployable, survivable, and lethal, but it would incorporate only off-the-shelf technology to ensure that it could be rapidly fielded.

The interim force would not really be transformational, therefore, according to Shinseki's notion, although it might provide good experience that would help train officers and support the development of doctrine for the real transformational force —the objective force, which we will consider presently.

The critical factor in transformation according to Shinseki was deployability. In the "Army Vision," which he released in October 1999, Shinseki declared that the Army must be able to put a brigade combat team anywhere in the world within ninety-six hours, a division within 120 hours, and five divisions in thirty days.[37] This was an ambitious goal, promising to move well over 100,000 soldiers and all of their equipment anywhere in the world within one month. Shinseki was well aware that the Army would not be able to accomplish this goal within the foreseeable future, but he thought it was essential as a mark to aim at in the development of the interim and objective forces.

The truly transformational part of Shinseki's proposal was the "objective force," centered around a new family of vehicles called the Future Combat System (FCS). Actually an amalgam of ideas from several sources, the objective force took its organization and basic fighting concept from wargames conducted by the Army After Next program, an effort begun in the middle of the decade to examine alternate routes toward transformation using the sophisticated wargaming facilities at the Army War College at Carlisle, Pennsylvania.

The Army After Next (AAN) program had several interesting features. The most prominent and influential aspect was the gaming of various different technologies, doctrines, and organizational structures of future forces in scenarios usually set in 2020 or beyond. These efforts involved relatively unconstrained red vs. blue wargames with highly skilled and qualified players on both sides. The results were interesting and enlightening, as talented red teams pressed future U.S. forces with innovative strategies. Among the other results of these games was the increasing conviction that future enemies would take advantage of cities to cover their forces from U.S. precision-strike capabilities, a development borne out to a very limited extent in the most recent Iraq war.

Another major learning point to emerge from several games was the notion that future battlefields would be cellular and not linear. There would not be clear "front" lines with safe zones behind them, but instead areas that the U.S. controlled intermingled with areas controlled by the enemy. For a variety of reasons, the AAN games seemed to suggest that such a cellular battlefield would favor internetted U.S. forces and disadvantage enemies that were more traditionally organized and commanded. Initial AAN games also seemed to suggest that a shift toward a flatter military hierarchy based on brigade-sized units was desirable.

Still another extremely important feature of the AAN games, particularly the first several iterations, was that the military portion of the games was preceded by a political portion that set the parameters of the military operations. The military portion also included a robust "green" team that represented all of the third-party countries and NGOs that might affect or be affected by the conflict. There was ample opportunity, therefore, to explore possible future political scenarios and to examine the ways in which political considerations would affect the conduct of future military operations. The games also tended to highlight the importance of civilians on or near the battlefield, an issue that operations in Bosnia and Kosovo had helped bring to the forefront of the Army's thinking.

By the end of the decade, unfortunately, the AAN games had begun to lose their focus on political-military interactions and to concentrate instead on testing out technological concepts in more perfunctory political contexts. The program was shut down entirely shortly after Shinseki became Chief of Staff. It is worth noting that a similar effort called Air Force 2025, which involved a massive effort at thinking about possible future political constellations and their impact on future military operations, and also included an insightful "contrarian's view" about the utility of airpower, had far less impact on the Air Force modernization programs and was never widely disseminated. In the end, for a variety of reasons, the military services were not comfortable with wide-ranging speculation about future political developments and the future relationship between war and politics. As a result, a number of highly promising beginnings that might have helped prepared the military for the challenges it faced after 9/11 were cut short.

The notion of a cellular battlefield dominated by smaller land force units relying heavily on digitization and internetting, nevertheless, came increasingly to be a part of the Army's thinking about transformation. The objective force, therefore, came to have these characteristics in the minds of the Army leadership. If the expected nature of the organization and general doctrine of that force was fairly clear, however, the details of the future combat system (FCS), its mainstay vehicular program, were vague and variable from the beginning.

Army leaders were always careful to point out that FCS was not a single vehicle. It was not simply a replacement for the M1 or the Bradley. Instead, it was to be a family of vehicles based on certain common elements that could be enhanced or configured to perform various functions. There would, thus, be an FCS variant that would perform many of the functions of the M1 and one that would perform those of the Bradley. These large vehicles would be supplemented, however, by a host of robotic systems, including Unmanned Aerial Vehicles (UAVs) of various sizes and purposes, remote sensors, mine-detecting and mine-clearing robots, and so forth. All of these systems taken together would form the FCS.

The most traditional elements of that family of vehicles, the future quasi-tank and quasi-infantry carrier, were to benefit from the Army's investment in digitization. They would carry long range, over-the-horizon, non-line-of-sight (NLOS) weapons that could engage and destroy the enemy from great distances before the system itself came into the range of the enemy's weapons. This capability was essential to the whole system and, indeed, the whole concept of the objective force, because these vehicles would not be armored heavily enough to withstand close combat with the enemy. That decision resulted from the need to make the vehicles small and light enough to be airlifted in C-130 aircraft.

This constraint, imposed by the Army leadership on the system virtually from the outset, resulted in part from the experience of Kosovo, where the Army's heavy units had taken too long to arrive in theater and used up too many airlift resources. It was also the result of a refocusing on the "lessons" of Desert Storm.

Whereas Sullivan, under the influence of third-wave mania, looked at Desert Storm and saw the need for an information revolution, Shinseki and others saw evidence that the Army was not responsive enough in traditional ways to be relevant in future wars. Kosovo only reinforced this trend that had already been gathering steam, as could be seen from the references in the NDP to the need for a 30–35 ton future armored vehicle.

Like the assumption that an "information revolution" was inevitably underway, the assumption that the Army was too heavy to be relevant also required much more investigation than it received. For one thing, it did not, in fact, take six months to move the Desert Storm force into the theater. When the Desert Shield deployment ended in early October (about two months after it had begun), the Army had most of four divisions (82nd Airborne, 101st Air Assault, 24th Mechanized, and 1st Cavalry) and the 3rd Armored Cavalry Regiment (ACR), while the Marines had one division ashore as part of the I Marine Expeditionary Force (MEF). Between mid-November 1990, when Bush authorized the deployment of an additional corps for purposes of launching a counter-attack, and early January 1991, the Army deployed three more heavy divisions (1st and 3rd Armored and 1st Infantry) and the 2nd ACR. That is a deployment rate of about one corps of three or four divisions every sixty days.

This deployment thus put fewer forces in the theater in sixty days than Shinseki's transformational program would have done in thirty, but the real issue was not the time from the thirtieth to the sixtieth day of deployment but the period from day 1 to day 15. In that period, the 82nd Airborne had had to face the full weight of the Iraqi Republican Guard without sufficient anti-tank capability to have confidence in its own survival. The purpose of being able to move Army heavy forces faster was to ensure that future such dangerous scenarios would not recur.

Reasoning from this example is complicated, especially with the benefit of hindsight. It is quite true that the 82nd Airborne faced a dangerous situation and that it would be preferable to avoid such risks in the future. It is also a fact that Saddam did not attack it. The military likewise had all the time it needed to plan and execute Operations Deliberate Force and Allied Force —as well as Operation Iraqi Freedom. Nor is it at all clear, as we will see, that Operation Enduring Freedom would have suffered importantly from taking the time to get a limited number of ground forces into Afghanistan.

As was the case with the digitization effort, it is patently clear that having lighter, more deployable forces would be a good thing. It is not clear, however, that developing such forces is the most important priority facing the U.S. military. Those who wish to make that argument must address the fact that the relative lack of deployability of American heavy forces has never yet proved to be an actual problem in the post-Cold War environment, however counterintuitive that seems. There is certainly not enough historical basis to justify subordinating all other priorities to ensuring that any future combat system can be flown in a C-130 airlifter.

The notion of making the Army "lighter" and more deployable was nevertheless greeted with a fair amount of enthusiasm in Congress and among defense analysts, and Shinseki worked hard to lock C-130-deployable vehicles into the procurement process both for the interim force and for the objective force. The immediate result was the Stryker system, which has now seen combat in both Iraq and Afghanistan. Stryker is a wheeled vehicle capable of transporting infantry and of carrying a number of possible armaments itself. It is relatively lightly armored and, in theory at least, c-130-deployable. The details of the development of the Stryker are too complex to present here, including the debate about whether it should have wheels or tracks, how much it should weigh, and how much armor and gun it could therefore have. The system has proven capable enough of providing a lightly-armored and highly-maneuverable vehicle to light infantry units, greatly increasing their combat capability without dramatically reducing their strategic deployability.

The Stryker solved no problem that had led to the Task Force Hawk debacle, however. There the Army had been asked to do something very difficult—cobble together a heterogeneous force for a mission it had never foreseen in a land without any of the necessary infrastructure, and on a moment's notice. That it failed in that task had nothing to do with the weight of the M1, since only fifteen M1s were deployed in an operation that required more than 400 airlift sorties. This was a relatively minor point, however, since Shinseki had really been using Task Force Hawk to sell a concept he had already decided upon.

Nor is it at all clear that the Stryker would have solved the Desert Shield dilemma, however. It had neither sufficient armor nor sufficient armament to face Iraqi tanks, and would therefore not have been a substantial improvement over the vehicles the 82nd Airborne fielded in 1990. It is quite true that by 1999 the light tanks that division had relied on in the Saudi desert had been retired and it now fielded only Humvees as its ground vehicles. The Stryker was, indeed, an improvement on that situation, but the net result was pretty much to return the division to the state of capability it had had during Desert Shield.

Another part of the selling process thus also complicated the early discussions of the interim force. The Stryker actually did not and could not have replaced the M1. Of the units eventually converted to Strykers, only one was a heavy (M1-equipped) formation; all the others were light infantry units. The Stryker really did virtually nothing to "lighten" the Army, therefore—on the contrary, the overall effect has been to make the total force rather heavier, since units that had previously had only Humvees now had Strykers.

This development, in truth, was a positive one. U.S. light infantry had, indeed, been far too light, and the Stryker provides a useful and important improvement to the capability of light infantry formations. Nevertheless, the degradation of combat power from the M1 to the Stryker is significant, both in terms of firepower and protection. The M1 is an overpowering weapons system that very few enemies can kill and very few can survive. The Stryker does not have those characteristics. The decision not to replace many M1s with Strykers, therefore, made excellent sense.

Yet the fact remained that the M1 was too heavy to be rapidly deployable. Only the FCS, relying on a series of assumptions and the development of a number of leap-ahead technologies, could actually solve the deployability problem, and the first such unit was not initially expected to be fielded until after 2010. Given the complexity of the system and the lead-time necessary for such a weapons program to mature, even this date was optimistic (and it was ultimately abandoned, in fact). If the Army's relevance was to be defined by its ability to field a "heavy" force that was deployable in days, the task of transformation would be truly monumental.

The Stryker, finally, is in no way transformational in itself. Similar vehicles have existed in second- and third-rate armies around the world for years, and the information technology deployed in the Stryker was the result of the Force XXI program, not any new program designed specifically for that vehicle. To be sure, Shinseki never thought that the Stryker would be transformational. Others, however, including Secretary of the Army Louis Caldera, did, and the Stryker came to be portrayed as a transformational system. The Army's transformation program thus came to seem wavering and inconsistent even as Shinseki tried to give it coherence and drive.

A more fundamental problem with the change in the course of Army transformation was that it promised to make the Army even more redundant by stripping it of the ability to engage in close combat. The digitization effort had focused on using information technology to enable ground attack from stand-off distances. The emphasis on lightness made that approach an absolute requirement. With no technology on the horizon to provide armor protection comparable to that of the M1 in a 20-ton vehicle, the Army's Future Combat System would survive, according to an increasing body of Army literature, by seeing and killing the enemy before it came within range of his weapons.

An Army "white paper" describing the Objective Force declared,

> Objective Force Units will see first, understand first, act first and finish decisively as the means to tactical success. Operations will be characterized by developing situations out of contact; maneuvering to positions of advantage; engaging enemy forces beyond the range of their weapons; destroying them with precision fires; and, as required, by tactical assault at times and places of our choosing. Commanders will accomplish this by maneuvering dispersed tactical formations of Future Combat Systems units linked by web-centric C4ISR capabilities for common situational dominance.[38]

To solve the dilemma caused by the lack of armor protection of the FCS, the Army increasingly redefined survivability for the

Objective Force: "Objective Force survivability will be linked to its inherently offensive orientation, as well as its speed and lethality. By seizing the initiative and seeing, understanding, and acting first, the Objective Force will enhance its own survivability through action and its retention of the initiative."[39]

The Army's transformation program, in fact, came to rely even more heavily than the airpower visionaries on acquiring and disseminating perfect intelligence.[40] The airpower enthusiasts needed this intelligence to target the enemy systems effectively, but Army units would require it merely to survive on the battlefield. Even if they did survive, moreover, they would contribute few capabilities that airpower did not already provide, considering that they could not close with the enemy or even safely occupy positions within range of the enemy's weapons systems. The Army was consciously or unconsciously embracing the concept that war is nothing more than a targeting drill without recognizing that such a vision, whatever its merits, would make the Army less relevant than ever.

CONCLUSION

By the beginning of the new millennium there was broad agreement within the armed forces and the defense community as a whole on several key points. First and foremost, that a revolution in military affairs based on information technology was underway and that U.S. forces had to "adapt" to this ongoing process or be left hopelessly behind. Second, that it was impossible to foresee any particular likely enemy in the middle or distant future, although Iraq and North Korea seemed obvious but manageable threats in the short term. No one in national defense circles seriously contemplated the possibility of war with China or the requirements preparing for such a conflict might impose. Third, that even without knowing whom America might be fighting, it was possible to know with reasonable certainty how that enemy would fight, and to develop an appropriate counter for it. Finally, that war was fundamentally a targeting drill and the only systems in the future that would matter would be those that improved America's ability to put metal precisely on target.

A number of important considerations had fallen by the wayside, however. Although the ongoing OOTW missions in the Balkans and elsewhere suggested that such operations would be much more common in the future, and although all service visions and defense reviews spoke of their importance, none of the service visions really considered what the requirements of those missions might be in any detail. All treated them primarily as lesser-included missions within a force structure designed for major war, and all assumed that even a military transformed to rely on information technology and superior targeting would be able to handle such collateral missions gracefully and without excessive strain.

A related problem was the failure to consider in any detail what victory meant in post-Cold War conflicts. The assumption during the Cold War, after all, had been that any war with the Warsaw Pact would be global, possibly even apocalyptic. If the belligerents managed to limit the war, then a negotiated peace would follow that would, at a minimum, ensure the tranquility of whatever was left of Western Europe. The U.S. did not foresee defeating the Soviet Union so decisively as to be able to dictate a peace in Moscow or impose a draconian treaty on the beaten foe, and so the detailed development of post-war thinking or programs seemed unnecessary.

But such thinking did not apply to post-Cold War conflicts. The U.S. was quite capable of defeating Iraq or North Korea utterly and would then be faced with the task of developing a meaningful and stable peace. As we shall see later, it turns out that the way a war is waged powerfully affects the sort of peace that emerges after it. The failure to consider this problem in any meaningful way in the 1990s was therefore a major failure in the strategic thought of the period, and laid the groundwork for future such failures of greater import.

To criticize the leaders and thinkers of the 1990s for this failure is not simply inserting the concerns of 2006 anachronistically into a prior era, however. By 1999 it was perfectly clear that the "peace" that ended the first Gulf War had fundamentally failed to achieve its major aims. Despite significant ex post facto efforts at spinning, it is now clear that the first Bush administration and the military really had hoped and expected that the attack would unseat Saddam, which it failed to do. U.S. leaders had certainly expected in the aftermath of that war to be able to disarm Saddam and prevent him from developing WMD capabilities. By 1999, however, the inspection regime had collapsed in the face of Iraqi opposition. By contrast, no U.S. leader had expected or wanted to be drawn into a protracted program of sanctions and periodic military actions from bases in Saudi Arabia, where the U.S. presence was increasingly resented. It should have required very little imagination to see that the nature of the peace following even a successful "information-age war" required much more thought than it was receiving.

The U.S. strategy community in the 1990s was in general so caught up with the minutiae of technology that it lost sight of the larger purpose of war, and therefore missed the emergence of a challenge even more important than that of technology— the challenge of designing military operations to achieve particular political objectives. As it would turn out, that challenge would prove the most important for U.S. forces in the post-9/11 world.

CHAPTER SEVEN

Reinventing Transformation: Network-Centric Warfare

T HE EARLY VISIONARIES of information age warfare, like Sullivan, derived their impressions of it from the theories of the Tofflers and others and what they could imagine based on the early stages of the "information revolution." By the end of the 1990s, information-age visionaries had much more tangible "proof" of their theorems in the form of the growing list of U.S. companies using information technology and new ways of doing business to gain enormous advantages over their competitors. The growth of a body of theory in the business world to explain and proselytize for these new approaches rapidly encouraged a revitalization of such theorizing in the realm of military affairs. Thus was "network-centric warfare" born.

From its origins in 1997 and 1998, network-centric warfare (NCW) had significant advantages over competing theories. Since it was based on business theories and practices, it started with a much more sophisticated theoretical basis than its competitors, and it had a host of real-world examples both to mine for meaningful similarities to warfare and to prove the validity of its concepts. It was both more persuasive and less easily refuted than, say, Tofflerism or Shock and Awe.

There is clearly a great deal of value in the concepts of

NCW—and much more that is helpful than in the more wild-eyed theorizing of some contemporary visionaries. But there was also a large amount of "reinventing the wheel" that resulted from exaggerations by the authors of NCW treatises and the limitations of their understanding both of military history and, in some cases, even of the recent history of U.S. military transformation efforts. As a result, NCW was presented as a new capability and a new set of requirements when, in fact, it was largely a limited logical progression from efforts already well underway in the 1990s.

That fact, by itself, does not diminish the importance or utility of NCW. As we have seen, transformation efforts were confused and somewhat incoherent, and a well-developed theory would have gone a long way toward solving important problems that had developed them. But NCW focused narrowly on one aspect of warfare, and it retained many of the false assumptions and theoretical errors of its predecessors. It has had the effect, therefore, of codifying and galvanizing all that was wrong with U.S. military transformation, as well as much that was right.

THE BUSINESS MODEL

Network-centric warfare was first described in detail in 1998 by David S. Alberts, John J. Garstka, and Frederick P. Stein. All three were involved in various Department of Defense digitization and transformation efforts; Garstka was also a retired Air Force officer and Stein a retired U.S. Army colonel. From the beginning, the concept had the enthusiastic support of retired Admiral Arthur K. Cebrowski, who co-authored an article with Garstka promoting it early in 1998.[1]

Network-centric warfare was an explicit attempt to translate business practices into warfare. Although its authors freely acknowledge that such translations are difficult and that the worlds of war and business are not entirely parallel, they argue that it is as foolish to ignore business models that might be helpful as it is to adopt them blindly.[2] This assertion is, of course, quite valid, as long as the limits of the resulting model are kept constantly in mind.

The "network-centric" business model was drawn from a series of corporations that had appeared, by the late 1990s, to use innovative organizations and techniques combined with the new capabilities of information technologies to achieve significant advantages over their competitors. The marquee names from among these companies are still familiar today, although not all of them have retained dominant positions in their respective markets: Cisco Systems, Dell Computers, Wal-Mart, American Airlines, Charles Schwab, Capital One, Deutsche Morgan Grenfall, Amazon.com, and Federal Express.[3]

The authors of NCW singled out Wal-Mart, Dell, and Capital One for particular mention, because they went furthest in creating vast webs of information to facilitate their operations. Dell, for instance, had pioneered what might be called "just-in-time production," by creating the capability to produce computers in response to individual customer requests on very short notice. As a result, Dell did not have to maintain warehouses full of products that might or might not sell and could be maximally adaptive to a constantly changing computer hardware and software environment.

Capital One focused on creating the capability to mine large amounts of data on prospective creditors, so that it could select those most likely to repay loans in a timely fashion. Wal-Mart used point-of-sale scanning technology to flash a report of each purchase to the relevant producer. As a result, Wal-Mart was able to reduce overstockage dramatically without risking stocking shortfalls, its producers were kept aware of its inventory so that they could plan their own production accordingly, and costs were kept down, allowing Wal-Mart to undersell the competition dramatically.

In all three of these cases, as well as the others cited, the use of information technology appeared to give an important or, in Wal-Mart's case, dominating advantage over "industrial-age" competitors. Network-centric warfare simply proposed to apply analogous principles to the organization and performance of the U.S. military.

There are a number of problems even with this evaluation of the business model, let alone with NCW's attempt to apply it to the very different realm of warfare. First, the NCW study was made at the height of the "information" boom in the U.S. economy. Two years after the publication of *Network-Centric Warfare*, the information economy suffered a horrible stock correction that rippled throughout the U.S. and world economies. In the course of that correction, some of the companies NCW identified as models did well; others did not.

Another problem with the direct translation of network-centric business concepts to war is that those concepts apply only to a certain very narrow part of the problem militaries face. The IT systems used by the NCW model corporations all allowed them to have a better understanding of their own systems, inventory, and capabilities. They did not, on the whole, provide a great deal of insight into the capabilities, inventories, etc., of their competitors, functions that would seem to come under the heading of industrial espionage rather than net-centric operations.

As a result, IT in the business world was used primarily to allow the organization to make decisions based on better information and to reduce internal friction in executing those decisions. It was almost entirely inwardly-focused in the advantages it would provide—the business would run more smoothly, be more adaptable, and its leaders would make better decisions. The assumption, which the markets seemed to bear out for a time, was that corporations with these characteristics would perform better than those without them. In the business world, naturally, there was no consideration given (at least publicly) to using these capabilities to make other corporations work less well, make worse decisions, or suffer from higher friction in executing them. This is another respect in which business is very different from war.

Even so, there can be no doubt that armies that are capable of reducing friction within their own structures, and making more rapid and better decisions, will generally outperform armies without those capabilities, all other things being equal. Depending upon what advantages, precisely, the NCW advocates promised would result from the adoption of their vision, therefore, it seemed clear that the U.S. military would benefit from proceeding down this path.

THE MILITARY APPLICATIONS OF RMA

The promises of NCW in the military realm were far from moderate, however. The proponents of NCW promised a dramatic revolution in American military capabilities if their vision were pursued, warning, as had their predecessors, that failure to follow that vision would leave the U.S. vulnerable to potential adversaries who surely would do so. They thus embraced the inevitability of the information revolution even more firmly than previous transformation thinkers had.

The basis of NCW was the belief that a close tie exists between the nature of the economy and the nature of war. As the most aggressive and articulate exponent of this theory, Admiral Cebrowski, stated: "nations make war the same way they make wealth." He compared "Economy A," the industrial age economy, with "Economy B," the information age economic system, and argued that "In Economy B, a product or product standard attains such a dominant position that consumers drop competing products because of concerns about the availability of 'content' or product support or because they prefer a familiar product based on existing skills or content." This phenomenon is called "lock-out," because the dominant position one technology achieved locked out competitors. He declared, "We seek an analogous effect in warfare."[4]

He expanded on this theme to claim that "Network-centric operations deliver to the U.S. military the same powerful dynamics as they produced in American business." The key attributes of these dynamics were "a detailed understanding of the appropriate competitive space; . . . the close linkage among actors in business ecosystems [which will be] mirrored in the military by the linkages and interactions among units and the operating environment;" and speed at the tactical level.

The result of these new dynamics applied to war would be fundamental:

> Network-centric warfare enables a shift from attrition-style warfare to a much faster and more effective warfighting style characterized by the new concepts of speed of command and self-synchronization. Attrition is the traditional "Economy A" analogue because it yields decreasing returns on investment. Reversals are possible, and frequently the outcome is in doubt.
>
> Network-centric warfare, where battle time plays a critical role, is analogous to the new economic model, with potentially increasing returns on investment. Very high and accelerating rates of change have a profound impact on the outcome, "locking-out" alternative enemy strategies and "locking-in" success.[5]

The primary mechanism for obtaining these benefits would be speed of command, which had three key parts: information superiority, the concentration of effects rather than of forces, and the ability to ensure the "rapid foreclosure of enemy courses of action and the shock of closely coupled events." Cebrowski concluded, "Speed of command facilitates the lock-out phenomenon observed in Economy B, but with even more powerful effects. Lock-out often takes years to achieve in business, but in warfare it can be achieved in weeks or less." He also revealed something fundamental about his understanding of warfare with the declaration that "It is easy to focus on the number of sites destroyed, but the payoff is in the initial very high rate of change. When 50 percent of something important to the enemy is destroyed at the outset, so is his strategy. That stops wars—which is what network-centric warfare is all about."[6]

Another virtue of NCW, according to Cebrowksi and Garstka, was that it would eliminate the "traditional" sequential approach to planning and conducting operations that, among other things, generates "operational pauses" that allow the enemy potentially to regain the initiative.[7] They also warned that the spread of global news coverage and the availability of information on the world wide web, which they called the "Circus Maximus" effect, "introduces a dose of chaos, and the Wired World makes the process nonlinear." They concluded, "All of this challenges our most basic assumptions about command and control and the doctrine developed for a different time and a different problem. One of the most enduring lessons derived from the history of warfare is the degree to which fog and friction permeate the battlespace." Although fog and friction would never completely disappear, they argued, the ability of NCW to reduce them to minimal levels meant that military structures and procedures designed to deal with larger amounts of confusion would have to be changed fundamentally.[8]

The authors of NCW initially offered relatively few insights into the concrete ways in which their proposals would actually change the way the U.S. armed forces waged war. The focus of the early writings was on describing the concept, educating suspicious readers, and creating a vocabulary to discuss the new ideas. Insofar as they did consider warfighting in detail, however, the results sounded fairly familiar:

> At the strategic level, senior leaders and leading military strategists are asserting the potential for the cumulative effect of closely spaced events (such as a rapid sequence of local tactical disasters, occurring over a period of hours) to dislocate and confuse an enemy to the point that his warfighting structures quickly disintegrate, and his feasible courses of action are rapidly reduced, resulting in an unequivocal military decision with minimum cost to both sides.[9]

They continued,

> The effects of a series of improvements, such as illustrated above, are highly synergistic, making the resulting force much more effective and efficient. In fact, this synergy allows NCW, for the first time, to provide us with the possibility of moving beyond a strategy based upon attrition, to one based upon shock and awe. Shock and awe are achieved not simply as a function of the number of targets destroyed, but as a result of the destruction or neutralization of significant numbers of critical targets within a short period of time and/or the successful targeting of the right target at the right time.[10]

Network-centric warfare, then, was to provide the military capabilities to implement the ideas encapsulated in Ullman and Wade's Shock and Awe idea.

The connection between NCW and Shock and Awe emphasized the fact that NCW offered relatively little that was new in the realm of warfighting, either compared to previous military thought or even compared to previous campaigns. The discussions of "attrition" warfare and sequential operations with inevitable long pauses between them were strawmen that did not accurately describe American military campaigns in the 1990s. The authors of NCW appeared to be unfamiliar with the theories of Warden and Deptula, and the idea of parallel warfare that had already found its way deep into Air Force planning procedures.

One of the essential characteristics of the Gulf War air campaign, after all, was that it was *not* sequential. Suppression of enemy air defenses took place simultaneously with attacks on command and control nodes, critical infrastructure, and even the enemy's fielded forces. Thirty-nine days of bombing followed by one hundred hours of ground combat offered the Iraqis no pause in operations that an NCW-approach would not also have offered. In 1991, the Iraqi were continuously under attack from the air, and the only ground pressure for the first thirty-nine days was the presence of a large U.S. force, the use of which Saddam hoped to deter with threats of high American casualties. Under the NCW concepts there would be even less pressure, given the emphasis on having a "light footprint" in the theater and the preference for airpower-pure solutions.

The essence of Warden's approach to the air campaign, moreover, is the antithesis of attrition. Warden proposed, we should recall, to avoid targeting the enemy's fielded forces at all, relying instead on the disaggregation of the enemy system through the destruction of its ability to communicate among its various forces. This idea, presented as a novel and even revolutionary one by the authors of NCW, dated, in fact, back to Boyd (actually, the first clear exposition of it was made in 1918 by J. F. C. Fuller). It was thus twenty years old (or possibly seventy-nine) when it was re-promulgated as a fundamental insight in 1998. By 1998, in other words, the capabilities promised by the authors of the NCW concept were no longer revolutionary. The U.S. had already demonstrated the ability to link its forces together through battlefield intranets, and was well advanced in experiments in all the services to do this. Ideas of parallel war and center-of-gravity targeting, developed in much more sophistication than NCW offered, had already informed two extremely successful air campaigns. It was not at all clear that the "new" capabilities promised by NCW would be very new at all. NCW also solidified a number of important errors that had emerged with the transformation theories that had gone before. First, it accepted the Tofflerite depiction of the ongoing information revolution, and assumed, like many other transformation visions, that this "revolution" would lead inevitably to a revolution in military affairs of a certain variety. It did not consider this proposition in much detail, promising only that computerization would lead to world changes similar to those caused by the steam engine, the internal combustion engine, and the airplane.[11]

A second fundamental problem with the 1990s transformation thinking that NCW repeated was the idea that war is simply a targeting drill. Network-centric warfare documents virtually ignore the political aspects of war. To the extent that they discuss warfighting, they only address the destruction of targets with precision weapons. The emphasis in NCW is slightly shifted from that of Shock and Awe or parallel war, in that NCW focuses more on creating a networked system to allow decision-makers at all levels to make the right decisions in choosing targets and the weapons with which to attack them, and doing so rapidly. The consideration of how to select the *right* targets, already atrophied in Shock and Awe, falls away almost completely in NCW.

This trend highlights another problem carried over from previous transformation thought to NCW—the internal focus of all of these theories. The vast majority of the writings on NCW address issues internal to the U.S. military—how to get information from sensors to shooters, how to help commanders make the right decisions, how to ensure that those decisions are executed perfectly and quickly, and so forth. Very little of the corpus addresses the enemy at all, either as a system to be explored or as a potential hindrance to U.S. military operations. The result is an increasing tendency to view the enemy as an inert, lifeless mass against which U.S. precision capabilities operate to the full extent of their potential. Concepts like "locking-out" enemy options reinforce this notion of a helpless and inactive foe.

Still another problem NCW shared with other transformation visions of the 1990s was its tangential reference to OOTW. Cebrowski and Garstka promised to "show that the application of NCW concepts have proven useful in Operations Other Than War including Desert Fox, Deliberate Force, and in Bosnia." They noted that "our collection systems are not currently designed for OOTW," but declared that "this does not negate the promise the NCW has for improving on our current approaches to these kinds of operations." "But even in the case where information is far less than perfect," they concluded, "it could reasonably be argued that being able to have a shared understanding of what is known and what is not known would be preferable to a situation in which units operated in isolated ignorance."[12] It is impossible to argue with the truth of this statement, of course, but the statement is itself irrelevant. American military forces in Bosnia, Kosovo, and elsewhere never "operated in isolated ignorance" from one another. Military units have not had to operate in such a fashion since the fielding of the military radio, and increasing efforts to link units with one another by various technologies had already achieved great success by the mid-1990s. The question was not whether U.S. units should be allowed to operate "in isolated ignorance" or instead "to have a shared understanding," but how much of an improvement NCW would actually offer. Because the treatise focused on defeating a strawman rather than addressing the real question, it did not provide a fair assessment of the concept, its advantages, and the problems it faced. As with Shock and Awe, finally, NCW focused excessively on the aspect of OOTW that looked most like conventional war—the use of airpower to compel an adversary to curtail its activities and allow the U.S. and its allies to undertake certain operations in peace. It did not really consider the central feature of OOTW, the operation of forces in a complex civilian environment, at all.

Network-centric warfare was thus neither more revolutionary nor more accurate than previous concepts such as Shock and Awe or Force XXI had been, and it would probably have had little more effect and staying power than those concepts but for an accident of politics. For as George W. Bush put together his campaign team, his military advisors gravitated toward a transformation vision based on NCW, and his designee as Secretary of Defense, Donald Rumsfeld, embraced the concept and put it at the heart of his defense program. In January 2001, therefore, network-centric warfare became the basis of U.S. military thinking, planning, and budgeting.

FROM THEORY TO POLITICS: BUSH, RUMSFELD, AND RMA

From early in his campaign for the White House, Bush accepted and promoted a vision of information-age warfare that meshed well with the concepts of NCW, Shock and Awe, and the other infowar theorists, although it was vague enough not to distinguish among them. At the defining campaign speech on national security issues he gave at the Citadel in September 1999, then candidate Bush declared that he would seize on "a tremendous opportunity . . . to extend the current peace into the far realm of the future." He continued,

This opportunity is created by a revolution in the technology of war. Power is increasingly defined, not by mass or size, but by mobility and swiftness. Influence is measured in information, safety is gained in stealth, and force is projected on the long arc of precision-guided weapons. This revolution perfectly matches the strengths of our country—the skill of our people and the superiority of our technology. The best way to keep the peace is to redefine war on our terms.[13]

Emphasizing his commitment to the new vision, he complained, "today our military is still organized more for Cold War threats than for the challenges of a new century—for industrial age operations, rather than for information age battles. There is almost no relationship between our budget priorities and a strategic vision. The last seven years have been wasted in inertia and idle talk."

He then laid out a bold vision for transformation drawing ecumenically on many trends in the debate to that point:

As president, I will begin an immediate, comprehensive review of our military. . . . I will give the Secretary a broad mandate—to challenge the status quo and envision a new architecture of American defense for decades to come. We will modernize some existing weapons and equipment, necessary for current tasks. But our relative peace allows us to do this selectively. The real goal is to move beyond marginal improvements—to replace existing programs with new technologies and strategies. To use this window of opportunity to skip a generation of technology. This will require spending more—and spending more wisely. . . .

Our forces in the next century must be agile, lethal, readily deployable, and require a minimum of logistical support. We must be able to project our power over long distances, in days or weeks rather than months. Our military must be able to identify targets by a variety of means —from a Marine patrol to a satellite. Then be able to destroy those targets almost instantly, with an array of weapons, from a submarine-launched cruise missile, to mobile long-range artillery.

On land, our heavy forces must be lighter. Our light forces must be more lethal. All must be easier to deploy. And these forces must be organized in smaller, more agile formations, rather than cumbersome divisions.

In the same speech, however, Bush distanced himself from those in the transformation community who were trying to embrace OOTW. The U.S. military, he declared, "needs the rallying point of a defining mission. And that mission is to deter wars—and win wars when deterrence fails. Sending our military on vague, aimless and endless deployments is the swift solvent of morale." He continued,

The problem comes with open-ended deployments and unclear military missions. In these cases we will ask, "What is our goal, can it be met, and when do we leave?" As I've said before, I will work hard to find political solutions that allow an orderly and timely withdrawal from places like Kosovo and Bosnia. We will encourage our allies to take a broader role. We will not be hasty. But we will not be permanent peacekeepers, dividing warring parties. This is not our strength or our calling.

He concluded, "I will replace diffuse commitments with focused ones. I will replace uncertain missions with well-defined objectives. This will preserve the resources of American power and public will."

It is important to put the two messages of this speech

together to see their real implications. Bush rejected peace-keeping missions because they are vague, indefinite, and messy. He supported transformation defined in a certain way because it was swift, decisive, and clean. These two points together reveal the image of war that Bush was really campaigning on: war is about the destruction of the enemy's ability to fight much more than about achieving the political objectives of the campaign. From the very beginning, war for Bush was really a targeting drill.

Bush continued to advance this viewpoint aggressively after his inauguration. At the christening of the USS Ronald Reagan, he said,

> The island on the *Reagan*'s main deck is almost the same height as that of its predecessors, but it has one less level. The empty space will be filled with cables that will tie the ship into a vast network that connects information and weapons in new ways. This will revolutionize the Navy's ability to project American power over land and sea, ensuring access for all our forces, wherever our vital interests are threatened.
>
> These new capabilities are the future of our military, not just the Navy, but of all our services. It is the future of where a revolution in technology will change the face of war, itself. We'll keep the peace by redefining the terms of war.[14]

At his graduation address to the Naval Academy a few months later, he declared,

> we must build forces that draw upon the revolutionary advances in the technology of war that will allow us to keep the peace by redefining war on our terms. I'm com-

mitted to building a future force that is defined less by size and more by mobility and swiftness, one that is easier to deploy and sustain, one that relies more heavily on stealth, precision weaponry and information technologies.[15]

He thus remained committed both to the general concept of the information RMA and to certain specific elements of military transformation. Bush hastened to insert his vision into Defense budget reality, promising to "Shape a 21st Century Force Structure," as opposed to the Cold War force structure he asserted the military still retained.[16]

He challenged the "defense technology community to use the present window of relative peace not just to modernize the force but to move beyond incremental improvements on defense systems already deployed and develop the military forces the nation will need for the 21st Century." He specifically proposed to devote $20 billion between 2002 and 2006 to increased research and development funds, and to "allocate 20 percent of the R&D budget to especially promising programs that propel America's Armed Forces generations ahead in military technology." Transformation-mania had seized the White House completely.

Bush's nominees to head the Defense Department did not at first focus heavily on transformation, however. In his opening statement at his confirmation hearing, Secretary-Designate Donald Rumsfeld said that Bush had assigned him three primary tasks: to restore the health of the military personnel system; to develop effective missile defense systems; and only then to "take advantage of the new possibilities that the ongoing technological revolution offers to create the military of the next century."[17]

Rumsfeld himself identified five major "key objectives" that he intended to pursue: 1) strengthening deterrence, especially against adversaries armed with WMD; 2) improving the readiness and sustainability of U.S. forces; 3) modernizing command, control, communications, intelligence, and space capabilities "to support twenty-first century needs;" 4) reorganizing and streamlining Department of Defense acquisitions procedures; and 5) reforming Department of Defense business and operating procedures. Deputy Secretary-Designate Paul Wolfowitz mainly echoed these priorities in his own confirmation hearing.[18]

These priorities emerged from the perceptions of the major problems facing the military in the 1990s that had been the basis of Republican criticisms of Clinton. By the end of Clinton's second term, the military was suffering from serious difficulties in the areas of recruitment, retention, and training. The "readiness levels" of certain units—formal military measures of a unit's ability to deploy and fight with no notice—had dropped alarmingly; others were undermanned. The services were also encountering problems with recruitment, and a large number of high-quality officers and NCOs were leaving. The Air Force faced a crisis as pilots left in droves; the Army found that many officers scarred by the downsizing of the early 1990s were leaving for what they perceived to be more stable careers.

The stresses of maintaining tens of thousands of active and reserve soldiers deployed in numerous contingency operations were also contributing to these recruitment and retention problems. Certain units that the military called "high-demand/low-density" because they were needed in many different kinds of contingencies but were few in number, found themselves deployed from one operation to another with little or no rest. Unfortunate soldiers moved from one unit when it returned home to another that was just about to deploy. This personal turbulence generated tensions in the home lives of servicepeople, leading to career dissatisfaction and departure from the service.

The overall inadequacy of the defense budgets of the 1990s,

especially in light of the high operational tempo of that period, led to significant shortfalls in training funds. The continual deployment of essential support units further hindered home-station training. An increasing number of units were not, therefore, able to train adequately in their permanent garrisons, leading to worse-than-normal results at the Army's training centers.

Clinton's critics had been quick to blame his defense policies for these problems, in addition to the blame some heaped upon him for failing to place enough emphasis on transformation. The Bosnia and Kosovo operations became lightning rods for this sort of criticism, as some of Bush's early speeches attest.

In truth, Clinton was only partly to blame. He had been determined to keep military spending "under control" in order to maintain his focus on domestic priorities even as he increased U.S. military commitments abroad. Such a policy was certainly short-sighted. But the Congress, dominated after 1994 by the Republican Party, was equally reluctant to increase the defense budget dramatically. The "Contract with America" championed by incoming House Speaker Newt Gingrich and his allies committed the Republicans to a Balanced Budget Amendment. Such an amendment is inherently harmful to the defense budget, which is the largest single block of "discretionary" spending in the Federal Budget. The focus on balancing budgets virtually precluded Republican support for increased defense spending.

Nor did the Republicans demand such an increase. They focused, instead, on attempting to prevent Clinton from using U.S. forces to support peacekeeping operations, or U.S. money to assist the U.N. in such endeavors. Although they bemoaned the stresses being placed on the shrinking U.S. military—in 1994!—their general solution was to eliminate the stresses by contracting the strategy, rather than to make more resources available for defense. Although they called for a "blue-ribbon panel" to make a detailed and objective assessment of the military's needs, the focus of the Republican Revolution was to prevent any further *reduction* in defense spending rather than to increase it.[19]

At the same time, a sizable body of Republicans came increasingly to the conclusion toward the end of the 1990s that military action against Saddam was essential to prevent him from restarting his WMD programs. Their belief in the importance of being able to fight another war against Iraq conflicted with their gloomy impressions of U.S. military capabilities and with their desire not to increase defense spending. It is not surprising, therefore, that many of these Republicans who came to form the inner sanctum of the Bush administration's national security team saw high-tech transformation as the solution to their problems.

Rumsfeld and Wolfowitz, however, in the days before 9/11, continued their own previous focus on making good the perceived deficiencies in Clinton's defense policy, with improvements in military readiness and quality of life and renewed efforts toward creating a national missile defense system receiving high priorities.

As Rumsfeld settled in to his Pentagon office, however, he began to shift his focus more and more toward transformation. He outlined his overall approach to national security in great detail at a June 2001 hearing of the Senate Armed Services Committee. He declared that the U.S. was still in the midst of a strategic pause in which "Cold War threats have receded, but the dangerous new threats of the twenty-first century have not yet fully emerged." He concluded that "we need to take advantage of this period to ensure that we are prepared for the challenges we will certainly face in the decades ahead," and "if we are to extend this period of peace and prosperity, we need to prepare now for the new and different threats we will face in the decades ahead—not wait until they fully emerge. Only if we act now will we be able to live in peace in that quite different world."[20]

Rumsfeld then picked up and expanded upon a core element of the transformation visions of the 1990s: "while it is difficult to know precisely who will threaten, or where, or when in the coming decades, it is less difficult to anticipate how we will be threatened." He then identified the four major threats he thought the U.S. would face in the coming decades: terrorism, cyber-warfare, adversaries' acquisition of PGMs, and WMD and ballistic missile proliferation. It is notable that, in keeping with a growing focus on capabilities rather than intentions, this list of "threats" is really a list of methods a generic enemy might use to attack the U.S. It is the sort of list that emerges less from a consideration of what specific potential foes are doing than from an evaluation of the vulnerabilities Rumsfeld could see in the U.S. national security system. It was in many respects, therefore, a projection of perceived American weaknesses and fears onto the future capabilities of America's enemies.

Rumsfeld also embraced the argument that an information revolution in military affairs was inevitable and imminent and the U.S. could either lead it or suffer the consequences:

If harnessed by us, these advanced weapons can help us to extend our current peace and security well into the new century. If harnessed by our adversaries, however, these technologies could lead to unpleasant surprises in the years ahead—and could allow hostile powers to undermine our current prosperity and our ability to contribute to peace. . . .

The new threats are on the horizon. And with the speed of change today—where technology is advancing not in decades but in months and years—we cannot afford to wait until they have emerged before we prepare to meet them.

After the new threats emerge, this opportunity may not be available. The risks of transformation could be much greater then—perhaps unacceptably so.

The urgency of transformation in Rumsfeld's mind was thus becoming clear. It became even clearer in his discussion of the possibility of abandoning the two-MRC force-sizing construct.

By March 2001, rumors had begun to circulate that Rumsfeld was thinking in these terms and that he might reduce military personnel in order to pay both for transformation and for missile defense. Some speculated that he intended to reduce the number of Active Army divisions from 10 to 8, possibly designating 2 of those 8 for peacekeeping operations; to cut the number of National Guard combat divisions from 8 to 4, and to reduce the number of Navy carriers from 12 to 10.[21]

Rumsfeld addressed these rumors more or less directly in his June testimony before the Senate Armed Services Committee. He began by offering the traditional justification of the two-theater capability:

> The two MTW [MRC] approach was an innovation at the end of the Cold War. It was based on the proposition that the U.S. should prepare for the possibility that two regional conflicts could arise at the same time. If the U.S. were engaged in a conflict in one theater, an adversary in a second theater might try to gain his objectives before the U.S. could react. Prudence dictated that the U.S. take this possibility into account.[22]

He then repeated the by-now standard criticism that this "approach" was primarily a "force-sizing" mechanism that allowed the services to defend their structures against efforts to change them. He added that the two-theater approach was explicitly conditioned on conflicts in southwest and northeast Asia (Iraq and Korea, primarily), even though only his predecessor Les Aspin had actually tied the concept so tightly to potential enemies.

Rumsfeld then argued that although it had been helpful as a transitional guideline from the Cold War to the post-Cold War world, it was no longer appropriate for the twenty-first century. His first point was fascinating and alarming:

> First, because we have underfunded and overused our forces, we find we are short a division, we are short airlift, we have been underfunding aging infrastructure and facilities, we are short high-demand/low-density assets, the aircraft fleet is aging at considerable and growing cost to maintain, the Navy is declining in numbers, and we are steadily falling below acceptable readiness standards. I have no doubt that should two nearly simultaneous conflicts occur that we would prevail in both. But the erosion in the capability of the force means that the risks we would face today and tomorrow are notably higher than they would have been when the two MTW standard was established.

He continued by pointing to the problems in recruitment and retention that had emerged through the consistent underfunding of quality-of-life, military pay, and other "people" issues. He added that it was necessary now to reduce the "waste, inefficiency, and distrust that result from the way Department of Defense functions," although the relationship of these problems to the two-war capability was not at all clear.

But the thrust of his attack on the concept was very clear. He argued:

an approach that prepares for two major wars, by its very nature, focuses military planning on the near-term, to the detriment of preparing for longer-term threats. Because we can't predict threats of the future, we tend not to plan for them. As a result, too much of today's military planning is dominated today by what one scholar of Pearl Harbor called "a poverty of expectations—a routine obsession with a few dangers that may be familiar rather than likely."

The result of this "poverty of expectations," he continued, had been a habitual under-investment "in dealing with future risks. We have failed to invest adequately in the advanced military technologies we will need to meet the emerging threats of the new century." Since research, development, and acquisition of new capabilities takes such a long time, he concluded, "waiting further to invest in twenty-first century capabilities will pose an unacceptable risk. We are, in essence, risking our future security."

Rumsfeld did not stop his attack there, however. He continued, "We also know that in the decade since the two MTW approach was fashioned, we have not had two major regional wars—which, of course, is good and may well be an indication of the success of the approach. On the other hand, we have done a host of other things, such as Haiti, Bosnia, Kosovo, noncombatant evacuations, humanitarian missions, etc." Any new strategy, therefore, had to take such smaller-scale contingencies into account (although Rumsfeld did not appear to notice that Bush had rejected the wisdom of undertaking such operations almost without exception).

Rumsfeld did not state during this testimony whether he intended to abandon the two-war standard or not, contenting himself with explaining that detailed reviews conducted together with the military service chiefs and regional combatant commanders were going on at that moment to hammer out a solution to the problem. It was clear, however, that he opposed the simple retention of the two-war standard and would work to reduce it in favor of increasing funding for transformation.

By far the most interesting attack Rumsfeld made against the two-MRC capability was the first one, in which he appeared to claim that it was foolish to maintain such a standard since the armed forces could not really execute it anyway. He was quite right, of course—the Army was "short a division," the Air Force "short airlift," and all services "short high-demand/low-density assets." These problems had existed since the early 1990s, and had led a series of senior officers, civilian officials, and outside analysts to point out the steadily rising risk the U.S. military faced in having to fight two wars at once. Rumsfeld was telling nothing less than the truth when he argued that this "standard" had already become strategically irrelevant through a decade-long failure to adhere to it.

The argument that the 1990s showed that "smaller-scale contingencies," including peacekeeping operations, were by no means "lesser included cases" of MRCs, was also cogent and correct. The strain of the Bosnia and Kosovo deployments was, in truth, out of all proportion to the actual size of the forces maintained in the Balkans: an Army with thirty-two deployable brigades in the active force should have been able to maintain several in peacekeeping operations for a long time without going to pieces. The strain resulted in part from the Army's continued reliance on a divisional system of deployment, which meant that the movement of one brigade adversely affected the combat readiness of two others not involved in the deployment, and from the inadequate number of certain critical support units. The real significance of all of this for the two-war construct was, thus, not immediately apparent, although the strain on the Army was very real.

It was a very strange argument, nevertheless, to assert that the military was incapable of executing a particular strategy within acceptable levels of risk, and should therefore abandon that strategy without evaluating the consequences of such an abandonment. It was particularly odd to note that the armed forces could not reasonably be expected to win two nearly simultaneous major wars in part because of the heavy burden that smaller contingencies were placing on them, note that they would likely continue to be involved in such smaller contingencies, and yet offer no suggestions for addressing this problem.

Since one of the charges Rumsfeld leveled at the two-MRC capability was that it had become irrelevant in the twenty-first century context, it is worth noting that it was not a novel idea or capability in 1991 when it became a prominent part of the U.S. national security debate, and was in no way particularly tied, except by rhetoric and terminology, to the immediate post-Cold War period. The U.S. has regularly fought multi-theater wars throughout its history. They are, indeed, the norm rather than the exception up to the most recent period. The French and Indian War, the American Revolution, the War of 1812, the Mexican War, the Civil War, the Spanish–American War (which first saw U.S. armed forces engaged in simultaneous operations at the opposite ends of the globe), World War I, and World War II were all multi-theater conflicts for America. Korea and Vietnam were not, it is true, but in both cases the U.S. military maintained its primary focus on the potential for a Soviet invasion of Western Europe, thus supporting a two-war capability without having to fight both. Desert Storm was the first major war America has fought that *was not* a multi-theater war or a sideshow in the shadow of a larger threat. By invading Iraq in 2003 while hostilities continued in Afghanistan, the U.S. seemed to be returning to the more normal pattern.

But Rumsfeld was not really interested in the historical validity of the two-war requirement, because he had accepted the argument that transformation was a much more urgent necessity. He believed that the U.S. was still in a "strategic pause" that left it without serious immediate threats, but that the arrival of an information RMA was inevitable and imminent. The attack on the two-war standard was really an attack on maintaining forces to support present strategic needs and an argument for refocusing defense policy primarily on the perceived requirements of future war.

Rumsfeld hinted at another important conceptual shift that supported this line of thinking by arguing that the U.S. should abandon its traditional "threat-based" strategic approach in favor of "capabilities-based" planning. He explained that, "because of the uncertainty about the future strategic environment," it was important to stop thinking so much about threats "while turning instead to a 'capabilities-based' approach to make certain we develop forces prepared for the longer-term threats that are less easily understood." He defined this approach as follows: "we would work to select, develop and sustain a portfolio of U.S. military capabilities—capabilities that could not only help us prevail against current threats, but, because we possess them, dissuade potential adversaries from developing dangerous new capabilities."

There was once again little new in this concept. Since 1991, the U.S. military had not been adjusting its force structure constantly based on shifting perceptions of North Korean or Iraqi plans or capabilities. Successive administrations, rather, had identified a desired capability—the need to be able to fight two major wars—and then, theoretically, crafted armed forces that would be able to do so against enemies somewhat more powerful than Iraq then was, and somewhat less powerful than North Korea then was. It was nothing if not a "capabilities-based" strategic approach.

The transformation visions of the 1990s were even more focused on developing certain desired capabilities and even less concerned with current or imminent threats. Virtually none of them, in fact, ever addressed any specific country, coalition, or non-state actor against whom their suggested approaches would best succeed. They regularly argued, as did Rumsfeld, however, that the information revolution was establishing the requirement for a certain very specific set of capabilities without which the U.S. would fall hopelessly behind in the global competition for military power.

But if there was nothing novel in 2001 in adopting a "capabilities-based" approach to defense planning, it was, however, extremely dangerous to have such an approach formally accepted as the point of departure for Bush administration budgeting and force planning. There can be no question that, at the end of the day, a military is designed to have certain capabilities. The question is how the leadership determines what those capabilities should be. One approach is to look at current and likely future threats, explore their vulnerabilities and the vulnerabilities in friendly forces and allies they might exploit, and from that evaluation determine what capabilities would be needed to defeat them. If the leadership wishes to focus on the future, then it would look in more detail at the transformation programs of likely foes, including their published records, their investment patterns, and any available intelligence about internal discussions. If it emerges that no likely enemy is actually pursuing a given line of military development—network-centric warfare, say—then preparations to meet the threat such a development would pose would receive secondary priority unless they clearly offered a capability U.S. forces would need to attack enemy vulnerabilities. This is the only procedure that is likely to ground transformation in reality.

The other approach is to attempt to determine in advance how warfare will change without considering who will be changing it. This is the approach pioneered by the transformation visionaries of the 1990s. It has the advantage of simplifying the problem—if global technological trends indicate that infowar is the way to go, then there is no need to scour the globe to find a potential enemy against whom such an approach might be necessary or particularly valuable. This approach suffers from the weakness that it is not grounded in reality at all. If the visionaries are true prophets, then the pursuit of the vision will prove wise. If they are not, then the military runs the risk of being unprepared for situations that could have been foreseen, even if only dimly, through a more pedestrian analysis of potential threats and their real trendlines. Rumsfeld, nevertheless, preferred this approach, and he established it firmly as U.S. policy in the Quadrennial Defense Review of 2001.

THE QDR OF 2001

The Quadrennial Defense Review (QDR) was published twenty-one days after the September 11th attacks. It was modified slightly to take account of the emerging "global war on terror," but it naturally reflected primarily the thoughts and ideas that had shaped it over the previous months—the last few months of America's "strategic pause." The review embodied both the information RMA as Bush and Rumsfeld had described it—which is to say, rather vaguely—and the "capabilities-based" approach to force planning. The QDR resolved the two-war capability problem by not really resolving it. It declared,

The new force-sizing construct specifically shapes forces to: Defend the United States; Deter aggression and coercion forward in critical regions; Swiftly defeat aggression in overlapping major conflicts while preserving for the President the option to call for a decisive victory in one of those conflicts—including the possibility of regime change or occupation; and Conduct a limited number of smaller-scale contingency operations.[23]

It continued,

> Second, the approach shifts the focus of U.S. force planning from optimizing for conflicts in two particular regions—Northeast and Southwest Asia—to building a portfolio of capabilities that is robust across the spectrum of possible force requirements, both functional and geographical. This approach to planning responds to the capabilities-based strategy outlined above. It focuses more on how an adversary might fight than on who the adversary might be and where a war might occur. The shift is intended to refocus planners on the growing range of capabilities that adversaries might possess or could develop.[24]

In the absence of any particular threats, of course, this "refocusing" of strategists on "the growing range of capabilities that adversaries *might* possess" gave free rein to speculation and to the sort of self-referential arguments that dominated the information revolution discussions of the 1990s.

Although the QDR did commit the military to being able to *fight* two major wars that overlapped in some way (but were no longer necessarily "nearly simultaneous"), it did not commit the military to being able to *win* them both *decisively*. It might be necessary, in other words, simply to halt one attack and then, presumably, negotiate a settlement while focusing on winning the other completely—presumably by occupying the enemy's territory. This capability was even weaker than the "win-hold-win" approach Aspin had advocated, as it contemplated the possibility that the U.S. might have to accept something less than victory in the second conflict. As a description of the focus and preferred approaches of some of the hawkish conservative Republicans who had entered the Bush administration, this approach was pretty accurate. Many, like Wolfowitz, wanted to attack and decisively defeat Saddam Hussein, but would probably have been content with just preventing North Korea from attacking or defeating the South. It is not clear, therefore, how totally free from concerns with particular immediate threats this "new" force-sizing approach really was.

The QDR attempted to rephrase the entire discussion: "The United States is not abandoning planning for two conflicts to plan for fewer than two. On the contrary, the Department of Defense is changing the concept altogether by planning for victory across the spectrum of possible conflict."[25] This assertion was little more than a fan dance. The QDR clearly was planning for fewer than two *major theater wars*, although it contemplated fighting more smaller conflicts simultaneously. And it ignored once again, as Rumsfeld had before, the strategic rationale behind the need to maintain the capability to fight two such wars.

Despite all the discussions about how revolutionary the new force-sizing construct was, however, the QDR did not actually recommend *any* significant changes in the actual size, composition, or organization of the U.S. military.[26] Worse still, it acknowledged that that force size remained inadequate to handle even all of the more restricted crisis scenarios the new force-sizing construct envisioned, noting that "certain combinations of warfighting and smaller-scale contingency scenarios present high risk."[27] The shift from a two-war capability to a one-war-plus-smaller-contingencies, thus, did not really relieve the strain or reduce the danger the U.S. military faced.

The QDR also highlighted two other aspects of U.S. force planning and military operational planning: global deployment and deterrence. One of the main purposes of the U.S. military, the QDR argued, was to deter conflict, both major and minor, including terrorist attacks. The best way to accomplish such deterrence was through developing capabilities that would be clearly sufficient to destroy any adversary's ability to fight. The review repeatedly noted that it did not matter, from the standpoint of deterrence, where those capabilities were based. Enemies of the U.S. would know that B-2 bombers in the United States were only hours from their heartland, wherever they were.

The major purpose of forward-deployed forces, such as American troops in Europe and Korea, was not, therefore, to deter aggression as much as to be able to defeat it should deterrence fail. The QDR declared, "One of the goals of reorienting the global posture is to render forward forces capable of swiftly defeating an adversary's military and political objectives with only modest reinforcement."[28] It naturally followed that this goal would require a fundamentally different global footprint from the Cold War model that focused on deterrence.

The QDR did not make very many specific recommendations on this point—that debate would come later on—although it bizarrely demanded that the Army base one of its Stryker-equipped Interim Brigade Combat Teams in Europe by 2007.[29] Since the entire point of those formations was to facilitate global deployment from the United States—the difference in travel time from Germany to the Middle East compared to that from the U.S. to the Middle East is negligible when the forces are all flying—this demand seemed to make little sense.

It is also worth pointing out what the QDR did not recommend—the fundamental reorientation of the domestic basing of U.S. military forces. Whatever the problems involved in moving U.S. forces from Germany or Korea to other areas of interests in Europe, the Middle East, or Asia, they are smaller than the problems involved in moving soldiers and their equipment hundreds of miles by rail from bases in Colorado, central Texas, Kansas, and so forth. The U.S. Army infrastructure was last fundamentally reoriented at the end of the Indian Wars of the nineteenth century. The Army still maintains garrisons as though it were preparing to subdue the Sioux and the Apaches once again. This disposition imposes significant delays on Army deployment, increases its complexity, and in the future will offer enemies numerous bottlenecks to strike with precision weapons if they actually acquire them. Creating a strategically deployable military should, in principle, require a wholesale reorientation of the military's bases within the U.S., but such a suggestion is politically naïve in the highest degree.

Perhaps the most important single announcement of the 2001 QDR was the creation of an Office of Force Transformation reporting directly to the Secretary and the Deputy Secretary of Defense.[30] This office was given broad guidance: it would "evaluate the transformation efforts of the Military Departments and promote synergy by recommending steps to integrate ongoing transformation activities." To assist with this monitoring function, the QDR directed the services to "develop transformation roadmaps that specify timelines to develop Service-unique capabilities necessary to meet the six critical operational goals described below," which included protecting the U.S., its forward bases, and allies; protecting information systems and "conducting effective information operations;" projecting U.S. forces despite enemy efforts at area-denial; "Denying enemies sanctuary by providing persistent surveillance, tracking, and rapid engagement with high-volume precision strike, through a combination of complementary air and ground capabilities, against critical mobile and fixed targets at various ranges and in all weather and terrains;" improving U.S. space systems; and "leveraging information technology and innovative concepts to develop an interoperable, joint C4ISR architecture and capability that includes a tailorable joint operational picture."[31] The Office of Force Transformation thus had no small or easily-accomplished mandate.

Another noteworthy aspect of the 2001 QDR was its failure to address the political aims, complexities, and limitations of war in any systematic way. It is one of the first such documents to state directly that the U.S. military must be capable of unseating an enemy government and occupying an enemy country. Its open recognition of the likelihood that "small scale contingencies"—read "peacekeeping"—would be a prominent part of the twenty-first century should also have been a warning that the political aspects of military force would be a critical factor to be considered. The document nowhere considered that factor. It had inherited from the growing momentum of the infowar movement the conviction that war was about the destruction of the enemy's ability to fight, either by precision attrition or by targeting centers of gravity. It did not consider the consequences of the policy of regime change that it openly accepted as a possible military mission. This focus and this lacuna would play an important role in the planning and conduct of U.S. military operations in Afghanistan, which commenced a few days after the publication of the QDR.

CHAPTER EIGHT

A Revolutionary War

THE WORLD CHANGED fundamentally on September 11, 2001 . . . or did it? The attacks on the World Trade Center and the Pentagon were the most visible, dramatic, and destructive acts of terrorism in history. They were the first major foreign attack on targets in the Continental United States since 1814 and the first successful attacks on American soil since Pearl Harbor. They immediately plunged the U.S. into a global struggle with a nebulous, networked enemy of a sort America had never really fought before. And they destroyed the notion that the U.S. was in a "strategic pause."

Although the attacks were in a new mode, President Bush responded to the attacks in a fairly traditional way—he launched a military attack against the state that had been harboring and aiding al Qaeda. The armed forces used an approach to that war that was innovative in execution if not really in concept, but it was still an approach that relied on the ideas and doctrines developed in the 1980s and 1990s, to say nothing of the technology with which it was executed. In the aftermath of that war, the senior military leadership proclaimed at the same time that it was a revolutionary way of fighting and that it vindicated the approach to war they had been pursuing all along. Fifteen months later, the U.S. invaded Iraq using an approach that was an amalgam of the "new way of war" supposedly pioneered in Afghanistan and more traditional techniques first showcased in Desert Storm. The results of that conflict were also said to have proven the validity of the transformation program Bush had brought with him to the White House and Rumsfeld to the Pentagon.

That transformation program, in the meantime, had picked up a great deal of steam. The creation of the Office of Force Transformation and the appointment of its first leader, Admiral Cebrowski, focused all military transformation programs on the development of a "network-centric warfare" capability. The process of preparing for future threats continued and even gained emphasis despite the rapid emergence of chaos in Afghanistan and a major insurgency in Iraq. The tension within U.S. strategy and military theory evident in the 1990s was translated into practical problems as the conflicts in Iraq and Afghanistan began to strain the ground forces very badly.

Since Bush and Rumsfeld and their associates repeatedly claimed that the wars in Afghanistan and Iraq demonstrated the validity of the "new American way of war" and stayed the course on their military transformation programs, it is appropriate to evaluate the conduct and results of those wars to verify these assertions. But even if it seems that these conflicts do not bear out the claims of the transformation enthusiasts, it is important to examine the obvious defense those enthusiasts will inevitably offer: that the technology was not yet sufficiently mature and the process of transformation still in its infancy so that time and rededication to the transformation program will fix any deficiencies that were seen in 2001 and 2003.

OPERATION ENDURING FREEDOM— AFGHANISTAN, 2001

Even before the dust from the World Trade Center began to settle, the Bush administration was certain that the attacks were the work of Osama bin Laden and his al Qaeda network. The U.S. government had been tracking this network for years, and Bush had received several briefings before the attacks about the extreme danger it posed to America. He knew that it was based in Afghanistan, where it was "joined at the hip" to the radical Islamist Taliban government that was on the verge of finally suppressing the insurgency it had been battling since taking power in 1994. He was determined to strike back at bin Laden immediately and do as much damage to al Qaeda as rapidly and as visibly as possible.[1]

There was little else that the Bush administration was clear about, however. Most senior decision-makers were almost totally unfamiliar with Afghanistan and its history. This unfamiliarity led to a number of mistaken assumptions that powerfully shaped the campaign plan. The administration was not clear about whether its objective was simply to destroy al Qaeda, to remove the Taliban from power and leave Afghanistan to its fate, or to take control of the country and work to reconstruct it on a more stable basis. The true objective of the military campaign was never really determined or enunciated before military operations began.

One of the reasons for this confusion about objectives resulted from the shock and fear the September 11 attacks had generated in the U.S. leadership. In the immediate wake of the attacks, the Bush administration was almost frantic about the possibility of additional attacks and was preoccupied with finding ways to defend the hundreds of obvious and critical targets the terrorists could strike next. Bush eagerly seized upon the suggestion to freeze the assets of a number of people and governments linked to al Qaeda, and he quickly signed an authorization allowing the CIA to seek out and capture or kill known terrorists around the world. He and others repeatedly proclaimed that this would be a "new kind of war" that would require innovative thinking, flexibility, and creativity.

At the same time, it became apparent that any dramatic retaliation, which the President felt that the American people hungered for, would have to come against targets the U.S. military could attack, which meant, in the first instance, Afghanistan. Although some within the administration, notably Paul Wolfowitz, pushed for an attack on Iraq instead, Bush refused to be diverted from an immediate counter-attack against those who had actually perpetrated the atrocities. The attack on Afghanistan was thus born in confusion, fear, controversy, and determination.

The Bush administration's ignorance of Afghanistan prior to the attacks was astounding. Only National Security Advisor Condoleezza Rice, a former Soviet specialist, was familiar with it at all, and the immediate information about the country on which Bush made his most critical decisions came from the CIA and its agents in the field. The CIA argued that any insertion of significant American troops into the country would raise a nationalist/Islamist reaction against the "invader," as had happened in 1979 against the Soviets and in the nineteenth century against the British. It would rally the people around the Taliban, a government that, to this point, had enjoyed a very thin veneer of popular support. The CIA advocated instead working with local tribal leaders who were already in the field opposing the Taliban to overthrow that regime by providing them with cash, weapons, and, above all, air support to help them win their battles.

This advice was, in truth, neither unconventional nor surprising. It was almost precisely the method the Agency had used in the 1980s to help defeat the Soviet Union in Afghanistan (the U.S. had not then supplied its own air power, of course); it was the method CIA agents were most comfortable and familiar with, and it offered the best hope for an early start to the operation. The only thing that was unusual or surprising was that the Secretary of Defense, who would ordinarily be expected to fight off Agency suggestions for taking over what should have been "his" war, instead supported this approach, offering the use of Special Operations Forces to work in association with the CIA and the tribal chiefs.

It is not entirely clear why Rumsfeld supported this CIA plan with such relative enthusiasm. It may be that he saw it as the opportunity to validate the "new American way of war," already germinating in his mind, although the published record neither supports nor refutes this possibility. It is certain that he did not feel comfortable with any of the military plans laid before him, partly because it took a very long time for the CENTCOM planners to get him any detailed plans at all.

In all of the controversy surrounding the performance of the Bush administration and the military in the run-up to September 11, it is remarkable that CENTCOM has received virtually no criticism for its failure to have developed a plan for dealing with Afghanistan. There was, after all, considerable basis for imagining in the 1990s that such a plan might become necessary. By the end of the decade, it was known that al Qaeda had orchestrated the 1993 World Trade Center bombing, that bin Laden had declared a *jihad* against the United States, and that he maintained extensive training camps in Afghanistan. President Clinton had even gone so far as to launch a meaningless cruise missile strike at empty training camps in that country in retaliation for the African embassy bombings in 1998, which were also clearly linked to al Qaeda. (The suicide bombing of the USS Cole in 2000 was also known to be bin Laden's handiwork, although it occasioned no response at all.) When Bush took office, finally, he was warned that al Qaeda was among the most serious threats the United States faced. How was it possible that CENTCOM, which had responsibility for Afghanistan, could have failed to develop multiple contingency plans for preempting or retaliating for an al Qaeda attack?

The answer is probably complicated. Central Command is

an unusual regional command in the U.S. military because it has no forces permanently assigned to it even though it has responsibility for a vast, complex, and dangerous area of the world from which many of the threats to the United States now emanate. This situation is a legacy of the late Cold War, for CENTCOM was the lineal descendant of the Rapid Deployment Joint Task Force first established under Carter to be prepared for an unexpected Soviet attack against the Middle East or other surprises in that area. With the focus of the U.S. military on Europe, however, the Rapid Deployment Force never received adequate resources or attention, and CENTCOM did not fare much better.

The command proved itself in Operation Desert Storm, of course, but then fell into a period of strain and tension. For the next decade, CENTCOM was responsible for policing the "no-fly" zones over northern and southern Iraq, operations that led to nearly daily threats and attacks. It was also intimately involved with the enforcement of U.N. economic sanctions against Iraq and with all the complexities posed by Saddam's efforts to smuggle oil out of his country and to circumvent the "oil-for-food" program designed to relieve the suffering of the Iraqi people. It is likely that these activities preoccupied the command and prevented it from considering other potential trouble spots with sufficient care.

The increasing focus of the Defense Department on "capabilities-based" planning rather than on the analysis of threats, a movement codified but not originated by Rumsfeld, as we have seen, was probably also a significant part of the problem. The refusal to take seriously the possibility that America faced significant short-term threats for which it might not be adequately prepared, common throughout the Defense Department, surely penetrated CENTCOM as well. It also made it unlikely that any Secretary of Defense would ever pound his desk and demand a report on contingency plans for dealing with al Qaeda. It may also be, of course, that the prospect of a war in Afghanistan just seemed to be too hard to plan for, a phenomenon that is not at all uncommon in militaries.

Whatever the case, when al Qaeda struck on 9/11, the military had no contingency plan for an attack on Afghanistan. Central Command commander Tommy Franks tried frantically to put one together, but the challenge was daunting. Since Afghanistan is a landlocked country, the U.S. could take no action there (apart from missile strikes) without obtaining the assistance of one or more of Afghanistan's neighbors, principally Pakistan, Uzbekistan, or Tajikistan. But it is difficult for the State Department or CENTCOM itself to make requests for basing rights without knowing what the military operations will look like, since the nature of the operations dictates the kind of rights the U.S. needs. The military's inability to develop a plan rapidly therefore delayed and hindered the formation of an effective coalition. The administration's failure to develop a clear set of objectives did not help either.

As a result, Rumsfeld had to go along with the CIA's "new approach" primarily for want of any better alternative. Central Intelligence Agency operatives worked their way into Afghanistan with suitcases full of cash, and Special Forces teams ready to direct precision air-strikes on Taliban and al Qaeda forces followed. The State Department put together a large coalition that was not expected to support the deployment of significant American ground forces, because there was no military plan in place to make such a deployment. When the Joint Chiefs of Staff criticized the plan, Tommy Franks dismissed them as service hacks who were not able to think outside the box.[2]

Considering the haste and confusion with which it was drawn up, it is not surprising that the plan for Operation Enduring Freedom, as it came to be known, contained a number of serious flaws. First, it was based on an overestimation of the capability of the Taliban and al Qaeda to resist American and Afghan attacks. Second, it was based on a false assumption about the dangers of inserting foreign forces into Afghanistan. Third, it contained no plan for the establishment of favorable conditions in post-war Afghanistan. Fourth, it therefore did not consider the problems that would emerge after the war resulting from the CIA's efforts to arm and build-up would-be regional warlords. Fifth, the failure to prepare for the deployment of any significant number of American ground forces deprived the U.S. of any real control over the developing situation on the ground. Sixth, the plan did not account for the enormous differences in objectives between the U.S. and the Afghan tribal leaders it was supporting. And, finally, the plan did not recognize how unique was the opportunity to fight al Qaeda forces in the open field and did not therefore adequately consider how to take advantage of that opportunity.

Although the administration did not realize it, the Taliban was, in fact, a weak government. It did not control all of the territory of Afghanistan, and it did not have strong support among the population. Afghanistan does not have a tradition of widespread radical Islam, although the war against the Soviets strengthened the more radical elements of Afghan society. The Taliban's brand of utterly intolerant and violent Islam, therefore, was not broadly popular, especially outside of the Pashtun south and southwest of the country, which was its base.

Decades of war, chaos, and poverty had also done little to create a combat-worthy Taliban military. Afghans have long been renowned as infantrymen, able to endure great physical hardships in their difficult terrain and utterly implacable as enemies. But it remains the case that without modern air defenses, armor, artillery, and communications, such forces are not able to fight toe-to-toe with modern militaries. It must be recalled that American aid, especially in the form of surface-to-air missiles, was critical in enabling the *mujahideen* to overcome the Soviets in the 1980s. The Taliban had no outside assistance on such a scale. The emphasis on the hardihood of Afghans, furthermore, which Rumsfeld highlighted repeatedly during the operations, ignored the impressive hardihood of American soldiers, who also undergo extremely rigorous physical training. And it completely ignored the fact that the U.S. plan called for using one set of Afghans to fight the others when there was no reason to imagine that the Afghans allied to the U.S. were any weaker or poorer fighters than their enemies.

America's ability to remove the Taliban from power, either with or without the use of U.S. ground forces, should therefore never have been in question. But in addition to its ignorance about conditions in Afghanistan, the Bush administration misread Afghanistan's history. Americans have long been impressed with the determination the Afghans showed against a vicious Soviet attack and occupation, holding out far longer than any would have expected and, ultimately, defeating the largest and most powerful military on earth. Those more familiar with Afghan history recalled the destruction of an entire British army in the nineteenth century as well, proof, to many, that the Afghans would reflexively band together to fight any Western invader. This view proved to be utterly false—American troops, when they finally arrived, were greeted as liberators, not conquerors, and have even to this day generated remarkably little opposition or resistance among the vast majority of the Afghan population, even in the Pashtun lands. This outcome should not have been a surprise. The British invaded Afghanistan for the purpose of imperial conquest, a policy Afghan leaders had been actively resisting for decades before the attack. The Soviets invaded to support a phenomenally unpopular government, whose leader they had, in addition, just overthrown and assassinated, pursuing policies hated throughout the country. These were the exceptional contexts that led the Afghans to come together to fight such foes so bitterly. To imagine that the Afghans would respond in an identical fashion to American troops coming to avenge an attack launched by foreigners from Afghan soil by striking an extremely unpopular, violent, and repressive government that had little support from the population reflected the most simplistic analysis of Afghanistan's history and culture and a poor grasp of the current situation in the country. The result, however, was profound.

From the beginning of the discussion, the fear of inciting an Afghan reaction against Western invasion precluded any real consideration of the deployment of ground forces. In the immediate wake of September 11, coalition partners such as France urgently requested to be allowed to send ground forces in support of U.S. operations in Afghanistan, but their requests were turned aside.[3] It does not appear that significant contingency planning for the deployment of large numbers of ground forces was even conducted, although the published sources have not focused on this important issue. The misreading of the political and social situation in Afghanistan seems to have taken this option off the table from the outset.

The next major problem with the plan for Operation Enduring Freedom was its failure even to consider the desired post-war configuration of Afghanistan. Part of the problem was that the Bush administration was not clear about its own objectives. Some of the time senior officials talked about removing the Taliban; at other times they talked about removing Mullah Omar, the leader of that movement, and allowing a reformed Taliban to remain in power, having "yielded up" al Qaeda in some fashion. The failure to establish a clear objective caused serious problems for the military operation and, especially, the post-war reconstruction and stabilization effort that is limping along even today.

The Taliban government was not, in fact, a threat to the United States by itself. It did not arm, train, or equip terrorists on its own to attack America or its allies. Simply toppling that government, therefore, did not remove the terrorist danger to the U.S., which resulted almost as much from the Taliban's failure to control the country as from its active connivance with bin Laden. Simply destroying the Taliban without developing a clear plan for creating a new, stable Afghan government that was able to control its own territory, would accomplish little.

It was not possible, however, to go after al Qaeda without also attacking the Taliban, if for no other reason than that such operations inevitably would be interpreted as an act of war against the sovereign state within which they were conducted. The Taliban's sympathy for al Qaeda, moreover, meant that Mullah Omar and his lieutenants were willing to place their limited military means at bin Laden's disposal during the fight. Any successful operation against bin Laden would necessarily result in the destruction of the Taliban regime, which relied upon that combat power (and on bin Laden's money) to keep itself in power.

In no circumstance, therefore, could the U.S. hope to avoid destroying the government of Afghanistan and its limited military forces. Leaving the country in anarchy, however, was clearly an invitation for a reconstituted al Qaeda or any other radical Islamist terrorist organization to take root there in the future and recreate the conditions that had led to the 9/11 attack. It should have been entirely obvious, therefore, that the only acceptable objectives of U.S. military operations were the destruction of al Qaeda, the removal of the Taliban from power, *and the replacement of that government by a new one able to achieve its own legitimacy, stability, and control of the country*. None of the discussions of the war plans in September and October seriously addressed this issue, and the initial phase of war was not, therefore, conducted with any real eye to the post-war situation.

From published accounts it appears that the senior leadership did not carefully consider the desired post-war situation in Afghanistan until the first week of October, long after the nature and many of the details of the military plan had been settled. At an NSC meeting on October 4, Bush asked, "'Who will run the country?' ... We should have addressed that, [National Security Advisor Condoleezza] Rice thought."[4] The timing was not accidental. Central Command's failure to have even a contingency plan to offer for a retaliatory strike against al Qaeda had forced the senior-most leadership to focus extensively on developing such a plan and getting it moving. With all of the pressure to act rapidly and all of the difficulties to be surmounted, it is not surprising that no one could spare a thought for the seemingly less-important problem of what to do after winning.

It may seem, in fact, that these priorities were the correct ones. Taking one thing at a time is a common feature of U.S. war planning. The intense focus on getting the "military part" right, which is an enormously complex and dangerous task in itself, frequently overwhelms any thinking about what to do after the victory. Even asking or thinking about that question before operations have begun seems to be hubristic.

But presidents are not just like normal people, and "common sense" does not always apply in affairs of state. Military operations must be designed to achieve particular political objectives. The only way to design them in that way is to identify in advance what the political objectives are and to think through the difficulties that will have to be overcome both during and after the war in order to achieve them. To develop a military operational plan without considering the details of the desired post-war settlement risks running a plan that will hinder rather than help with the attainment of that settlement. This is precisely the problem the Bush administration encountered in Afghanistan.

When the leadership began considering the problem of a post-war Afghanistan in early October, a number of things became clear. First, that it was not really possible to imagine leaving any part of the Taliban in power. There would have to be a new government. Second, that the Northern Alliance, by itself, could not be that government. That alliance, itself fractured along tribal and ethnic lines, represented a coalition of Afghanistan's minorities. Any attempt simply to put its leaders in power was likely to fan the flames of further civil war and chaos. Third, that it was therefore undesirable for the Northern Alliance to take Kabul by itself. Such an event would seem to signal the likelihood of minority government in Afghanistan, undermine support for the U.S. among the majority Pashtuns, and lay the groundwork for future disorder. And, fourth, it would be necessary to insert some sort of substantial peace-keeping force to prevent the country from falling entirely into anarchy and to facilitate a yet-to-be-established process for rebuilding Afghanistan's political system. In other words, the objectives the U.S. would need to accomplish at a minimum militated powerfully against certain decisions that had already been made, including the refusal to consider or prepare for inserting U.S. ground forces in numbers, the determination to rely upon the Northern Alliance for the bulk of the soldiers fighting the war, and the failure to plan for a post-war political transition before commencing hostilities.

Even after the leadership began considering these issues, moreover, it was slow to change powerful and harmful precon-ceptions. As late as October 12, five days after the bombing cam-paign had begun, Bush told his team, "Look, I oppose using the military for nation building. Once the job is done, our forces are not peacekeepers. We ought to put in place a U.N. protec-tion and leave, but if fighting resumes and the Taliban come back from the hills, who has to stabilize the situation?" The only answer offered to this prescient question came from Colin Powell: "Well, the new entity has to have a capacity to defend itself," and from George Tenet: "Well, our covert action network will remain." Neither was a remotely satisfactory solution to what would turn out to be the critical problem of the post-war situation.[5]

The failure to think through the problem of achieving

America's post-war objectives, or even of deciding what those objectives were exactly, led to still another problem in execution. In looking for Afghans to bribe to fight the Taliban, the CIA prioritized those that had meaningful armed forces and a history of hostility to Mullah Omar's government. Central Intelligence Agency agents then handed over bags of dollars to such tribal leaders and encouraged them to build up their armies. This was an effective technique for creating mercenary forces. But it was also an effective technique for enabling those tribal leaders to establish their own semi-independent palatinates in various regions of Afghanistan in despite of any post-war central Afghan government. Since Afghanistan has a history of relatively weak central governments struggling with powerful local chieftains, this was a policy that threatened to doom any effort to establish a stable central government in Kabul able to control all of the territory of Afghanistan—a primary objective of the war. The failure to think through the political objectives and to incorporate them into the military planning, once again, led to the development of military plans that would actively hinder the accomplishment of those objectives.

These problems would not necessarily have been overwhelming had the U.S. been prepared to deploy significant ground forces into the country. American ground forces would have been able to allow or prevent the Northern Alliance from taking Kabul, for instance. They would have minimized the need to build-up regional warlords. They would have allowed the U.S. to shape the collapse of the Taliban and the beginnings of the new order that would replace it rapidly and from the start. They would have given the U.S., in other words, far greater leverage and much more ability to control the rapidly developing situation in the country. The failure to deploy ground forces, by contrast, left the development of the campaign, both military and political, largely in the hands of the tribal allies. The problem was that those allies did not share the objectives of the Bush

administration, especially the most important objectives relat-
ing to al Qaeda.

For the administration and Americans in general, the
destruction of al Qaeda was the number one priority in the
attack on Afghanistan to which all other considerations should
have been subordinated. Over the course of the campaign, U.S.
leaders repeatedly complained when too much time was spent
talking about the Taliban or even the post-war situation at the
expense of the destruction of al Qaeda. But the Afghan tribal
leaders were not really interested in destroying al Qaeda. For
them it was enough to drive the foreigners out of their regions,
clearing the way for them to establish their own rule—which was
their main preoccupation. Considering that the al Qaeda soldiers fought fanatically to the death, moreover, their deliberate
and focused destruction was more than most tribal leaders were
eager to undertake, with or without American air power. This
fundamental disagreement about basic aims shaped the military
campaign, and the administration's failure to deploy ground
forces gave it little leverage. As Tenet noted on October 11,
"They had put their fate in the hands of the Afghan tribals, who
were going to act at a time, place and pace of their own choosing.
They had their own issues, endgames, ambitions and internal
power plays. It was a mercenary force—not under U.S. command. That was the price of admission when it was decided at
the front end that the tribals were going to do the bulk of the
ground fighting and not the U.S. military."[6] This observation
would have been much more valuable and to the point had he
made it several weeks earlier, before the administration had
already committed to that course of action.

The result of these miscues and failures to think problems
through in a timely fashion was that the U.S. did not destroy
al Qaeda's forces in Afghanistan and did not "kill or capture"
bin Laden or most of his lieutenants. The Bush administration
can point to significant damage inflicted upon the enemy, to be

sure—the U.S. and its Afghan allies certainly killed hundreds of al Qaeda fighters and captured a certain number of fighters and sympathizers. But it is essential to consider the magnitude of the opportunity the enemy offered us in September—October 2001 before making a claim of success.

The characteristic that makes organizations like al Qaeda so terribly difficult to fight is that they disperse and hide. It is hard to find targets in such dispersed organizations, and hard to use military force to attack them. As a result, they can largely negate America's greatest advantage in most conflicts—our overwhelming military power. When such organizations do, for whatever reason, concentrate large numbers of their members in visible locations, it is absolutely imperative to kill or capture as close to one hundred percent of them as possible. Simply killing some and scattering the rest is really a defeat, for they are unlikely to repeat the mistake of concentrating again in the future.

Osama bin Laden clearly did not expect Bush to respond to 9/11 by attacking his sanctuaries in Afghanistan, toppling the Taliban, and taking control of the country. Terrorists are not immune to the common disease of believing their own propaganda. As a result, it seems clear that there were several thousand al Qaeda operatives in Afghanistan at the time of the U.S. attack, including around one thousand in the so-called Brigade 055 of the Taliban Army. These al Qaeda troops were foolish enough to take the field in combat formations to defend their erstwhile sponsors against American attack.

The Bush administration was aware of this opportunity, but apparently did not grasp its full significance. Every effort should have been bent to killing or capturing all or nearly all of these fighters. Military planners should have been examining possible routes of withdrawal, since experienced Afghan fighters are expert at finding such routes, and determining ways to block them. The ample Soviet military experience, readily available to those planners in the form of translations of Soviet "after action reviews," suggested the difficulty of using either indigenous Afghan allies or stand-off weapons to block such "bolt holes." [7] Nor would any reasonable estimate of the aims and capabilities of the Northern Alliance forces suggest that they would be willing or able to undertake such a campaign of annihilation.

At the beginning of hostilities, the bulk of al Qaeda's forces were north of Kabul, preparing to resist the expected attack of the Northern Alliance supported by the U.S. This was the best possible location, from the American standpoint, for these soldiers to occupy. Many of their escape routes would take them across the Shamali plain north of Kabul, an area as accessible to U.S. ground forces and bombers as any in the country, before bringing them to the mountain fastnesses along the Pakistani border. The deployment early in the operation of even a relatively small number of American light infantry along these likely routes of withdrawal would probably have netted a much higher percentage of the al Qaeda forces in the north when they broke under the pressure of Northern Alliance attack and U.S. bombing. The failure to deploy such forces meant that the concentrated al Qaeda forces in the north were shattered and dispersed rather than rounded-up. The result was a series of operations, one in the caves around Tora-Bora and the other in the Shah-i Kot valley (Operation Anaconda), aimed at capturing and killing those stragglers under much less favorable conditions. The Tora-Bora operation was not very successful in this aim; Anaconda was rather more so, but both were aimed even so at only part of the al Qaeda organization that had dispersed. Others had simply melted away into Pakistan and beyond, safely out of the reach of American military power and free to raise new recruits and plan new operations against the U.S.

No military plan would have captured or killed all of these fighters, of course, and it is impossible to determine with precision what the best case might have been. What is distressing, rather, is that the need to seize the golden opportunity that bin

Laden's arrogance had presented played very little role in the planning of the military operation. America's leaders seem to have taken it seriously only when it was too late—when it was already becoming plain that al Qaeda was breaking and that the Afghan allies were not preventing their escape.

It has been argued in response that it would have been impossible to get ground forces into Afghanistan in time to be useful. It is certainly true that the deployment of military force to Afghanistan was the most difficult force-projection mission the U.S. has ever undertaken. Afghanistan's neighbors were reluctant to offer bases to be used as staging areas for an invasion (although Uzbekistan and Tajikistan seem to have been more concerned about whether the U.S. would protect their borders than anything else, a concern that a ground presence might well have allayed). The sheer logistics of putting U.S. troops in such a far-off, landlocked country were extremely daunting, and the prospect of doing it rapidly enough for them to take part in meaningful operations was unlikely.

We should consider, however, the following facts. In the Gulf War, for instance, the 82nd Airborne Division was in Saudi Arabia ready to fight literally within days of the order to deploy. It is the purpose of that unit, and a handful of others, to be ready for such no-notice rapid deployments. Granted all of the additional difficulties involved in Afghanistan's terrain and location, it is ridiculous to imagine that that unit, or a substantial portion of it, could not have been in place north of Kabul in early November, when the critical fights took place, if it had been ordered there in mid-September when Bush decided to take the war to Afghanistan.

Moreover, the U.S. was able to position significant elements of a Marine Expeditionary Unit near Kandahar during the combat phase of the operation. Like the 82nd Airborne Division, Marine units are designed to make such rapid and deep deployments, and to sustain themselves in those positions for a period of time. The movement from Kandahar to north of Kabul would have been difficult, but it could certainly have been undertaken successfully with the stakes so high.

It is also true that the race to begin military operations was dictated not by military considerations but by political concerns. Bush repeatedly pressed the CIA and the Defense Department to get the operation underway even before they were ready, out of fear that the American people might lose their will for the fight if he delayed too long. This was an important consideration, to be sure, and the president's job is to ensure success both abroad and at home, but it should not have been allowed to overwhelm the even more important objective of doing as much harm as possible to such a dangerous foe. The argument that haste was needed to prevent the much-vaunted Afghan winter from shutting operations down also collapses in view of the fact that the largest military operation of the war, Anaconda, would take place in January, as had numerous major Soviet operations in the Soviet–Afghan War.

Despite all of these difficulties, however, Operation Enduring Freedom succeeded beyond the wildest expectations of Bush and his colleagues. The bombing began on October 7, and by mid-November the Taliban was gone. The speed with which the Taliban collapsed led quickly to extravagant claims that the operation had ushered in a "new American way of war" and would provide a model for future such undertakings.

In a speech at the Citadel on December 11, 2001, Bush made the argument that Afghanistan had proven the validity of the new approach to warfare he had championed on the same stage two years earlier. "We are fighting shadowy, entrenched enemies," he declared, "enemies using the tools of terror and guerrilla war—yet we are finding new tactics and new weapons to attack and defeat them. This revolution in our military is

only beginning, and it promises to change the face of battle."
He continued:

Afghanistan has been a proving ground for this new
approach. These past two months have shown that an
innovative doctrine and high-tech weaponry can shape
and then dominate an unconventional conflict. The brave
men and women of our military are rewriting the rules of
war with new technologies and old values like courage
and honor. . . .

Our commanders are gaining a real-time picture of the
entire battlefield, and are able to get targeting information from sensor to shooter almost instantly. Our intelligence professionals and special forces have cooperated
in battle-friendly—with battle-friendly Afghan forces—
fighters who know the terrain, who know the Taliban,
and who understand the local culture. And our special
forces have the technology to call in precision air strikes
—along with the flexibility to direct those strikes from
horseback, in the first cavalry charge of the twenty-first
century. . . .

This combination—real-time intelligence, local allied
forces, special forces, and precision air power—has really
never been used before. The conflict in Afghanistan has
taught us more about the future of our military than a
decade of blue ribbon panels and think-tank sympo-
siums.

"Precision-guided munitions also offer great promise," he continued. "We're striking with greater effectiveness, at greater
range, with fewer civilian casualties. More and more our
weapons can hit moving targets. When all of our military can
continuously locate and track moving targets—with surveillance from air and space—warfare will be truly revolution-

ized." He concluded with a clarion call to redouble the efforts to transform the U.S. military which he and Rumsfeld had already decided to pursue.

Bush's decision to stake this claim and to see in Afghanistan the need to redouble his efforts at transformation was truly epochal. Transformation, we should recall, had always been aimed at providing the U.S. military with capabilities supposedly needed to face enemies in the middle and distant future. It had been predicated on the existence of a "strategic pause." No one had ever claimed that transformation was needed in the 1990s in order to defeat current threats. Throughout the decade, in fact, transformation and current readiness had been constantly at odds, leading to a series of important stresses on the military as it undertook operations for which transformation was nearly irrelevant.

The beginning of the "global war on terrorism" gave the Bush administration the opportunity to reassess the importance and the role of transformation. It could well have decided that preparing for future threats was less important than ensuring that the military was ideally configured to fight the war then underway. Particularly since it is now clear that Bush was already contemplating war against Iraq in the very near future even as he addressed the Citadel cadets, it is remarkable that he continued to emphasize the need to prepare the military to face threats that were decades away. This decision laid the groundwork for a series of subsequent critical decisions during and after the Iraq war that have shaped that campaign and the difficulties the U.S. military has faced in prosecuting it.

The explanation for this decision is probably two-fold. First, Bush really was a true believer in the cause of military transformation. He had become convinced that the information age presented both dangers and opportunities that it was essential to meet, and he felt that it would be negligent to ignore those long-term risks and potential gains in order to focus on immediate problems. If his evaluation of the information age and its significance for military affairs was accurate, this was far from being a foolish thought.

Second, Bush and his entourage seem really to have believed that Afghanistan proved the validity of the "transformational" approach even thus in its infancy and even for unusual situations for which it would not, at first, have seemed likely to be helpful. A simplistic view of Operation Enduring Freedom supports this view, especially when the faulty pre-war assumptions that governed the planning for that operation are kept in mind. The U.S. defeated a battle-hardened, radical Muslim regime in a landlocked country thousands of miles from any major U.S. base using only long-range airpower, precision-guided munitions, Special Operations forces, and indigenous allies. And this "victory" came in less than two months.

Considering the irrational fear that the Taliban had inspired in the administration, the feeling of accomplishment following their collapse was natural, but it was no less irrational. By the end of November 2001, the U.S. military had accomplished only the least important of the three major objectives it should have been pursuing in Afghanistan. It had removed the Taliban from power, but it had neither destroyed enough al Qaeda forces in that country nor established the preconditions for the erection of a new regime to follow the Taliban in power. But just as the Bush administration had begun its evaluation of Operation Enduring Freedom by dramatically overestimating the degree of success it had attained and underestimating the difficulties for the subsequent political settlement it had caused, so too the evaluation of the military campaign itself and the lessons drawn from it were also inadequate and inaccurate. The dominant impression most people have taken away from Operation Enduring Freedom was that U.S. precision-strikes directed by Special Operations Forces won the war by itself. This view is wrong. The Northern Alliance forces and the indigenous troops raised in southern Afghanistan by Hamid Karzai and Gul Agha Sherzai won the war, supported by U.S. airpower.

The Taliban did not surrender to any "shock and awe" attack because there was none. It proved impossible to use the principles of "shock and awe" or even of Warden's five rings against an enemy whose state structure and military were as primitive as those of the Taliban. Throughout the planning phase and much of the conduct of the war, Rumsfeld and his team remained at fever pitch, desperately trying to find appropriate targets to attack with U.S. precision airpower. The initial list was, as they had anticipated, quickly exhausted without making much of an impact on the Taliban. Thereafter, U.S. aircraft would loiter over the theater waiting for special forces teams or other reconnaissance assets to identify fleeting targets for them to attack. This was an effective use of airpower, but it had nothing at all in common with the dominant theories for the use of those capabilities developed in the preceding decade. It was little more, in fact, than very high-tech close air support.

The desperate search for appropriate targets, moreover, led to some foolish decisions that hindered subsequent operations. U.S. forces, for example, were quick to bomb Afghanistan's airfields. This decision is almost inexplicable except by sheer military inertia. The Taliban's air force was decrepit, poorly equipped, poorly supplied, and poorly trained. The Deputy Commander of CENTCOM estimated that it could not have posed any challenge to the U.S. Air Force, which would without question have shot Taliban planes down without any difficulty and with little risk.

Bombing the airfields only made more difficult the task of getting supplies and reinforcements, including humanitarian aid, about which Bush was most insistent, into the country. Since the logistical difficulties of operating in Afghanistan were foremost in everyone's mind, and since the key to resolving those difficulties should have been preserving if at all possible every means of flowing troops and supplies into the theater, the pride with which Rumsfeld announced the destruction of some of the best of those means for no important military purpose is difficult to understand.

As the most authoritative study of the operation as a whole has argued, Enduring Freedom was, in fact, a rather traditional military campaign. Ground forces supported by significant and precise air power destroyed an enemy without air support or defense against air attack. What was novel was that the ground forces came from one country and the airpower from another. But this idea itself was not new: as early as the 1950s, Eisenhower had proposed using precisely this model as the basis for America's military relationship with its allies. The U.S. would provide the airpower and the allies the troops.

The real question was whether the U.S. should be willing to pay the important price in risking political failure involved in relying entirely upon indigenous forces, not whether wars could be won entirely from the air. Since the Bush administration was unwilling to admit that its political objectives—nebulous from the outset—had not been achieved, it could not evaluate this question or this problem objectively. Rightly or wrongly, therefore, the Bush–Rumsfeld transformation program only picked up speed from the ambiguous success in Afghanistan.

Transformation between Afghanistan and Iraq

As we have seen, the concept of a "revolution in military affairs" has a substantial historical lineage and a significant body of theoretical support. The debates about whether or not there really are sudden RMAs, or whether war proceeds in a more evolutionary pattern—or, indeed, whether war ever really changes its nature at all—were and are healthy components of an important discourse. Both sides can bring to bear numerous historical

examples, pro and con, and make use of the theoretical framework for the concept first developed by the Soviets and then
elaborated on by Western theorists and practitioners in the
1980s and 1990s. Although it is impossible to imagine ever
resolving the debates to everyone's satisfaction, it is perfectly
possible to conduct the debates in such a way as to enrich the
general understanding of an important question: How does
war change?

"Transformation" is a much weaker concept. It was a term
coined with no historical referent in the 1990s, and its concrete
meaning comes exclusively from the specific defense policy
program it is used to describe. Transformation, after all, means
nothing more than change. It is used now to imply a large change,
but there is no way in advance to know even what "large" means.
The objective of transformation is also unclear: Is the goal
changing the nature of war or changing the nature of the U.S.
military? At the end of the day, something is "transformational"
if someone says it is, and not otherwise. It is not really possible to
insist upon any more rigorous or exclusive definition than that.

This problem emerged with stunning clarity in the wake of
Operation Enduring Freedom. While combat operations were
still underway, even before the beginning of Operation Anaconda, the largest U.S. military undertaking of the Afghanistan
war, in fact, the Bush administration and the advocates of transformation declared that the operation had proved the validity of
their concepts. Andrew Krepinevich declared in early December, "This war is kind of a wake-up call for transformation. . . .
This war is Exhibit A in the list of evidence that warfare is
changing." Cebrowski said, "The need for transformation, I
think, has been well-established as compelling, and certainly
after 9-11 it should be self-evident."[8]

The list of "transformational" technologies and techniques
identified at that time by senior military leaders and independent analysts indicates the shifting meaning of transformation

itself. General Tommy Franks noted that the war "is allowing the armed services to make creative use of new 'transformational' technologies such as the Predator unmanned aerial vehicle." Air Force Chief of Staff General John Jumper pointed to the first use of the experimental Global Hawk UAV, and to the use of advanced targeting pods on F-16s. A Navy officer declared that "Another 'transformational' development in the campaign has been the basing of U.S. special operations troops and their helicopters on the aircraft carrier USS *Kitty Hawk*." Another Navy officer recalled that in the first Gulf War, the critical air tasking orders that controlled the movements of aircraft in a theater had to be sent in hard copy, whereas in Afghanistan they were sent by data link. "That's transformation," he added. "Transformation is occurring."[9]

Transformation enthusiasts were also quick to praise Tommy Franks' strategy itself as transformational. The very fact that there were no heavy forces in the theater at all was advanced as proof of that assertion. Another example of the "transformational" nature of the strategy was that "Army Rangers parachuted into Afghanistan and staged a nighttime raid on an airfield near Kandahar on Oct. 19. And lightly armed Army and Air Force special operations troops have performed missions, such as spotting targets for Navy and Air Force planes."

In reality, none of these examples were transformational. The use of Unmanned Aerial Vehicles (UAVs) in combat dates back to the early 1980s, when the Israelis used them to great effect over the Bekàa Valley. The use of armed UAVs was novel, to be sure, but it played a very marginal role in the overall campaign in Afghanistan. The use of the Army Rangers and the services' special forces soldiers was entirely in accord with the traditions of those units and not in any important way innovative except for the fact that they were supporting Afghan tribal militias instead of heavier Marine forces for much of the campaign. As far as transforming war, this was no change at all. And it goes without saying that the nature of war remains unchanged whether Army special operations forces base on Navy carriers or on land. Transformation had come to be synonymous with "innovative" or simply "good" and had lost all real meaning.

Attempting to find a common definition of "transformation," one reporter discovered that it varied from service to service and even from individual to individual:

> Top Air Force and Navy officers generally describe trans-formation as improving computer and communication links to network their forces. The goal is to give them a shared, comprehensive view of the battlefield so they can pinpoint enemy forces or targets better and strike them on sight.
>
> The Army also has been striving to "digitize the battle-field." But for many in the service, "transformation" refers to the quest to create lighter, more mobile forces yet keep them heavy enough to fight and win once they get to the battlefield. . . .
>
> [W]hen Marine Corps officers discuss "transforma-tion," they tend to bring up equipment they'd like to have that would get them places faster, such as the V-22 Osprey tilt-rotor aircraft.

The reporter concluded, "One task for the new Office of Force Transformation will be to help the services figure out what 'transformation' means;" another analyst said simply, "Nobody knows."[10] Another ominous note also appeared at this time, moreover: "for most scenarios, the force mix and tactics used in Afghanistan could be the model, officers and other experts said, and that will require continued transformation."

The opinions of outside experts and senior military officers who offer comments on anonymous background do not, of course, necessarily reflect those of the political leadership. But

Rumsfeld himself immediately adopted a vaguer and more confusing definition of transformation than he had previously been using in order to argue that the war in Afghanistan validated his concepts. In a speech in January 2002, he began by describing part of the Battle for Mazar-e Sharif:

> On the appointed day, one of [the special forces] teams slipped in and hid well behind the lines, ready to call in airstrikes, and the bomb blasts would be the signal for others to charge. When the moment came, they signaled their targets to the coalition aircraft and looked at their watches. Two minutes and 15 seconds, 10 seconds—and then, out of nowhere, precision-guided bombs began to land on Taliban and al Qaeda positions. The explosions were deafening, and the timing so precise that, as the soldiers described it, hundreds of Afghan horsemen literally came riding out of the smoke, coming down on the enemy in clouds of dust and flying shrapnel. A few carried RPGs. Some had as little as 10 rounds for their weapons. And they rode boldly—Americans, Afghans, towards the Taliban and al Qaeda fighters. It was the first cavalry attack of the twenty-first century.[11]

He continued, offering an analysis of this critical action:

> Now, what won the battle for Mazar and set in motion the Taliban's fall from power was a combination of ingenuity of the Special Forces, the most advanced precision-guided munitions in the U.S. arsenal delivered by U.S. Navy, Air Force and Marine crews, and the courage of the Afghan fighters, some with one leg. That day on the plains of Afghanistan, the nineteenth century met the twenty-first century, and they defeated a dangerous and determined adversary, a remarkable achievement. . . .

But really, this is precisely what transformation is about. Here we are in the year 2002, fighting the first war of the twenty-first century, and the horse cavalry was back and being used, but being used in previously unimaginable ways. It showed that a revolution in military affairs is about more than building new high tech weapons, though that is certainly part of it. It's also about new ways of thinking, and new ways of fighting.

It appears that the actual events of the Battle for Mazar-e Sharif are less supportive of this triumphalist view than Rumsfeld's presentation. General Dostum, the commander of the Northern Alliance troops there, actually charged the defenses twice. The first time, it appears, he received no air support despite his requests and the promises of Special Forces forward air controllers, and was driven back in disorder. The second time, he seems to have misinterpreted a warning from his Special Forces companions to prepare to attack and charged prematurely. His troops arrived at the walls of Mazar-e Sharif seconds after the last bomb exploded—so close to the detonations that the Americans thought they had killed Dostum and his men. The timing was accidentally perfect, however, as Dostum's troops charged into al Qaeda forces still stunned from bomb impacts. It was an action no one in his right mind would have planned that way because the risk to friendly forces was far too high, but luck was with the U.S. and its Afghan allies.[12]

Rumsfeld's distortion of this incident is less important than his use of it as an example of transformation. It was, in fact, a perfectly ordinary assault on a defended position. Through some mistake, Dostum had attempted to take the position by storm without close air support following a two-day bombing to soften it up. He then attacked again with close air support and took the position. The fact that his troops were on horseback was unusual, but since no one imagined that the U.S. was thereby going to replace its tanks and Bradleys with horses, it was also irrelevant. The fact that Special Forces troops had called in the air strike in support of their Afghan allies was also unusual in U.S. practice, but it was not any sort of "transformation" in the nature of warfare.

Rumsfeld drew another conclusion from this story that was essential to his changing vision of transformation. He offered the analogy of the German development of blitzkrieg techniques in World War II, noting two salient facts. First, that the Germans revolutionized warfare when their military "was really only about 10 or 15 percent transformed." Second, "What was revolutionary and unprecedented about the blitzkrieg was not the new capabilities the Germans employed, but rather the unprecedented and revolutionary way that they mixed new and existing capabilities."

Both of these statements are true, of course. The bulk of the German army in 1939 and even 1940 was still basically World War I infantry, although a vast and powerful Luftwaffe was now supporting that infantry. And, since the French, British, Russians, and Americans all had tanks, the initial German victories clearly came from the way they used those tanks rather than from their mere possession of the technology. The assertion that it was as important to think about how to use new technology as it was simply to develop that technology was sound and important. But Rumsfeld missed two other critical characteristics of the blitzkrieg that made the analogy more problematic than he supposed. First, the fact that so little of the German army was "transformed" was actually one of the main reasons for Germany's failure in the 1941 campaign against the Soviet Union. In that campaign, the World War I infantry could not keep up with the panzer spearheads, and there were not enough panzers for the Germans to maintain operational reserves. When they arrived at Moscow, therefore, they were exhausted and depleted beyond the point at which they could really be expected to fight any more. A partially transformed military is likely to succeed only in limited cases, especially against a transformed enemy.

Secondly, Rumsfeld's comparison of the change in war between 1918 and 1939 with the war in Afghanistan was fatuous. Warfare in 1939 looked nothing like warfare in 1918. The speed of movement, the capability and firepower of individual soldiers and larger units, the use of air power in meaningful support of ground troops for the first time on a large scale—these were innovations that changed the face of war fundamentally. The use of Special Forces forward air controllers to call in air strikes in support of a cavalry charge in 2001 was not a change in the nature of warfare at all. Armies and air forces had been conducting such operations since, well, 1939.

The problem is that Rumsfeld was focused on the different way in which the U.S. military accomplished these tasks without noticing that the tasks themselves were not new and were not carried out to particularly better effect than they had been many times before. It is easier for soldiers with laser designators, GPS, and data uplinks to identify targets to aircraft or artillery, but soldiers have been accomplishing those missions the hard way for decades. It was unusual for Army troops to stage off of a Navy ship, but their doing so had no impact on the actual fighting. And in terms of this analogy, what mattered about blitzkrieg was not that the Germans were doing things differently within their army, but *that they were doing different things*. This point was entirely lost as U.S. military leaders scrambled to show that they were being "innovative" and, thereby, "transformational."

If Rumsfeld wanted to argue that transformation was relevant to the ongoing war on terror, he needed to argue that it would yield immediate benefits to that war. Such an argument flowed naturally from the extreme introversion of network-centric warfare thinking. Because of its roots in the business world, as we have seen, NCW focused on changing the way the military did business rather than on changing the business the military did. When Wolfowitz, testifying before the Senate Armed Services Committee, identified as "transformational efforts in the past" the 1947 National Security Act, the 1973 All-Volunteer Forces Act, and the 1986 Goldwater–Nichols Act, he highlighted this internal focus.[13] Another troubling trend in the discussion of transformation following Afghanistan was the assertion that transformation had already been preparing the U.S. to handle unforeseen contingencies such as the 9/11 attacks. This assertion flowed from the claim that any innovative approach to war was transformational. Thus Rumsfeld argued,

> Our challenge in this new century is a difficult one. It's really to prepare to defend our nation against the unknown, the uncertain and what we have to understand will be the unexpected. That may seem on the face of it an impossible task, but it is not. But to accomplish it, we have to put aside the comfortable ways of thinking and planning, take risks and try new things so that we can prepare our forces to deter and defeat adversaries that have not yet emerged to challenges.
>
> Well before September 11th, the senior civilian and military leaders of the Department of Defense were in the process of doing just that.[14]

The way in which Rumsfeld claimed to have been "doing just that" prior to September 11th was by eliminating the two-MRC capability as the basis of U.S. force planning and by abandoning "threat-based" planning in favor of "capabilities-based" planning. As one reporter put it: "In the weeks after Sept. 11, in places where men argue about the future of war, you could detect an unmistakable mood of vindication. Since the gradual demise of the Soviet Union, certain scholars of combat had been arguing that the great lumbering military machine constructed for the Cold War was stubbornly ill suited to the new threats of a disorderly world and slow to exploit the new technologies of the information age. As they watched American airliners explode into American landmarks, and then monitored the subsequent rout of the Taliban, the reformers could barely contain the urge to gloat: this is the sort of threat we were warning you about. 'The changing nature of war is now in your living room,' proclaimed a post-9/11 manifesto posted on one of the several Web sites where the wonks of war congregate." [15]

Before September 11th, of course, these shifts in policy had resulted from the determination to free up resources allocated to defense against short- and mid-range threats to focus on transformation for the future. And in those days, transformation was rather clearly defined as network-centric warfare. The refocusing of transformation on anything that is innovative made it easy to claim that it was the best approach for dealing with unanticipated threats. The problem was that the specific transformation programs being developed before September 11th—and expanded upon after it—were anything but open-ended in the capabilities they promised to provide.

Network-centric warfare, as we have seen, is intended to give the U.S. military the ability to identify and strike targets with great accuracy from stand-off distances. To the extent that its advocates had attempted to develop a concept of war based on this capability, it was something like "shock and awe"—using this precision targeting to attack critical nodes in the enemy's system to degrade the performance of that system and simultaneously so stun the enemy's leadership as to convince it to yield.

The trouble is that no part of that concept is useful against an enemy such as al Qaeda. The U.S. does not have the human intelligence capabilities to understand the terrorist network in real time well enough to identify the critical nodes—read individuals—target, and kill them. Nor is it clear that there are "nodes" in that network whose destruction would break it apart or force its leaders to yield—always assuming that the surrender of the leadership would be sufficient to end the struggle. Of all the enemies that "shock and awe" might be effective against, al Qaeda is absolutely not one. It turned out, in fact, that even the Taliban was not susceptible to such an attack, as we have seen. The notion, therefore, that transformation prior to 9/11 was somehow preparing the nation for the unforeseen trouble ahead is nonsense.

Had Rumsfeld actually changed the definition of transformation he was using to encompass developing and implementing concrete programs, the shift might have been advantageous. It might have been used to encourage real innovation and out-side-the-box thinking about how to move the armed forces forward. The selection of Admiral Cebrowski as the first head of the Office of Force Transformation, however, ensured that there would be no such shift.

In February 2002 Cebrowski made it clear that his ideas about transformation had not changed, saying "the overarching change occurring in the military is a transition from the Industrial Age to the Information Age. . . . 'There is no doubt about it—that is the fundamental transition, and all other elements of transformation are subordinate to it.'"[16] Testifying before the Senate Armed Services Committee in April 2002, Cebrowski declared, "First and foremost amongst this process is the transformation from the industrial age into the information age. And in the department, we call that network-centric warfare." He added, "If we do not succeed in transforming from the industrial age to the information age, then all of our other efforts in transformation will likely not bear fruit."[17]

As Cebrowski repeated almost verbatim the sorts of distant-future threat arguments that had been common before 9/11, he, Rumsfeld, and other RMA enthusiasts regularly castigated opponents for persisting in old-think. One reporter characterized the struggle in this fashion: "With but a handful of loyal appointees, President George W. Bush has dragged the Pentagon's Apatosaurus-like bureaucracy into the twenty-first century, kicking and screaming as it goes. Under the day-to-day leadership of his defense secretary, Donald H. Rumsfeld, Bush has reached into the military to force long-resisted changes, while showing confidence in the officers carrying out a 'transformation' of the armed forces from their obsolete Cold War configurations."[18] With "transformational" redefined as "innovative," it was easy enough to argue that anyone who opposed transformation also opposed innovation and was simply defending some self-serving bureaucratic objective. Considering that these were charges leveled by senior Defense Department civilians and external analysts against senior military officers, they were readily and unquestioningly accepted on the whole. Everyone expects service chiefs to defend the bureaucratic and budgetary prerogatives of their services, and when they criticized Tommy Franks' plan for the war in Afghanistan, even he dismissed their objections on those grounds.

This process is natural and, indeed, inevitable. Any change in the military is inordinately difficult, and many senior—and junior—officials and officers do attempt to preserve their own fiefdoms even at the expense of national interests as a whole. But when transformation is used both as code for a particular vision of a future military and as a synonym for innovation, it is far too easy to dismiss real critiques as the cries of dinosaurs who simply cannot adapt. Rumsfeld and his allies in and out of government surely did not create this confusion intentionally— it is doubtful, in fact, if they even recognized it as they perpetrated it—but it became extraordinarily helpful to them in deflecting any criticism of their programs.

Through this convoluted linguistic and pseudo-logical process, therefore, it became an article of faith that the war in Afghanistan had validated the concepts of network-centric warfare, that those concepts were also ideal for designing a military to prosecute its part of the war on terror, and that anyone who opposed NCW had not adjusted to the new realities after 9/11. In other words, while broadly chastising all opponents for failing to change their views after September 11, Rumsfeld and his allies determined to implement their pre-established defense program unchanged and at an accelerated rate even as the U.S. plunged into wars, counter-insurgencies, and peacekeeping operations for which those programs were spectacularly ill-suited.

CHAPTER NINE

Iraq and the Future of Transformation

OPERATION IRAQI FREEDOM

THE WAR IN Iraq differed from the war in Afghanistan in almost every imaginable way. American military and civilian leaders had been thinking about the possibility of such a war since 1991. Central Command already had a complete war plan ready, prepared for several possible contingencies. U.S. intelligence had been focused on Iraq for more than a decade. The war would begin entirely on President Bush's timetable, which meant that he could in theory wait as long as necessary for the military to get ready. The enemy was thought to be a powerful, conventional foe with weapons of mass destruction. On the one hand, the military was confident that the U.S. would defeat Saddam conventionally in 2003 even more handily than it had in 1991. On the other, it had to fear that his use of WMD would gravely complicate that conventional military campaign. None of these facts, beliefs, assumptions, or fears had had significant parallels in the Afghanistan campaign.

Another critical difference between the two wars was that there was no confusion in anyone's mind about the objective of a war with Iraq. George Bush intended to remove Saddam from power and to install a stable, democratic government in his place. There was no notion that he might accept any lesser goal.

At some points, the administration seemed to imagine that simply killing Saddam and his sons might provide a shortcut to victory, a belief that accounted for the attempt to assassinate Saddam by bombing shortly before the war was to commence. For the most part, however, it was understood that only a large-scale conventional military campaign could lead to real success.[1]

Still another critical difference is that an enormous amount of work went into efforts inside the government and outside to think about the probable post-war situation in Iraq and to plan intelligently for the transition from hostilities to the desired political objective—a free, democratic, and independent Iraq. The State Department, the CIA, CENTCOM, the Strategic Studies Institute at the U.S. Army War College, USAID, the Office of Reconstruction and Humanitarian Assistance (ORHA), the RAND Corporation, the American Enterprise Institute, and other agencies all developed post-war planning efforts of various scales.[2] The war in Afghanistan had seen no such preparation, and the scale of this preparation before Operation Iraqi Freedom was so large that the Bush administration's apparent failure to benefit from it requires considerable explanation.

The earliest such effort, the State Department's Future of Iraq program, began in October 2001 and was formally announced to the public in March 2002.[3] This program brought together a number of Iraqi exiles and refugees and formed them into working groups to consider critical elements of the transition from Saddam Hussein's dictatorship to a new regime in their country. The groups considered issues such as government, economics, military, oil and energy, and so forth. The results of these efforts were compiled in thirteen volumes of more than 2,500 pages, some in Arabic and some in English.

Parts of these reports were certainly prescient. The exiles focused on the need to restore power, water, sewage, and other critical elements of the infrastructure immediately. They warned that the collapse of the Saddam regime would lead to disorder, violence, crime, and chaos that must be checked. They also warned that disbanding the army at once would lead to problems, that corruption would be endemic and problematic for efforts to establish a new regime, and so forth.[4] These accurate predictions of likely difficulties are commonly used to point up the arrogance of the Bush administration and its blind submissiveness to the dogma that simply installing Ahmed Chalabi and his Iraqi National Congress would solve all problems in Iraq easily and without further U.S. intervention.[5]

Nor was the Future of Iraq project the only one to point to the importance of establishing security in the post-war environment. Almost all of the pre-war studies and projects made that point, and many highlighted one or another of the various other issues developed by the State Department's team of Iraqi exiles. The Army War College's report was particularly insightful and ominous in this regard.[6] Whatever else is true about pre-war planning for the Iraq war and post-war, therefore, it cannot be said that the security, corruption, infrastructure, or governance problems that the U.S. encountered after the end of hostilities were unforeseen, let alone unforeseeable, or that the decision simply to disband the Iraqi army was generally accepted as the wisest course of action.

Why, then, did the U.S. military seem so unprepared in the aftermath of major combat? Why did the U.S. armed forces permit the widespread violence and looting that broke out after the fall of the regime? Why was so little effort made to prevent the formation of the power vacuums in critical regions that so many experts had warned about? Why, in short, did the U.S. do so little to prevent the collapse of order and so create the preconditions for the insurgency it would soon have to combat?

There is certainly some merit in the charges customarily leveled against Rumsfeld, Wolfowitz, and others in this regard. Some senior leaders apparently did trust too much in Chalabi and other exiles' promises that U.S. forces would be received as liberators and would not cause hostility that would lead to violent opposition. Some may have been reluctant to address these likely difficulties publicly for fear that it would weaken the already shaky support for a war they believed was necessary. Others believed that Powell and the State Department were doing everything in their power to sabotage the war effort, and therefore mistrusted any projects they undertook that tended to underline the difficulties the U.S. would face during or after the war. From the outset, Bush and his team were aware that the war would be a hard sell both domestically and internationally. As they saw exactly how hard, they naturally became focused on that problem. The emphasis in war planning rapidly came to focus on the diplomatic difficulties the administration faced. Rumsfeld was determined to come up with a deployment plan that would have U.S. forces ready to go if and when Bush decided to attack, but that would not prematurely undermine the president's formal position in support of disarmament and a negotiated settlement. This determination to preserve Bush's diplomatic options was a powerful impetus behind Rumsfeld's constant tinkering with the military deployment plan, and, as a result, behind his determination to keep the U.S. military footprint as small as possible. Only by doing that could he avoid an obvious and massive build-up that would make a mockery, as he thought, of Bush's claims that he had not yet decided on war.[7]

The intense hostility with which the idea of war was met, moreover, also focused the attention of Bush's lieutenants on defending that idea. This defensive mindset made it easier to dismiss problems proposed by known opponents of the war, such as Powell, as mere devices to derail a policy of which they did not approve. It was an easy step from that position to one in which anyone who proposed major problems must be doing so only because he opposed the war—a method for unwittingly assuring that possible problems do not receive adequate consideration.

But these problems are not enough, by themselves, to explain the failures to prepare properly for the post-war situation in Iraq. Had the U.S. military simply developed and executed a plan as it normally would have to attack and defeat Saddam's armies, there would have been enough troops on the ground to respond rapidly to a deteriorating situation, even if the pre-war planning had proved inadequate. There was considerable momentum behind such a normal planning process, moreover. The initial CENTCOM plans called for hundreds of thousands of troops, and Franks was able to pare forces away only with great difficulty and over a long period of time. Even at that, General Shinseki, the Army Chief of Staff, undertook his own parallel planning process and testified to Congress that "several hundred thousand" troops would be needed to deal with the post-war problems the armed forces would likely encounter.[8] It took all of Rumsfeld's determination to overcome this inertia and force the military to go to war with a much smaller force than it would normally have done, even with the devoted assistance of Tommy Franks, who seems sincerely to have believed in Rumsfeld's vision of war. The coincidence of having a CENTCOM commander who was inclined to follow the wishes of a decisive Secretary of Defense in this direction may prove to be peculiar to this situation. It will continue to be a problem, however, that the transformation vision so earnestly embraced by all the services now drives toward a repetition of the sort of war the U.S. fought in 2003. It will also continue to be a problem that the military defines war and war planning in a particular way that focuses first on defeating the enemy's armed forces and only then on pursuing the political objectives of the war.

Shock and Awe in Iraq

Rumsfeld and his team in the Pentagon largely took away from the war in Afghanistan the conclusion that their transformation program worked. They did not notice the limitations of that lesson, the problems with their changing definitions of transformation, or the problems that developed in Afghanistan as the result of the nature of the U.S. military campaign. They thus prepared for a war in Iraq based upon many of the presuppositions they had had before 9/11, oblivious of the fact that these theories had not really been tested in Afghanistan or anywhere else.

Rumsfeld in particular was determined to import "lessons" from Afghanistan into the planning for the new conflict. He was outraged to learn in 2001 that the war plan for Iraq then on the shelf called for the deployment of 500,000 troops—as well he might be in one sense, since there were not 500,000 soldiers in the Active Army at the time. In December 2001, Franks briefed Rumsfeld on a revised plan that called for only 400,000 troops. Rumsfeld was still not satisfied.

> "I'm not sure that that much force is needed given what we've learned coming out of Afghanistan," Rumsfeld said, citing what that war showed about their advanced precision weapons with laser guidance and the improvement in intelligence, surveillance and reconnaissance (ISR). The new Predators, the small, unmanned aerial vehicles or drones that provided real-time video, could stay airborne for 24 hours, and could fire two Hellfire missiles. He looked at the charts. "I'm not sure we're going to have to do that."
>
> "You'll get no argument out of me," Franks replied. "I don't think we have to do it either, but it is what it is," he repeated.[9]

A month later, Rumsfeld pressed further, asking, "If dozens of key targets could be destroyed simultaneously, would that put pressure on the regime, cause it to crumble and preclude the need for a long war requiring a large force? If you had the intelligence database, could you pinpoint the most critical targets to accelerate the fall of Saddam?"[10] Over the next several weeks, Franks continued to revise the plan to use fewer troops and to be able to start before all the forces had assembled in the theater. By mid-January Franks reported that he would only need 105,000 soldiers in the theater to begin operations.[11]

Central Command's war planning for the Iraq war was sophisticated and innovative. Franks adopted a centers-of-gravity approach to taking down Saddam's regime, and carefully considered which U.S. assets were best suited for which target sets. He always believed that an American ground presence would be essential to convince Saddam's regime of the futility of continuing the struggle, and that assumption was never seriously questioned in the war planning discussions between him and Rumsfeld. The question was how large that force should be, and both men wanted to keep it as small as possible.

From the purely military standpoint, this pressure to keep the force small was wise. There were and are many in the military who prefer more troops simply because the numbers make them feel more comfortable, or because they cannot think beyond the vast armies rolling forward that they saw in 1991 or in previous maneuver wars. The fact is that U.S. air power with its current level of superiority obviates the need for enormous armies to steamroller the enemy. But at times, even Franks feared that the paucity of troops and the narrowness of their advance from Kuwait to Baghdad would expose them to attacks on their flanks—despite the ability of U.S. airpower to prevent such attacks by large formations of Iraqi maneuver units. If the purpose of the war was simply to render the Iraqi military incapable of fighting, then the small footprint that Rumsfeld and Franks were focused on was appropriate. Considering the widespread fear that Saddam would use WMD against advancing American troops, moreover, it was even wise. And, indeed, the small American ground force supported by an intelligent air campaign aimed at destroying vital centers of gravity did destroy Iraq's ability to continue to fight in short order.

The trouble is that destroying the Iraqi military's ability to continue to fight was never the major problem facing the U.S. armed forces in 2003. It was well and widely known that a decade of sanctions following a disastrous war had left the Iraqi military a hollow shell. Both in overall numbers and in the quality and training of its personnel, there was no doubt that the Iraqi army had nowhere near the capability it had in 1991 —a capability that even then had been unable to avoid a complete and disastrous rout in a little over five weeks.

The major problems facing the U.S. army did not result from anything the Iraqi military as an organized force would undertake, but in actions Saddam himself might take. He might use weapons of mass destruction. He might try to destroy the oil fields. He could certainly be expected to destroy the bridges over the Euphrates. He might attack Israel. None of these tasks, with the exception of destroying the bridges, involved the Iraqi military as a conventional force. The only "nightmare" scenario that did was that he might withdraw the Republican Guard into Baghdad and try to fight a modern Stalingrad. The U.S. ground campaign, thus, did not need to focus on the destruction of the enemy's ground forces, as is traditional in a land campaign, but instead on moving rapidly enough to prevent Saddam from undertaking any of a number of strategic actions that might complicate the war or its political support. The destruction of Saddam's army would be almost a by-product of the campaign.

The U.S. air campaign was also unique. American aircraft had been flying over much of Iraq's airspace since 1991, enforcing the northern and southern "no-fly" zones, regularly attacking anti-aircraft radars, missile sites, and gun emplacements in those zones, and gathering phenomenal amounts of intelligence about Saddam's air defenses and their capabilities.

In the run-up to the war, in fact, the U.S. military launched a series of attacks that helped cripple the already weak Iraqi air defenses under the guise of "no-fly zone" strikes even before hostilities began. With little need to take much time to establish air supremacy, the U.S. could proceed at once with strikes against critical targets and troop concentrations. The "rolling start" that Franks ultimately launched, in which ground forces began moving simultaneously with air strikes and there was no period in which establishing air supremacy was the primary objective of U.S. air power, depended on the weakness of Iraq rather than on any new strength of the U.S. military.

For all the dangers inherent in the movement of military forces against one another, therefore, that movement was never the major issue in Iraq. The question was whether the U.S. would be able to prevent Saddam from taking any or all of the strategic actions at his disposal and whether the war plan would create the preconditions for a successful post-war transition. Franks and his planners focused heavily on the first problem. Their emphasis on the need for speed and on bypassing cities and centers of resistance during a race to Baghdad aimed primarily at preventing Saddam from preparing for the twenty-first century Stalingrad. But the second part of the problem received insufficient attention.

The pre-war consideration of post-war problems should have made several things clear to the war planners. The destruction of Saddam's regime would leave a massive power vacuum in a country that had been subjected to decades of totalitarian rule. Since the Iraqi army had been the principal entity responsible for keeping order in Iraq, its destruction would leave Iraq without any indigenous ability to enforce the rule of any sort of law. Any democratically elected post-war government would give the Iraqi Shi'ites much greater power than they had ever had before, and the Sunnis were certain to see this development as an epochal defeat. It was also known that Saddam had sown the country with "Saddam Fedayeen," guerrilla warriors intended to attack the flanks and rear of advancing U.S. forces. These troops, as well as internal security forces deployed to prevent Iraqis from rising up during the hostilities, would remain interspersed within the population after the war, able to form the basis for any insurgency that should begin to develop. In addition, the Iraqi infrastructure was weak and liable to collapse even if not deliberately targeted during hostilities. The Future of Iraq groups and others emphasized the importance of preventing that collapse to sustaining the support of the population for the new order. The Iraqi economy, moreover, was a command economy that would require massive reorientation to function within a democratic system. The destruction of the leadership of that command economy could well lead to its total collapse. It was essential for the coalition to be ready with plans for preventing massive unemployment and the resulting chaos. Finally, the remnants of the Iraqi army would be a major issue in the aftermath of the war. Numerous post-war planning groups warned that simply disbanding the army was likely to lead to chaos as trained soldiers melted away with their weapons. No one had a very good idea for what to do with the Iraqi army if it was not disbanded.

By far the most important points all revolved around a simple truth. When a regime is destroyed, especially a dictatorial one, domestic order will inevitably collapse unless some other force intervenes. The collapse of domestic order, furthermore, is a terrible blow to hopes for a smooth transition. The ensuing lawlessness breeds violence and looting and creates fertile ground for insurgency as the elements of the population that feel as though they will lose in the transition take advantage of the absence of order to try to oppose the transition with force. In addition, local leaders rapidly emerge to try to control the chaos around them. These leaders are likely to gain the support of the population based more upon their effectiveness in gaining control of the situation than on the general support for them or their messages. The occupying force can thus find itself confronted with the emergence of local strongmen very much not to its taste.

This wisdom is, indeed, 20/20 hindsight, but it is hindsight looking no farther back than to the war in Afghanistan, where all of these events occurred. Power vacuums bred violence and lawlessness and encouraged the establishment of regional strongmen whom the U.S. has been working ever since to tame or unseat in favor of the government of Kabul. The Afghan troubles were entirely visible in 2003, independent of the post-war planning cells' reports identifying the same potential problems, and the failure of Rumsfeld and Franks to develop and execute a war plan to prevent a repetition of these problems is the most important mistake they made in the conduct of the war.

This mistake resulted from all of the problems identified above, but it was really driven by an even deeper flaw in U.S. military practice. Franks did not think that the reconstruction of Iraq was primarily his problem. The Defense Department commonly shrugged that problem off onto the shoulders of ORHA, the State Department, the allies, and others. The focus of the U.S. war plan in 2003, as in almost all previous wars, was on defeating the enemy first and worrying about the consequences only later. That is why serious war planning began in late 2001, but serious planning for the post-war situation, apart from the Future of Iraq Project, started more than a year later.[12]

This timetable in itself demonstrates the terrible flaw of U.S. military planning efforts. It highlights the gap that American military planners see between war fighting and the transition to peace. In reality, how one fights a war powerfully determines the nature of the peace that follows. In the case of Iraq, the potential difficulties identified above called for the rapid occupation of Baghdad with a force sufficient to maintain order there, and for a rapid occupation of the Sunni areas, mostly north and west of Baghdad, and the Shi'ite areas, mostly to the south. The occupation of Kurdish lands was important for more strategic reasons—to prevent the long-standing Turko-Kurdish tension from flaring up. On the one hand, the semi-autonomy those regions had enjoyed since the Gulf War meant that a collapse of public order there was less likely. On the other hand, by failing to occupy those lands, the U.S. reduced its already thin leverage in determining who would lead the Kurds and what their policies would be.

Fear of Turko–Kurdish problems led to the decision to airlift the 173rd Airborne Brigade, reinforced with some Bradleys and M1s, into the north, although those forces were far from large enough to maintain order or be more than a token presence. Franks had always wanted to send the 4th Infantry Division (1D), along with British forces, through Turkey into the north to open a second front, to be sure. The collapse of that effort for diplomatic reasons led to the belated shift of the 4th 1D to Kuwait, where it arrived too late to take part in the combat phase of the war.

The movement of the 4th 1D requires further consideration, however. It became clear as the date set for beginning operations approached that the Turkish government probably would not allow the division to land. Franks decided to move the division to Kuwait instead, knowing that it would not arrive there until after the war had begun.[13] This division represented some 25 percent of the American force committed to the initial invasion, perhaps 20 percent of the total force (the other major combat forces came from the 3rd Infantry Division, the 101st Airborne Division, the 1st Marine Division, and the 1st UK Armored Division, and a number of separate brigades).[14] It was also the most technologically advanced U.S. division and the best suited, because of its improved communications, to operate in a dispersed fashion over great distances. In most other wars, the commander might well have pushed back the beginning of hostilities to ensure that he would have the necessary force in theater. Franks did not do so, partly because of Rumsfeld's insistence on allowing diplomatic initiatives to drive the timetable for war, but mainly because he did not think that he needed the division to win. He defined victory solely as removing Saddam from power and did not factor the critical post-war tasks into his plan, which was already largely complete before there was any serious consideration of the post-war problem at all.

The Centcom "Phase IV" Plan

Central Command did not entirely ignore the problem of post-war planning, nevertheless. On the contrary, a team headed by Colonel Kevin Benson worked hard to develop a sophisticated plan for the transition from hostilities to peace. It has become common wisdom that this team received the less capable officers, less support, and much less interest than the teams developing the plans for combat operations, and the "Phase IV" plan suffered from important flaws. But the work Colonel Benson and his team did would have provided Franks and Rumsfeld with a good basis for thinking about establishing the conditions for a successful transition period, had they heeded it.

The Benson team began by considering the mission of the Combined Forces Land Component Commander (CFLCC), Lieutenant General McKiernan—their boss:

When directed, CFLCC attacks to defeat Iraqi forces and control the zone of action, secure and exploit designated sites, and removes the current Iraqi regime. On order,

335

CFLCC conducts post-hostilities stability and support operations; transitions to CJTF–7.[15]

The critical element in this mission statement that defined the "Phase IV" planning effort was the last phrase: "transitions to CJTF–7." Combined Joint Task Force–7 was the headquarters to which CFLCC expected to turn over responsibility for post-war Iraq. It was to be built around ORHA and serve as the headquarters for Jay Garner, the head of the Coalition Provisional Authority that then governed Iraq. The CFLCC planners divided "Phase IV" into three subphases: stabilization, recovery, and transition. They imagined that their responsibility would end when Iraq had been stabilized and that CJTF–7 would take over at that point, whereupon CFLCC would redeploy.[16] If any long-term planning for the sustained U.S. presence in Iraq after the initial sub-phase of Phase IV were to take place, therefore, it would have to come out of Garner's office. Since that office only started to work, albeit feebly, in January 2003, however, the prospects for such long-range planning were dim. Expectations about an early "battle handover" therefore severely hampered efforts to think through the military requirements of establishing a stable new regime in Iraq.

The relatively short-range thinking that underlay the CENT-COM Phase IV planning effort was reflected in the priorities Colonel Benson's team set for the period following the end of major combat:

1. Defeat pockets of resistance
2. Secure key infrastructure
3. Secure EPWs [enemy prisoners of war]
4. Locate/Secure WMD/Conduct SSE [sensitive site exploitation]
5. Provide emergency HA [humanitarian assistance]
6. Assist in control of DCs [displaced civilians]

7. Support the maintenance of public order and safety
8. Exercise military authority at local levels
9. Support the restoration of critical utilities/basic services
10. Support sustainment HA [humanitarian assistance]
11. Repair mission essential LOCS [lines of communications]
12. "Empower" selected Iraqi officials at local/state/ national level (Provisional Commissions)
13. Begin reintegration of Iraqi military[17]

Had CENTCOM brought enough forces to accomplish all of these tasks, the prioritization might not have been that important. As it was, placing the maintenance of public order and safety at priority 7 and the restoration of critical infrastructure at priority 9 had important consequences for the transition from war to peace in Iraq. This prioritization would have been important even had the "battle handover" occurred as planned. Since it did not, it ensured an unnecessary scramble to address issues that should have received higher priority from the outset.

Colonel Benson's group nevertheless did fairly well identifying most of the major challenges the U.S. would face in the post-war period, with one glaring exception: the group did not understand that the Sunnis would see the fall of Saddam's regime as a fundamental defeat and begin a widespread insurgency to prevent the rise of a Shi'ite-dominated democratic government. Although Benson's team worried a great deal about "score-settling" by the Shi'ia and the Kurds against Sunnis, they did not recognize the danger posed by Sunni irredentists themselves. This failure of vision resulted in an incorrect estimate of the number of forces that would be needed in the post-war order and their likely areas of deployment.

The failure to consider or plan for a Sunni insurgency was surely partly an intelligence failure and partly a failure of imagination—things that can happen in any military planning effort. But it also resulted from a systemic problem. Because Benson's team saw its task primarily as stabilizing Iraq and only secondarily as establishing the preconditions for a stable new regime—it appears, indeed, that the group regarded those two tasks as largely identical—it did not consider in any detail what the new regime would look like, let alone what the political consequences of trying to establish it would be within Iraq. That is because CENTCOM did not see the establishment of a new regime as its responsibility—that task belonged to ORHA or the State Department. Since neither of those organizations was producing any clear guidance about what the new regime would look like, apart from the fact that it would be stable and democratic, the CENTCOM planners did not think about it very much. The misunderstanding of the nature of stability and support operations in a "transition from hostilities," therefore, led in large part to the total failure to foresee an entirely foreseeable Sunni revolt.

In addition to missing this critical piece of the post-war puzzle, Benson's team produced a plan based on three faulty assumptions. First, it assumed that there would be significant coalition military support for the post-war reconstruction effort. Since the entire administration was operating on this assumption, the CENTCOM planners can hardly be blamed for making it themselves, although the result was to produce an inaccurate impression even within the military of the sort of American troop commitment that would be needed.

Second, it assumed that the Iraqi Army would not simply melt away or be disbanded. The CENTCOM planners knew that it would be necessary to disband the various special security organs Saddam had used to keep himself together, as well as what was left of the Republican Guard. They thought, however, that there would be a substantial residuum of Iraqi regular army soldiers. On the one hand, they were concerned with the future

of those soldiers, and the plans called for eliminating dangerous Ba'athists from among the leadership but otherwise reconstituting the force. On the other hand, it appears that they
believed that this force would be available relatively quickly after
the end of hostilities to assist with keeping order in the country—
an assumption at odds with political reality in the country,
since such an effort would have alienated the Shi'ites, perhaps
permanently.[18] They certainly did not imagine, and would not
have supported, the decision simply to disband the Iraqi regular army completely two weeks after the end of hostilities.

Third, it assumed that forces would continue to flow into
the theater to sustain the stability and support operations even
after major combat operations ceased. When it became clear
that COBRA II, the plan for the "rapid decisive operation" that
took down Saddam, would not bring enough troops into the
country to carry out the plan for the post-war missions, General
McKiernan assured Benson's team that he would continue to
send troops in after combat had ended to bring CFLCC up to
the force levels the planners thought were needed. In the event,
Rumsfeld effectively "turned off the spigot" on reinforcements
as soon as Baghdad fell, leaving CFLCC below even the strength
Benson's team had thought would be necessary for Phase IV.

The CENTCOM planners developed a proposed deployment
for coalition forces during the stabilization period for which they
were planning. The main features of this deployment were: six
brigades in Baghdad; two in Basra; three in the vicinity of
Kirkuk; two around Tikrit; one each in Sulaymaniyah, Anbar,
and Ninawa provinces; one near Nasiriyah; one in Najaf; two
battalions in Karbala; and smaller elements along the other
borders. The total deployment would come to some twenty
brigades—nearly seven divisions, of which almost half would
be in the areas north of Baghdad.[19]

Notably absent from this plan, however, was any focus on
what would become known as the Sunni triangle. No forces were

339

earmarked for Fallujah or Samara, for instance. Apart from the two brigades near Tikrit, in fact, the bulk of the forces north of Baghdad would be deployed either in the Kurdish areas, on the border between the Kurdish and Sunni areas, or along Iraq's international borders. The CENTCOM Phase IV plan thus seriously underestimated the force that would be required, since its predictions for the troop levels needed in the places it did consider were not far off and were probably even low themselves—Najaf and Karbala, for example, probably merited more than a brigade each.

The assumptions the planners used to derive their proposed deployment were also interesting: "Iraq is a country bigger than California. This troop to task analysis was done to identify a *minimum* level of forces needed to exert *some* control over the populated areas of the country. Our start point was equating the number of troops to the number of police and security forces in [California]. We had fewer troops than Governor Schwarzenegger had police." [20] This analysis might have been sufficient had there been no serious danger of insurrection—had the problem, in other words, been only one of policing a disorganized society. This *minimum* level of troops needed to exert *some* control in a peaceful society would itself have been woefully inadequate to prevent the emergence of an insurgency during the chaos following the complete collapse of law and order in Iraq. Even so, coalition troop strength was slow to reach even this proposed minimum level, and apparently no serious thought was given to the contingency that Iraq might not behave like California. Errors and mistaken assumptions had therefore led to the development of a flawed and inadequate plan for "Phase IV" operations—which Rumsfeld and Franks did not, in the end, even adhere to.

★   ★   ★

Operation Iraqi Freedom and Its Consequences

The movements of military forces in Operation Iraqi Freedom are easily described. On March 20, 2003, the 3rd Infantry Division (ID) began its race from Kuwait up the west bank of the Euphrates toward the Karbala Gap, where it paused briefly before marching to positions in front of Baghdad. The 1st Marine Expeditionary Force (1 MEF) marched at the same time from Kuwait to the northeast, seized the Rumaila oilfields, and advanced on Baghdad from the southeast. The UK 1st Armored Division charged rapidly toward Basra. As events unfolded and Franks became concerned for his lengthy supply lines, he committed the 101st Air Assault Division to pacifying bypassed urban centers, particularly Najaf, and a brigade of the 82nd Airborne Division to securing the lines of communications further back. After another brief pause in front of Baghdad, the 3rd ID launched a massive armored raid—the "thunder run" —through the capital and then a second armored thrust into the center of the city, where it established itself. The 173rd Airborne Brigade (reinforced) established itself in the north around Bashur airfield, supported by a small contingent of armor flown in from the 1st ID. When the 3rd ID was clearly established in Baghdad, the regime fell and Saddam and his sons went into hiding. Major military operations were over.

The coalition at that point had approximately fourteen combat brigades operating in Iraq.[21] Significant reinforcements were on the way, however, including another three brigades each from the 1st Armored, 4th Infantry, and 1st Cavalry Divisions, and the brigade-equivalent 2nd and 3rd Armored Cavalry Regiments. These reinforcements would have brought the total number of brigades in Iraq up to twenty-five. But Rumsfeld cancelled the movement of the 1st Cavalry Division almost the minute Baghdad fell, the brigade of the 82nd Airborne left the theater rapidly, and elements of the I MEF also began to withdraw. Plans to pull the 3rd ID out of Iraq shortly after the end of hostilities fell victim to the rising insurgency. If that plan had been executed it would have left fewer than seventeen brigades in Iraq. At all events, the immediate post-war deployment left virtually no forces in the Sunni Triangle, and no plans to occupy that region quickly.

The Bush administration was convinced, of course, that help would soon be on the way in the form of international contributions to the post-war stabilization and reconstruction effort. Such assistance would have helped offset the lack of adequate numbers of American forces in Iraq, but it was poor planning not to have troops in readiness to make up the deficit if aid was not forthcoming. The cancellation of the 1st Cavalry Division's deployment orders was particularly irresponsible in this regard.

Another unexpected development that complicated efforts to secure a stable post-war order was the immediate and thorough collapse of the Iraqi regime and military. The military began to fall apart virtually from the first moment of the attack, with demoralized Iraqi soldiers melting into the countryside and heading home. Cease-fire agreements like the one reached in Mosul on April 11 accelerated this process, perhaps unwisely. The seizure of Baghdad accelerated the process further. At least one entire Republican Guards division that had been stationed in the Sunni Triangle melted away with its weapons and its expertise, and there were no U.S. forces around to take note or to hinder that process. Nor were there enough forces available to guard many of the vast ammunition and weapons dumps that dotted Saddam's Iraq. Soldiers and officers have reported watching Iraqis loot those dumps regularly without being able to do anything to prevent it. Those looted weapons helped supply Iraqi insurgents liberally in the months that followed.

The paucity of American troops in Baghdad also led to an

immediate crisis, as widespread looting and violence broke out across the city. Ministries and museums were looted and burned, private homes and individuals were attacked, and domestic order broke down fundamentally. The American troops in the capital were too overextended and still worried about resurgent attacks from undestroyed Iraqi military units to prevent this disorder, and the military leadership at first claimed that there was no need. Rumsfeld declared, "freedom is untidy." [22] This statement was a weak dismissal of a fundamental problem— civil society in Iraq was breaking down, that collapse would badly compromise efforts to make a transition to stable democracy, and the U.S. military was unable to respond because there were not enough troops in the country to do so.

In this context, the decision simply to disband the remnants of the Iraqi army on May 23 was foolish. Whatever the problems that might have resulted from attempting to use Iraqi troops in domestic disorders, and those problems were indeed enormous, the decision simply to throw tens of thousands of armed and trained men out of work, to shame them in front of their peers, and to make it clear that they were definitely "losers" in the transition process was intellectually and politically delinquent. The blame rests on shallow thinking—Bremer and civil administrators were worried about the Iraqis perceiving the U.S. as "just another dictator" and becoming associated with Saddam in the minds of the people. This fear somehow did not prevent the military from using one of Saddam's most infamous prisons, Abu Ghraib, as a detention center, however.

Individuals will make bad decisions periodically, operating as they do with their own assumptions and limited information. There is no defense against such errors in general. But the systemic problem that enabled and even encouraged these mistakes can be fixed. Rather than developing plans for military operations and then considering the post-war conditions, U.S. military planners should reverse the process. It is essential to consider the desirable post-war situation and the problems that will hinder its achievement *first*, and only then to develop military plans that will get there. Even a proper planning process would not have made the transition to democracy in Iraq smooth. But it might well have avoided some of the more disastrous mistakes that resulted from a failure to think about problems in the correct order.

The determination to use "shock and awe" contributed to these problems, of course, since that model pays no heed to the post-war situation in the country at all. It is entirely focused on persuading the enemy to surrender as quickly as possible rather than on creating the preconditions for political success after the "major combat operations" are over. It shares that flaw with network-centric warfare and with the notion that destroying enough things of value will be sufficient to force any enemy to stop fighting. The enemy may or may not stop fighting, but the destruction of things of value may well complicate the development of an acceptable post-war environment badly.

The U.S. military understood that fact in a limited way during Operation Iraqi Freedom. That is why there was no effort to destroy the Iraqi power grid, for instance, and numerous efforts were made not only to avoid civilian casualties and collateral damage, but to avoid destroying critical parts of Iraq's infrastructure. One result of this wise self-limitation was that the "shock and awe" campaign that Pentagon officials talked up in the weeks prior to the war was immediately condemned by Harlan Ullman, the author of the concept, as the war was going on: "What they announced at the beginning of the war as shock and awe seems to me was largely PR. . . . It did not bring the great shock and awe that we had envisaged."[23]

It also failed to achieve its purpose. Saddam did not surrender because of the "shock and awe" attacks of the first week of the war—in fact, he never surrendered. His regime only fell when U.S. tanks, Bradleys, and soldiers physically occupied his capital. So much for the notion that occupying territory is irrelevant in modern war. Ullman's complaint that the air campaign was not sufficiently shocking and awful misses the point. Given the determination with which Saddam continued to try to orchestrate an insurgency even while running for his life, it is impossible to imagine any air campaign the U.S. could have conducted that would have persuaded him to surrender. The effort to interact with the enemy's psychology central to both "shock and awe" and network-centric warfare relies on assumptions about that psychology. If the enemy truly is irrational (at least, by our standards) and his determination is, in fact, unbreakable, then efforts to take short-cuts to victory by operating on his psyche are doomed in advance to failure. The willingness to devastate the enemy's *society*, moreover, in order to persuade his leadership to give in a critical element to the "shock and awe" approach is in reality a willingness to do grave harm to any reconstruction or transition effort—and therefore to the prospect for accomplishing the political objectives of the war. All of the flaws and poor thinking that had crept into U.S. military thinking through the transformation programs of the 1990s thus emerged with all their contradictions in March and April 2003.

Programmatic Lessons from Operation Iraqi Freedom

These problems of conception and planning were clearly the most significant issues to emerge from Operation Iraqi Freedom from the standpoint of long-term American national security. The immediate focus, however, was instead on the shorter-term issues related to budgetary and programmatic decisions. Did Operation Iraqi Freedom validate network-centric warfare? What did it portend for the future of armored vehicles? Was the Department of Defense on the right course in its transformation programs—meaning the technology it was planning to purchase? The debates began quickly but were, unfortunately, settled quickly by the Pentagon leadership.

It is difficult, in reality, to say whether or not Operation Iraqi Freedom "validated" any particular concept. The Iraqi military was so weak that just about any American plan would have succeeded in driving Saddam from power, so success in the war can hardly be said to have proved that one approach was better than any other. This was not, however, the conclusion drawn by the administration in the immediate aftermath of the war.

The day Baghdad fell, Cheney immediately declared the victory "proof positive of the success of our efforts to transform our military." Steven Cambone, the Undersecretary of Defense for Intelligence, added, "What you see in Iraq in its embryonic form is the kind of warfare that is animating our desire to transform the force."[24] Testifying before the Senate Armed Services Committee in July 2003, Rumsfeld and Franks presented a series of "lessons learned" that constituted a complete and total validation of their previously held beliefs and concepts.

Rumsfeld thus identified four major learning points from Operation Iraqi Freedom: the importance of speed, jointness, intelligence, and precision.[25] He added,

> Another lesson is that in the twenty-first century "over-matching power" is more important than "overwhelming force." In the past, under the doctrine of overwhelming force, force tended to be measured in terms of mass. . . . In the twenty-first century, mass may no longer be the best measure of power in a conflict. After all, when Baghdad fell, there were just over 100,000 American forces on the ground. General Franks overwhelmed the enemy . . . by overmatching the enemy with advanced capabilities, and using those capabilities in innovative and unexpected ways.[26]

Rumsfeld also addressed the post-war situation in this testimony, of course, since the deterioration in that situation was making headlines at the time of his testimony. "In Iraq," he declared,

> coalition forces drove the country's leaders from power. But unlike traditional adversaries of wars past that sign a surrender document and hand over their weapons, the remnants of the Ba'ath regime and Fedayeen death squads in Iraq did not surrender. Some were killed or captured, but many others faded into the population, and are forming pockets of resistance against coalition forces.

Rumsfeld seems to have made no connection whatever between the "innovative and transformational" war plan he described and the problems U.S. troops were encountering even as he presented his testimony. It did not occur to him that the presence of only 100,000 troops in Iraq when Baghdad fell was a major contributing factor to the violence he was then attempting to explain away.

General Franks also seemed oblivious to that connection. In his briefing, he identified "things that worked:" jointness; precision munitions; command and control which provided "unprecedented situational awareness;" equipment readiness; training; coalition support; and Department of Defense/CIA synergy. His list of "areas requiring additional work" was even more interesting: fratricide prevention; deployment planning, which he rightly called "too cumbersome;" coalition information sharing; human intelligence; communications bandwidth; certain aspects of the Global Hawk UAV; the "integrated common operational picture," which is the key to NCW and which Franks called "very powerful but [in need of] further development;" and strategic lift and tanker capacity.[27] Once again,

Franks concluded that Operation Iraqi Freedom had validated NCW and the military's approach to war and found the only major problems that needed addressing were those that might improve that approach. Absent was any consideration of the possible links between the approach he had taken to fighting the war and the problems that had resulted after the end of major combat operations.

Paul Wolfowitz also joined in the euphoric self-congratulation, declaring in June 2003 that Iraqi Freedom allowed the world "to see some remarkable changes in our military:"

- First has been the application of new networking and communications technologies, which has taken the integration of air and ground forces to an entirely new level and gave our soldiers and Marines on the ground nearly instantaneous access to precision air support. The presence of those brave soldiers and Marines in turn enabled our long range striking power to find targets with precision. And that, too, represents a quantum leap. Precision weapons are only good if you have precision targeting. We can now combine the two in dramatic new ways.

- That new capability, in turn, enabled our ground forces to advance at an astonishing speed over distances far exceeding those of Desert Storm. It also made possible the use of Special Forces on a scale that would have been difficult to conceive in the past. More than 100 Special Forces A teams were deployed throughout Iraq in this conflict. And that in turn led to the disappearance of a "front" in the traditional sense, to be replaced by the concept of "battle space."

- We also saw some remarkable organizational innovations. Who would have imagined a conventional tank unit under the command of a Special Forces lieutenant colonel? Or the first-ever combined forces land component commander integrating U.S. Army, U.S. Marine Corps and coalition forces in a single, brilliant land combat campaign?

- And we saw revolutionary application of new technologies, such as unmanned aerial vehicles and hit-to-kill anti-missile systems.[28]

Once again, we see transformation used to describe anything that is good and novel, while also meaning the application of network-centric warfare principles and capabilities, together with the assertion that everything that went right in Iraq was historically unprecedented.

Looking more concretely at specific systems, Cebrowski concluded that the solution to problems with NCW in Iraq was more NCW.

Another "fertile area" to research for lessons learned, he said, is the level of network-centric warfare practiced by small units or isolated systems—the "last mile of connectivity."

A key focus will be studying "differences in performance and tactics by people who were well-connected at the tactical level and who were not. . . ."

The next question for network-centric warfare in Iraq will be at the command and control (c^2) level, he said. For example, has the military reduced the decision-making cycle for striking time-critical targets?

"What happened to the c^2 delay time?" Cebrowski asked.

Asked about lessons for the Army's 70-ton tanks, Cebrowski said he does not agree with those who claimed the campaign proved the need for heavy tanks, or those who argued the opposite.

"It's a polarization of what's going on," he said. "What you'd like to have is a mix" of systems. Cebrowski added, however, that the Army's tanks should be at most half the weight they are now, but equipped with better sensors to improve situational awareness.

"I come down more on the speed and information side," he said.[29]

These statements came just three weeks after the fall of Baghdad, weeks that had been filled with images of looting and disorder in the capital—images that appear to have troubled Cebrowski not at all, nor shaken his confidence in the vision of war that had produced them.

A closer look at the role of NCW, sensors, communications, and tanks in the actual fighting, moreover, reveals that the proponents of NCW were too quick to assert that the war had validated their theories for more practical reasons. The official Army history of the operation casts serious doubt on the notion that "network-centric warfare" was the key to the rapid success of the ground forces. Serious problems with the interoperability of various command, control, and communications systems prevented the military from using the network to clear close air support missions, for instance, from using network-centric approaches to logistics, or from communicating information rapidly and accurately through the network to the units that needed it. The authors of that study concluded, "joint coalition forces did not fight a netcentric campaign in Iraq. It is accurate to say they fought a net-enabled campaign."[30] The consequences of these flaws were not trivial: "Most tactical unit commanders claimed that they made every assault as a movement to contact," that is, they advanced without knowing exactly where or when they would encounter Iraqi forces, nor the precise size and disposition of those forces. "There is no reason to dispute that claim, other than to argue that most of these same commanders *generally anticipated* when contact was likely, whether they knew precise locations of the enemy or not."[31] But the goal and promise of NCW is not to allow tactical commanders to "generally anticipate" when they will meet the enemy. If, as seems clear, that is what the war actually looked like to the tactical commanders, then it can in no way be said to have proven anything about NCW, other than, perhaps, the impossibility of attaining those capabilities.

Cebrowski's repeated assertions that NCW capabilities would obviate the need for heavy tanks, since future vehicles could rely on the network to provide advanced warning of threats, found no real support in the events of Operation Iraqi Freedom. The official Army history points out one problem that resulted from an effort to "lighten" certain Army units:

> [S]cout platoons and brigade reconnaissance troops exist to provide the means for tactical commanders to "see" the enemy. Mounted in lightly armored HMMWVs, battalion and brigade scouts are vulnerable to RPG [rocket-propelled grenades] and cannon fires. This design is intentional and reflects a widely held view in the late Cold War era that armored and armed scouts would fight rather than conduct reconnaissance. As a consequence of this, if contact seemed imminent, commanders often chose not to use their scouts and brigade reconnaissance troops. In short, they elected to give up their "eyes" rather than risk losing them.[32]

The official history left unspoken the corollary: because the units meant to be following the scouts had M1s and Bradleys, they felt safer conducting a movement to contact in which they were certain that their armor would protect them. They could afford to do without their "eyes," in other words, because of the protection the main body had. If, as Cebrowski proposed, heavily armored vehicles were stripped from the entire force, the result would be that no commander would feel safe to advance except with perfect knowledge of the enemy, since none could afford to risk a surprise engagement at close range. Considering the significant failures of intelligence and the network in Operation Iraqi Freedom, this fact is extremely worrisome.

In contrast to Cebrowski's easy dismissal of the importance of armor in the fight, the officers of the 3rd Infantry Division had no doubt of its centrality. They concluded, in fact, that more than a decade of theorizing about the role of armor in urban warfare—theorizing that largely concluded that urban warfare is a light infantry fight—was totally wrong:

> This war was won in large measure because the enemy could not achieve effects against our armored fighting vehicles. While many contributing factors, such as air interdiction (AI), close air support (CAS), Army aviation, and artillery helped shape the division battlespace, ultimately any war demands closure with an enemy force within the minimum safe distance of supporting CAS and artillery. U.S. armored combat systems enabled the division to close with and destroy heavily armored and fanatically determined enemy forces with impunity, often within urban terrain. Further, the bold use of armor and mechanized forces striking the heart of the regime's defenses enabled the division to maintain the initiative and capitalize on its rapid success in route to Baghdad. During MOUT [Military Operations in Urban Terrain], no other ground combat system currently in our arsenal could have delivered similar mission success without accepting enormous casualties.[33]

It may perhaps be objected that this defense of the tank by one of the premier tank divisions in the Army is self-serving, but it is no more self-serving than statements by Cebrowski, Rumsfeld, and Wolfowitz that defend their own transformation programs. During the first "thunder run," in fact, virtually every vehicle in the convoy had been hit by enemy fire, and many had been hit repeatedly by enemy RPG rounds, yet only a single M1 was disabled (and the crew recovered alive).[34] Nor was this situation confined to the combat phase of the operation—one officer commanding a tactical unit during the counter-insurgency struggle reported that his unit would have had over three times as many soldiers killed had it not been equipped with M1s and Bradleys.

The fact is simply that passive armor protection at the level offered by the M1 is an enormous force multiplier on the battlefield, and one totally ignored by the advocates of NCW. It allows commanders to advance into unknown situations utterly without fear. It allowed the 3rd ID to charge through Baghdad in two "thunder runs" without using air support to devastate the surrounding blocks in an effort to "clear" them for the passage of light-skinned vehicles. Armor protection is essential for maneuver in the open, for urban warfare, and for counter-insurgency, and this unsung capability, created in the 1970s for a very different sort of war, was one of the most important factors that led to U.S. military success in Iraq at such speed and such a low cost.

CONCLUSION

The wars in Iraq and Afghanistan do not prove that network-centric warfare does not work any more than they prove that it does. Since neither one was really fought by a military that actually had the full range of promised NCW techniques, neither one really tested the concept at all. The claims by NCW advocates that their theories were validated are without foundation and very dangerous; counterclaims that the war shows the bankruptcy of the NCW approach are also problematic.

Robust networks, excellent communications, good intelligence-gathering, and excellent precision-strike capabilities are good things to have. Commanders at every level reported being pleased with such systems as they had (that worked) and wanted to improve those systems that did not function as well as they should have. There is no doubt, based on Operation Enduring Freedom and Operation Iraqi Freedom, that the military should proceed with developing these capabilities rather than abandoning them.

Many of the conclusions drawn by NCW advocates about the implications of their systems, however, are overdrawn to a dangerous degree. The fact that neither Operation Enduring Freedom nor Operation Iraqi Freedom was actually fought with NCW capabilities is mostly important in calling into question the value of pursuing those capabilities to the degree demanded by their proponents. The U.S. military did not destroy Saddam's regime in three weeks because of NCW, but instead because of the excellence in people and technology developed over the preceding two decades. If that degree of excellence was sufficient to produce such a lopsided result, what greater benefit can we really expect from an NCW-enabled force?

One benefit frequently asserted is that it will be possible in the future to use NCW to do even more with even less. War can be even faster and more decisive, advocates claim, using even fewer and much lighter ground forces. But if current pre-NCW capabilities are sufficient to provide decisive military victory in three weeks, how much is it really worth to be able to win in one week? It seems clear that there is a point of diminishing returns in this equation beyond which additional capabilities of the same variety are not worth the enormous costs required to generate them.

More worrisome still are the capabilities NCW would strip away from the force as it is in pursuit of this marginally greater speed. The elimination of passive armor protection would have devastating consequences to the psychology of maneuver commanders, as well as to the lives of soldiers. The reliance on "near-perfect" intelligence to offset the elimination of that armor is virtually certain to prove misguided.[35] The reduction of the "footprint" of ground forces still further will virtually ensure the same sort of post-war chaos and loss of focus that bedeviled the U.S. in both Iraq and Afghanistan and created the preconditions not for political success, but for large-scale insurgency.

Network-centric warfare has always had three fundamental flaws. First, it is a solution in search of a problem. Second, the technical requirements needed to produce the capabilities sought and promised are unattainable in the real world. Third, it proceeds from a misunderstanding of the nature of war. Taken together, these flaws argue for disassociating the benefits that limited NCW approaches have offered the force so far from both the excessive demands and exaggerated promises insisted upon by NCW advocates.

Network-centric warfare provides no capability that the U.S. armed forces do not already have. The American military can track and target an enormous number of objects and strike them with tremendous precision and few errors. Military units can communicate with one another, using both pictures and words, at an unprecedented level, allowing them to conduct complex, flexible, dispersed operations over vast stretches of terrain in contact with enemy forces. The principles of identifying and attacking enemy centers of gravity are well established and incorporated into most planning efforts. The idea of using rapid movement combined with precision strikes to shock the enemy has also become the norm. All of these developments occurred prior to and largely independent of the adoption of NCW as Department of Defense dogma.

Pursuing the NCW vision at this point offers little except more of the same. Spending what will surely end up being billions of dollars to achieve the "last mile of connectivity" will not offer any revolutionary new capabilities. Recent wars, furthermore, have demonstrated *no important problem* with America's ability to do any of the things NCW promises. If it were, in fact, possible to achieve the real NCW goal of all units seamlessly integrated with one another from the highest level to the lowest and sharing a "common operational picture" that was *completely accurate*, then the improvement over the current capabilities might be worth the outlay. Unfortunately, there is no prospect of such a development because it is impossible to attain.

Improvements in the connectivity of U.S. forces are possible and, indeed, inevitable. The problems once identified, the solutions will come, although the process will be slow and painful because of the size and complexity of military systems. It is quite possible to imagine a day when all U.S. forces from the soldier to the admiral share the same picture of the battlefield and can communicate with one another seamlessly. It is not possible to imagine, however, that that picture will be entirely accurate.

Several factors preclude the possibility of having "near-perfect situational awareness," a precondition demanded by NCW advocates for their theories to work. First, the Earth's surface is fantastically complex, especially when urban centers, foliage, and underground facilities are added to the mix, as they inevitably are. The ability to see anything anywhere on the Earth at any time would require the development of technologies that would profoundly revolutionize human life on the planet. Nothing short of that will completely eliminate confusion caused by terrain.[36]

Second, the enemy constantly adapts and will always find ways to confuse our sensors. The NCW visionaries imagine a world in which the eternal race between offense and defense ends in our favor—we will be able to see everything and the enemy will be able to do nothing about it. This notion is preposterous. The enemy will always find ways to obscure our intelligence gathering, to infiltrate our network, and to feed us wrong information. Our systems, however perfect, will always have data-processing vulnerabilities that skillful enemies will identify and exploit. What we "see" with our sensors, therefore, will always reflect, at least partly, what the enemy wants us to see.

Third, just as human beings are imperfect, so are all human artifacts, including computers and software. As we have already considered, the programs on which our expert systems depend will have bugs and flaws. They will be subtly skewed to perceive certain developments in certain ways, reflecting the assumptions and beliefs of their programmers. These distortions will add up as the complexity of the network and its supporting systems increases, and they will be harder and harder to track down. They will inject elements of error that we will not readily perceive.

These arguments consider only the problem of identifying and tracking physical things, of course. In reality, "near-perfect intelligence" also requires the ability to predict with a high degree of accuracy what the enemy intends to do. This requirement is utterly unattainable. Human beings are rarely able to predict each other's behavior, especially in war. Their artifacts may be able to find patterns more quickly and increase the ability of their human masters to perform this task, but "near-perfection" is a standard that will be forever out of reach because the enemy frequently does not know what he intends to do until he does it.

War is an interaction of opposing forces. The enemy's actions are driven not only by his background, aims, and experiences, but also by what we do. To be more precise, his actions result from *his perception* of what we do. The distinction is critical. In order to understand how the enemy sees the battlespace it is not enough to know what the battlespace actually looks like—itself an impossible task. We must then know precisely what the enemy's mechanical systems tell their operators, how those operators individually synthesize and analyze that information, and how they report it, suitably adjusted to the known desires of their leaders, to their commanders. Distortions enter at every level of this process, and almost none of them are discernible to an outside observer. It is objectively impossible, therefore, to know how the enemy sees the battlespace, and therefore impossible to predict how he will react to that perception.

The final flaw in NCW is that it proceeds on the basis of a fundamentally wrong understanding of war. NCW, like its predecessors in transformation theory, treats war as a targeting drill. It defines the basic problem in war as identifying and destroying the correct targets in order to force the enemy to capitulate. It focuses, therefore, entirely on the use of the military to destroy things and kill people, and thereby misses the point of war entirely.

War is not about killing people and blowing things up. It is purposeful violence to achieve a political goal. The death and destruction, though the most deplorable aspect of war, are of secondary importance. The pursuit of the political objective is all, in fact, that separates killing in war from murder. The history of U.S. military transformation efforts since the end of the Cold War has been the story of a continuous movement away from the political objective of war toward a focus on killing and destroying things. The result of this trend, which was already present in the military even before transformation made it dominant, can be seen today in Iraq and Afghanistan.

In those countries, the U.S. military demonstrated a remarkable ability to identify critical targets and destroy them with phenomenal accuracy and unprecedentedly low levels of collateral damage. The focus on that controlled destruction helped blind military and political leaders to a serious focus on the political objective of the war. That blindness, induced in part by more than a decade of military dogma arguing for the primacy of destruction over planning for political outcomes, largely explains the amazing failure to take obvious post-war dangers and problems into account in the development of the military campaign. It is virtually the only way in which network-centric warfare actually affected the wars in Iraq and Afghanistan, and the effect so far has been disastrous.

CHAPTER TEN

The Way Forward

THE EXAMPLE OF the military transformation of the 1970s offers an important insight into the nature of such successful undertakings. States have most commonly revolutionized their own militaries, or even war itself, not by setting out to do so but by trying to solve concrete technical, procedural, and strategic problems they faced. The Germans and Soviets worked to resolve the conundrum posed by trench warfare in the 1920s, not to take advantage in the abstract of the "mobility revolution" then occurring in civil societies as the result of the mass marketing of the automobile and the agricultural tractor. The Germans were trying to find a way to defeat Poland and possibly France without allowing the war to degenerate into a long-lasting slugging match that they were certain to lose. The Soviets were trying, on the one hand, to build on their experiences with more mobile warfare during the Russian Civil War and, on the other, to solve the trench problem with an eye to a war against Germany. In both cases there was considerable abstract theorizing about the future of war, but all of that theorizing was based on the need to resolve known problems posed by the prospect of war with real enemies. Neither Germany nor the Soviet Union, moreover, would have devoted desperately scarce resources to military modernization and experimentation without the perception of dangerous threats and serious military problems. It is not an accident that the British, for whom both the threats and the problems were much more remote, never did devote adequate resources, either intellectual or financial, to solving the problem in the Interwar Years, and so did not develop effective armored forces before World War II despite having invented the tank two decades before.

An earlier revolution in warfare reveals the same pattern. Helmuth von Moltke the Elder was a visionary. He believed that the development of a dense rail network and the military systems to use it properly would transform war. He was right, of course, and he persuaded the legendarily parsimonious Prussian king to support him despite considerable opposition. His arguments were not based on the simple promise that a railroad revolution was coming in civil society, even though that was true. He argued instead that a dense rail network would solve the single most important strategic problem Prussia faced: how to move forces rapidly from one side to the other of a monarchy surrounded by the most powerful states in Europe. Had he not tied his vision to the primary strategic dilemma of the day, it is inconceivable that the Prussian king would have supported him adequately, and there is no telling when or even if railroads would have come to have the particular revolutionary effect on war that Moltke pioneered.

U.S. transformation following Vietnam was no different. Army officers, determined to avoid any repetition of that horrible experience, focused on large-scale maneuver war in Europe. The collapse of the conscription system compelled them to make certain changes to the military, but more visionary officers and analysts drew conclusions about future war from the experience of the Arab-Israeli Wars as well. Without the overwhelming danger of the Soviet threat, however, to which all reformers clearly tied their arguments, there is no chance that the U.S. military would have transformed itself in the 1970s.

The transformation efforts of the 1990s through today have followed an entirely different path. Eschewing the traditional threat- or problem-based approach to thinking about war, transformation enthusiasts have argued instead for the urgent necessity of exploiting certain technologies to transform war. Some in the 1990s rejected the notion that the U.S. faced any significant short-term threat at all and dubbed the period a "strategic pause." Others argued that the long-term danger of *not* seizing the opportunity they perceived was much greater than any short- or mid-term threat. Considering that none of these visionaries tied their programs to any particular threat or to the solution to any pressing military problem, it is astonishing how successful they have been. It is not at all surprising, however, that over time their programs have lost focus and become diffuse and confused, that "transformation" has steadily lost whatever meaning it might have had, and that the technological projects undertaken with such enthusiasm have run into significant setbacks. Nor is it surprising that, focused on their vision without careful connection to reality, transformation advocates have allowed the serious flaws to develop within their thinking that we have already considered. The only way out of a policy that looks increasingly like a dangerous trap is to change the way we are thinking about the problem, and return to a more traditional method of contemplating the present and future of war.

A New (Old) Way to Think about War

One of the casualties of the September 11th attacks was the idea of the "strategic pause." Since that tragic day, we have heard much discussion of a new type of war, a new type of enemy, a more difficult challenge to face—but no discussion of any strategic pause. America knows now that it faces a major threat to its security and to its way of life, and discussions about defense policy since 9/11 have rightly focused on how to defeat that threat. Both those attacks and subsequent developments, moreover, have awakened many in the national security community to the fact that there are other threats to worry about besides terrorism alone. China seems to be not only an economic but a military competitor. The acquisition of nuclear weapons by North Korea and Iran seems a much more serious problem today than it did five years ago. The danger of the collapse of secular rule in Pakistan is now nothing short of terrifying.

In truth, none of these threats, including terrorism, is new. The roots of the problems in China, North Korea, Iran, and Pakistan go back to the end of the Cold War and beyond. Even terrorism is not a novel threat—as we have seen, among the first briefings Bush received upon taking office in 2001 was a warning of the imminent danger al Qaeda posed to U.S. security, a warning based on eight years of study following the unsuccessful first attack on the World Trade Center in 1993. Even that attack, moreover, was novel mainly because it took place on U.S. soil and because of its scale—Reagan abandoned Lebanon, after all, because of a massive car bomb attack (what we would now call a "vehicle-borne improvised explosive device"), and the U.S. military during the 1980s was engaged almost exclusively in counter-terrorism operations. The novelty after 9/11 came not from the nature of the threat, but from the sudden perception of its importance. With the bubble of the strategic pause dreadfully burst, Americans re-awoke to the fact that the world is a dangerous place.

In a marvelous piece of irony, the transformation enthusiasts, who had prided themselves on pioneering a new way of thinking about war for a new era, suddenly became guilty of old-think. Their programs had not been designed to fight terrorism, as we have seen, but to defeat relatively poorly equipped enemies in conventional combat. The forces they were designing were supposed to be ready for wars like Iraq much more than for wars like Afghanistan, let alone the more nebulous campaigns that make up the rest of the "global war on terror." Rather than re-orienting those programs, however, they modified the definition of transformation, as we have seen, to include any military approach that is "novel"—and they identified almost anything positive the military accomplished as novel whatever historical precedents there might have been. In order to retain the right to call themselves new-thinkers, therefore, they defined transformation as innovation of any variety and use a very broad definition of innovation indeed.

Instead of this effort to salvage a "strategic pause" military policy through linguistic legerdemain, we should capitalize on the fact that Americans have returned to a more realistic understanding of the world and their place in it. Like previous successful military transformation efforts, we should shorten our gaze and focus on immediate operational challenges and problems first, on visible near- and mid-term threats second, and only then on long-term threats and opportunities. There are, after all, no lack of immediate problems to solve or near-term threats to consider, and programs based on the realities of those problems and threats are much more likely, if history is any guide, not only to be successful, but to transform warfare in ways yet to be foreseen.

Challenges and Problems in Current Operations

By far the most pressing problem facing the United States today is the task of reconstructing defeated former enemies while conducting counter-insurgency and counter-terrorism operations in those states. Since the beginning of the U.S. commitment to Iraq, transformation enthusiasts have behaved as though this was a short-term problem that would vanish as quickly as the counter-insurgency and not reappear. Although some made half-hearted attempts to argue that transformational approaches would ultimately offer solutions to these problems, the deteriorating situation on the ground in Iraq gave the lie to those arguments, which have largely faded away.

But the problems the U.S. is facing in Iraq and Afghanistan today are not transient difficulties dependent upon unique circumstances in those countries. The mere fact that the U.S. faces very similar problems in two countries with nearly totally different histories, geographies, ethnicities, and economic systems (about the only things Afghanistan and Iraq have in common is that they are both Muslim countries bordering Iran) should provide ample warning that the challenges the U.S. has encountered there are likely to be the norm rather than the exception.

President Bush enshrined the policy of pre-emptive war and regime change in his 2002 National Security Strategy. Although the imminence of the threat Iraq posed before the coalition attack is arguable, the arguments for those two policies in general are sound. In a world that has both well-organized and networked international terrorism aimed at destroying the West and weapons of mass destruction that can accomplish that aim, the U.S. must do everything possible to prevent these two threats from merging into one. In this context, it is not acceptable to wait for the blow to fall and then respond—preemption may well be necessary not merely to prevent an attack in preparation, which is extremely difficult, but to prevent the circumstances from arising that would make such an attack possible. Judgment will always be essential in these matters, and no decision to preempt will be without controversy—decisions for war never are. But for all the ambivalence toward Bush's decision in 2003, it is highly unlikely that Operation Iraqi Freedom will turn out to be the last preemptive strike in the war on terror.

It is even more unlikely that future such strikes will not also lead to regime change. If the U.S. were to find itself at war with North Korea or Iran, whether preemptively or reactively, it is almost inconceivable that such a conflict would not result in the fall of the current leadership in Pyongyang or Teheran. Both states have a history of supporting terrorism; both states have more or less openly avowed their determination to acquire weapons of mass destruction. What American leader having defeated their armies in war would not then go on to depose those regimes, even assuming that the regimes survived the destruction of the military force on which their power rests? Regime change as U.S. policy is here to stay.

The Nature of Regime-Change Wars

Confusion among several concepts has led to confusion about the nature of regime-change wars. Most people are accustomed to thinking that insurgency, revolutionary war, guerrilla war, and unconventional war are all pretty much the same. Even experts frequently use these terms interchangeably. All these concepts are commonly contrasted with conventional war, a disarmingly and deceptively simple phrase. Since regime-change wars *look* much more like conventional war than like guerrilla or unconventional war, we tend to think of them in such terms. This tendency is a dangerous error.

Insurgency and revolutionary war are terms that describe the political purpose of military undertakings. Any movement that has as its aim deposing a sitting government is an insurgency. Any war with such a purpose is a revolutionary war. Guerrilla war and unconventional war, however, describe not the purpose of the conflict but the methods used to prosecute it. Guerrilla tactics, defined originally by the operations of Spanish rebels fighting Napoleon in 1808–1812, are hit-and-run raids, ambushes, sabotage, and so forth. Unconventional war is an even broader term that can include just about any form of military activity other than the deployment of regular combat units in traditional formations.

Guerrilla war and unconventional war are not equivalent to

366

revolutionary war or insurgency, however. Soviet partisans operating behind German lines after 1941 were engaged in guerrilla
operations and unconventional war, but not in revolutionary
war or insurgency; they were acting as unconventional auxiliaries of a sitting government trying to defend itself against
a conventional, foreign invader. By contrast, Maoist armies
maneuvering in traditional formations during the latter part of
the Chinese civil war were engaged in revolutionary war, or insurgency, but not primarily in guerrilla war. The same holds true
of American revolutionary forces at Saratoga, Guilford Court-
house, or Yorktown, which were conventional battles—but not at
Lexington and Concord, which were guerrilla-style ambushes.
The form of the war does not drive or result from the political
purpose of the war.

Determining which type of war one is embarked upon is,
however, essential to planning and waging it properly. "Conventional" war (that is, war fought not for the purpose of unseating a regime whether by conventional, unconventional, or
guerrilla methods) falls readily into the Clausewitzian character-
ization of war as a duel. Two (or more) opposing states struggle
with one another for the purpose of overthrowing each other's
will to continue to fight. When the enemy's will has been broken,
according to Clausewitz and a great deal of historical example,
he will make peace and the war will be over. The focus in such
wars on the destruction of the enemy's military as the means of
forcing the enemy to surrender is natural and frequently effective, although there have been notable exceptions, including,
unfortunately, Saddam Hussein in 2003. Military transformation programs in the 1990s and through to today have focused
on this shortcut to victory by designing systems whose sole aim
is to persuade the enemy by the destruction of his military
capability that further resistance is hopeless.

Revolutionary wars do not fit this "duelistic" model, however. As students of such wars have argued for decades, revolu-

tionary wars (or insurgencies) are not duels, but triangular struggles. Two sides compete with one another in order to gain the support of the bulk of the population. The triangular nature of these conflicts helps explain why counter-insurgency efforts focused primarily on defeating the armed forces of the rebels generally fail, while successful examples normally involve positive efforts to win over the population as well as to destroy the rebellion's military power. Revolutionary wars have a much more overtly political character than non-revolutionary wars for this reason.

Another characteristic of revolutions and revolutionary wars is that initial success can frequently lead to ultimate failure. The revolutionary movement generally has two major objectives. The first is to discredit the sitting government and cause it to fall. The second is to establish a new, revolutionary government more suitable to the insurgents. Examples of movements able to bring down a government but unable to install a new one abound. Russian revolutionaries brought down the tsarist regime in 1917 and then went through numerous failures to establish a new government before the Bolsheviks succeeded after a years-long civil war. Cycles of violence in Africa and Central and South America frequently result from precisely this dilemma—governments fall, but no new government can establish itself sufficiently to break the cycle.

Regime-change wars are revolutionary wars. Their purpose is the removal of one government and its replacement with another. The second task is generally more difficult than the first for the United States today because of America's great superiority in conventional warfighting techniques. Successful revolutionaries do not, on the whole, wait until they have taken power or are on the verge of doing so before deciding what their new government will look like and how they will win the support of the population for it. On the contrary, the vision of the new order is frequently what motivates revolutionaries to fight in the first place. Just so should the U.S. approach planning for and conducting regime change wars.

The first task in that planning should be determining what the political end-state should look like in as much detail as possible. Flexibility will of course be needed in the application of this plan to the fluid circumstances surrounding the war's termination, but the requirement for flexibility does not obviate the need for a plan from which to be flexible. If nothing else, the process of devising such a plan in great detail is likely to highlight many, if not all, of the major tasks and challenges that a victorious army will have to face and overcome in order to succeed in the phase of the war that actually matters, the phase frequently called now "Phase IV."

The importance of planning for the post-war period is not news to the Army. Even the plan for the invasion of Iraq had a significant sub-plan devoted to that period, as we have seen. But the way the military thinks about post-war planning now is misguided, despite recent attempts to improve it, and still rests on a flawed understanding of the purpose of war and the various parts of a war plan.

"Phase IV" itself is a revealing phrase. It is part of a continuum that begins with Phase I, engagement and deterrence, Phase II, building-up forces for a possible attack, and Phase III, major combat operations. Phase IV, "post-conflict" or "stability and support operations," is at the end of the line. This phasing structure suffers from two major problems, only one of which the military has noticed and tried to correct. It is obvious now that "Phase IV" begins even before Phase III is over—military units engaged in combat also engage in stability and support operations (SASO) in areas they occupy even as hostilities continue. While major combat is still taking place in some parts of the theater, therefore, the primary mission of combat units in other parts will be SASO. In recognition of this fact, the military has largely abandoned the use of the term "Phase IV" and doctrine now emphasizes the simultaneity of combat operations with SASO.

Another critical problem with the way the military thinks about the transition from war to peace remains unaddressed, however. Even today, officers talk about "decisive" combat operations and see SASO as the mopping-up afterwards. The war in Iraq has convinced many that that mopping-up may be prolonged, complicated, and even more troop-intensive than the "decisive" operations that preceded it, but it is still seen as the mission that follows the main mission. The recognition that this secondary mission is important and takes place simultaneously with the main mission has not changed their relative prioritization. Above all, it has not changed the way the military thinks about SASO.

In regime-change wars, however, "decisive combat operations" are conducted *for the purpose of being able to conduct stability and support operations afterwards.* Since the goal of the war is to replace one regime with another, victory cannot be attained until the new regime is in place. The military victory over the incumbent government is therefore only the prelude to the operations that will actually determine the outcome of the effort. Its primary importance lies in creating the precondition for the successful conduct of those operations rather than for anything accomplished in itself. The destruction of the enemy's ability to fight, which is the current focus of transformation efforts, only matters because it makes possible the installation of a new regime.

"Phase IV" or "transition operations" or "SASO," or whatever the regime-installing operations are to be called, is therefore not subordinate to or even equal with "decisive combat operations" in regime-change wars—it must predominate. If these operations do not succeed, then the war will end in defeat however stunning the initial military successes might have been. All of the operations preceding these final missions should be designed to help them achieve success.

This is not an entirely new principle in war. As early as the 1920s, Soviet military theorists argued that military operations of any scale should be planned from back to front. The planner must first decide what forces he will need at the *final* battle to win, and then plan the preceding battles in order to ensure that those forces will be present when necessary. The Germans, by contrast, pursued the opposite approach. Most of the energy of the "blitzkrieg" theorists went into planning the initial battles. The most stunning result was Operation Barbarossa: despite unprecedented success in its first weeks, the German army ran out of steam at the gates of Moscow. Because it had done its planning from front to back, the Wehrmacht had not considered what force would be needed at the decisive point, did not have that force available, and lost. The U.S. military, whose thinking about war is generally much closer to that of the Wehrmacht than that of the Soviets, has made the same mistake twice within the past five years.

The "transformation" involved in changing the way the military does its planning is enormous. Because of the danger, death, and destruction entailed in major combat operations, as well as the obvious difficulty of coordinating so many pieces all moving so quickly, planning for such operations has always been the centerpiece of U.S. military thought. To relegate the planning of those operations to second priority will require a cultural shift of significant proportions in the military.

A second problem is that U.S. military culture predisposes officers to be deeply nervous about intruding into political decisions. Soviet theorists, after all, were only proposing to shift the focus from one part of a military operation to another. The current proposal calls for shifting the focus of military planning from military to political operations. Both the military and the civilian leadership will simply have to work to get over this traditional reticence, however.

The military is inevitably involved in the political decisions that affect both war planning and war termination. As it stands now, military planners de facto make a host of decisions that powerfully shape the post-war environment and that facilitate or harm the prosecution of the political objectives of the war. Most of those decisions today are taken without really considering those effects, however. Having the military involved directly in planning for the post-war political reconstruction of a defeated state will not, in fact, change the civil-military balance —it will simply make it more likely that the inevitable military contribution will be helpful and not harmful.

A third difficulty is that there is not now any organ in the U.S. government capable of producing a detailed and executable plan for the post-war reconstruction of a defeated enemy. Military combatant commands have the expertise in planning, but do not have enough regional expertise or political and cultural savvy to produce plans that will work, not to mention the current cultural bias toward prioritizing operational military issues over reconstruction tasks. The State Department, CIA, and certain other organs of the government have regional expertise and political savvy, but they do not have the capability to produce executable plans. Efforts to have the National Security Council or some other body coordinate joint planning endeavors have so far failed, in part because of the military's determination to fence off major combat operations as too important to allow "political" interference and in part from the organizational weaknesses of the NSC. The legacies of Vietnam continue to affect American military thinking and planning.

From a pragmatic standpoint, the simplest fix would be to augment the staffs of combatant commanders with the necessary regional experts, State Department, CIA, and other liaison officials, and so forth, and have them do the political planning.

But the military is resistant to the idea of requiring officers to give priority in planning to "post-war" operations rather than "decisive combat operations," and it would encounter resistance in the other agencies at the subordinate role they would be asked to play in planning for operations that are fundamentally their responsibility and area of expertise.

A more complex solution would be to augment the NSC dramatically and give it the capability to devise such plans on its own. Apart from the bureaucratic nightmare involved in doing such a thing, this procedure would run the risk of over-centralization. A given organization can rarely conduct more than one major planning operation at one time. If the NSC, even greatly augmented, were required to develop multiple contingency plans simultaneously, the likelihood is that one or all would suffer. The division of planning and execution responsibilities among regional combatant commands makes a great deal of sense, and not just for military operations.

There are other ways of solving this problem, but for now the most important thing is simply to acknowledge that finding a solution is one of the most important tasks facing the U.S. national security community today. Until and unless America changes the way it plans for regime-change wars, the conditions that have led the U.S. into grave difficulties in Iraq and Afghanistan will recur each time such a war is fought.

THE OUTLOOK FOR CONFLICT

In contrast to the "strategic pause" of the 1990s, it is now possible to discern a host of scenarios that might lead to U.S. military intervention or large-scale combat. The continuing improvements in the Chinese military, coupled with increasingly bellicose Chinese policy toward Taiwan and recent Chinese efforts to establish client relationships with Iran and Sudan, all raise the specter of a conflict between the U.S. and China in the not-so-distant future. Furthermore, the dangerous instability of Pakistan is always worrisome. Since Islamabad's acquisition of nuclear weapons, that instability now seems to be potentially a mortal threat to the U.S. and could generate any of several possible scenarios for U.S. military involvement in that country. What is more, the ability of terrorist organizations to take root in chaotic, war-torn lands means that any collapsed or collapsing state is potentially an area of military interest for the U.S. Numerous large countries in Africa fall into this category, as do some of the Central Asian states and even certain South American countries, where chaos is combined with indigenous terrorism, drug networks, and organized crime groups that could support militant Islamist terrorist groups either directly or indirectly. The possibility of war against North Korea and Iran remains real, as does the more remote prospect of conflict with Syria or any of several other smaller Arab states.

China

Possible scenarios for conflict with China have multiplied as Chinese interests have grown, and this process will continue unless it is interrupted by war or by a change of policy in Beijing that rejects the current trend toward expanding Chinese reach beyond the Asian mainland. The most likely and the scariest scenario at the moment, however, remains the possibility of a Chinese attack on Taiwan. The basic features of the Chinese threat to Taiwan are well known, as are the difficulties Beijing would face in executing an attack. Hundreds of Chinese missiles are poised to reduce Taiwan to a smoldering ruin, but such an attack would deprive China of the fruits of victory. The vast People's Liberation Army would make mincemeat of the Taiwanese land forces—if it could get across the Taiwan Strait in force. Chinese paratroopers could almost certainly land, but probably could not hold without reinforcements coming by sea. For these reasons and others, the Chinese leadership has always held back from trying to retake Taiwan by force, and may well continue to show restraint in the future.

If, however, a Chinese government became convinced, rightly or wrongly, that the U.S. might not defend Taiwan, or might not do so promptly, and if internal Chinese politics and conditions were such as to press for an attack, it is quite possible that Beijing might launch any of a number of more or less limited strikes against its island neighbor. A restrained missile salvo might send a message without destroying Taipei; the dispatching of a fleet with an invasion force, possibly coupled with paratrooper landings, might be undertaken in the hopes of driving Taipei to capitulate out of fear. Beijing might also launch such an attack in the hopes of actually seizing Taiwan before the U.S. could intervene effectively. It will remain unlikely for some years to come that the Chinese leadership would deliberately court a full-scale war with the U.S. over Taiwan, but it is very easy to imagine a series of miscalculations that might lead to conflict.

If a conflict began, it is virtually certain that one of the major objectives of both the U.S. and the Chinese leadership would be to keep it limited. There is no question that neither state wants to have a full-scale nuclear exchange, or even a massive conventional war. The U.S. objective in such a war-by-mistake would be to persuade or compel the Chinese to abandon their ambitions in Taiwan without forcing them to escalate the conflict; the Chinese objective would almost certainly be to find some way to yield without entirely losing face. One fact emerges starkly from the consideration of such a scenario—the theory of warfare enshrined in NCW, especially "shock and awe," would be entirely counterproductive in such a fight.

It is nearly certain that a U.S. president faced with a rapid

Chinese attack on Taiwan would not immediately decide to launch wave after wave of airstrikes on critical targets throughout mainland China. Such an action would only too clearly run the risk of forcing the Chinese to escalate the conflict. It is thus likely that the U.S. Air Force and Navy would face a Chinese air force that still had the use of many of its ground-based radars and ground control stations. It is not even certain that the U.S. would undertake to destroy all of the SAM batteries that might fire on American aircraft over the Taiwan Strait. At sea, the U.S. might have to undertake aggressive anti-submarine warfare against Chinese subs that approached U.S. battle groups, but it might well avoid attempting to destroy submarines outside of the immediate battle area so as not to raise the stakes too high. In this moderately likely scenario the priority would be on the limited and discriminate use of force to deter the Chinese from pressing an attack, rather than to destroy their ability to continue to fight.

Many of the techniques and technologies of NCW would be very helpful in this fight. The ability to identify and destroy targets precisely and with minimum collateral damage would be particularly useful. But the focus of the warfighting theory that underlies NCW could be very harmful. The U.S. could not reliably identify and destroy strategic centers of gravity, could not try to shock or awe the Chinese regime into submissiveness, and might even have to limit the damage done to the Chinese military.

The focus of NCW architects on offensive rather than defensive functions at all levels would be a major hindrance to such an operation. Right now, the only reliable way the U.S. could protect its own forces or Taiwan from Chinese missile strikes would be by destroying the missiles before they were launched. Such an effort, however, could well unintentionally raise the stakes too high for the Chinese, leading to an unwanted escalation of some variety. It would be far better to have the capability to shoot down Chinese missiles in flight, an action that would not have remotely the same effect as a direct attack on the Chinese mainland to *preempt* the launch of those missiles.

A revival of some of the key concepts Warden developed for Desert Storm would also prove very helpful, especially if divorced from some of the larger conclusions subsequently drawn from them. It is quite possible to conduct a centers-of-gravity analysis not of China-as-a-system, but of the specific forces the Chinese would be using to attack Taiwan and fight U.S. forces. A key insight of the official Air Force history of the Bosnia air campaign would also help here—we must identify the centers of gravity of the U.S.–Taiwan coalition, of Taiwan itself, and of the U.S. in order to protect them. The trend in transformation literature toward focusing on a centers-of-gravity analysis of the enemy regime and society as a whole tends to obscure the real breakthrough Warden made, namely that such an analysis can provide ground-breaking insight when applied to any subordinate problem in war as well.

For this scenario, as for the scenarios of regime-change wars we have already considered, then, the best approach is to dissociate the capabilities being developed to support NCW from the concepts currently used to justify them. It is important to be able to use force precisely and discriminately in order to increase the options available to the political leadership. By tying that increase in offensive capabilities to a decrease in defensive capabilities and, even more, by tying it tightly to a particular vision of how to fight war, however, NCW advocates risk constraining available military options instead.

Pakistan

Those looking for nightmare scenarios need look no farther than Pakistan. The stability of the regime of General Pervez Musharraf is impossible to gauge accurately. There is a significant militant Islamist faction within the country, and although Musharraf has made every effort to keep the Pakistani army and security services pure of that faction, he has assuredly not succeeded. What would happen if a coup d'état occurred, if Musharraf were assassinated, or if militants were able to seize one of Pakistan's nuclear weapons even with Musharraf still in power? The answer surely is that the United States would need to be ready with a plan to intervene rapidly if needed to prevent terrorists from acquiring those weapons.

Pakistan is a large country with a population nearly six times Iraq's. Its terrain is in places nearly as daunting as Afghanistan's. It is difficult to contemplate the size of a military force that would be required to keep order in Pakistan, should the present regime collapse, but it is certainly far beyond anything the United States and its allies could muster at the moment. Yet the Western World could not simply stand idly by and allow Pakistan to collapse utterly without risking disaster. At a minimum, it would be essential to be prepared to send in military teams to secure Pakistan's nuclear weapons. Special Forces teams alone would not be sufficient, since it might be necessary to defeat significant regular or irregular forces guarding the sites, and to hold the sites against counterattack. In the worst case, U.S. troops might have to chase weapons that militants had seized and begun to move about the country. Such operations might require considerable force.

The actual force requirements for such an operation are very difficult to calculate. There would certainly be an initial premium on speed to seize the weapons before they could be moved. Long-distance sensing and precision-strike capabilities would be important in this phase, but would remain secondary efforts supporting the movement of teams of ground forces, since it is absurd to imagine that the U.S. could content itself with simply firing missiles at suspected Pakistan weapons sites. Depending upon the circumstances in the country, however, small teams might require significant reinforcement rapidly. Here complexities emerge most starkly. If the Pakistani army remains loyal or simply disintegrates, then relatively lightly-armored units such as Stryker Brigades would be valuable and might well be sufficient. If Pakistani army units go over to the rebels, however, then heavier vehicles might be required.

Heavy armored vehicles could be sent to Pakistan in two ways. They could be flown laboriously one at a time on large airlifters, or they could be landed at one of Pakistan's ports and driven overland. The first approach would dramatically limit the speed of any build-up and, therefore, the speed of reinforcing units trying to seize or defend weapons sites. The second approach would create long supply lines vulnerable to attacks and would require the securing of the ports as well. This approach could also have the most dramatic ramifications on the internal situation in Pakistan, since it would establish an immediate heavy U.S. presence in prominent locations in the country. The prospect of mob attacks on U.S. positions in and around Pakistani ports can also not be dismissed.

This scenario best emphasizes the dilemma U.S. forces face because of the weight of the M I tank. The solution proposed by N C W advocates is unacceptable, however. It would reduce the weight of the vehicle by reducing its passive defensive capability and relying instead on the ability to sense and destroy potential enemies before they can fire on the vehicle. Such an approach could lead to catastrophe in a scenario such as the one considered here. In the chaos of a post-collapse Pakistan, it may well be impossible to know whether a Pakistani army unit has remained loyal or gone over until it reacts to the presence of U.S. forces. Simply destroying all such units before American vehicles arrive would virtually ensure the opposition of all that survive. In chaotic scenarios, as well as in urban scenarios, it remains vital to have vehicles in which soldiers are confident of their own ability to survive, so that they can allow the enemy to fire first before returning devastating fire if necessary. The M1 provides that capability today; none of the network-enabled systems proposed to replace it do.

The goal of fielding a 20-ton tank is thus both laudable and important, but it cannot be done by trading off armor for killing power. It must instead be accomplished by finding new ways of producing passive defensive capabilities equal to or better than those of the M1 without the weight. The solutions will be found, in all likelihood, in the realm of materials technology rather than information technology. Experiments with ceramic armor have already suggested that such capabilities are possible. If U.S. transformation programs once broke away from the unique preoccupation with long-range precision strike and started to devote significant efforts to lightweight passive protection systems, there is a good chance that solutions could be found. We should recall the skepticism with which the continued viability of the tank met in the late 1960s, and the revolution in armor technology that saved it. That development was fortuitous. The problem is now urgent enough to demand a concerted effort to find a similarly effective solution so that some future Army Chief of Staff can declare, as Creighton Abrams famously did, "the tank is back in business."

The development of a lightweight tank with the survivability of the M1 will not, of course, solve the problem of Pakistan today. That is, in truth, a problem with no real solution right now. Even if American forces could secure and remove all of the Pakistani warheads in a timely fashion, the disintegration of Pakistan into a vast haven for militant Islamist terrorists would be wholly unacceptable. The U.S. could not now prevent that from happening because the requirement for ground forces would be far beyond what the Active Army and the Reserves could provide, even if both were significantly expanded. For the moment, we can only hope that this scenario never arises or that, if it does, it does not take the worst possible path.

North Korea

The balance of the Korea problem is shifting. For fifty years the danger was that North Korea would invade the South, triggering a repetition of the first Korean War. That danger remains, but it is growing more remote. North Korea's military power has been steadily decreasing relative both to South Korea and to the United States over the past two decades, and there is now very little prospect that Pyongyang could succeed in such an undertaking. An attack would be devastating to South Korea's economy and could cause thousands or even tens of thousands of casualties, but it is extremely unlikely that the result would be North Korean control over the peninsula. Pyongyang retains this option now more as an exercise in potential terrorism on a mass scale, or as a last throw in desperation than for any rational purpose.

Two scenarios are emerging, however, that are more likely paths to conflict on the Korean peninsula. The first is that the Kim Jong Il regime might collapse; the second that its development of nuclear weapons might demand an American attack. The pressure on Pyongyang is growing daily as the North Korean economy weakens, revealing the utter bankruptcy of the *"juche"* policy of autarky invented by Kim Il Sung. Unless North Korea's neighbors intervene to prop up the regime—something that is not altogether improbable now given the efforts to barter South Korean aid for Kim Jong Il's agreement to slacken the pace of nuclear developments—then it is likely that the time will come when Pyongyang will either have to change course dramatically or face collapse. The effort to change course, if attempted, might also lead to collapse in North Korea as it did in the Soviet Union.

What would be the result of a collapse of the North Korean regime? It is impossible to say, of course, but there are several possibilities. Assuming that Pyongyang does not launch a desperate and hopeless attack on the South in its last agonies, the result of a collapse will be chaos throughout a country accustomed to slavish obedience to a lunatic dictator. Civil order will break down and there will be an immense humanitarian crisis —even greater than the one that is already underway in North Korea today. Three candidates will at once emerge to step into the resulting vacuum—China, South Korea, and the U.S. The goal of any South Korean government will be to "reunify" the peninsula under Seoul's rule. The U.S. will certainly support that goal. China will certainly oppose it. All will be under pressure to act rapidly to prevent political and humanitarian catastrophe. Endless contingencies emerge from the possible actions of these three states, ranging from a tripartite war to a peaceful resolution of the problem.

The U.S. will have an important stake in determining the outcome. At the moment, America and China have a great deal in common over Korea. Neither wants war on the peninsula. Neither wants nuclear weapons on the peninsula. Neither wants to drive Pyongyang to desperation or war over the issue of nuclear weapons. And since the U.S. is now relying on Chinese pressure to contain the North Korean nuclear threat, neither can afford for Beijing to take steps that would destroy its leverage with Kim. The moment the North Korean regime collapses, however, the Sino–American confluence of interests will also collapse. At that point, neither Washington nor Beijing will be willing for the other to acquire predominance in North Korea. The fall of the Kim Jong Il regime will thus create another potential flashpoint in U.S.-Chinese relations.

The U.S. can affect the development of such a crisis dramatically by changing its posture in the region. If American forces continue to be present in South Korea, then the U.S. will automatically be a significant player in determining the fate of the North. The U.S. will retain its leverage in Seoul and in Beijing at the critical moments of the crisis. If the U.S. presence in South Korea is eliminated, as Rumsfeld wishes to have happen, then Washington will have relatively little leverage in the ensuing discussions. It will neither be able to control the South as effectively, nor easily be able to enter into discussions with the Chinese without threatening or beginning a provocative military build-up in the region.

Whether or not such a crisis leads to war on the Korean peninsula, the ability of the U.S. to provide forces to help maintain or reestablish order in North Korea may well be essential. In the aftermath of a successful struggle with China it will be vital, but it may be important to prevent the situation from escalating to that point. The use of the Korea example, in sum, simply to prove the utility of NCW concepts by demonstrating their value against a North Korean attack into the South is yet another example of NCW old-think. The situation on the peninsula is rapidly moving beyond the point where that is the critical problem, and the new problems emerging there are not generally susceptible to NCW solutions.

The scenario in which the North Korean fielding of nuclear weapons or, perhaps worse, delivery of such weapons to terrorists or other rogue states, might seem at first glance to support the NCW model better. In such a scenario, the U.S. president might well decide on one or more surgical strikes to destroy critical facilities in North Korea, accepting the risk that such an action might lead to a North Korean attack on the South that, however costly, was doomed to fail. This scenario includes two contingencies. If it is simply a matter of raiding North Korean weapons sites, then current U.S. capabilities should be sufficient. Because of the depth of certain key sites, additional work on "bunker-buster" bombs may be necessary, but the systems that identify targets and vector weapons onto them are now more than sufficient to undertake limited strikes of this variety. The biggest challenge will be acquiring the requisite intelligence, a challenge that is probably not amenable to solution by electronic measures.

If, however, the strike on North Korean nuclear sites triggers either a regime collapse of some sort or an attack on the South, then all of the considerations discussed above come into play, and the problem again becomes primarily one of handling the transition to a post-communist regime in the North. In either case, additional work on NCW methods will add little to American capabilities to perform the essential tasks. Maintaining a sizable presence in the theater with ground forces available to reinforce it rapidly, on the other hand, will be vital.

Iran

The problems posed by Iran are similar to those posed by Korea. The collapse of the regime of the ayatollahs is less likely, at least in the short term, than that of the North Korean communists. U.S. involvement in Iran is therefore likely to come either as the by-product of Iranian actions in Afghanistan or Iraq or as the result of the growing Iranian nuclear program. In either case, the same two contingencies are likely in Iran as in North Korea: either the U.S. might launch a limited strike to destroy Iranian nuclear weapons facilities, or the president might decide for that reason or for some other to remove the regime. Considering that Iran borders two countries in which the U.S. is now maintaining a large ground force combating an insurgency, it would be irresponsible to launch a limited strike without having the capability to remove the Teheran regime if it retaliated by escalating its support to either insurgency dramatically. Even if the goal is simply a surgical attack, therefore, the U.S. military must have the ability to change the Iranian regime if that becomes necessary.

As impossible as it is to imagine the U.S. simply allowing

North Korea or Pakistan to disintegrate without attempting some sort of reconstruction, such a policy is even more inconceivable in Iran. The Teheran regime has long been a direct supporter of terrorist networks throughout the Middle East. Even the civilian nuclear program inevitably brings fissionable materials into the country, along with equipment to carry weapons designers well down the road toward a nuclear device. The U.S. would not be able to sit back and allow Iran to sink into chaos, creating the likelihood that terrorists would avail themselves of the opportunity.

The basis for the argument that the U.S. cannot simply fight wars and leave chaos behind—summed up accurately if sarcastically as the "you-break-it-you-buy-it" argument—is not so much moral and ethical or a response to the "CNN effect" as it is pragmatic. It is not just that in the world today America cannot tolerate the odium that would be attached to any smash-and-withdraw attack. It is simply that, in many cases that might draw U.S. involvement, leaving chaos and wreckage behind would harm American security directly. It is not true that the U.S. can tolerate no failed states, that every weak government requires an American invasion followed by reconstruction. It is, however, true that the increasing number of states with potentially weak governments, weapons of mass destruction programs, and links to terrorism makes successful hit-and-run raids far less desirable or likely.

Apart from the possibility of a limited war with China over Taiwan, almost every other apparent threat in the world today that might require the commitment of significant U.S. military forces is also likely to require the capability to perform successful regime-change operations and post-war reconstruction efforts. In almost every case, moreover, those "Phase IV" operations are almost certain to prove much more challenging than any "decisive combat operations" needed to destroy the old regime. Iraq and Afghanistan are therefore likely to prove to be good models for future U.S. military operations, although not in the sense Rumsfeld and the transformation enthusiasts suppose.

Some Implications for Force Planning

Certain salient features of the forces required to respond to the immediate and near-term challenges the U.S. military faces stand out from this brief overview.

First, the defense budget overall is far too small to sustain an adequate military posture today. This fact should surprise no one. The current defense budget was fundamentally shaped in the wake of the first Gulf War, and it was designed explicitly to support forces appropriate for a protracted strategic pause. That pause is now over, and the U.S. is at war, but the defense budget is still largely funding a peacetime program. The sorts of trade-offs demanded of the military today—whether to respond to present conventional threats, sustain long-term reconstruction efforts, deploy new technology today, or develop new technology for tomorrow—are inappropriate for a military at war. There is no easy way to estimate the size of the increase that would be needed, but it seems clear that nothing less than an additional percent of GDP per year or more will be adequate. The nation could undertake such an expansion of the defense budget and still be within historically low levels of *peacetime* expenditures as a proportion of GDP.

Second, the ground forces are far too small. America's land forces today were designed to face a limited number of badly degraded conventional enemies in an environment in which American air power was expected to have decimated those enemies' ability to fight before the ground war even began. They were not designed to sustain long-term deployments of any variety, let alone long-term deployments on the scale necessary to succeed in reconstruction efforts following regime-change wars. In addition, since there is every reason to imagine that the U.S. will have to continue the struggles in Iraq and Afghanistan for some time and that other such conflicts and requirements are likely to occur, an expansion of the active-duty ground forces is essential.

Once again, it is impossible to evaluate the requirement in detail, but it seems clear that an expansion of at least 200,000 or so active duty soldiers and Marines will be necessary. To maintain a force of twenty brigades in reconstruction and counter-insurgency operations without breaking the ground forces would require a total force of at least sixty brigades. That would account for the entire active Army and Marine Corps today—and the twenty brigades deployed in Iraq after the end of Operation Iraqi Freedom proved inadequate to the task. Such a deployment, moreover, leaves no forces available for other contingencies. It seems likely that a total force of at least one hundred deployable brigades would be necessary to assure a *minimum* capacity in this regard, and the additional forty-some brigades required to reach that goal would need at least about 200,000 soldiers.

Some may object that these calculations ignore the role of the National Guard and Reserves, forces that have borne a large part of the burden of operations in both Iraq and Afghanistan. The burden they have borne is, in fact, far too large. The National Guard and Reserves exist to be a grand strategic reserve for the nation. They are the hedge against the possibility that something will go disastrously wrong either in an ongoing operation or in some part of the world in which trouble had not been foreseen. The commitment of those forces to day-to-day operations such as Iraq and Afghanistan not only runs the risk of destroying morale, recruitment, and retention in them, but also of leaving the nation with no trained reserve whatever to handle unexpected dangers at home or abroad. This situation is wholly unacceptable. The active forces must be increased to the point at which the Guard and Reserve can return to their original and vital role as true reserves for the nation.

It might also be objected that it will not be possible to recruit such a large number of volunteers, especially in this economic environment and in the midst of a war. It is true that the all-volunteer force does not have a track record of trying to recruit during a protracted counter-insurgency, but it does have an excellent record of recruiting during periods of economic growth. All throughout the economic boom of the 1980s the Army maintained itself at a level more than 200,000 soldiers above the current force size. It did so through a combination of recruiting bonuses and skillful advertising, supported by a president who highlighted the external threats to the United States. Recruiting such a large force in the midst of war will almost certainly be more expensive now than it was in the 1980s, and it will require a clear call to arms from the President, but there is no reason to imagine that it is impossible.

It is impossible to imagine failing to increase the size of the active military without putting the nation's security at grave risk, and it is also impossible to imagine returning to conscription except in the event of a real calamity. The military has just spent thirty years learning how to function within the parameters of the all-volunteer force. There are now no officers in the military below the rank of general who have ever served with conscripts. Just as officers like DePuy in the 1970s failed to recognize the qualitative advantages volunteers would bring to the force, so current senior leaders now take those advantages entirely for granted. In addition, the military has not maintained the training structures necessary to turn large numbers of recruits into soldiers rapidly. Any attempt to do so would lead to the demolition of current combat units in a scramble to find trainers—who would even so be totally unaccustomed to the training problems specific to conscripts. Even the enormous experience American soldiers are gaining in training Iraqi and Afghan recruits is still experience in training volunteers.

Any draft today, finally, would inevitably seem to be even more unfair and inequitable than the conscription system of the 1970s. Although the military needs more soldiers, it does not need enough more to make any sizable dent in the population of young men who come of military age every year. It is virtually impossible to imagine any system of selective service that would not create a nightmare of recriminations, resentment, and hostility among those called to serve against their will. Apart from the enormous political difficulties entailed in a return to conscription, therefore, it makes no sense from a military perspective either.

The terrible strains the military is suffering from sustaining operations in Iraq and Afghanistan should be a clear warning to the national security community. Although there were flaws in the assumptions that underlay the campaign, problems with the way it was executed, and errors in the early post-war decision-making, it simply should not have been so devastating to the Army to sustain this operation for this long. The fact that it is so painful to do so reveals the degree to which the policies of the 1990s, continued with little change after 9/11, Afghanistan, and Iraq, have left the military unbalanced and unprepared to handle obvious and likely contingencies in the present and the near future.

TOWARD THE DISTANT HORIZON

Challenging as it will be to develop a military and a political-military planning system able to handle the threats facing the U.S. today and in the immediate future, however, even responding to those changes may not be enough to secure America in the longer term. The transformation enthusiasts are right about this fact, but for the wrong reason. The danger does not come from the inevitability of an information revolution that will necessarily transform warfare in a certain way. It arises, rather, from the certainty that states contemplating war with the United States will work hard in the intervening years to find ways to counter American military predominance.

Such efforts are already underway. China has been working for years on systems to deny the U.S. access to Chinese territorial waters and airspace. North Korea has developed numerous techniques for closing all of the ports and airfields in South Korea in order to achieve a similar effect. Foreign engineers around the world are working on the problem of penetrating the M1's armor either with kinetic energy rounds, RPGS, or missiles, and there are already some solutions out there. Software designers will be working on viruses and other techniques, both physical and cybernetic, to confuse, obscure, or disintegrate essential U.S. military networks.

It is not the case, as many now believe, that future adversaries will simply cede the realm of conventional war to the U.S. and pursue purely "asymmetric" challenges. Ceding conventional war to the U.S. means abandoning any possibility of defending one's national territory and sovereignty. Over the long run, states will not accept such a posture and they will endeavor to find ways to defeat the U.S. conventionally, with or without asymmetric auxiliaries.

One particular threat nearly certain to arise is the possession by American adversaries of increasingly advanced systems similar to U.S. precision-strike capabilities. Whether or not this development was inevitable before the U.S. created those capabilities, now that their effectiveness has been repeatedly demonstrated potential U.S. foes will bend every effort to acquire them. This is the universal fate of revolutions in military affairs. The end result of every RMA to date has been the possession by all major powers of the technology and capabilities originally pioneered by one. This RMA will be no different.

Many of the transformation enthusiasts explicitly or tacitly recognize that current technologies will spread. Some use that assumption to argue for increased efforts to develop new systems to maintain the American lead over the long-term. Such efforts are likely to fail. The truth is that the RMA the transformation enthusiasts are chasing so eagerly has already arrived. It is the precision-strike RMA, and new systems are extremely unlikely to add sufficient new capability to bring about another revolution along the same lines. The challenge in the future will not be about finding new systems to keep the revolution going, but about finding ways to defeat enemies rapidly acquiring equivalent or nearly-equivalent capabilities themselves.

This is indeed a daunting challenge. So far, U.S. military thought has focused almost exclusively on using RMA-capable armed forces against pre-RMA enemies. Military thinkers and force planners have devoted far less effort to figuring out how to defeat enemies with similar abilities. The failure of British armored warfare enthusiasts in the Interwar Years to think through the problems of fighting armored enemies seriously harmed the development of British tanks, armored formations, doctrine, and training in that period and led to several years of defeat at the hands of superior German armored units. Similarly, while it was Napoleon who pioneered a new system for waging war at the beginning of the Napoleonic Wars, it was his adversaries who adopted and improved that system and then rode it to victory at the end. The U.S. would not be the first country to revolutionize warfare initially only to lose ultimately to a state that built more effectively on the revolutionary ideas over time.

Changing the focus of U.S. military thought to consider this problem offers a partial solution, but the real solution will come only with the interaction between American military development and that of its potential enemies. It is essential to devote significant resources to understanding current military programs in China, North Korea, Pakistan, India, and elsewhere, but even more important to try to divine the intellectual developments that will lay the bases for future transformations in those countries. By far the most important work done to prepare Germany for World War II took place in the 1920s, was theoretical, and did not involve building a single tank. Important as it is to have an eye to the possibilities new technologies or theories might offer the U.S., it is at least as important to tie future American military development to concrete, if theoretical, developments in the armies of potential enemies.

Above all, it is essential to recognize that "skipping generations" of military development is not only impossible, but meaningless. Because there is no inevitable direction in ongoing changes in warfare, it is not possible to know in advance what the "generation after next" of military systems will look like. The only way to proceed is step by step through the process of designing a military to meet obvious current threats, solve apparent near- and mid-term problems, and keep an eye on long-term dangers and possible opportunities. Changing the U.S. military today to deal with the challenges of today will generate ripple effects throughout the rest of the world's militaries. Only when those effects have been observed will it make sense to enter into the next iteration of identifying key threats and problems and attempting to solve them. This is the method that has produced RMAs in the past, and it is the only one likely to produce another RMA, of a variety that cannot now be determined, in the future.

CONCLUSION

MILITARIES CAN TRANSFORM themselves. War can be revolutionized. Scholars have rightly pointed out that these processes are extremely complex both to study and to carry out, and that the results are almost always less clear-cut than many claim. But some go too far in arguing that there is no such thing as a revolution in military affairs and that military transformation is an inherently meaningless term.

The flaw in the development of the American military over the past decade is not that it has been pursuing a meaningless concept but that it has been approaching the problem incorrectly. Transformation enthusiasts have explicitly divorced their programs both from history and from current reality. The main justifications for their efforts are intellectually weak theories based on neo-Marxist views of history that have been repeatedly proven wrong. In their attempts to rescue their programs from dangerous irrelevance after the 9/11 attacks, they have so diluted the meaning of transformation as to render the concept useless. They may even succeed unintentionally in discrediting the notion of transformation completely.

This result would be unfortunate. There is value in thinking about how war might change, although not in deciding *a priori*

393

that we know how it will, and there is value in imagining how the military might change either to bring about a revolution in military affairs or to react to one. Intellectual efforts along these lines are much more likely to produce concepts that will change dramatically when the tests of history and current reality are applied to them than they are to produce executable programs, but they are nevertheless important.

But however valid the abstract search for a transformation strategy that would lead to a theoretical RMA might have been before 9/11, it cannot receive priority while America is engaged in a deadly war. There is no task in U.S. national security more important now than succeeding in Iraq, and no challenge beyond that more important than preparing for the numerous grave scenarios which confront us today. These requirements must have the highest priority in our thinking and in the allocation of scarce resources. Efforts to transform the military must take second place.

Failure to prioritize transformation does not mean that transformation will not occur. As we have seen, it appears that the bulk of the transformation for *this* revolution in military affairs has already taken place. Most of what remains to be done is completing a suite of capabilities the significance of which is already clear. The "last mile of connectivity" to which Admiral Cebrowski frequently refers is not the mile that separates the U.S. military from some fundamental change in warfare. It is merely the completion of a process from which the U.S. has already derived most of the available benefits.

It is highly likely that there will be another revolution in military affairs in the next decades. Depending on how one counts them, there have been significant changes in the face, if not the nature, of war an average of every thirty to forty years for the past two centuries, and we are already a decade or so into the current RMA. It is also likely that the next RMA will result from additional changes in technology imaginatively integrated into military operations, although it is unlikely that information technology will be the real engine of such a change. It is more likely to play the ancillary role of making the real technological driver possible —in materials technology furthered by the availability of high-speed computers, say.

Any of a variety of over-the-horizon technologies today could revolutionize warfare tomorrow. The invention of storage batteries with massive capacity, for instance, would make possible both hyper-velocity guns and dramatically reduced logistical requirements for vehicles, as well as a host of other new capabilities that can not yet be imagined. Ultra light-weight armor, as we have seen, could have a dramatic effect on the nature of war, as could the fielding of truly effective and reliable anti-missile, anti-mortar, and anti-artillery defenses. Directed energy weapons, also far more feasible in the context of some revolution in energy storage techniques, could also change warfare fundamentally. Or they might not—sometimes armies field "super-weapons" that turn out to have far less impact than imagined, at least at first. The specific way in which new systems are used will be a critical determinant of their ultimate impact on war. There will be no way to know for sure what the next RMA will bring until it actually arrives.

It is also possible that the next change in the nature of warfare will result not from technology, but from a transformation in the way human beings think about their world. As the historian Alan Beyerchen and others argue, the world has been dominated for several centuries by a Newtonian approach not only to physics but to human affairs as well. Both natural scientists and political scientists have searched for a small set of relatively simple rules that govern not only the physical world, but the world of human beings too. This analytical approach has worked very well in creating technological marvels and relatively less well in helping us to understand how people work, but it is possible that it has run its course.

CONCLUSION

Beyerchen suggests that we may be entering the age of biology, in which both scientists and humanists do not try to analyze problems, breaking them down into simpler components for study, but to consider systems holistically. Biologists must work in this fashion, since biological systems die when they are "analyzed" or broken into their component parts. It turns out that applying this thought-process both to the physical world and to the world of human interactions can also be very fruitful. One manifestation of this way of thinking—chaos theory—has already proven valuable in science. It has helped meteorologists, for example, understand better both the weather and the limitations of their ability to predict it. It holds out great promise for helping warriors as well.

Seeing the enemy as a system and performing centers-of-gravity analyses of that system can be the beginning of a more sophisticated application of this way of thinking to war. All that is really required to make this leap is the understanding that the enemy system, like any living thing, reacts both to external stimuli and to attacks. Those reactions will never be fully predictable, because biological systems are too complex to permit completely accurate predictions of their behavior. If we abandon the extreme goals of NCW, effects-based operations, and other such programs that require such predictability, but focus instead on the higher degree of flexibility and responsiveness they can bring to military organizations and on ways of studying a system as an integrated whole rather than breaking into sub-systems to study, they may also serve as points of departure for the development of a real next-generation theory of warfare. Or they may not—it may emerge instead that such apparently new ways of thinking will offer little practical benefit to those who undertake them.

The basis for the critiques of current military doctrine and theory is not the stupidity or ignorance of the developers and the proponents of those ideas. On the contrary, all of them are intelligent, able, and experienced military thinkers and practitioners and they have produced much of value. The task they set themselves, however, was inordinately hard. By far the most difficult thing about dealing with revolutions in military affairs is understanding when you are in one and identifying how to pursue it further. The track record of attempts to deal with this problem in the past is poor—most states, leaders, and thinkers fail at it.

Some fail through lack of imagination, as the French did before World War II. Although aware of the potential of new technology in some ways, they did little but graft it on to their predetermined concepts and programs and so were defeated by German leaders with more creativity. Others fail through too much imagination. J. F. C. Fuller developed a variety of brilliant insights into the nature of tank warfare, but he also developed a host of extremely silly ones. His vision of tank-pure armies, including flying tanks and swimming tanks, but no dismounted infantry, was utter folly, for instance. His vaunted Plan 1919, which was supposed to presage the armored developments of the Interwar Years, was unachievable with the technology of his day. His excessive imagination, and the excessive promises he made on behalf of his new way of war, helped to discredit him and it, and set back the cause of transformation he wanted so much to advance. A similar problem has bedeviled airpower theorists virtually from the birth of air forces.

If the enthusiasts for transformation have fallen into a similar trap and exposed their programs to a similar danger, they can well plead the enormous difficulty of their task. Those who truly appreciate the importance and possibility of change in warfare will neither blindly follow their programs nor simply discard their ideas. They will instead mine them for the wisdom they offer, the benefits they have already conferred, and the reasonable promise they hold, while developing new frameworks and ways of thinking with which to carry them forward. Such efforts, tied carefully to the reality of the world and the challenges facing the U.S. today, stand the best chance of securing America, and also of transforming warfare once again.

ACKNOWLEDGMENTS

THIS BOOK HAS really been ten years in the making, although I only began actively researching and writing it about twelve months ago. From the moment I arrived at West Point to teach in the Fall of 1995, I was caught up in the debates swirling throughout the Army of the mid-1990s about the future of that institution, and of America's security. It was the best possible place to learn the ins and outs of that debate, for I was surrounded by some of the most intelligent, thoughtful, educated, and articulate officers in the military. Dave Fautua, Con Crane, Ty Seidule, Chris Kolenda, Gunner Sepp, and numerous others taught me much about how to understand war and how to think about the issues of military transformation then being discussed excitedly if nervously throughout the halls of the United States Military Academy. Several of them were kind enough to spare time they did not have to read portions of this manuscript and to offer advice and assistance that helped improve it enormously. I owe them all too many intellectual debts to recount or repay.

No one shaped my thinking about war more decisively than H. R. McMaster, the commander of the 3rd Armored Cavalry Regiment in Nineveh Province, Iraq at the moment of this writing. To have had the opportunity to share an office with H. R., and then to maintain a devoted friendship with him and his lovely wife, Katie, in the decade that has followed, has been a blessing in my life for which I will always be thankful. Much of what is of value in the pages that follow resulted from that friendship.

I am also thankful that my time at USMA brought me into contact with Dennis Showalter, who served as the visiting professor in the Department of History twice while I was there. Dennis has been a fount of insight, wise counsel, and support to me for many years, laboring through my work and helping me to improve it. He is also a wonderful friend.

I must also express my gratitude to Generals Casey Brower and Bob Doughty, who brought me to the History Department and supported my efforts to learn about the U.S. military, warfare, and its history. My time at USMA was truly life-changing, and I will always cherish it in memory. I am equally grateful to Chris DeMuth, Danielle Pletka, and my colleagues at the American Enterprise Institute for giving me the opportunity to concentrate my efforts on understanding military transformation in a supportive and intellectually challenging environment.

A special word of thanks must go to Melissa Wisner, my research assistant at AEI who was indefatigable in hunting down references, offering good advice, keeping me on track, and manhandling this manuscript into shape. Her presence at AEI has helped make my time there a real joy.

The present work also owes a great deal to a series of editors: Neal Kozodoy of *Commentary*, Tod Lindberg of *Policy Review*, Bill Kristol of *The Weekly Standard*, and Roger Kimball of *The New Criterion*, all of whom, under the guise of "editing," helped me develop and refine my thoughts about military transformation in a number of articles in their various journals. This work itself was the brainchild of Peter Collier of Encounter Books, who had no idea what he was letting himself in for when he

ACKNOWLEDGMENTS

asked me to write it, but has been unfailingly supportive and patient in the process.

I am especially grateful, as always, to my family, deluged with tales of weapons systems and military theory for weeks on end, but always supportive and helpful. My father not only listened to weary hours of these discussions, but also read every page dutifully and kept me on the right track when I was ready to veer off. And I am ever grateful to my wife, Kim, without whom neither this nor anything else I have ever undertaken would have been possible or meaningful.

Whatever is of significance in the pages that follow comes from this remarkable group of people who have educated and supported me over the years. Whatever faults and errors remain are mine alone.

NOTES

INTRODUCTION

1 Geoffrey Parker, *Military Revolution: Military Innovation and the Rise of the West, 1500–1800* (New York: Cambridge University Press, 1988); Clifford Rogers, *The Military Revolution Debate: Readings on the Transformation of Early Modern Europe* (Boulder: Westview Press, 1995).

2 The Russian word *delo* is rather hard to render into English, as it is more similar to the Latin *res* than to any single English word; "affair" is not too bad an approximation.

3 Stephen Biddle, *Military Power: Explaining Victory and Defeat in Modern Battle* (Princeton: Princeton University Press, 2004); Colin Gray, *Strategy for Chaos: Revolutions in Military Affairs and the Evidence of History* (Portland, Oregon: Frank Cass, 2002).

CHAPTER ONE

1 John Lewis Gaddis, *Strategies of Containment: A Critical Appraisal of Postwar American National Security Policy* (New York: Oxford University Press, 1982), p. 297.

2 Don Oberdorfer, *The Two Koreas: A Contemporary History,* revised edition (New York: Basic Books, 2001), pp. 84ff.

3 See Kenneth J. Coffey, *Strategic Implications of the All-Volunteer Force: The Conventional Defense of Central Europe* (Chapel Hill: University of North Carolina Press, 1979), pp. 6–35, for a good brief overview of the growth of opposition to the draft and the government's responses, and *Defense Manpower Commission, Defense Manpower: The Keystone of National Security: Report to the President and the Congress* (Washington, DC: Government Printing Office, 1976), pp. 40–48 for a brief summary of the technical and legal history of modern U.S. conscription.

4 *Defense Manpower*, p. 47. Johnson only called up about 40,000 reserves in a "token mobilization" in 1968.

5 Coffey, pp. 40–43.

6 Ibid., pp. 157–59.

7 *Defense Manpower*, p. 46.

8 This is not to say that there are no racial or ethnic tensions within the military services, but that the armed forces have done a superb job of mitigating such problems compared with the dire predictions being made in the 1970s about the consequences of the changing military demographic.

9 The Total Force concept and its early development is described in detail in *Defense Manpower*, pp. 97ff.

10 Conrad Crane, "Avoiding Vietnam: The U.S. Army's Response to Defeat in Southeast Asia" (Carlisle, Penn.: U.S. Army Strategic Studies Institute, 2002), p. 5, esp. note 12. Lewis Sorley, *Thunderbolt: General Creighton Abrams and the Army of His Times* (New York: Simon and Schuster, 1992), pp. 361–64, asserts that Abrams was motivated by the desire to tie the hands of future presidents, offering the evidence of contemporaries to corroborate it. He does not consider the larger context of the decision, however, and so probably places too much of the credit or blame on Abrams. Although Abrams' decision took on a peculiar cast in the 1990s, when even small deployments to the Balkans required the mobilization of reservists, it is far more likely that he had not considered such operations than that he had meant to require the president to seek the approval of the nation even for the movement of a brigade to Bosnia. Abrams, after all, was thinking about the deployment of hundreds of thousands of soldiers at the height of the Cold War, and it is dangerous to read the issues of the 1990s back into his early 1970s decision-making.

11 *Defense Manpower*, pp. 420–21.

12 Ibid., pp. 422–23.

13 Robert H. Scales, *Certain Victory* (Washington, DC: Government Printing Office, 1993), pp. 9–10.

14 Quoted in Coffey, p. 79.

15 Sorley, *Thunderbolt*, p. 362.

16 Ibid., pp. 362–63.

17 "Department of Defense Active Duty Military Personnel Strength Levels, Fiscal Years 1950–2002" from the Department of Defense Military Personnel Statistics website, http://www.dior.whs.mil/mmid/military/ms9.pdf, accessed on 31 March 2005.

18 *Department of the Army Historical Summary: Fiscal Year 1975*, Chapter II, p. 6 (available from

http://www.army.mil/cmh/books/DAHSUM/1975/, accessed 6
November 2005).

19 Sorley, *Thunderbolt*, pp. 362–67 describes Abrams' fights and accomplishments in this regard.

20 "Department of Defense Active Duty Military Personnel Strength Levels, Fiscal Years 1950–2002" from the Department of Defense Military Personnel Statistics website, http://www.dior.whs.mil/mmid/military/ms9.pdf, accessed on 31 March 2005.

21 See Chapter 2 for a consideration of the impact of the transition to the AVF on the Navy.

22 Benjamin Lambeth, *The Transformation of American Airpower* (Ithaca, New York: Cornell University Press, 2000), p. 13.

23 Richard Hallion, *Storm over Iraq* (Washington, DC: Smithsonian Institution Press, 1992), p. 20; Lambeth, p. 48.

24 Gaddis, *Strategies of Containment*, pp. 127–99.

25 Lambeth, *The Transformation of American Air Power*, pp. 35–36.

26 The best study of Boyd's impact is Grant T. Hammond, *The Mind of War: John Boyd and American Security* (Washington, DC: Smithsonian Institute, 2001).

27 Hammond, *The Mind of War*, pp. 70–72.

28 Ibid., pp. 67–82; Hallion, *Storm over Iraq*, pp. 40–41.

29 Hallion, *Storm over Iraq*, pp. 39–40.

30 Ibid., pp. 210–211; Lambeth, *The Transformation of American Air Power*, pp. 72–73.

31 Lambeth, *The Transformation of American Air Power*, p. 43.

32 See below for a more detailed consideration of changes in Air Force and Navy training programs.

33 Hallion, *Storm over Iraq*, pp. 309–10.

34 Lambeth, *The Transformation of American Air Power*, pp. 12–53.

35 Ibid.

36 Ibid., p. 40.

37 Hallion, *Storm over Iraq*, pp. 39–45.

38 Orr Kelly, *King of the Killing Zone* (New York: W. W. Norton, 1989), p. 13.

39 Ibid., p. 97.

40 Ibid., pp. 107–108.

41 Sorley, *Thunderbolt*, p. 338.

42 Kelly, *King of the Killing Zone*, p. 89; Robert H. Scales, *Certain Victory: The U.S. Army in the Gulf War* (Washington, DC: Government Printing Office, 1993), p. 20, attributes the Big Five decision to Abrams.

43 W. Blair Haworth, *The Bradley and How It Got That Way: Technology, Institutions, and the Problem of Mechanized Infantry in the United States Army* (Westport: Greenwood, 1999).

44 Hallion, *Storm over Iraq*, pp. 30–31.

45 Lambeth, *The Transformation of American Air Power*, p. 60.

46 Cited in ibid., p. 62.

47 Ibid., pp. 62–63.

48 Hallion, *Storm over Iraq*, p. 32.

49 We will consider the evolution of airpower doctrine at the operational and strategic levels presently.

50 Lambeth, *The Transformation of American Air Power*, pp. 62–68.

51 Ibid., p. 69.

52 Ibid., p. 71.

53 Basic sources for the transformation of Army training are: Anne W. Chapman, *The Origins and Development of the National Training Center, 1976–1984* (Fort Monroe, VA: Office of the Command Historian, U.S. Army Training and Doctrine Command, 1992) and *The Army's Training Revolution, 1973–1990: An Overview* (Fort Monroe, VA: Office of the Command Historian, U.S. Army Training and Doctrine Command, 1991); John L. Romjue, Susan Canedy, and Anne W. Chapman, *Prepare the Army for War: A Historical Overview of the Army Training and Doctrine Command, 1973–1993*; Romie L. Brownlee and William J. Mullen III, *Changing an Army: An Oral History of General William E. DePuy, USA Retired* (Carlisle Barracks, PA: U.S. Military History Institute, 1988); and Major Paul H. Herbert, *Deciding What Has to Be Done: General William E. DePuy and the 1976 Edition of FM 100–5, Operations* (Fort Leavenworth, Kansas: Combat Studies Institute, 1988). The section that follows is drawn from these works.

54 Charles E. Heller and William A. Stofft, eds. *America's First Battles, 1776–1965* (Lawrence, KS: University Press of Kansas, 1986).

55 Herbert, *Deciding What Has to Be Done*, p. 30.

56 The Army already possessed relatively advanced training areas in Germany and Korea for its forces stationed overseas, but the bulk of the Army stationed in the U.S. lagged woefully behind them in training facilities.

57 Brownlee and Mullen, *Changing an Army*, p. 181.

58 The basic sources for the doctrinal revolution of the 1970s are Herbert, *Deciding What Has to Be Done* and John L. Romjue, *From Active Defense to AirLand Battle: The Development of Army Doctrine, 1973–1982* (Fort Monroe, VA: Historical Office, U.S. Army Train

ing and Doctrine Command, 1984), as well as the manuals themselves, FM 100–5, *Operations*, 1976 and 1982 editions.

59 Cited in Romjue, *From Active Defense to AirLand Battle*, p. 6.

60 Herbert, *Deciding What Has to Be Done*, p. 64.

61 Ibid., p. 68.

62 Ibid., p. 97.

63 Robert J. Hamilton, "Green and Blue in the Wild Blue: An Examination of the Evolution of Army and Air Force Airpower Thinking
and Doctrine since the Vietnam War" (Maxwell Air Force Base,
Alabama: School of Advanced Airpower Studies, Air University,
1993), pp. 19–20.

64 Ibid., p. 20.

65 Herbert, *Deciding What Has to Be Done*, p. 69.

66 Ibid., p. 68.

67 Ibid., p. 70; Hallion, *Storm over Iraq*, pp. 75–82; Lambeth, *The
Transformation of American Air Power*, p. 84.

68 Herbert, *Deciding What Has to Be Done*, pp. 70–71.

69 Lambeth, *The Transformation of American Air Power*, pp. 84–85.

70 Some Air Force students of these developments misunderstand the
operational focus of the 1982 draft of FM 100–5, asserting that only
with the 1986 edition did the Army refocus on the operational level.
This view is without foundation, as a careful examination of both
documents will show. ("Green and Blue in the Wild Blue," p. 27).

71 For Soviet thought, see Shimon Naveh, *In Pursuit of Military Excellence: The Evolution of Operational Theory* (Portland, OR: Frank Cass,
1997); David Glantz, *Soviet Military Operational Art: In Pursuit of
Deep Battle* (Portland, OR: Frank Cass, 1991), along with many
other works; and A. B. Kadishin, ed., *Voprosy strategii i operativnogo
iskusstva v sovetskikh voennykh trudakh, 1917–1940* (Moscow: Voennoe Izdatel'stvo, 1965). Romjue, *From Active Defense to AirLand
Battle*, interestingly, does not make any mention of the obvious
Soviet influence in the 1982 doctrine.

72 Hallion, *Storm over Iraq*, pp. 78–79.

73 Lambeth, *The Transformation of American Air Power*, p. 89.

CHAPTER TWO

1 Peter Schweitzer, *Reagan's War: The Epic Story of His Forty-Year
Struggle and Final Triumph over Communism* (New York: Doubleday,
2002), describes Reagan's attitudes toward the Soviet Union in
great detail. See also U.S. National Security Strategy, April 1982,

pp. 1–3 (available in declassified form from the Digital National Security Archive [henceforth DNSA]).

2 Ibid.

3 PD/NSC–18, Zbigniew Brzezinski, August 24, 1977, DNSA.

4 George W. Baer, *One Hundred Years of Sea Power: The U.S. Navy, 1890–1990* (Stanford: Stanford University Press, 1994), pp. 411–12.

5 U.S. National Security Strategy, April 1982, DNSA; Schweitzer, *Reagan's War*, pp. 141–42.

6 Cited in Schweitzer, *Reagan's War*, p. 141. Emphasis added.

7 Schweitzer, *Reagan's War*, p. 154. Emphasis added.

8 Schweitzer, *Reagan's War*, pp. 131–32. Throughout 1981, 1982, and 1983, U.S. ships and aircraft aggressively shadowed Soviet fleet elements, occasionally buzzing them, as on one occasion in April 1981 when a Navy P–3 aircraft buzzed a Soviet flagship with Admiral Sergei Gorshakov on board. At other times, a U.S. destroyer sailed through the middle of a Soviet anti-submarine training exercise, and U.S. ships and aircraft repeatedly flew into the Sea of Okhotsk and other areas that the Soviets claimed as territorial waters.

9 Defense Budget Green Book, FY 2006, table 6–13, p. 143. Calculations based on constant-dollar outlays (as opposed to authorizations). These increases were accompanied by a nearly 50% reduction in "Defense-wide" activities.

10 Department of Defense Annual Report, FY 1990, p. 221.

11 Active Army manpower remained constant between 1981 and 1987 at 781,000, and the number of Active Army divisions increased only from 16 to 18 by 1986. Army National Guard and Reserve strength, however, grew by 186,000 men and women (or 32%) between 1980 and 1987. The U.S. fleet, on the other hand, grew from 479 ships to 565 ships between 1980 and 1988 (or 18%) while Naval personnel strength grew by 15% in the same period. Air Force manpower remained nearly constant, while the number of fighter and attack aircraft increased by 12%. Department of Defense Annual Report, FY 1990, pp. 226 and 232; Defense Budget Green Book, FY 2006, table 7–5, p. 213.

12 Defense Budget Green Book, FY 2006, table 6–12, p. 137.

13 Schweitzer, *Reagan's War*, pp. 138 ff; *Daniel Wirls, Buildup: The Politics of Defense in the Reagan Era* (Ithaca: Cornell University Press, 1992), pp. 35–36. Reagan approved an increase in the Carter defense budget for 1981 of $32 billion less than two weeks after taking office.

14 Problems with the All-Volunteer Force led to a significant body of

work in the late 1970s and early 1980s, much of which bears reconsideration in light of current concerns over the viability of a volunteer military. See, e.g., Kenneth Coffey, *Strategic Implications of the All-Volunteer Force*; Lawrence Korb, "Defense Manpower and the Reagan Record" in Stephen J. Cimbala, ed., *The Reagan Defense Program: An Interim Assessment* (Wilmington: Scholarly Resources, 1986); John B. Keeley, ed., *The All-Volunteer Force and American Society* (Charlottesville: University Press of Virginia, 1978); and Jerald G. Bachman, John D. Blair, and David R. Segal, *The All-Volunteer Force: A Study of Ideology in the Military* (Ann Arbor: The University of Michigan Press, 1977).

15 Korb, "Defense Manpower and the Reagan Record" in Cimbala, ed., *The Reagan Defense Program*. It is worth noting in passing that the American military mobilization rate, calculated as the ratio of active duty military personnel to the overall estimated labor pool, has fallen from 2.3% in 1975 to under 1% in FY2006. It was under 2% for the entire Reagan period. (Defense Budget Green Book, FY 2006, table 7–6, p. 215.)

16 See Wirls, *Buildup* and Cimbala, *Reagan Defense Program* for considerations of the continuities and discontinuities between the late Carter and early Reagan defense policies.

17 Schweitzer, *Reagan's War*, pp. 150ff.

18 Baer, *One Hundred Years of Sea Power*, pp. 423–24; Frederick H. Hartmann, *Naval Renaissance: The U.S. Navy in the 1980s* (Annapolis: Naval Institute Press, 1990), p. 69; John F. Lehman, Jr., *Command of the Seas* (Annapolis: Naval Institute Press, 1988), p. 118.

19 Cimbala, *Reagan Defense Program*, p. 13; NDSM 344, Navy Shipbuilding Program, January 18, 1977, DNSA. Carter relented on this opposition after the Soviet invasion of Afghanistan, and the 1980 defense appropriation included funding for the *Theodore Roosevelt*, a Nimitz-class carrier that cost $2 billion.

20 Baer, *One Hundred Years of Sea Power*.

21 Ibid., pp. 403–407, discusses changing ideas (and competing terminology) of control of the seas or sea control.

22 Hartmann, *Naval Renaissance*, p. 40.

23 John B. Hattendorf, *The Evolution of the U.S. Navy's Maritime Strategy, 1977–1986* (Newport: Naval War College, Newport Paper 19, 2004), esp. chapter 2; Baer, *One Hundred Years of Sea Power*, pp. 418ff.

24 Ibid.

25 Ibid.

26 Baer, *One Hundred Years of Sea Power*, pp. 432ff.

27 National Security Strategy, April 1982, DNSA.

28 Ibid., p. 17.

29 Ibid.; Jeffrey Record, *The Rapid Deployment Force and U.S. Military Intervention in the Persian Gulf* (Cambridge, Mass.: Institute for Foreign Policy Analysis, 1983), esp. p. 12.

30 See Hallion, *Storm over Iraq* and Lambeth, *The Transformation of American Air Power* for the best exemplars of this approach.

31 Daniel P. Bolger, *Americans at War: 1975–1986: An Era of Violent Peace* (Novato, Cal.: Presidio Press, 1988), chapter 2.

32 Ibid.

33 Ibid., chapter 4.

34 Lambeth, *The Transformation of American Air Power*, pp. 100–102; Bolger, *Americans at War*, chapter 7; Hallion, *Storm over Iraq*, pp. 104–109.

35 Ibid.

36 Schweitzer, *Reagan's War*, pp. 139–40.

CHAPTER THREE

1 The idea of seeing the enemy's military as a system was not entirely new—elements of that view formed the basis both for German armored doctrine before and during World War II, and for Soviet "deep battle" doctrine of about the same time. Boyd was very familiar with German doctrine, although he does not seem to have known much about Soviet techniques, but his approach to the problem was broader and more synthetic, and therefore reached deeper and more significant conclusions. See Shimon Naveh, *In Pursuit of Military Excellence*, for a discussion of the systemic views inherent in German and Soviet armored doctrine.

2 Hammond, *The Mind of War*; John Boyd, "A Discourse on Winning and Losing" (unpublished briefing slides, August 1987). I am very grateful to Grant Hammond for providing me with a copy of Boyd's unpublished work. The slides are now also available on-line at http://www.d-n-i.net/second_level/boyd_military.htm along with a number of articles and bibliographic references about Boyd.

3 Naveh, *In Pursuit of Military Excellence*.

4 Antulio J. Echeverria II, "Clausewitz's Center of Gravity: Changing our Warfighting Doctrine—Again!" (Carlisle, Penn.: U.S. Army Strategic Studies Institute, 2002) and "Clausewitz's Center of Gravity: It's Not What We Thought," *Naval War College Review*, vol. LVI, no. 1 (Winter 2003), pp. 108–123; Joseph L. Strange and Richard Iron, "Center of Gravity: What Clausewitz Really Meant,"

Joint Forces Quarterly, issue 3 5, pp. 2 0–2 7 and "Understanding
Centers of Gravity and Critical Vulnerabilities," available at
http://www.au.af.mil/au/awc/awcgate/usmc/cog1 .pdf and
http://www.au.af.mil/au/awc/awcgate/usmc/cog2 .pdf; and Seow
Hang Lee, "Center of Gravity or Center of Confusion: Understanding the Mystique" (Maxwell Air Force Base, Alabama: Air
University, Air War College, 1 9 9 9).

5 Strange and Iron, "Center of Gravity: What Clausewitz Really
Meant."

6 Although he also uses it more loosely on certain occasions, sometimes meaning simply "important fact" and at other times "critical
element," as in "the battle must always be considered the true center of gravity of the war." (Carl von Clausewitz, *On War*, trans. Peter
Paret and Michael Howard [Princeton: Princeton University Press,
1 9 8 9], p. 2 4 8. See also p. 2 5 8 for a similar usage.)

7 Clausewitz, *On War*, pp. 4 8 6 and 5 9 7 .

8 Boyd, "Patterns of Conflict," slide 4 1 .

9 Ibid., slides 4 2 , 6 0 , 7 1 , among others.

1 0 Ibid., slide 7 8 .

1 1 I am grateful to Professor Cliff Rogers of West Point for pointing
this out to me, and for helping me in general to understand Clausewitz's concepts more clearly.

1 2 Clausewitz, *On War*, pp. 4 8 8–8 9 .

1 3 Clausewitz did note that the center of gravity might not be a military
force—it might be the seizure of a key piece of terrain, the enemy
leadership, the people's morale, or other less tangible factors. He did
not, however, ever discuss how to attack these intangibles and consistently stated or implied that striking the most important military
force was almost invariably the right way to proceed.

1 4 Echevarria, "Clausewitz's Center of Gravity," p. 1 1 .

1 5 *On War*, p. 1 6 3 .

1 6 Azar Gat, *A History of Military Thought from the Enlightenment to the
Cold War* (New York: Oxford University Press, 2 0 0 1), pp. 1 1 3–1 2 1

1 7 John Warden, *The Air Campaign* (New York: toExcel, 1 9 9 8), pref-
ace and epilogue. Legends surrounding these events are plentiful
and gloss over several important points, eliding the concepts of *The
Air Campaign* with the much more developed concepts that Warden
and his colleagues used to develop the Iraqi air war plan and then
presenting the history of that intellectual development as a continuous path from the 1 9 8 0 s into the following decade. In truth, the
development of Warden's ideas, and airpower theory in general, was
far from continuous or inevitable. The Gulf War and especially the

post-war interpretation of the air campaign and its results, in fact, created a sharp break in that development and mark a decisive turn in the development of modern U.S. airpower thought.

18 John Warden, interview with the author, 14 June 2005.

19 Warden says that he was only vaguely aware of Boyd's work, and, although Boyd briefed the Checkmate team, he did so before Warden took command of it. David S. Fadok, *John Boyd and John Warden: Air Power's Quest for Strategic Paralysis* (Maxwell Air Force Base, Alabama: Air University Press, 1995), p. 21, n. 23.

20 Warden, *The Air Campaign*, p. 13.

21 This assertion required Warden to make a complicated elliptical argument about Vietnam, of course, where the North Vietnamese never enjoyed air superiority but nevertheless defeated an American adversary that always had it. The closest Warden comes to addressing this problem is by asserting that U.S. air superiority prevented the North Vietnamese from undertaking a large-scale conventional offensive, something that only occurred in 1975 after American airpower had been withdrawn.

22 Warden, *The Air Campaign*, p. 7.

23 Boyd, "A Discourse on Winning and Losing," slides 41–42.

24 Warden interview. He noted that he was probably more familiar with the concept initially from his days as a cadet studying physics and engineering, although he relied on Clausewitz's discussions of the idea as his intellectual point of departure in *The Air Campaign*.

25 Warden, *The Air Campaign*, p. 34.

26 Ibid., pp. 34–35.

27 Ibid., pp. 34–44.

28 Warden interview.

29 Warden, *The Air Campaign*, p. 44.

30 Ibid., p. 45. In his interview with the author, Warden explained that he has come to reject the concept of the OODA loop completely, on the grounds that both experience and psychological studies of cognitive functions show that it is simply not an accurate depiction of how human beings or human organizations actually function.

31 Warden, *The Air Campaign*, p. 46.

32 Ibid., p. 46.

33 Ibid.

34 Ibid., pp. 48–50. See also Lambeth, *The Transformation of American Air Power*, pp. 92–96.

35 Warden, *The Air Campaign*, pp. 116–17.

36 Ibid., p. 121.

37 Warden interview.

38 Ibid.

39 Ibid.

40 Warden, *The Air Campaign*, pp. 144–46.

41 Warden interview.

42 Ibid.

43 Warden, *The Air Campaign*, p. 147.

44 Ibid., pp. 144 ff.

45 Ibid., pp. 144–45.

46 Michael R. Gordon and General Bernard E. Trainor, *The General's War* (New York: Little, Brown and Company, 1995), chapter 1.

47 Thomas A. Keaney and Eliot A. Cohen, *The Gulf War Air Power Survey* (Washington, DC: U.S. Government Printing Office, 1993—hereafter GWAPS), vol. I, p. 109.

48 Warden, *The Air Campaign*, p. 151.

49 Ibid., p. 145.

50 Gordon and Trainor, *The Generals' War*, p. 90.

51 George Bush and Brent Scowcroft, *A World Transformed: The Collapse of the Soviet Empire, the Unification of Germany, Tiananmen Square, The Gulf War* (New York: Knopf, 1998), pp. 326–28.

52 Gordon and Trainor, *The Generals' War*, p. 91.

53 Cited in Williamson Murray, *The Air War in the Persian Gulf* (Baltimore: The Nautical and Aviation Publishing Company of America, 1995), p. 21.

54 Gordon and Trainor, *The Generals' War*, p. 93.

55 Ibid.

56 Murray, *The Air War in the Persian Gulf*, p. 21.

57 Gordon and Trainor, *The Generals' War*, p. 93.

58 Ibid., p. 96.

59 Lambeth, *The Transformation of American Air Power*, p. 106.

60 Gordon and Trainor, *The Generals' War*, p. 96.

61 Ibid., p. 99.

62 Ibid., p. 137. Bush and Scowcroft, *A World Transformed*, pp. 380–81 generally confirms the trend of this briefing.

63 Gordon and Trainor, *The Generals' War*, p. 101.

64 Ibid., p. 137 and Bush and Scowcroft, *A World Transformed*, pp. 380–81.

65 Gordon and Trainor, *The Generals' War*, pp. 134–35.

CHAPTER FOUR

1 William W. Kaufmann, *Assessing the Base Force: How Much is Too Much?* (Washington, DC: Brookings Institution, 1992), p. 11.

2 Donald Kagan and Frederick W. Kagan, *While America Sleeps: Self-Delusion, Military Weakness, and the Threat to Peace Today* (New York: St. Martin's Press, 2000), p. 296.

3 Ibid., pp. 272–73.

4 Les Aspin, *Report on the Bottom-Up Review* (1993—hereafter BUR), Section IV.

5 Department of Defense Annual Report for 1996, p. D–2. Marine Corps strength did not vary over this period, holding steady at three active division/wing expeditionary forces and one in reserve.

6 In truth, the defenses he actually offered for his structure were rather weak, and, since he died in 1994, it is not possible to know now how sophisticated a defense he could have mounted. Other elements in the BUR and in his statements, however, allow the development of the theoretical rebuttal that follows.

7 BUR, Section III.

8 Kagan and Kagan, *While America Sleeps*, p. 312.

9 The failure to get National Guard units into the Kuwait Theater of Operations in time to participate in Desert Storm raised hackles both in the Guard and in the Active Army. Some in the active force used it as evidence that the Guard was irrelevant and could not be made combat-worthy. Some in the Guard argued that it proved, rather, an active force bias against the Guard, including an unwillingness to train and equip the Guard on a par with the Regular Army and a refusal to evaluate Guard units' readiness fairly. Whatever the truth of this argument, and it is probably complicated, it is important to remember that the Guard and Reserve were less then a decade away from the nadir of their recruitment and capabilities in the late 1970s and early 1980s, having been deliberately neglected by a Carter administration focused on winning the first battle of a short war.

10 Richard H. Shultz, Jr. and Robert L. Pfalzgraff, Jr., *The Future of Air Power in the Aftermath of the Gulf War* (Maxwell Air Force Base, Alabama: Air University Press, 1992), p. 11.

11 Ibid., p. 12.

12 Ibid., pp. 75–82.

13 Lt. Col. Price T. Bingham, "Air Power in Desert Storm and the Need for Doctrinal Change," *Airpower Journal*, Winter 1991.

14 Shultz and Pfalzgraff, *The Future of Air Power*, p. 85.

15 Lt. Col. Phillip S. Meilinger, "The Problem with Our Air Power Doctrine," *Airpower Journal*, Spring 1992.

16 Col. Dennis M. Drew, "Desert Storm as a Symbol," *Airpower Journal*, Fall 1992.

17 Shultz and Pfalzgraff, *The Future of Air Power*, p. 19.

18 John Warden, "Employing Air Power in the Twenty-first Century," in Schultz and Pfalzgraff, *The Future of Air Power*, pp. 57–82.

19 Robert L. Pfalzgraff, Jr. and Richard H. Shultz, Jr., *The United States Army: Challenges and Missions for the 1990s* (Lexington, Mass.: Lexington Books, 1991), p. 84.

20 Cited in General Gordon R. Sullivan and Colonel James M. Dubik, *Land Warfare in the 21st Century* (Carlisle, Penn.: U.S. Army Strategic Studies Institute, 1993), publication 247, p. xiii.

21 Sullivan and Dubik, *Land Warfare in the 21st Century*, p. xiv.

22 Ibid., p. xv.

23 Headquarters, Department of the Army, FM 100–5, *Operations* (Washington, DC: Government Printing Office, 1993), pp. 2–6 to 2–9.

24 Ibid., pp. 2–0 to 2–1.

25 Ibid., Chapter 13, "Operations Other Than War."

26 Sullivan and Dubik, *Land Warfare in the 21st Century*, p. xv.

27 Ibid., p. xxiii.

28 Ibid.

29 Ibid., p. xx.

30 Ibid., p. xxv.

31 Ibid.

CHAPTER FIVE

1 *A National Security Strategy of Engagement and Enlargement* (Washington, DC: Government Printing Office, July 1994—hereafter NSS 1994).

2 Ibid., p. i.

3 Secretary of Defense Dick Cheney, *Defense Strategy for the 1990s: The Regional Defense Strategy*, January 1993, p. 3.

4 NSS 1994, p. 19.

5 Ibid., p. 7.

6 Ibid., p. 7.

7 *National Military Strategy of the United States of America, 1995: A Strategy of Flexible and Selective Engagement* (Washington, DC: Government Printing Office, 1995), pp. 15–16.

8 NSS 1994, p. 10.

9 Kagan and Kagan, *While America Sleeps*, pp. 338, 358–59, and 385–86.

10 Ibid., p. 359.

11 Major General Charles D. Link, "An Airman's View," in *Clashes of*

Visions: Sizing and Shaping our Forces in a Fiscally Constrained Environment, A CSIS–VII Symposium, 29 October 1997 (Washington, DC: CSIS, 1997). See also Earl H. Tilford, Jr., *Halt Phase Strategy: New Wine in Old Skins . . . With Powerpoint* (Carlisle, Penn.: U.S. Army Strategic Studies Institute, 1998), for a review and critique of the "halt phase" argument.

12 Colonel Robert C. Owen, *Deliberate Force: A Case Study in Effective Air Campaigning* (Maxwell Air Force Base, Alabama: Air University Press, 2000), p. 119.

13 Ibid., p. 122.

14 Ibid., p. 123.

15 Richard P. Hallion, "Precision Guided Munitions and the New Era of Warfare" (Fairbairn, Australia: Air Power Studies Centre, 1995), Working Paper Number 53.

16 John A. Tirpak, "Deliberate Force," *Air Force Magazine,* October 1997.

17 Ibid.

18 Tim Ripley, "Air Power Vindicated," *Flight International,* 1 November 1995.

19 Lambeth, *Transformation of American Air Power,* p. 218.

20 Operation Allied Force produced a number of excellent and detailed studies, including Anthony H. Cordesman, *The Lessons and Non-Lessons of the Air and Missile Campaign in Kosovo* (Westport, Conn.: Praeger, 2001); Andrew J. Bacevich and Eliot A. Cohen, *War Over Kosovo: Politics and Strategy in a Global Age* (New York: Columbia University Press, 2001); and Benjamin S. Lambeth, *NATO's Air War for Kosovo: A Strategic and Operational Assessment* (Arlington, VA: RAND, 2001).

21 Tirpak, "Lessons Learned and Re-Learned," *Air Force Magazine,* August 1999.

22 Ibid.

23 Paul Richter, "Crisis in Yugoslavia: Air-Only Campaign Offers a False Sense of Security, Some Say," *Los Angeles Times,* 4 June 1999.

24 Cited in Lambeth, *Transformation of American Air Power,* p. 223.

25 The F/A–22 "Raptor" has been under development for more than two decades, and has been under attack for budgetary and strategic reasons for virtually that entire period. The first prototypes flew in 1990, the aircraft was first approved for low-rate production in 2001, and debates about how many to purchase have swirled in Congress ever since.

26 Tirpak, "Lessons Learned and Re-Learned."

27 F. Whitten Peters, "Are We Ready To Lose the Next Air War?" *New York Times*, 24 July 1999.

28 Lambeth, *The Transformation of American Air Power*, p. 214.

29 Cordesman, *The Lessons and Non-Lessons of the Air and Missile Campaign in Kosovo*, p. 38; Department of Defense, Annual Report, 1999, Appendix D.

30 Lambeth, *The Transformation of American Air Power*, pp. 215–16.

CHAPTER SIX

1 Alvin Toffler, *The Third Wave* (New York: Bantam, 1980).

2 Gen. Jimmy D. Ross, "Winning the Information War," *Army*, February 1994, p. 27.

3 Gordon Sullivan, "A New Force for a New Century," *Army*, May 1994, p. 26.

4 Ross, "Winning the Information War," p. 28.

5 Gordon Sullivan, "America's Army—Focusing on the Future," *Army*, October 1994, pp. 21–23.

6 U.S. Army Training and Doctrine Command Pamphlet 525-5, "Force XXI Operations: A Concept for the Evolution of Full-Dimensional Operations for the Strategic Army of the Early Twenty-First Century," 1 August 1994, p. 2–10. Emphasis added.

7 TRADOC Pamphlet 525-5, p. 3–6. Emphasis in the original.

8 LTG Paul E. Blackwell, "Winning the Wars of the 21st Century," *Army*, October 1994, p. 126.

9 Stuart Johnson and Martin Libicki, eds., *Dominant Battlespace Knowledge* (Washington, DC: National Defense University Press, 1995).

10 Ibid., Introduction.

11 Paul Bracken, "The Significance of Dominant Battlefield Awareness," in Johnson and Libicki, *Dominant Battlespace Knowledge*. Emphasis in the original.

12 Martin C. Libicki, "DBK and Its Consequences," in Johnson and Libicki, *Dominant Battlespace Knowledge*.

13 Bracken, "The Significance of Dominant Battlefield Awareness."

14 Admiral William A. Owens, "The Emerging U.S. System of Systems," in Johnson and Libicki, *Dominant Battlespace Knowledge*.

15 Harlan Ullman and James P. Wade, *Shock and Awe: Achieving Rapid Dominance* (Washington, DC: NDU Press, 1996).

16 Ibid., Chapter 3.

17 Ibid.

18 I am indebted to Professor Jennie Kiesling of West Point for this

observation, which forms the basis of her forthcoming work, tentatively entitled *Annihilation: America's Infatuation with "Total" War*.

19 CSIS, "Clashes of Visions," p. 27.

20 Ibid., p. 28.

21 Ibid., p. 30.

22 The Commission on the Roles and Missions of the Armed Forces, *Directions for Defense: The Department of Defense Report* (Washington, DC: Brassey's, 1995)

23 The Navy and the Marine Corps naturally developed mission statements as well, although they did not play a critical role in shaping the overall defense debate at this time.

24 Chairman of the Joint Chiefs of Staff, *Joint Vision 2010* available from http://www.dtic.mil/jv2010/jv2010.pdf, p. 2.

25 Ibid., p. 8.

26 Ibid., p. 11.

27 Ibid., p. 16.

28 Ibid., p. 20.

29 General Ronald R. Fogleman and Sheila E. Widnall, *Global Engagement: A Vision of the 21st Century Air Force*, available from http://www.au.af.mil/au/awc/awcgate/global/nuvis.htm.

30 William S. Cohen, *Report of the Quadrennial Defense Review*, May 1997, available from http://www.defenselink.mil/pubs/qdr/ (hereafter cited as QDR), Section IV.

31 *Transforming Defense: National Security in the 21st Century: Report of the National Defense Panel*, December 1997, available from http://www.dtic.mil/ndp/FullDoc2.pdf (hereafter cited as NDP), p. ii.

32 Ibid., p. 47.

33 See, for example, Dennis Reimer, "Projecting the Force: FORSCOM's Use of Technology in the 21st Century," *Army* (May 1994), p. 45.

34 These events are narrated in many of the basic works on Operation Allied Force, including Cordesman, *The Lessons and Non-Lessons of the Air and Missile Campaign in Kosovo*; Bacevich and Cohen, *War Over Kosovo*; Lambeth, *NATO's Air War for Kosovo*, and several articles in Army and elsewhere.

35 Lieutenant General Theodore G. Stroup, Jr., "Task Force Hawk: Beyond Expectations," *Army*, August 1999, pp. 8–10; General Frederick J. Kroesen, "We Won?," *Army*, November 1999, p. 8, does not make claims for Task Force Hawk but instead challenges the notion that the airpower-pure campaign actually accomplished its objectives.

36 General Eric Shinseki, testimony before the Senate Armed Services

Committee, Airland Forces Subcommittee Hearing on Army Transformation, 8 March 2000.

37 Department of the Army, *Army Vision*, October 1999.
38 United States Army White Paper, *Concepts for the Objective Force*,
available from http://www.army.mil/features/WhitePaper/Objective-
ForceWhitePaper.pdf, p. 6.
39 Ibid., p. 14.
40 H. R. McMaster, "Crack in the Foundation," unpublished paper.
The author is grateful for this and all of the other assistance
Colonel McMaster has provided throughout this project.

CHAPTER SEVEN

1 Vice Admiral Arthur K. Cebrowski and John J. Garstka, "Network-
Centric Warfare: Its Origin and Future," Proceedings, January 1998.
2 David S. Alberts, John J. Garstka, and Frederick P. Stein, *Network
Centric Warfare: Developing and Leveraging Information Superiority*,
2nd ed., (Washington, DC: CCRP Publication Services, 1999),
p. 26.
3 Ibid., p. 35.
4 Cebrowski and Garstka, "Network-Centric Warfare: Origin and
Future."
5 Ibid.
6 Ibid.
7 Ibid.; Alberts, Garstka, and Stein, *Network Centric Warfare*, p. 70.
8 Alberts, Garstka, and Stein, *Network Centric Warfare*, p. 71.
9 Ibid., p. 83.
10 Ibid., p. 184.
11 Ibid., p. 16.
12 Ibid., p. 8.
13 George W. Bush speech at The Citadel, 23 September 1999, at
http://citadel.edu/pao/addresses/pres_bush.html accessed on 7 July
2005.
14 George W. Bush, speech at the christening of the USS Ronald Reagan, 4 March 2001.
15 George W. Bush, speech at the U.S. Naval Academy, 25 May 2001.
16 George W. Bush, *A Blueprint for New Beginnings* (Washington, DC:
Government Printing Office, 28 February 2001), p. 53.
17 Donald Rumsfeld, statement before the Senate Armed Services
Committee, 11 January 2001.
18 Ibid.; Paul Wolfowitz, statement before the Senate Armed Services
Committee, 27 February 2001.

19 Ed Gillespie and Bob Schellhas, eds., *Contract with America: The Bold Plan by Rep. Newt Gingrich, Rep. Dick Armey, and the House Republicans to Change the Nation* (New York: Times Books, 1994).

20 Donald Rumsfeld, statement before the Senate Armed Services Committee, 21 June 2001.

21 Tom Bowman, "Pentagon Faces Transformation: A Secretive Review, Fashioned by a Small Team at the Pentagon, Could Mean Radical Changes for U.S. Forces," *Baltimore Sun*, 13 March 2001; Thomas E. Ricks and Walter Pincus, "Pentagon Plans Major Changes in U.S. Strategy: Rumsfeld Envisions Shift in Size, Focus of Military," *Washington Post*, 7 May 2001, p. A1.

22 The term "major regional conflict" shifted to "major theater war" at the end of the 1990s for no very good reason.

23 *Quadrennial Defense Review Report*, 30 September 2001 (hereafter QDR 2001), available from http://www.defenselink.mil/pubs/qdr2001.pdf, p. 17.

24 Ibid.

25 Ibid., p. 18.

26 Ibid., p. 22.

27 Ibid.

28 Ibid., p. 26.

29 Ibid., p. 27.

30 Ibid., p. 29.

31 Ibid., p. 30.

CHAPTER EIGHT

1 The best narrative of the Bush administration's decision-making at this time remains Bob Woodward, *Bush at War* (New York: Simon and Schuster, 2002). The recent appearance of Michael DeLong's book (with Noah Lukeman), *Inside CentCom: The Unvarnished Truth about the Wars in Iraq and Afghanistan* (Washington, DC: Regnery, 2004) and Rowan Scarborough's brief study, *Rumsfeld's War: The Untold Story of America's Anti-Terrorist Commander* (Washington, DC: Regnery, 2004), adds relatively little to Woodward's account of the decision-making related to the military and political campaigns. The best analysis of the military operations remains Steven Biddle, "Afghanistan and the Future of Warfare: Implications for Army and Defense Policy" (Carlisle, Penn.: U.S. Army Strategic Studies Institute, November 2002). The ensuing account relies heavily on Woodward and Biddle.

2 DeLong, *Inside CentCom*, p. 28.

3 Ibid., p. 31.

4 Woodward, *Bush at War*, p. 193.

5 Ibid., p. 237.

6 Ibid., p. 230.

7 Two excellent studies of the Soviet experience in Afghanistan were available at the time in Lester W. Grau, ed. and trans., *The Bear Went Over the Mountain: Soviet Combat Tactics in Afghanistan* (Washington, DC: NDU Press, 1996) and Lester W. Grau and Ali Jalali, *The Other Side of the Mountain: Mujahideen Tactics in the Soviet–Afghan War* (Quantico: U.S. Marine Corps Combat Development Command, 1998). Additional such information was posted at the time on the Foreign Military Studies Office webpage (http://fmso.leavenworth.army.mil/products.htm), where much of it still is. The author had occasion to explore this site in the years prior to Operation Enduring Freedom, and it was rich with material about the manner of warfare in the country even then.

8 Richard Whittle, "War Speeds Up Pace of Change for Military: Pentagon Resistance Diminished after Sept. 11, Analysts Say," *Dallas Morning News*, 5 December 2001, p. 16A.

9 Ibid.

10 Ibid.

11 Donald Rumsfeld speech at the National Defense University, 31 January 2002.

12 Biddle, "Afghanistan and the Future of Warfare," and DeLong, *Inside CentCom*, pp. 46–48. The accounts do not coincide perfectly, and this is my best effort at a reconstruction; the primary sources needed to correct the account are still classified. It is certain, however, that Dostum charged twice, was repelled once, and succeeded the second time immediately following an air strike.

13 Paul Wolfowitz, testimony before the Senate Armed Services Committee, 9 April 2002.

14 Donald Rumsfeld speech at the National Defense University, 31 January 2002.

15 Bill Keller, "The Fighting Next Time," *The New York Times Magazine*, 10 March 2002.

16 Vernon Loeb and Thomas E. Ricks, "1's and 0's Replacing Bullets in U.S. Arsenal: Success in Afghanistan Propels Shift to Equipping Forces with Digital Arms," *Washington Post*, 2 February 2002, p. A01.

17 Admiral Arthur K. Cebrowski, testimony before the Senate Armed Services Committee, 9 April 2002.

18 J. Michael Waller, "Command Performance," *Insight on the News*,

11 February 2002, available from
http://www.insightmag.com/main.cfm/include/detail/storyid/
179930.html.

CHAPTER NINE

1 See Bob Woodward, *Plan of Attack* (New York: Simon and Schuster,
2004), pp. 383ff.for a discussion of the abortive effort to kill
Saddam.
2 James Fallows, "Blind into Baghdad," *The Atlantic Monthly*, Janu-
ary/February 2004; for the American Enterprise Institute efforts,
see http://www.aei.org/events/seriesID.6/series_detail.asp.
3 Fallows, "Blind into Baghdad;" the State Department's "Future of
Iraq" effort had been available at
usinfo.state.gov/regional/nea/iraq/future.htm, although this site was
not working as of 8 November 2005.
4 Fallows, "Blind into Baghdad."
5 This is, unfortunately, the rather simplistic conclusion that Fallows
comes to after a detailed excursion into the post-war planning and
a fairly nuanced consideration of some of the issues. (Fallows,
"Blind into Baghdad").
6 Conrad C. Crane and W. Andrew Terrill, *Reconstructing Iraq:
Insights, Challenges, and Missions for Military Forces in a Post-Conflict
Scenario* (Carlisle, Penn.: U.S. Army Strategic Studies Institute,
February 2003).
7 Woodward, *Plan of Attack*, passim.
8 General Eric Shinseki, testimony before the Senate Armed Services
Committee, 25 February 2003.
9 Woodward, *Plan of Attack*, pp. 40–41.
10 Ibid., p. 76.
11 Ibid., p. 83.
12 Woodward, *Plan of Attack*; Fallows, "Blind into Baghdad."
13 Thomas Donnelly, *Operation Iraqi Freedom: A Strategic Assessment*
(Washington, DC: The AEI Press, 2004), p. 49; Colonel Gregory
Fontenot, Lieutenant Colonel E. J. Degen, and Lieutenant Colonel
David Tohn, *On Point: The United States Army in Operation Iraqi
Freedom through 01 May 2003* (Fort Leavenworth, Kan.: Combat
Studies Institute Press, 2004), p. 78.
14 A full order of battle is in Fontenot, Degen, and Tohn, *On Point*,
and available from www.globalsecurity.org.
15 Colonel Kevin Benson, "CFLCC OPLAN ECLIPSE II: CFLCC
Stability Planning Phase IV," Powerpoint presentation delivered at

the U.S. Army TRADOC/Combat Studies Institute Conference, "Turning Victory into Success: Military Operations After the Campaign," Fort Leavenworth, Kansas, 14–16 September 2004, slide 4.

16 Ibid., slide 17.

17 Ibid., slide 7.

18 Ibid. Slides 17, 19, 20, 25, and 26 taken together indicate that the planning group did not imagine that Iraqi forces would be available immediately, but they clearly did believe that they would begin the process of reorganizing and restoring those forces almost immediately upon the termination of hostilities, and that they would begin operating as CFLCC handed over responsibility for Iraq to the follow-on headquarters, CJTF-7, which it expected to do shortly after that point.

19 Ibid., slide 18.

20 Ibid., slide 18, notes. Emphasis added.

21 Three brigades each came from the 3rd Infantry and 101st Air Assault Divisions; the I MEF provided four regiments (the Marine equivalent of brigades); the UK 1st Armored Division added one armored and one air assault brigade; the 173rd Airborne Brigade; and one brigade from the 82nd Airborne Division.

22 Donald Rumsfeld press briefing, 11 April 2003.

23 Rowan Scarborough, "U.S. air attack found lacking in 'shock and awe,'" *Washington Times*, 31 March 2003.

24 Toby Harnden, "'Fight Fast, Fight Light' Theory Advances," *Telegraph*, 14 April 2003.

25 Donald Rumsfeld, testimony before the Senate Armed Services Committee, 9 July 2003.

26 Ibid.

27 From the Powerpoint presentation prepared for the testimony of General Tommy Franks and Donald Rumsfeld before the Senate Armed Services Committee on 9 July 2003, from http://www.oft.osd.mil/library/library_files/lesson_223_Summ_Rumsfeld_Franks.ppt.

28 Paul Wolfowitz, address to the Naval War College Commencement, 20 June 2003.

29 "Cebrowski: Iraq War Offers Clues For Transformation Agenda," *Aerospace Daily*, 23 April 2003.

30 Fontenot, Degen, and Tohn, *On Point*, p. 417.

31 Ibid., p. 423.

32 Ibid.

33 Third Infantry Division (Mechanized) After Action Report,

Operation Iraqi Freedom, July 2003, from
http://www.globalsecurity.org/military/library/report/2003/
3id-aar-julo3.pdf, p. 22.

34 Donnelly, *Operation Iraqi Freedom*, p. 80.
35 McMaster, "Crack in the Foundation"
36 Biddle, *Military Power*, pp. 72–73.

BIBLIOGRAPHY

Alberts, David S., John J. Garstka, and Frederick P. Stein. *Network Centric Warfare: Developing and Leveraging Information Superiority*, 2nd ed. Washington, DC: CCRP Publication Services, 1999.

Aspin, Les. *Report on the Bottom-Up Review*. October 2003.

Bacevich, Andrew J. and Eliot A. Cohen. *War over Kosovo: Politics and Strategy in a Global Age*. New York: Columbia University Press, 2001.

Bachman, Jerald G., John D. Blair, and David R. Segal. *The All Volunteer Force: A Study of Ideology in the Military*. Ann Arbor: The University of Michigan Press, 1977.

Baer, George W. *One Hundred Years of Sea Power: The U.S. Navy, 1890–1990*. Stanford: Stanford University Press, 1994.

Benson, Colonel Kevin. "CFLCC OPLAN ECLIPSE II: CFLCC Stability Planning Phase IV." Powerpoint presentation delivered at the U.S. Army TRADOC/Combat Studies Institute Conference, "Turning Victory into Success: Military Operations After the Campaign," Fort Leavenworth, Kansas, 14-16 September 2004, slide 4.

Biddle, Stephen. *Afghanistan and the Future of Warfare: Implications for Army and Defense Policy*. Carlisle, Penn.: U.S. Army Strategic Studies Institute, November 2002.

———. *Military Power: Explaining Victory and Defeat in Modern Battle*. Princeton: Princeton University Press, 2004.

Bingham, Lt. Col. Price T. "Air Power in Desert Storm and the Need for Doctrinal Change." *Airpower Journal* (Winter 1991).

Blackwell, Lieutenant General Paul E. "Winning the Wars of the 21st Century," *Army*, October 1994.

Bolger, Daniel P. *Americans at War: 1975–1986: An Era of Violent Peace*. Novato, Cal.: Presidio Press, 1988.

Bowman, Tom. "Pentagon Faces Transformation: A Secretive Review, Fashioned by a Small Team at the Pentagon, Could Mean Radical Changes for U.S. Forces." *Baltimore Sun*, 13 March 2001.

Boyd, John. *A Discourse on Winning and Losing* (1987). Retrieved from http://www.d-n-i.net/second_level/boyd_military.htm on 16 November 2005.

BIBLIOGRAPHY

Bracken, Paul. "The Significance of Dominant Battlefield Awareness." In *Dominant Battlespace Knowledge,* ed. Johnson and Libicki.

Brownlee, Romie L., and William J. Mullen III. *Changing an Army: An Oral History of General William E. DePuy, USA Retired.* Carlisle Barracks, PA: U.S. Military History Institute, 1988.

Bush, George, and Brent Scowcroft. *A World Transformed: The Collapse of the Soviet Empire, the Unification of Germany, Tiananmen Square, the Gulf War.* New York: Knopf, 1998.

———. *A Blueprint for New Beginnings.* Washington, DC: Government Printing Office, 28 February 2001.

———. "A Period of Consequences," speech at The Citadel, 23 September 1999, at http://citadel.edu/r3/pao/addresses/pres_bush.html accessed on 7 July 2005.

———. "Remarks at Christening Ceremony for the USS *Ronald Reagan*," 4 March 2001. Retrieved from http://www.whitehouse.gov/news/releases/2001/03/20010305.html on 16 November 2005.

———. "Remarks by the President at U.S. Naval Academy Commencement," 25 May 2001. Retrieved from http://www.whitehouse.gov/news/releases/2001/05/20010525-1.html on 16 November 2005.

Cebrowski, Admiral Arthur K. "Iraq War Offers Clues For Transformation Agenda." *Aerospace Daily,* 23 April 2003.

——— and John J. Garstka. "Network-Centric Warfare: Its Origin and Future." *Proceedings,* January 1998.

———. Testimony before the Senate Armed Services Committee. 9 April 2002.

Chapman, Anne W. *The Origins and Development of the National Training Center, 1976–1984.* Fort Monroe, VA: Office of the Command Historian, U.S. Army Training and Doctrine Command, 1992.

Cheney, Dick. *Defense Strategy for the 1990s: The Regional Defense Strategy.* 1993.

Coffey, Kenneth J. *Strategic Implications of the All-Volunteer Force: The Conventional Defense of Central Europe.* Chapel Hill: University of North Carolina Press, 1979.

Cohen, William S. *Report of the Quadrennial Defense Review.* [PDF online], May 1997, accessed November 9, 2005; available from http://www.defenselink.mil/pubs/qdr/.

Cordesman, Anthony H. *The Lessons and Non-Lessons of the Air and Missile Campaign in Kosovo.* Westport, Connecticut: Praeger, 2001.

Crane, Conrad C. and W. Andrew Terrill. *Avoiding Vietnam: The U.S.*

BIBLIOGRAPHY

Army's Response to Defeat in Southeast Asia. Carlisle, PA: U.S. Army
Strategic Studies Institute, 2002.

———. *Reconstructing Iraq: Insights, Challenges, and Missions for Military
Forces in a Post-Conflict Scenario.* Carlisle, Penn.: U.S. Army Strategic Studies Institute, February 2003.

Defense Manpower Commission. *Defense Manpower: The Keystone of
National Security: Report to the President and the Congress.* Washington,
D.C.: Government Printing Office, 1976.

DeLong, Michael, and Noah Lukeman. *Inside CentCom: The Unvarnished Truth about the Wars in Iraq and Afghanistan.* Washington, DC:
Regnery, 2004.

Department of the Army. *Army Vision*, October 1999.

———. *Department of the Army Historical Summary: Fiscal Year 1975.*
Retreived November 6, 2005 from
http://www.army.mil/cmh/books/DAHSUM/1975/.

———. FM 100-5, *Operations.* Washington, DC: Government Printing
Office, 1993.

———. FM 100-5, *Operations.* Washington, DC: Government Printing
Office, 1986.

———. FM 100-5, *Operations.* Washington, DC: Government Printing
Office, 1982.

———. FM 100-5, *Operations.* Washington, DC: Government Printing
Office, 1976.

———. *The Army's Training Revolution, 1973–1990.* Fort Monroe, VA:
Office of the Command Historian, U.S. Army Training and Doctrine Command, 1991.

Department of Defense. Annual Report. FY 1990.

———. *Department of Defense Military Personnel Statistics.* (2005).
*Department of Defense Active Duty Military Personnel Strength Levels,
Fiscal Years 1950–2002.* Retrieved March 31, 2005 from
http://www.dior.whs.mil/mmid/military/ms9.pdf.

Donnelly, Thomas. *Operation Iraqi Freedom: A Strategic Assessment.*
Washington, DC: The AEI Press, 2004.

Drew, Col. Dennis M. "Desert Storm as a Symbol." *Airpower Journal*
(Fall 1992).

Echeverria II, Antulio J. Clausewitz's *Center of Gravity: Changing our
Warfighting Doctrine-Again!* Carlisle, Penn.: U.S. Army Strategic
Studies Institute, 2002.

———. "Clausewitz's Center of Gravity: It's Not What We Thought."
Naval War College Review. vol. LVI, no. 1 (Winter 2003).

Fadok, David S., John Boyd, and John Warden. *Air Power's Quest for*

Strategic Paralysis. Maxwell Air Force Base, Alabama: Air University Press, 1995.

Fallows, James. "Blind into Baghdad," *The Atlantic Monthly* (January/February 2004).

Fogleman, General Ronald R., and Sheila E. Widnall. *Global Engagement: A Vision of the 21st Century Air Force*. [PDF online], accessed November 9, 2005; available from http://www.au.af.mil/au/awc/awcgate/global/nuvis.htm.

Fontenot, Colonel Gregory, Lieutenant Colonel E. J. Degen, and Lieutenant Colonel David Tohn. *On Point: The United States Army in Operation Iraqi Freedom through 01 May 2003*. Fort Leavenworth, Kan.: Combat Studies Institute Press, 2004.

Franks, General Tommy, and Donald Rumsfeld. "Summary of Lessons Learned," from the Powerpoint presentation prepared for testimony before the Senate Armed Services Committee on 9 July 2003, available at http://www.oft.osd.mil/library/library_files/lesson_223_Summ_Rumsfeld_Franks.ppt, accessed on 16 November 2005.

Gaddis, John Lewis. *Strategies of Containment: A Critical Appraisal of Postwar American National Security Policy*. New York: Oxford University Press, 1982.

Gat, Azar. *A History of Military Thought From the Enlightenment to the Cold War*. New York: Oxford University Press, 2001.

Gillespie, Ed, and Bob Schellhas, eds. *Contract with America: The Bold Plan by Rep. Newt Gingrich, Rep. Dick Armey, and the House Republicans to Change the Nation*. New York: Times Books, 1994.

Glantz, David. *Soviet Military Operational Art: In Pursuit of Deep Battle*. Portland, OR: Frank Cass, 1991.

Gordon, Michael R., and General Bernard E. Trainor. *The General's War*. New York: Little Brown, 1995.

Grau, Lester W., ed. and trans. *The Bear Went Over the Mountain: Soviet Combat Tactics in Afghanistan*. Washington, DC: NDU Press, 1996.

——— and Ali Jalali. *The Other Side of the Mountain: Mujahideen Tactics in the Soviet-Afghan War*. Quantico: U.S. Marine Corps Combat Development Command, 1998.

Gray, Colin. *Strategy for Chaos: Revolutions in Military Affairs and the Evidence of History*. Portland, OR: Frank Cass, 2002.

Hallion, Richard. *Storm Over Iraq*. Washington, D.C.: Smithsonian Institution Press, 1992.

———. "Precision Guided Munitions and the New Era of Warfare," (Fairbairn, Australia: Air Power Studies Centre, 1995), Working Paper Number 5.

Hamilton, Robert J. *Green and Blue in the Wild Blue: An Examination of the Evolution of Army and Air Force Airpower Thinking and Doctrine Since the Vietnam War*. Maxwell Air Force Base, Alabama: School of Advanced Airpower Studies, Air University, 1993.

Hammond, Grant T. *The Mind of War: John Boyd and American Security*. Washington, DC: Smithsonian Institute, 2001.

Harmann, Frederick H. Naval Renaissance: *The U.S. Navy in the 1980s*. Annapolis: Naval Institute Press, 1990.

Harnden, Toby. "'Fight Fast, Fight Light' Theory Advances." *Telegraph* (14 April 2003).

Hattendorf, John B. *The Evolution of the U.S. Navy's Maritime Strategy, 1977–1986*. Newport: Naval War College, 2004.

Haworth, W. Blair. *The Bradley and How It Got That Way: Technology, Institutions, and the Problem of Mechanized Infantry in the United States Army*. Westport: Greenwood, 1999.

Heller, Charles E., and William A. Stofft, eds. *America's First Battles, 1776–1965*. Lawrence, KS: University Press of Kansas, 1986.

Herbert, Major Paul H. *Deciding What Has to Be Done: General William E. DePuy and the 1976 Edition of FM 100–5, Operations*. Fort Leavenworth, KS: Combat Studies Institute, 1988.

Johnson, Stuart and Martin Libicki, eds. *Dominant Battlespace Knowledge*. Washington, DC: National Defense University Press, 1995.

Kadishin, A.B., ed., *Voprosy strategii i operativnogo iskusstva v sovetskikh voennykh trudakh, 1917–1940*. Moscow: Voennoe Izdatel'stvo, 1965.

Kagan, Donald, and Frederick W. Kagan. *While America Sleeps: Self-Delusion, Military Weakness, and the Threat to Peace Today*. New York: St. Martin's Press, 2000.

Kaufman, William W. *Assessing the Base Force: How Much Is Too Much?* Washington, DC: Brookings Institution, 1992.

Keaney, Thomas A. and Eliot A. Cohen. *The Gulf War Air Power Survey*. Washington DC: Government Printing Office, 1993.

Keeley, John B. ed., *The All Volunteer Force and American Society*. Charlottesville: University Press of Virginia, 1978.

Keller, Bill. "The Fighting Next Time," *The New York Times Magazine*. 10 March 2002.

Kelly, Orr. *King of the Killing Zone*. New York: W.W. Norton, 1989.

Korb, Lawrence. "Defense Manpower and the Reagan Record." In Stephen J. Cimbala ed., *The Reagan Defense Program: An Interim Assessment*. Wilmington: Scholarly Resources, 1986.

Kroesen, General Frederick J. "We Won?," *Army*, November 1999.

Lambeth, Benjamin S. NATO's *Air War for Kosovo: A Strategic and Operational Assessment*. Arlington, VA: RAND, 2001.

———. *The Transformation of American Airpower*. Ithaca, NY: Cornell University Press, 2000.

Lee, Seow Hang. *Center of Gravity or Center of Confusion*. Maxwell Air Force Base, Alabama: Air University, Air War College, 1999.

Lehman, Jr., John H. *Command of the Seas*. Annapolis: Naval Institute Press, 1988.

Libicki, Martin C. "DBK and Its Consequences," in Johnson and Libicki, *Dominant Battlespace Knowledge*.

Link, Major Gen. Charles D. "An Airman's View," in *Clashes of Visions: Sizing and Shaping Our Forces in a Fiscally Constrained Environment, A CSIS-VII Symposium*, 29 October 1997 (Washington, DC: CSIS, 1997).

Loeb, Vernon, and Thomas E. Ricks. "1's and 0's Replacing Bullets in U.S. Arsenal: Success in Afghanistan Propels Shift to Equipping Forces with Digital Arms." *Washington Post*, 2 February 2002, p. A01.

McMaster, H.R. "Crack in the Foundation." Unpublished paper.

Meilinger, Lt. Col. Phillip S. "The Problem with Our Air Power Doctrine." *Airpower Journal*, (Spring 1992).

National Defense Panel. *Transforming Defense: National Security in the 21st Century: Report of the National Defense Panel*. [PDF online], December 1997, accessed November 9, 2005; available from http://www.dtic.mil/ndp/FullDoc2.pdf.

Naveh, Shimon. *In Pursuit of Military Excellence: The Evolution of Operational Theory*. Portland, OR: Frank Cass, 1997.

Oberdorfer, John. *The Two Koreas: A Contemporary History*. New York: Basic Books, 2001.

Owen, Colonel Robert C. *Deliberate Force: A Case Study in Effective Air Campaigning*. Alabama, Maxwell Air Force Base: Air University Press, 2000.

Owens, Admiral William A. "The Emerging U.S. System of Systems," in Johnson and Libicki, *Dominant Battlespace Knowledge*.

Parker, Geoffrey. *Military Revolution: Military Innovation and the Rise of the West*. New York: Cambridge University Press, 1988.

Peters, F. Whitten. "Are We Ready To Lose the Next Air War?" *New York Times*, 24 July 1999.

Pfalzgraff, Jr., Robert L., and Richard H. Schultz, Jr. *The United States Army: Challenges and Missions for the 1990s*. Lexington, Mass.: Lexington Books, 1991.

Quadrennial Defense Review Report, 30 September 2001, available from http://www.defenselink.mil/pubs/qdr2001.pdf

Record, Jeffrey. *The Rapid Deployment Force and U.S. Military Interven-*

tion in the Persian Gulf. Cambridge, Mass.: Institute for Foreign Policy Analysis, 1983.

Reimer, Dennis. "Projecting the Force: FORSCOM's Use of Technology in the 21st Century." *Army*, May 1994.

Richter, Paul. "Crisis in Yugoslavia: Air-Only Campaign Offers a False Sense of Security, Some Say," *Los Angeles Times*, 4 June 1999.

Ricks, Thomas E., and Walter Pincus. "Pentagon Plans Major Changes in U.S. Strategy: Rumsfeld Envisions Shift in Size, Focus of Military," *Washington Post*, 7 May 2001, p. A1.

Ripley, Tim. "Air Power Vindicated." *Flight International*, 1 November 1995.

Rogers, Clifford. *The Military Revolution Debate: Readings on the Transformation of Early Modern Europe.* Boulder: Westview Press, 1995.

Romjue, John L. *From Active Defense to AirLand Battle: The Development of Army Doctrine, 1973–1982.* Fort Monroe, VA: Historical Office, U.S. Army Training and Doctrine Command, 1984.

———, Susan Canedy, and Anne W. Chapman. *Prepare the Army for War: A Historical Overview of the Army Training and Doctrine Command, 1973–1993.* Fort Monroe, Va.: Office of the Command Historian, United States Army Training and Doctrine Command, 1993.

Ross, General Jimmy D. "Winning the Information War." *Army*, February 1994.

Rumsfeld, Donald. "DoD News Briefing—Secretary Rumsfeld and Gen. Myers," 11 April 2003. Retrieved from http://www.defenselink.mil/transcripts/2003/tr20030411-secdef0090.html on 16 November 2005.

———. "Secretary Rumsfeld Speaks on '21st Century Transformation' of U.S. Armed Forces (transcript of remarks and question and answer period)," 31 January 2002. Retrieved from http://www.defenselink.mil/speeches/2002/s20020131-secdef.html on 16 November 2005.

———. Statement before the Senate Armed Services Committee, 11 January 2001.

———. Statement before the Senate Armed Services Committee, 21 June 2001.

———. Testimony before the Senate Armed Services Committee, 9 July 2003.

Scales, Robert H. *Certain Victory.* Washington DC: Government Printing Office, 1993.

Scarborough, Rowan. *Rumsfeld's War: The Untold Story of America's Anti-Terrorist Commander.* Washington, DC: Regnery, 2004.

———. "U.S. air attack found lacking in 'shock and awe.'" *Washington Times*, 31 March 2003.

Schultz, Richard H., and Robert L. Pfalzgraff, Jr. *The Future of Air Power in the Aftermath of the Gulf War*. Maxwell Air Force Base, Alabama: Air University Press, 1992.

Schweizter, Peter. *Reagan's War: The Epic Story of His Forty-Year Struggle and Final Triumph over Communism*. New York: Doubleday, 2002.

Shinseki, General Eric. Testimony before the Senate Armed Services Committee, Airland Forces Subcommittee Hearing on Army Transformation, 8 March 2000.

———. Testimony before the Senate Armed Services Committee, 25 February 2003.

Sorley, Lewis. *Thunderbolt: General Creighton Abrams and the Army of His Time*. New York: Simon and Schuster, 1992.

Strange, Joseph L., and Richard Iron. "Center of Gravity: What Clausewitz Really Meant." *Joint Forces Quarterly* (Issue 35).

———. "Understanding Centers of Gravity and Critical Vulnerabilities." Retrieved from http://www.au.af.mil/au/awc/awcgate/usmc/cog1.pdf and http://www.au.af.mil/au/awc/awcgate/usmc/cog2.pdf on 16 November 2005.

Stroup, Jr., Lieutenant General Theodore G. "Task Force Hawk: Beyond Expectations," *Army*, August 1999.

Sullivan, Gordon. "A New Force for a New Century," *Army*, May 1994.

———. "America's Army-Focusing on the Future," *Army*, October 1994.

——— and Col. James M. Dubik, *Land Warfare in the 21st Century*. Carlisle, Penn.: U.S. Army Strategic Studies Institute, 1993.

Third Infantry Division (Mechanized) *After Action Report, Operation IRAQI FREEDOM*, July 2003, from http://www.globalsecurity.org/military/library/report/2003/3id-aar-jul03.pdf, on 16 November 2005.

Tilford, Jr., Earl H. *Halt Phase Strategy: New Wine in Old Skins . . . With Powerpoint*. Carlisle, Penn.: U.S. Army Strategic Studies Institute, 1998.

Tirpak, John A. "Lessons Learned and Re-Learned." *Air Force Magazine*, August 1999.

———. "Deliberate Force," *Air Force Magazine*, October 1997.

Toffler, Alvin. *The Third Wave*. New York: Bantam Books, 1980.

Ullman, Harlan and James P. Wade. *Shock and Awe: Achieving Rapid Dominance*. Washington, DC: NDU Press, 1996.

BIBLIOGRAPHY

U. S. Army, White Paper: Concepts for the Objective Force, available from http://www.army.mil/features/WhitePaper/ObjectiveForce-WhitePaper.pdf, last accessed on 16 November 2005.

U.S. Army Training and Doctrine Command Pamphlet 525-5. "Force XXI Operations: A Concept for the Evolution of Full-Dimensional Operations for the Strategic Army of the Early Twenty-First Century," 1 August 1994.

U.S. Chairman of the Joint Chiefs of Staff, *Joint Vision 2010*. [PDF online], accessed November 9, 2005; available from http://www.dtic.mil/jv2010/jv2010.pdf

U.S. Commission on the Roles and Missions of the Armed Forces. *Directions for Defense: The Department of Defense Report*. Washington, DC: Brassey's, 1995.

U.S. Joint Chiefs of Staff. *National Military Strategy of the United States of America, 1995: A Strategy of Flexible and Selective Engagement*. Government Printing Office, 1995.

Waller, J. Michael. "Command Performance." *Insight on the News*, 4 March 2002, available from http://www.findarticles.com/p/articles/mi_m1571/is_8_18/ai_83699603, last accessed on 16 November 2005.

Warden, John. *The Air Campaign*. New York: toExcel, 1998.

———. "Employing Air Power in the Twenty-First Century" in Schultz, Richard H. and Robert L. Pfalzgraff, Jr. *The Future of Air Power in the Aftermath of the Gulf War*. Maxwell Air Force Base, Alabama: Air University Press, 1992.

Whittle, Richard. "War Speeds Up Pace of Change for Military: Pentagon Resistance Diminished after Sept. 11, Analysts Say." *Dallas Morning News*, 5 December 2001, p. 16A.

Williamson, Murray. *The Air War in the Persian Gulf*. Baltimore: The Nautical and Aviation Publishing Company of America, 1995.

Wirls, Daniel. *Buildup: The Politics of Defense in the Reagan Era*. Ithaca: Cornell University Press, 1992.

Wolfowitz, Paul. Address to the Naval War College Commencement, 20 June 2003.

———. Statement before the Senate Armed Services Committee, 27 February 2001.

———. Testimony before the Senate Armed Services Committee, 9 April 2002.

Woodward, Bob. *Bush at War*. New York: Simon and Schuster, 2002.

———. *Plan of Attack*. New York: Simon and Schuster, 2004.

INDEX

INDEX

DESIGN AND COMPOSITION BY CARL W. SCARBROUGH